Human Services
for
older adults

Human Services for older Adults: Concepts and skills

Second Edition, Revised

Anita S. Harbert
San Diego State University

Leon H. Ginsberg
University of South Carolina

University of South Carolina Press

Published in Columbia, South Carolina, by the University of South Carolina
Press

Manufactured in the United States of America

Library of Congress Cataloging-in-Publication Data

Harbert, Anita S., 1937–
　Human services for older adults : concepts and skills / Anita S.
　Harbert, Leon H. Ginsberg. — 2nd ed., rev.
　　　p.　cm.
　Includes bibliographical references.
　ISBN 0-87249-682-1
　　1. Social work with the aged—United States.　2. Aging—United
States.　3. Old age—United States.　I. Ginsberg, Leon H.
II. Title.
HV1461.H36　1990
362.6'0973—dc20
89-24900
CIP

CONTENTS

Preface to the Second Edition   vii

One   The Elderly in Contemporary American Society   1

Chapter 1   The Impact of Aging on Society and the Individual   3

    Reading 1.1   Grays on the Go / *Time* Magazine   17
    Reading 1.2   Joie de Vivre / Simone de Beauvoir   25

Chapter 2   The Social Problems of Later Life   33

    Reading 2.1   Growing Old in America / Grace Hechinger   48

Chapter 3   Special Aging Populations: Minorities, Offenders, Rural, and Women Aged   54

    Reading 3.1   A Miracle Story / Rosalie K. Jackson   60
    Reading 3.2   The Older Woman / Irene de Castillejo   64
    Reading 3.3   The Elderly Prisoner / *The State* (Columbia, S.C.)   77

Two   Providing Counseling Services to Older Adults   81

Chapter 4   Reaching and Serving Older Adults: Interviewing, Case Management, and Follow-up Services   83

Chapter 5   Serving Groups of Older Adults   106

    Reading 5.1   Peer Group Counseling for Older People / Elinor Waters, Sylvia Fink, and Betty White   125

Chapter 6   Serving Older Adults and Their Families   135

Chapter 7   Working with Terminally Ill and Dying Older Adults   147

    Reading 7.1   The Social Worker's Role / Leon H. Ginsberg   159
    Reading 7.2   The Ritual Drama of Mutual Pretense / Barney G. Glaser and Anselm L. Strauss   165

Three   Program Planning and Development for Older Adults   175

Chapter 8   The Older Americans Act: The Structure of Aging Services in the United States   177

Chapter 9   Program Planning for Older Adults   190

Chapter 10   Support Services for Older Adults   203

   Reading 10.1   The Elderly: Prisoners of Fear / *Time*   210

Chapter 11   Advocacy and Protection on Behalf of the Elderly   215

Four   Service Programs for Older People   **226**

Chapter 12   Meeting the Economic Needs of the Elderly: Financial   227
Assistance, Housing, Transportation, Employment, and Training

   Reading 12.1   Shelter Issues in the 1990's / Leon Ginsberg   240

Chapter 13   Meeting the Health Needs of the Elderly: Physical   252
Health, Mental Health, Institutional Care

   Reading 13.1   Senility Is Not Always What It Seems to Be /   270
   Lawrence K. Altman, M.D.
   Reading 13.2   Nursing Home Reforms and the Politics of   273
   Long-Term Care / Catherine Hawes
   Reading 13.3   Older—but Coming on Strong / *Time*   285

Chapter 14   Meeting the Leisure-Time Needs of the Elderly: 291
Recreation, Volunteer, and Self-Help Programs

   Reading 14.1   Teaching Old Folks Is an Art / Robert Coles   307
Selected Statistics on the Aging   **312**

Glossary   **317**

Bibliography and Reference   **321**

Index   **337**

pREfACE TO THE SECONd EdiTION

Growing old in America is significantly different from what it was a decade ago when the first edition of this book was published. It would have been difficult to predict the major changes that have affected aging in the United States.

Perhaps the most dramatic examples of change are those of the relative economic situations of older people in the 1980's and 90's compared to their situations in the 1960's and 70's. Major reforms and increases in Social Security—particularly in indexing Social Security benefits to inflation and increases in the cost of living—have overcome the poverty encountered by many older people just a few years ago. Although the problem of poverty in late life is still significant, it is not as pervasive as it was prior to those reforms. Medicare has also been improved so that the problems of securing health services within one's financial means is much less a serious difficulty for many seniors than it once was.

Similarly, Supplemental Security Income, the national income support program for low-income adults, has been steadily increased. Although even its current levels—$340.00 per month for ann individual and $510.00 per month for a couple—are still not enough for adequate living in the 1990's, SSI has not fallen behind. Similarly, Food Stamps, which are available to low income seniors, have continued to increase with inflation and rises in the cost of living.

The severe poverty that was the lot of many older adults has been replaced by impoverishing circumstances for a relative minority. However, the programs and services for the elderly described in this book are as significant and perhaps more significant than ever before. It has been these services that have lifted America's older people out of the difficulties that were so much the focus of the first edition.

If these programs are changed in major ways or allowed to fall behind, the problem status of many older people may reemerge.

It was difficult to project, during the Carter presidency, that his administration would lose its efforts to be reelected and that it would be replaced by the Reagan administration (followed after eight years by that of George Bush). The Reagan presidency was dedicated, at least at it beginnings, to the reversal of the elimination of nearly fifty years of social legislation that began with the New Deal in 1933. Early in the Reagan years, there was question in the minds of many human services workers whether the social policy developments of the second half of the twentieth century would survive the efforts to create "block grants," and to turn programs that had been federal into state operations, instead. But toward the end of the Reagan years and at the time of transition to the presidency of Bush, human services administrators and workers began to take heart in what appeared to be the persistence and continued wide acceptance of human services programs for older adults by the American population. For example, President Reagan signed into law a bill reforming the U.S. welfare system. Although that legislation is primarily directed to children and their families and, therefore, has affected relatively few older people, it was still a sign that the Reagan administration and, in all likelihood its successor, could be persuaded of the virtues of programs of aid to the disadvantaged and the vulnerable.

Some problems that have become near-crises in American life were only beginning to emerge in the 1970's. For example, homelessness was understood as a program affecting a few "street people," some dischargees from mental institutions, and a few others—primarily eccentric sorts. However, it was clear, even then, that disproportionate numbers of the homeless were older rather than young. At the time of this second edition, the homeless were present in cities of any size in the United States. National programs to deal with the problem, including federal, state, and local funding for shelters to house the homeless, were a major factor in the social services field. The authors hope that by the time a third edition is published, even this problem will no longer be included because the relatively direct and obvious solutions to the problem of homelessness will have been implemented.

Although its major impact has not been on older people, the epidemic of Acquired Immune Deficiency Syndrome has been a major force in American social policy and has been a social as well as public health problem. Older gay men, and older intravenous drug users, are among those who have suffered from or who have modified their behavior and lives because of AIDS. Similarly, AIDS has had a major impact on the heterosexual population as well. Many older adults have changed their life styles because of it.

Forms and styles of human services have also changed as part of the ongoing evolution of the field. Approaches to serving the elderly such as case management are relatively new. The changes in social service delivery formats have followed upon major changes in the overall organization and delivery of human services programs. Intergovernmental planning has made it almost impossible to tell where federal, state, and local programs begin and end. In reality, today's human services are more likely to include policies and funding that represent not only all levels of government but the public and private sectors, as well.

The United States has also become a much more cosmopolitan nation. Workers with the aging are again finding that they must and do serve people from a broad spectrum of the world's nations. Immigration from Asia by older as well as younger people has been an important fact in the 1980's and programs of service for older Vietnamese, Koreans, and other members of what is coming to be called the "Pan-Asian" community are increasingly clients of the human services. The same is true to an extent for the large groups of immigrants from Latin America many of whom are elderly.

Of course, the authors have changed too. Barely into our forties when the first edition was written, we are now firmly in our fifties. Perceptions about aging not only change when one reads, studies, and conducts research and practice. Personal cases of arthritis, personal experiences with grandchildren, and personal encounters with negative stereotypes of older people have their impact on one's thinking and writing, as well.

So this edition, while retaining some of the pervasive truths of the first, also changes and brings up-to-date much of what the authors have learned since that first effort was made.

We hope that a new generation of human services faculty and students find this book a helpful introduction to the fascinating and essential field of services to America's older people.

acknowledgments

Book publishing is never an individual or even joint effort. The authors are indebted to several people who assisted in the preparation of the manuscript, with research, and with suggestions. We acknowledge with thanks the efforts of B.J. Charles, Elaine Glaser, Lee Hartley, Lynn Loring, and Joyce Shaw of the University of South Carolina; Lori Zornado of San Diego State University, Connie Ginsberg, and Earle Jackson of the University of South Carolina Press.

We especially thank Kenneth Scott, Director of the U.S.C. Press, whose encouragement was a major factor in the development of this second, revised edition of our book.

human services
for
older adults

PART ONE

THE elderly in CONTEMPORARY AMERICAN SOCIETY

Part One discusses the meaning of growing old in America from biological and social perspectives. In order to practice effectively, human services workers must understand their clients. In this case, the clients are older people and understanding them means knowing something about the physical strengths and problems they have as well as the social consequences of growing older.

Today's older adults have overcome many of the problems their predecessors in the senior years faced because of economic problems and lack of health services. The status of the elderly has improved remarkably since the late 1970's so that poverty is not the common lot of older people, as it was likely to be for many in the earlier years of this century. Still many older people face many problems; without programs for the aging and the human services workers who help older people use them, many more would be in difficult circumstances.

CHAPTER 1
THE IMPACT
OF AGING ON SOCIETY
AND THE INdividUAL

At the turn of the century people 65 and older composed only 1.2 percent of the total U.S. population; today they are the fastest growing age group in the country. Government documents indicate that between 1900 and 1984 the percentage of people aged 65 and over more than tripled, going from 4.1 percent in 1900 to 11.9 percent in 1984 (*Facts About Older Americans*, 1985). Their number increased about 9 times, from 3 million to 28 million. The same documents predict that by the year 2000 older people will represent approximately 13.0 percent of this nation's population of about 268 million, and this percentage will grow to 21.1 percent by the year 2030.

Within the aging population, those 85 and older constitute the fastest growing age group. This group is expected to triple in size between the 1980's and the year 2020 and be seven times larger in 2050 than in 1980. In addition, more older people are surviving to celebrate their 100th birthdays. As more and more elderly live longer life spans it is likely that many of those older individuals in their sixties and seventies may have surviving partners, which is a new phenomenon in our society.

Many elderly people are healthy, vital, and in good financial circumstances. The term "young-old" categorizes the health and social characteristics of the elderly rather than the very old. What was once considered old age is now applicable only to the vulnerable elderly, the "old-old," who are in need of special care (Pifer & Bronte, 1986).

The increased number of older people in the United States represents a paradox. On the one hand, improvements in health care and the quality of life have made it possible for people to live longer. On the other hand, for many older people survival into old age is not a blessing. Many suffer from poverty, isolation, and nonproductivity. The large population has become a problem for society, as we have not created channels for productive use of leisure time and means for old people to meet their own needs successfully. On the whole, our society is ill prepared to cope with the increasing number of older people.

Increased services and programs have been created because older people have become more visible to society as a whole. To work successfully with older people, it is important to understand their social status today in relation to changes that have occurred in this century. In addition, it is important to understand the aging process and the strengths and weaknesses of people in the later phases of life in coping with their status and problems. In this chapter we will examine the factors that have caused old age to emerge as a social problem and the effects of the aging process on the individual.

The increase of the elderly in the population can be attributed to several factors, the most important being a dramatic increase in life expectancy in this century (Atchley, 1977). "Life expectancy at birth is the average number of years a person can expect to live from the time of birth. Currently those arriving at age 65 can expect to live approximately 16.8 years more" (Cox, 1984). This change does not mean that the average human life-span has increased dramatically; we have not substantially increased longevity, that is, the total number of years we can expect to survive, so much as the total number of individuals who live to old age. The greatest gains occurred during the first half of the century largely because of dramatic reductions in deaths from infectious disease. Although in the early part of this century, increases in life expectancy were due to decreases in deaths of infants and children, most of the increasing life expectancy since 1970 has been due to decreased mortality among the middle-aged and elderly population (Special Committee on Aging, U.S. Senate, 1986).

We can see a more dramatic increase, however, when we look at the growing number of older individuals over the last century. Modern technology and improved health care have decreased the risks of pregnancy and childbirth and reduced deaths among infants and young adults. As a result more individuals survive adulthood and live to reach old age. In 1900, for example the life expectancy for an infant was approximately 48 years; a child born today can expect to live approximately 75 years. Thus in this century we have increased life expectancy at birth by approximately 27 years.

Throughout this century improvements in the years an individual can expect to live has been more significant for women than men. For instance, from 1950 to 1980, life expectancy at birth for the total population advanced by 5.5 years. For women, relative life expectancy is declining slightly. Between 1981 and 1985, life expectancy for males at birth increased by 0.8 year, slightly more than the 0.4 year gain for females. The male/female differential in life expectancy was 7.1 years in 1985, as compared to 7.6 years in 1980 and 7.8 years in 1970.

Since 1900, life expectancy at age 65 has advanced significantly. Although life expectancy at birth showed greater increases in the first half of the century than life expectancy at age 65, in recent years life expectancy at age 65 has been increasing more rapidly. According to estimates from the Social Security Administration, elderly men gained 3.1 years from 1900 to 1985 and elderly women gained 6.8 years. These projections for the future suggests that elderly men can expect to gain an additional 3 years by the year 2050, while women could expect to gain an additional 3.9 years.

Perhaps the most clear-cut issue raised by the change in the **demographic** makeup of this country is an economic one: How will the nation bear the cost of caring for so many older people? In a sense, the number of people each productive worker has to support won't have changed much, since the number of children is destined to shrink, but the elderly are considerably more expensive to maintain, living mainly in households of their own, having high medical costs, and needing more services. Maintaining a population made up largely of older adults requires more services on the whole and a new supply of labor to provide those services. We are now just beginning to make efforts to prepare those who will deliver the services.

The Changing American Life-Style

The rapid industrialization of the past century and its impact on family life have also had major effects on the lives of older adults. As our nation shifted from an agrarian to an industrial society, the American family changed considerably. In our early agrarian economy every family member was needed to produce the essential goods for life. Fathers, mothers, sons, daughters, grandparents, and sometimes aunts and uncles all worked together tilling, planting, hoeing, harvesting, weaving, cooking, and putting up preserves to support the family as an economic unit. Thus the extended family was important to survival, and elderly people tended to live out their years cared for by their families and contributing to the family group.

With industrialization and the mass production of goods came a gradual change from the extended to the nuclear family. Rapid urbanization opened up many new jobs in the cities, and many young people migrated from rural areas in search of good pay and a higher standard of living than they had known on the farm. At the same time there was a great influx of immigrants from central and southern Europe into American cities, further swelling the urban population. As families grew and the cost of land increased, it became more difficult to support all members of the family on the farm. As younger people found jobs and became established in the cities, other family members followed, until eventually only parents and grandparents remained behind. Extended families began to split up into smaller units, and older people no longer had their original family roles. Today a disproportionately high number of elderly live in rural areas.

The urban elderly were experiencing a different kind of problem created by immigration. Because of inadequate housing in the early part of the century, two- or three-generation urban families, especially immigrant families, usually shared a single dwelling. The cities developed, and as younger members of immigrant urban families became more affluent, they followed industry and the housing industry to single-family units in the suburbs. Again the elderly family members were left behind, this time in the deteriorating inner-city neighborhoods. In both shifts—from country to city and from city to suburbs—a precedent was set for older family members to maintain separate households and to function as economically independent units.

The problem created by the shift from the extended to the nuclear family is that although older people are expected to be independent economic units, in reality this is an impossibility. Too frequently independent older people are unable to live alone because of failing health or the problems of isolation, immobility, and poverty. Consequently, if the elderly are to survive, society must provide services or programs to subsidize them as independent economic units.

Establishing Economic
Independence for Older Adults

Before 1900, the ability of older people to maintain economic independence was relatively unimportant, since few people survived into old age, and those who did played a significant part in the economic survival of the entire family. Today neither situation is true. We no longer consider it the responsibility of the family to maintain its elderly parents, grandparents, aunts and uncles. We now think it desirable for the elderly to maintain their economic independence both for the good of the society and the good of the individuals themselves.

As our values and customs now stand, however, the means to this end are blocked. In our industrial society we aim at keeping everyone employed while maintaining a stable wage structure in which everyone can make enough money to live on. In recent times we have stabilized wage structures by reducing the number in the work force (i.e., supply of labor) and redefining what we mean by *employable*. In effect, we have kept two groups out of the labor market: the young and the old. The young are kept out by increasing the number of years of prework education required; the old are removed through mandatory retirement.

Once workers reach retirement age and leave the work force, it is virtually impossible for them to reenter; few employers want to hire older workers. Retired people generally have income from Social Security and private pensions. Increasingly, these sources of income are too small to meet the elderly's needs, however, and older people are stuck in the middle: The income they have is insufficient, yet they are blocked from obtaining additional income. Because of this double bind elderly people are increasing their demand on society to help them meet their needs. Their economic welfare has now become a social problem for which we have not yet developed solutions. Nor have we developed ways that older adults can enjoy their nonproductive years in our society, although by removing older people from the work force, we have created the problem for them of finding satisfactory uses of their leisure time.

We can see from the above discussion that, as it now stands, older people present very demanding problems for the country as a whole. We are trying to find ways of dealing with this group, but to date we have not been successful. One of the reasons we are not successful is that we do not understand old age as a process or as a phase of life. If we are to successfully serve older people, we must have a clear understanding of what it means to grow old: What are the social, physical, and psychological implications of the aging process? How do these factors affect the behavior of older people as they relate to the constantly changing environment? In the next part of this chapter we will examine the aging process and highlight its significance for those working with aging individuals.

What It Means to Grow Old

Aging is difficult to define. We generally associate increasing age with physical changes, such as graying hair, wrinkles, a bent back, a slow gait, and perhaps absentmindedness. These changes certainly occur, but they represent only a part of a complex process marked by physical, psychological, and social effects. Although we can discuss these three aspects of aging separately, they all interact and influence one another throughout the aging process. Similarly, although we can generalize about older people for the purpose of our discussion, keep in mind that the processes we discuss are characteristic of *most* older people but may not be true of specific individuals. One person may age faster than another physically or psychologically.

Physical Aging and Uneven Decline

We don't yet know when the aging process actually begins and what factors contribute to or control it. We know more about what creates life than we do about what causes it to cease. Researchers believe that **physical aging** begins when we reach middle age, since the physical changes that occur with advancing years are increasingly noticeable at this stage of life. Recently, however, researchers have begun to redefine aging as a continuing process that begins with conception and is distinct from chronological age.

One theory of physical aging suggests that changes in the body's retention of fluid and production of energy are the keys to physical changes (Calloway, 1974). Proponents of this theory point out that at conception the percentage of water found in the human fetus and the amount of heat produced are much greater than those found in later stages of life. As we grow older, our bodies progressively retain less water and generate less heat. The theory suggests that the faster we lose fluid and body heat, the faster we age.

There are various other theories of aging. The "wear and tear" theory based on a mechanical analogy (Kart, 1985) sees the body as a machine. Eventually, its parts wear out and the machine breaks down. The "waste product" theory ascribes to accumulated waste products in the body a key role in physiological aging. So far, however, there is no conclusive explanation of physical aging.

Although we may not understand why physical aging occurs, we do know that not all parts of the body age at the same rate. In those organs where cells are regenerated—for example, the skin and the stomach lining—the aging process is slower than in those body parts such as the nervous and muscular systems where cells are not regenerated. We assume that the wrinkled skin of old age is due to the aging of the skin. In fact, the skin ages at a slower rate than other parts of the body. Wrinkling of the skin is due to the degeneration of the muscular system that supports it.

The pattern of physical aging is a linear decline that begins about age 30 and continues throughout the life span. Figure 1.1 shows that certain body functions, including metabolic rate, percentage of body water, cardiac output, and breathing capacity, reach their peak at age 30 and decline from there on. Muscle tone and strength seem to peak between 20 and 30 years of age and then decrease. This fact is exemplified by the professional athletes who are at the height of their careers in their mid-20s and are seen as has-beens in their late 30s. All of the senses (vision, smell, hearing, taste, and touch) decrease in function with time. Hearing loss, for example, begins in adolescence, but there are significant losses between the ages of 40 and 50. What these facts tell us is that the physical characteristics of aging involve a gradual process beginning earlier than most people assume. Various body functions have their own characteristic pattern of change.

When we look at total body function over time, the speed of return to normal levels of functioning generally decreases after exposure to stress, such as extensive exercise or extreme fear. Blood sugar, pH factor, blood volume, per-

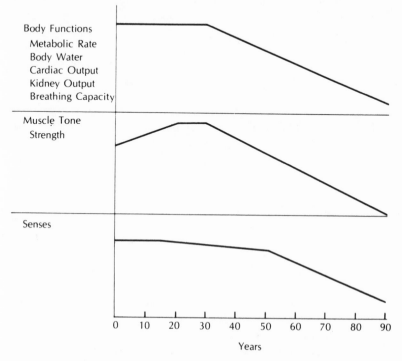

Figure 1.1   Rate of Physical Changes with Age.

haps even heart rate and blood pressure, of young and old subjects at rest may be quite close. This could lead to the assumption that homeostatic equilibria are not modified with age. However, significant differences in body functions are revealed during stress. For the older person, the magnitude of displacement is greater, and the rate of recovery is slower. When reactions to stress are measured, for example, by oxygen consumption, we find a maximum breathing capacity and a decrease in the residual lung volume. In addition, a decrease in vital capacity, such as blood pressure and heart rates, is revealed in older adults under stress.

Although the body changes, we should emphasize that normal aging is not a disease (Belsky, 1984). People do not die of old age. Death occurs because, over time, the body becomes more vulnerable to outside assault, less adaptable to the environment, and more subject to stress and crisis. Scientists predict that the major diseases affecting the aged will no doubt be significantly reduced if not eliminated by the beginning of the twenty-first century as a result of current medical and technical revolutions. With improved sanitation, nutrition, and antibiotic therapy, morbidity and mortality from infectious diseases will be virtually eliminated from our society.

The knowledge we gain about the physical aspects of aging that is most significant for those working with older people is in the fact that the physical deterioration that occurs with age is not an irreversible process. Research studies support the belief that some body functions can be restored with proper treatment or care. Muscle strength and muscle tone can be regained with an exercise regime of six to eight weeks for 60- to 90-year-old men. It is also possible to reverse some confusion, fatigue, irritability, and insomnia with changes in diet. Treatment in the form of correcting vitamin and protein deficiency and hormone balance and tender loving care will reverse many conditions of physical aging that were once thought to be irreversible.

Psychological Implications of Old Age

The psychological characteristics of the aging process can be viewed in the context of the life cycle. Individuals pass through various phases in life: infancy, childhood, adolescence, adulthood, middle age, and old age. We generally attach approximate years to these phases, but chronological age is only a clue to where one stands in relation to the phases of life. There are experiences characteristic of each phase of development. As we move throughout life, we successively make choices regarding education, career, marriage, children, and retirement. Though it is difficult to avoid viewing these events as problems, from a developmental perspective they are part of a normal life cycle. We become differentiated individuals depending on our characteristic pattern of coping with these challenging events. Old age is one phase in the life cycle, and the changes individuals experience at this time of life are thought by some to be characteristic of this stage of development.

Until recently old age was not given much attention in the study of human development, but now more emphasis is being placed on understanding this phase of life. It was once believed that old age began at 65 and continued until death. Psychologists assumed a 65-year-old person experienced the same developmental events as an 85-year-old person. This is no longer considered true. We now believe that 65- and 75-year-old individuals must learn to cope with different experiences in the late part of life. To reflect this belief, the later years of life are divided into three stages, middle age, later maturity, and old age, and a series of developmental events are identified for each. Figure 1.2 identifies the significant events for each phase of later life.

Middle Age	Later Maturity	Old Age
40 50	60 70	80 90
Events	Events	Events
Job Stabilization	Loss of Spouse	Major Loss of Health
Loss of Parenthood	and Friends	Increased Dependence
Minor Loss of Health	Chronic Health Problems	Loss of Life
	Loss of Status	
	Considerable Leisure Time	
	Increased Independence	
	Retirement	
	Reduced Income	

Figure 1.2   Significant Events in Later Life.

Psychological Capacities of Older People

Psychological age relates to the various adaptive capacities individuals use to cope with problems confronting them throughout life. Psychologists studying older people have occasionally found contradictions in their research because of differences in the educational levels or health status of those studied. Certain diseases, such as cerebral, vascular, and primary brain disease, can seriously impair mental functioning and limit effective behavior in later life. The presence of people with these conditions in a research sample often distorts what can be generally regarded as the developmental or normative changes of later life.

The adaptive capacities studied by psychologists include sensory and perceptual functioning, speed and timing, psychomotor skills, learning abilities, problem-solving abilities, and personality traits. How these capacities change with advancing years is our concern in understanding **psychological aging.**

Sensory and Perceptual Functions

The senses are the way we experience the world both outside and inside the body. In order to respond to our environment, we must be able to learn something about it; we depend upon our senses—vision, hearing, taste, smell, touch—to gather the information. The function of the sensory organs is to pick up information on to the brain. Research in the physiological aspects of aging has demonstrated that there is a decline in functioning of the sensory organs with increasing age.

The senses provide the means for assembling and classifying information, but they do not evaluate it. The process of evaluating the information gathered by the senses and giving it meaning is called **perception.** As for perception in later life, people appear to gradually suffer a decline in the general speed with which they can organize and evaluate stimuli. The available evidence concerning perceptual processes, however, is far less conclusive than that concerning sensory processes.

Speed and Timing

Whereas young adults generally behave quickly or slowly in accord with the demands of the situation, older adults exhibit generally slower behavior. This generalized slowness is seen as most likely an expression of a primary process of general neural aging (Belsky, 1984). One consequence of the slowing-down process is that aged individuals are often limited in the number of things they can do at a given time.

Older people adapt to their slowness by avoiding situations with unusual time pressures. Slowness itself can be partly a manifestation of adaptation. If the individual becomes less confident in walking, fearing the consequences of a fall, he or she may tend to slow movements considerably.

Psychomotor slowness of older people may also be affected by depressive mood. However, depression is not an adequate explanation for the slowness of advancing age, although it can be a factor that amplifies its consequence. As we can see, there is no single explanation for slowness in older people's behavior; several related factors may be at work. We do not know much about modifying conditions that would maintain an alert organism with a potential for precise and rapid responses. We do not know whether continuous high-level stimulation in later life will retard or advance psychomotor slowness.

Psychomotor Skills

Psychomotor performance refers to a complex chain of activity beginning with a sensory response and ending with some sort of reaction, usually through a muscle; in other words, " . . . a person's ability and dexterity on tasks involving physical actions." (Belsky, 1984). In the ideal situation, psychomotor performance involves taking sensory input, attaching meaning to it through perception, incorporating the perceived information into the mind alongside other ideas, making a decision concerning the act if one is required by the new information, and then sending instructions to the appropriate nerve and activating a nerve-muscle response. In lay terms we might refer to this behavior as hand-eye coordination.

Studies of psychomotor functioning in later life have shown that changes in the central nervous system and the peripheral sensory receptions result in reduced sensory input with age (Woodruff and Birren, 1985). The reduced sensory input of older people affects their level of activity. On the whole, older people have less muscular strength, take longer to react to many forms of stimuli, take longer to make a motion, and are generally less capable of performing athletic tasks such as running and swimming.

Psychomotor functioning is extremely important to certain types of employment, especially assembly-line work. Much of the evidence from industrial studies indicates that little change in worker performance is found up to about age 60-65 (Birren, 1974). It is believed that individual limits are not often taxed in occupational performance and tend to be well counterbalanced by experience and better work methods. Workers' capacities change so generally that adaptation is an almost unconscious process. When dramatic changes in skills do occur, they are likely to be the result of injury or disease with accompanying neurological damage. It is perhaps only after age 70 that a worker seems old, primarily because of the slowness of action and the tendency to work according to an internal tempo rather than an external pace.

Mental Capacity

Learning ability is another adaptive capacity examined by psychologists. Evidence in the study of both animal and human learning suggests that, counter to general belief, learning ability does not diminish with age. Learning continues throughout life, although the rate of learning is slower for the old than for the young. Because of the many sensory changes that occur with age, methods of teaching may need to be different, but advancing age is not a hindrance to learning.

Studies suggest there is no simple answer to the question of whether problem-solving abilities increase or decrease with age. Some evidence suggests that as people age, their knowledge increases, and this strengthens their problem-solving ability. Furthermore, how effectively older people solve problems is determined by whether the problem contains familiar or unfamiliar elements. Problems containing familiar elements are frequently solved more quickly by older people than by young people. Other evidence suggests that older individuals do not function as effectively where speed or pressure are concerned. Over the life span older people develop ready-made solutions to most problems and apply these in later life. The model of problem solving characteristic of old age is to search within the existing repertory of responses to problems rather than to generate new or creative approaches.

Whether intelligence declines with age has been a subject of study for some time. It was once thought that intelligence declined with age, but recent research suggests that it does not (Baltes and Schaie, 1974). This research maintains that declines in intelligence in older adults are related to their state of health. There appears to be a direct relationship between poor health and decline in an older person's mental capacity.

Personality Traits

There is much evidence to substantiate the stability and continuity of certain personality traits or underlying disposition into old age. Some evidence does suggest age-related changes in traits, motivational patterns, and ego energy. For example, the individual's drive and spontaneous physical and sexual behavior may be reduced. In general, personality traits may vary more than mental capacity over the adult years. Personal values and vocational interests remain stable into old age, but other traits such as self-regard or self-identity may change markedly with age. However, studies of personality traits in relation to age and intelligence indicate that age is less important than intelligence in adaptation over adult life. Adaptive people modify their behavior over time and age successfully. The internal habit system of the individual personality that promotes adaptation is not fully understood, and successful adaptation in old age can occur in quite different and almost opposite types of personalities.

Although a great deal of research has been conducted into the psychosocial aspects of aging, psychologists are still not sure which coping capacities contribute most to successful aging. Those working with older people must keep in mind that each individual takes into old age an individual coping pattern, and some can adjust better than others. On the whole, old people adapt better than we believe; perhaps with modification in the external factors influencing their lives, they would be able to age more successfully.

Social Aspects of Aging

The third set of characteristics of concern in examining the aging process are those related to social aging. Social aging refers to the habits and roles of aging individuals as they relate to groups or society. Sociologists are interested in determining the extent to which older people continue to interact socially. Social interaction refers to the behavior exhibited in groups or by classes of people without reference to specific individuals.

Socialization in Later Life

Sociologists are also interested in the process by which individuals learn to negotiate the social changes experienced throughout life. The term most often used to characterize this adaptation to change is socialization, which may be defined as the learning of new behaviors and orientations as one moves into new positions in the social structure.

The process of socialization is most obvious during childhood. One must learn to say please and thank you, to talk only at certain instances in school, to comb one's hair in a certain way, and to wear certain types of clothing. The list is endless. It is equally true but not as apparent that socialization occurs throughout the life cycle. Whenever people move into different social positions, they must learn many new behaviors in order to fill the position acceptably. In childhood one is helped— even forced—to learn the new behavior by institutions of socialization such as the family and the school; in adulthood one finds few institutions to program individual behavior into acceptable ways. The army or college are exceptions to this, but they pertain to very specialized positions and periods of life. This is what makes the normal transitions of adulthood, that is, the role changes, so difficult in our society. How does one learn the behaviors necessary to become a good mother? A happy retiree? A valued grandmother? A graceful widow?

Such questions reflect some of the fundamental problems in the natural course of adulthood and aging. For those working with older people, these problems are translated into more general terms: How does the social system change for individuals as they move into the later phases of the life cycle, and how may socialization into the roles associated with old age be characterized?

Social Age and Age Grading

Aging in the everyday interactional world is socially defined. To be "old" or "elderly" is to have reached some social milestone. The term *age-grading* refers to age positions and the system developed by a culture to give order and predictability to the individual's life course. Students entering college define themselves and behave differently than they did earlier as seniors in high school, because they now occupy a different position. Different things are expected of them, and their behavior is judged accordingly.

The points along the life cycle at which a person moves from "child" to "adolescent" to "adult" to "older adult" are socially defined but closely related to biological development. After physical maturity is reached, social age continues to be marked off by relatively clearcut biological or social events in the life cycle. For example, marriage marks the end of one social age period and the beginning of another. So does the appearance of the first child, the departure of children from the home, and the birth of grandchildren. At each stage we take on new roles, and our prestige is altered in relation to other family members. At each of these points we may be said to occupy a new position within the family.

Age Norms

Age norms and age expectation operate as probes and brakes to behavior, in some instances hastening and in other delaying it. Men and women are aware of their own timing and readily describe themselves as early, late, or on time with regard to family and occupational events, for example, "He married late," or "He is too young to marry." Age norms also operate in many less clear-cut ways and in more peripheral areas of adult life, as illustrated in such phrases as, "He's too old to be working so hard," "She's too young to wear that style of clothes," or "That's a strange thing for a man his age to say."

Norms are defined simply as expectations of behavior (Bengtson, 1973). They are rules that socially define what is appropriate or inappropriate in a situation. Norms are enforced by sanction, and a person is generally rewarded for conformity and punished for nonconformity.

From childhood to adulthood, much effort is made to socialize individuals to assume the roles of adulthood, while little or no training emphasizes the roles of later life, such as retirement or widowhood (Cox, 1988). This suggests that there are few norms specifically related to old age. Those things that are norms for older people apply as appropriately to adults of all age groups; for instance, religion, interest in grandchildren, maintaining contact with children, and remaining financially independent as long as possible. Behaviors disapproved for older people were related to social isolation and inactivity, solitude, and inattention to religion. The evidence confirms that there are few norms regarding appropriate or inappropriate behavior in old age.

Sociologists suggest that, in old age, there are positive as well as negative consequences to a lack of norms. Lack of norms allows greater range of personal choice in structuring one's life. In addition, lack of norms permits old people to be inwardly directed, expending all their energies on themselves. On the other hand, the lack of norms creates an environment without expectation, making it difficult to structure one's life.

Stereotypes

In this society the young people's attitudes about the old are often stereotypic. Aging individuals frequently accept such **stereotypes,** so that their own expectations concerning aging are inaccurate. On the basis of information about the small percentage of institutionalized elderly, for example, the erroneous generalization may be made that most old people are "senile." Similarly, it is often assumed that older people are politically conservative, lacking in sexual interest and motivation, and more religious than younger people, or that they dread death. Other stereotypes are that old people are rigid, narrow-minded, old fashioned, and crabby; that they do not care about their physical appearance, that they are always sick; and that they are generally neglected by their families. These attitudes about the elderly in general are false, but they encourage stereotypic thinking.

Role Loss in Old Age

Roles are defined as special positions for the division of labor within groups. Roles are generally derived from the various tasks an individual performs in a social system. For example, if a man works to support his family, he assumes the role of "breadwinner." There are expectations of behavior that are associated with certain positions or roles. Over time the social world of the aging person changes. In some instances he or she can no longer assume the roles of friend, parent, spouse, and worker. The number and kind of social contacts diminish, and various roles are lost through retirement, death of friends and relatives, and decreased mobility.

There are two significant aspects of role change associated with old age. One is role confusion: Many older adults are confused about the role they play in society. The other is related to the shrinking range of roles possible in old age. Fewer and fewer roles exist for individuals with advancing age. Role loss in later life may have severe emotional ramifications for older adults; for instance, the high incidence of suicide among older men is generally attributed to the effects of role loss.

Status

Status refers to one's position in the social order. Sociologists suggest that in most societies there are age status systems that determine how individuals are to behave in various age groups. For example, in many Eastern societies old age is a time when individuals are given a great deal of status. For the most part, status is given to the extent that an individual possesses something that is of value to the group. Status is generally obtained through two means: it is achieved or earned, that is, gained on the basis of something accomplished; or it is ascribed, that is, given on the basis of one's position. For example, a war hero may achieve status through his deeds; a princess has ascribed status on the basis of her position of high rank in the social order.

As we stated earlier, individuals are prepared for new positions and change in status in a society through the process called socialization. The goal of socialization is to assist the individual to personally reorganize the internal effects created by new positions and a change in status. Passage from childhood to adulthood is marked by many institutional arrangements—legal, interpersonal, and occupational—that prepare the individual for this transition. The transformation from middle age to old age is not characterized by similar socialization experiences. With retirement and the consequent change in status associated with it, for example, there is no formal process that prepares the individual for the role of nonworker.

Essentially, old age has a devalued status in our society. Being old has less value than being middle aged or young, and consequently no gain of status accompanies movement into old age. This devaluation is exemplified by the fact that, when speaking of themselves to others, older people often do not identify themselves as "old." Rather, they might say they are "senior citizens."

When people reach old age they are relegated to a position in society in which their skills are not demanded, and they are left to their own devices to

81

survive. As Robert Atchley (1975) suggests, the old, like mo
ments in society, are subject to poverty, illness, idleness, an   _lation.
Those working with older people should be aware that society has institutionalized means of systematically limiting the roles of older people, and, in many instances, the service programs provided for them are an effort to compensate for
this fact.

Summary

In the past decade the United States has been confronted with a tremendous
increase in the number and proportion of older people in the population. The
increased number of older people and the need to provide services for them have
resulted in a greater attempt to understand the aging process as it affects individuals. We know that old age is not characterized by physical changes alone. As individuals move into old age, they are confronted with physical, psychological, and
social changes that they may or may not be able to cope with.

As a nation we are not prepared to deal with the increased number of older
people. Since older people are viewed by society as unproductive, they are not
seen as an essential segment of our population, and their status in society reflects
this. The lives of older people are plagued with three major problems: poverty,
illness, and idle time. These problems will be discussed in chapter 2.

READING 1.1

Grays on the Go / *Time* Magazine
The following reading is taken from Time *Magazine and describes the current
state of the aging in America, through the eyes of a popular magazine's writers
and editors.*

No one ever expected America to age gracefully. How could the country of
adolescent spirit, reckless politics, marathons, short skirts, unbounded energy and
a restless imagination admit that its body is growing old? Not with Ronald Reagan
in the saddle at 77. Or Joe Niekro, a starting pitcher at 43, fluttering knuckle balls
past cross-eyed youngsters on a Saturday afternoon. Or Dr. Jonas Salk, 73, who
developed the first polio vaccine 35 years ago, searching for an AIDS vaccine. Or
Elizabeth Taylor at 55, flashing a luscious violet smile from a magazine cover. We
don't have to slow down, they seem to say. Why should you?

It may be that, with all the willfulness of youth, America is finding a new way to grow old. Far from fading away, the elderly seem to be brightening on the horizons of the mind, the family, the workplace, the community. Everywhere their role and presence are changing. Politicians rush to court the gray vote. Corporations and charities plumb a deeply skilled, reliable labor resource among the used-to-be and not-yet-ready-to-be retired. Madison Avenue prepares to tap a vast, long-ignored market. Where once the image of the elderly was of frailty, there are now energy and curiosity, courses to take, choirs to join, diets to break, children to counsel, battles to fight, whims to follow.

But with these come other, less cheering images and prospects. Among them is the still haunting presence of the elderly poor, most of them widows, many of them black, collapsing into a safety net that cannot support their weight. The well-being of America's senior citizens, though far greater than 20 years ago, is by no means universal. Many are sick and getting sicker, as health care becomes prohibitively, expensive. Every year as the baby boomers age and the nation's center of gravity shifts upward, the allocation of resources becomes ever more difficult and the potential for conflict between generations ever greater.

Budget-conscious policymakers must already balance the competing claims of education, child-care and welfare programs against Medicare, catastrophic health insurance and numerous benefits for the elderly. With each advance in medical technology, doctors and ethicists wrestle over how long people should be kept alive and how to ration health care between the young and the very old. And closest to home, many "sandwich" families will feel a terrible strain as they try to raise their children and sustain their parents on a squeezed household budget.

In many ways, America is not yet ready for a vast social change that came upon it rather suddenly. "It used to be," says Ken Dychtwald, a young, blunt-spoken gerontologist in Emeryville, Calif., "that people didn't age. They died." When the Republic was founded a new-born child could expect to reach 35. Today Americans could well live into their 90s—and live well too. In 1950 people 65 and over made up just 7.7% of the population. Now the number is up to 12% and it will reach 17.3% by 2020. Fastest growing of all is the group 85 and over. By 1995 the population of the average U.S. town will look like Florida's population today.

But it is not just that the elderly are living longer, healthier lives. They are living them differently. Look around the Sunbelt. Florida, Arizona, New Mexico and Nevada have some of the country's fastest-growing populations of those over 65. In some places it seems a wholly different, more leisurely universe, full of choices and passions long delayed. There is Hulda Crooks, 91, who has climbed 97 mountains since she turned 65, most recently Mount Fuji in Japan. And Dentist James Jay, 74, who finished, along with 51 other septuagenarians and four octogenarians, that 26-mile ribbon of pain, the New York Marathon. And Virginia Peckham, 69, known on San Clemente beach as "That Crazy Old Lady," riding an orange-and-white boogie board and shouting surfing mantras. And Etta Kallman, 77, writing knowingly about "The Metabolism of the Dinosaur" and winning awards for academic excellence from New York University. And Jane Stovall, 103 next week, a onetime milliner, author, tango dancer and seniors golf champion and, at 89, a student pilot.

Then there are the seasoned boys of summer: the Kids-Kubs softball league of St. Petersburg, Fla., where rookies must be at least 74 to don the white Good Humor man uniform and black bow tie. The team has its own special rules, Harry Rylee told TIME Correspondent Michael Riley. "You've got a couple of guys there that you could eat a sandwich while they're running to first base," muses the outfielder, whose brothers Morris and Michael play shortstop and infield. "But you can't tell 'em they can't play. That'd be like sticking a knife in them."

For many of the relentlessly young, the attitude is born out of a community life that resembles nothing so much as their college years of half a century ago: a life of options, dates, lessons and sudden, surprising fellowship. Florida Gerontologist Otto Von Mering, 65, refers to the "fictive kinship," whereby older people acquire a new support system long after their families and friends have dispersed. Take Liz Carpenter. At 65, the twangy-voiced former press secretary to Lady Bird Johnson started writing a book. At 66, she found romance—with a man she had known when she was 20. Now 67, she has devised her cardinal rules for aging: entertain a lot, never pass up an invitation, and by all means fall in love. On a hilltop outside her home in Salado, Texas, she entertains friends in the Jacuzzi she calls her "golden pond." Every month she gathers with fellow members of the Bay at the Moon Society, a group of large-lunged Texas who meet at a different ranch to sing and holler at the midnight sky. "Aging has become very stylish," Carpenter concludes happily. "All the best people are doing it."

But the elderly are doing far, far more than just playing. The "shadow work" of millions of volunteers—in schools, hospital wards, prisons and arts centers—has helped fill the hole left by younger women, once full-time volunteers, who have entered the work force. Many retirees view such service as a duty as well as a pastime. Lois Eiseman, 67, a former kindergarten teacher, travels to schools and day-care centers to test children for hearing disabilities. Restaurant Owner "Daddy" Bruce Randolph, 88 this week, serves thousand of dinners to Denver's homeless and shut-ins every Thanksgiving. Wayne Matson, 67, a retired Air Force colonel, volunteers full time for the humane society in Winter Haven, Fla. "If you're not committed to something," he declares, " you're just taking up space."

For others, the luxury of time and health has required some creative thinking. In the 1880s, when German Chancellor Otto von Bismarck set the retirement age at 65, the average life expectancy was 45. No problem there. But these days, many of those over 65 who prepared themselves for a life of leisure found they were not cut out for it. For them, the greatest luxury of retirement is returning to work—on their own terms. Robert Pamplin, 76, former head of the Georgia-Pacific Corp., prudently began plotting his corporate afterlife ten years before he reached his company's mandatory retirement age. In 1976, on his 65th birthday, he bought a small sand-and-gravel company in Portland, Ore. Ten years and two other acquisitions later, he oversees a small empire with revenues of $420 million. Pamplin too saw his postretirement course as a sort of duty. "God has given us certain talents," he says. "And he gave them to us to use."

Granted, many retirees looking to return to work have had a harder time. It often takes many months to find a suitable job, whether to supplement Social Security or fill spare time. But between 1980 and 1986 the number of part-time employees in the U.S. rose by 23%, twice the rate of full-time jobholders, in part because many large corporations were quick to respond to the widened applicant pool. McDonald's created McMasters, a four-week job-training program for people over 50. The part-time work has helped people like Katherine Gaik, 76, dodge an idle old age. The Travelers Insurance Co. of Hartford is saving more than $1 million a year by hiring back retired workers instead of paying fees to temp agencies. What is more, says Employment Director Donald K. Deward, "we get better, more competent, dedicated and highly motivated people."

The activity and prosperity of America's retirees have not gone unnoticed on Madison Avenue. There was a time when advertisers behaved as though no one past middle age ever bought anything more durable than panty hose. No more. Few marketing experts can ignore the fact that Americans over 50 earn more than half the discretionary income in the country. Magazine publishers are betting on the favorable demographics. Norman Lear's former wife Frances, 64, will next week debut Lear's, a glossy upscale bimonthly for women over 40. Major firms are forming special groups to study the senior market, and at least one company that offers ageless ads has opened. "My sense is we're on the leading edge right now," says Jerry Gerber of LifeSpan in Manhattan, "way out there, totally new, totally different."

In time, through sheer force of gravity, the products themselves, and not just the ads, will be shaped for an older consumer. "We have designed America to fit the size, shape and style of a country we used to be," says Gerontologist Dychtwald, "and what we used to be is young." Books and newspapers, with their tiny print, are designed for wide young eyes, as is the lighting in public places. Buttons, jars and doorknobs are obstacles to those with arthritis. Traffic lights are timed for a youthful pace. "In years to come," predicts Dychtwald, "huge industries will emerge as America changes its shape and form."

One huge industry has already emerged, based in Washington but reaching across the country: an industry of influence. Politicians for years viewed the aged as a uniform group—physically and often mentally feeble, politically compliant, socially inert. The candidate who does so now risks being trampled by what one Congressman sweetly calls the 800-lb. gorilla. The American Association of Retired Persons, with 28 million members, is bigger than most countries. The Gray Panthers, with 80,000 members, pressures Congress on everything from health insurance to housing costs. This year the formidable gray lobby is moving full force into grass-roots presidential politics. And when it moves, the ground shakes.

In New Hampshire, leading up to primary night, the AARP mailed out 250,000 pieces of literature detailing the candidates' position on Social Security, long-term health care and other incendiary issues. One booklet was called *You Can Select the President*—a brash enough claim, until you consider that in 1984 a total of 101,000 Democrats voted in the primary and that the AARP has 145,000 members in New Hampshire alone. A $250,000 television ad campaign aims to get out the gray vote. "The old folks," says Political Consultant Thomas Kiley, "are showing more political muscle in this election than ever before."

The candidates have been quick to respond. Most have produced either a touching story of an aged parent or, in the case of Michael Dukakis, the real thing. Jesse Jackson, invoking Social Security's creator, tells voters that he "would rather have Franklin Roosevelt in a wheelchair than Ronald Reagan on a horse." Virtually all have come out in support of the long-term health-care bill now stalled in Congress, which, if it ever passed, would cost the Government tens of billions of dollars over the next five years. Only Republican Pete du Pont has proposed radically restructuring Social Security, a notion that George Bush boldly dismissed as a "nutty idea."

The fervor with which the elderly lobby to protect their benefits seems incongruous—and unforgivably selfish—to younger people who see only the silvery lifestyle of the old rich. But the AARP campaign is born of stark realities: the persistence of nasty pockets of poverty among the aged, the threat of catastrophic illness that faces every old man and woman and, above all, the prospect of cutbacks in benefits as Washington struggles to balance its budget.

The programs that the elderly are fighting to preserve were created a generation ago, when the reform-minded leaders of the 1960s vowed to protect senior citizens from the shameful destitution that had terrorized earlier generations. At the time that Lyndon Johnson launched his immense rescue mission, the Great Society, more than a quarter of all old people lived below the poverty line. In the popular imagination, being old usually meant a frail and lonely dependency, in which old women lived on cat food in spartan apartments and relied on busy children or social workers for a ride to the doctor.

Washington waged war on poverty among the elderly through two programs that helped rich and poor alike. Congress created Medicare insurance in 1965. In 1972 it voted a 20% increase in Social Security benefits and linked them to the Consumer Price Index in an attempt to safeguard retirees from the double-digit inflation that was devastating young families. In 1980 alone, payments increased a record 14.3%. Now each month 91% of those 65 and over receive benefits totaling $13.6 billion. The percentage of elderly people living below the poverty line has been cut from 20% in 1970 to 12% in 1984.

These outlays, combined with other sources of income, have provided many of the elderly with a sense of security that their own parents never enjoyed and that they will not relinquish without a fight. The median income of couples 65 and over in 1986 was about $22,000, which can go a long way when mortgages are paid up, children have left home, and there are few large purchases, such as appliances, to worry about. A 1984 congressional report on aging concluded, "Today

. . . the act of retirement alone is no longer the source of poverty, isolation and poor health it once was."

Yet for all the improvement in the condition of America's senior citizens, there is a sharp divide between the vigorous "young old," those 65 to 75, and the far frailer "old old," those 75 and up. There also remain grave disparities among ethnic groups. Nearly a third of elderly blacks live on less than $5,300 a year. Among black women living alone, the figure is 55%. For all the creative thinking on Madison Avenue and in corporate boardrooms on how to make use of the elderly as a recourse, there still needs to be a comparable response from Washington when the aged become a burden.

But many young people do not see it that way. In their view, Washington is already doing too much for aged citizens, a perception that could bring about a serious breach between the generations. Already the emerging power of America's grandparents frightens many of their children and grandchildren. Some experts forecast a costly confrontation, in which embittered young people and embattled older ones fight with the most sophisticated political weapons over ever scarcer resources. In the shorthand of demographers and journalists, the scenario is known as the age wars.

Consider the following: Martha Dierdre is 72 and worth about $300,000. Widowed five years ago, she lives in a $150,000 condominium in Los Angeles, drives an Audi, consults her broker weekly, and plays bridge on Tuesdays over tea and crumpets. Her most solemn ritual takes place at the beginning of each month, when she walks to her bank and deposits a $420 Social Security check. She thinks of her husband, a warehouseman who worked hard and saved for 30 years. "A deal is a deal is a deal," she declares. "I don't care what I'm worth; that money is mine."

Dierdre's only grandchild Paul earns $16,000 a year working at a lumberyard in Portland, Ore. His wife Karen brings in an additional $6,000 as a part-time secretary. Since they cannot afford a house, they rent a two-bedroom apartment for $500 a month, where they raise their three-year-old daughter. They too have a ritual. Every two weeks, when they deposit their paychecks, they agonize over the 7% deduction for Social Security tax and wonder if they will ever see that money again—unless, of course, they visit Grandma. "This whole system just beats the hell out of me,' says Paul, 27. "It's like that old saying: robbing from the poor to pay the rich."

Paul does not personally blame the elderly. Few young people do, even when they sense, as they read the newspapers or go shopping for a house, that they are walking into a trap. Who is going to protect young families, they wonder, from an economic system that is eroding their living standards? Or a health system that promises at least partial care for the elderly but guarantees nothing for families with sick children? Or a political system that allows communities to outlaw residents under 19 to ensure peace and quiet—and reduce school taxes at the same time? Or a Social Security system that seems to assure only that the young will never draw out anything like the amount they are required to pay in? "I don't have a grudge against older people collecting Social Security because the Government told them to expect it," says Law Student Jeffrey Rosen, 28. "But what about us? Something has got to be done."

Jeffrey's is a generation that viewed progress as an American birthright, only to discover its expectations vastly exceed its prospects. For the past 15 years, even as their parents grew more financially secure, young workers have faced declining real wages, rising taxes, high interest rates and prohibitive housing costs. At times, the Government seems to be conspiring against them. During the Reagan Administration, payments to the elderly have risen 35%, so that now more than a quarter of all Government spending goes to the 12% of the population who are 65 or older. Meanwhile, America's infant-mortality rate remains one of the highest among industrialized nations, and one in five children lives in poverty. While Social Security remains off limits, Aid to Families with Dependent children was cut by 19% and school-meal programs by 41% between 1981 and 1984. The U.S., argues Senator Daniel Patrick Moynihan, may be the "first society in history in which a person is more likely to be poor if young rather than old."

Of such sentiments and statistics is the fear of an age war born. Lured by high stakes and intuitive appeal, the lobbyists are swarming around the "generational equity" issue. Three years ago, Republican Senator David Durenberger from Minnesota helped establish the youth-advocacy group AGE (Americans for Generational Equity) to advance the claims of the young and counterbalance the powerful gray lobby. "The AARP is almost totally focused on the well being of its clients," says AGE Executive Director Paul Hewitt, "but they are going to have to address ways to avoid putting unbearable burdens on the baby boomers' children." Other youth advocates in Congress are also sharpening their blades. John Porter, Republican Representative from Illinois, for example, calls the budget deficit an exercise in "fiscal child abuse."

When the social costs of the age quake—the arrival of the baby boomers into their golden years—are tallied, the figures become even more alarming. The $50 billion spent on health care for the old when Reagan came into office is expected to reach $200 billion by the year 2000. Between 1980 and 2040, experts project a 160% increase in physician visits by the elderly, a 200% rise in days of hospital care, a 280% growth in the number of nursing-home residents. Between now and the year 2000, a new 220-bed nursing home will have to be opened every day just to keep even with demand. Without a change in the present system, pension and health-care costs will account for more than 60% of the federal budget by 2040.

So who is going to pay for America to grow old? With each advancement in medical technology, the possibility of extending people's lives increases. Who is to decide who should get the organ transplant or have first access to kidney-dialysis machines? The questions have fired a debate about what society owes its elderly, what should constitute a natural life-span and how far doctors should go to keep elderly patients alive. Medical Ethicist Daniel Callahan, 57, suggests that health involves more than preventing death. "We should seek to advance research and health care that increase not the length of life," he argues, "but the quality of life of the elderly."

Senior citizens deeply resent critics who seem to begrudge them their independence or imply that anyone ever got rich on a $500-a-month check. Many retirees
worked hard, lived frugally and saved carefully to guard against the nightmare of a
destitute old age. And while it is true the elderly consume roughly a third of the
nation's medical resources, Medicare cannot begin to cover all the costs of a long
illness. Already senior citizens pay three times as much out of their own pockets for
health care as the young do. They view their benefits as a right, not a windfall. "I
spent years away from my family fighting in Europe," says Roger Davis, 68, of Los
Angeles. "Don't tell me the nation doesn't owe me something in my old age."

Such attitudes rile policymakers who are charged with slashing billions of dollars out of already hard-hit social programs. While no one proposes cutting off the
truly needy, those lobbying for reform point out that thousands of millionaires
receive a monthly check. Argues Horace Brock, president of Strategic Economic
Decisions Inc. in Menlo Park, Calif.: "There may have been a social contract that
what you put in you got back, but not six times what you put in." Unless the system
is revamped, he warns, when the baby boomers reach retirement age, Social Security will be in jeopardy. Just as alarming, the trust fund that supports the hospital-
insurance part of Medicare could be bankrupt by 2002.

That prospect worries older people as well as the young. In fact the reason
Social Security is unlikely to ignite an age war is that many elderly people acknowledge its flaws and admit the system needs to be changed, while many young people support its basic principles. Even some lobbyists for the aged privately accept
the need to adjust Social Security, by raising the age of eligibility or taxing benefits
for the wealthy, as part of a drastic deficit-reduction plan. While many retirees
defend Social Security, they are horrified by the legacy of a $2 trillion debt they will
leave behind. "The interest on it is about $1,000 a second," says George Toll, 82, of
Long Beach, Calif. "That's why I worry about my grandchildren."

Such signs of mutual concern and interdependence reassures social scientists
and policymakers. In fact the whole age-war scenario, some charge, is a political
distortion, designed to stir up passion and protest about what should be an issue
not of age but of social justice. "I don't think it should ever be put in terms of
equity, that there is a choice between the elderly and children," argues Alan Pifer,
co-editor of Our Aging Society. "There are many other questions." The central
issue, these experts agree, is how to protect those in society who are most vulnerable, regardless of age. "The 'intergenerational equity' debate," insists Ronald Pol-
lack, executive director of the Villers Foundation, an advocacy group for the
elderly, "is a diversionary and dangerous sideshow."

That view is supported by opinion polls, which reveal that most children are
grateful for Social Security because it relieves them of some of the responsibility for
taking care of their elders. Some, but not all. Financial responsibility is only one of
several kinds, and perhaps not the most burdensome. An ailing parent, even in a
distant city, can take an emotional toll on adult children. In many cases the parent
may be living in the same town—or the same house. Already, says Fordham's Marjo-
rie Cantor, former president of the Gerontological Society, "the family is the major

source of support for the elderly. And there is no indication in the future that families will abandon them." The notion of an age war rings false with many experts who work with both the elderly and their children. "Adult children spend a lot of time caring; they make a lot of personal sacrifices," says Dr. Carl Eisdorfer of the University of Miami. The support goes both ways. In fact private transfers of money and assets within families are just as likely, if not more likely to take place from old to young. "The traditional generosity of grandparents," says Author Lydia Bronte, formerly of the Carnegie Corporation, "now takes the form of helping with college tuition, down payment on a house, furniture—not just a check every Christmas."

So how will America adjust to its growing pains? It is possible that advances in science, steady economic growth, better education and some courageous and creative politics will allow the nation to mature gracefully. The signs of interdependence and cooperation encourage policymakers, who agree that a family is a far better source of compassion than a federal agency, however well funded. With that in mind, some politicians are urging that Congress consider tax breaks for families responsible for the care of an elderly parent. Others are lobbying for a broader national health plan that would provide care for the young and old alike.

Corporations too are looking for ways to support workers who are burdened by care-giving obligations. Such benefits, they expect, will raise productivity, reduce absenteeism and allow them to hang on to valued employees who might otherwise quit. Travelers Corp. has offered lunchtime support groups, flex-time hours and an information fair for employees to meet with social service experts. PepsiCo provides seminars and a handbook on care of the elderly. Remington Products Inc., of Bridgeport, Conn. pays half the cost of parent sitters who can take over for employees on evenings and weekends

Within many schools and communities, leaders are exploring ways to bring together retirees with skills and time to spare and young people in need of training and guidance. With the encouragement of the First Lady, the Foster Grandparent program is expanding rapidly. The assumption that one generation can serve as a resource rather than a rival to another, most advocates on both sides would agree, holds far more promise than any call to arms.

READING 1.2

Joie de Vivre / Simone de Beauvoir
Socialization is the process through which we learn new behavior and orientations. Age norms are rules, which vary from culture to culture, for those behaviors that are appropriate and those that are inappropriate at a given age. In this ex-

Reprinted by permission of G. P. Putnam's Sons from *The Coming of Age* by Simone de cerpt *Simone de Beauvoir takes issue with restrictive norms regarding sexuality among aged people, and she concludes that "sexuality, vitality, and activity are indissolubly linked."*

We have one most remarkable piece of evidence concerning an old man's relationship with his body, his image, and his sex: this is Paul Leautaud's *Journal*.[1] He provides us with a living synthesis of the various points of view that we have considered in this study.

Leautaud always looked at himself with a certain approval. It was from the outside that he learned he was aging, and it made him very angry. In 1923, when he was fifty-three, a railway official referred to him as "a little old gentleman." Furious, Leautaud wrote in his Journal, "Little old man? Old gentleman? What the devil—am I blind as all that? I cannot see that I am either a little or an old gentleman. I see myself as a fifty-year-old, certainly, but an exceedingly well preserved fifty-year old. I am slim and I move easily. Just let them show me an old gentleman in such good shape!" At fifty-nine he looked at himself with a critical eye: "Mentally and physically I am a man of forty. What a pity my face does not match! Above all my lack of teeth! I really am remarkable for my age: slim, supple, quick, active. It is my lack of teeth that spoils everything; I shall never dare to make love to a woman again."

In him we see with remarkable clarity how impossible it is for an old man to realize his age. On his birthday he wrote, "Today I begin my sixty-fourth year. In no way do I feel an old man." The old man is Another, and this Other belongs to a certain category that is objectively defined; in his inner experience Leautaud found no such person. There were moments, however, when his age weighed upon him. On April 12, 1936, he wrote, "I do not feel happy about my health nor about my state of mind: and then there is the sorrow of aging, too. Aging above all!" But at sixty-nine he wrote, "During my seventieth year I am still as lively, active, nimble and alert as a man can be."

Leautaud had every reason to be pleased with himself: he looked after his house and cared for his animals; he did all the shopping on foot, carrying heavy baskets of provisions; wrote his *Journal*: and he did not know what it was to be tired. "It is only my sight that is failing. I am exactly as I was at twenty. My memory is as good as ever and my mind as quick and sharp."

This made him all the more irritable when other people's reactions brought the truth home to him. He was seventy when a young woman lost her balance as an underground train started off with a jerk: she cried out. "I'm so sorry, Grandpa, I nearly fell on you." He wrote angrily, "Damm it all! My age must show clearly in my face. How impossible it is to see oneself as one really is!"

The paradox lies in the fact that he did not really dislike being old. He was one

[1] Leautaud was a critic and an editor of *Mercure de France*, a literary journal.

of those exceptional cases I have mentioned, where old age coincides with child-hood fantasy: he had always been interested in old people. On March 7, 1942, when he was seventy-two, he wrote, "A kind of vanity comes over you when you reach old age—you take a pride in remaining healthy, slim, supple and alert, with an unaltered complexion, your joints in good order, no illness and no diminution in your physical and mental powers."

But his vanity demanded that his age be invisible to others: he liked to imagine that he had stayed young in spite of the burden of his years.

He only gave way to discouragement at the very end of his life, when his health failed. On February 25, 1945, he wrote, "I am very low indeed. My eyesight. The horrible marks of age I see on my face. My *Journal* behind-hand. The mediocrity of my life. I have lost my energy and all my illusions. Pleasure, even five minutes of pleasure, is over for me." He was then seventy-five, and his sexual life had come to an end. But except in his very last years one of the reasons for his pride was that he still felt desire and was still capable of satisfying it. We can follow his sexual evolution in his *Journal*.

Leautaud only became fully aware of women when he was approaching his fiftieth year. At thirty-five he wrote, "I am beginning to regret that my tempera-ment allows me to enjoy women so little." He lacked the "sacred fire." "I always think too much of other things—of myself, for example." He was afraid of impo-tence and his lovemaking was over very quickly: "I give women no pleasure since I have finished in five minutes and can never start again. . . . Shamelessness is all I really like in love. . . . There are some things not every woman can be asked to do." He had a lasting affair with a woman called Bl__. He says he loved her very much, but he also says that living with her was hell. When he was about forty, although he was still rather indifferent, since he could give his partner no pleasure, he delighted in looking at pictures of naked women. Yet a few years later he speaks sadly of the "rare love-scenes in my life which I really enjoyed." He reproaches himself for being "timid, awkward, brusque, oversensitive, always hesitant, never able to take advantage of even the best opportunities" with women. All this changed when at fifty he met "a really passionate woman, wonderfully equipped for pleasure and exactly to my taste in these matters," and he showed himself to be "almost brilliant," although up until then he had thought that he was not very good—as he had only known women who did not suit him. From this time on sex became an obsession to him: on December 1, 1923, he wrote, "Perhaps Madame (one of the names he gave to his mistress) is right: my perpetual desire to make love may be somewhat pathological. . . . I put it down to a lifetime's moderation—it lasted until I was over forty—and also to my intense feeling for her, which makes me want to make love to her when I see so much as a square inch of her body. . . . I think it is also because I have been deprived of so many things, such as that female nakedness for which I acquired such a liking. I am quite amazed when I think of what has happened to me in all this. . . . Never have I caressed any other woman as I career Madame." In the summer they parted, and abstinence lay heavy upon him: he masturbated, thinking of her. "Of course I am delighted to be such an ardent lover at my age, but God knows it can be troublesome."

Madame was a little older than he: all his life he had loved only mature women. A twenty-three-year-old virgin threw herself at his head, and he agreed to have an affair with her: but it did not give him the least pleasure and he broke immediately. Except for this one fling he was faithful to Madame for years. He liked watching himself and her in a mirror during their lovemaking. From 1927—age fifty-seven—on, he was forced to take care not to make love too often; he found consolation in bawdy talk with the Panther (another name he gave to his mistress). He did not get on well with her; "we are attached to each other only by our senses—by vice—and what remains is so utterly tenous!" But in 1938 he did recall with great satisfaction the "seventeen years of pleasure between two creatures, the one as passionate and daring as the other in amorous words and deeds." When he was fifty-nine his affair with the Scourge, as he now called her, was still going on, though she was already sixty-four. He was shocked by couples where the woman was much younger than the man. "I myself at fifty-nine would never dare to make any sort of advance to a woman of thirty."

He was still very much attracted to the Scourge, and he took great pleasure in his "sessions" with her. Yet he did complain, "What a feeble ejaculation when I make love: little better than water!" Later he wrote, "I am certainly better when I do not make love at all. Not that it comes hard—far from it—but it is always a great effort, and I do not get over it as quickly as I did a few years ago. . . . What I miss most is female nakedness, licentious attitudes, and playing amorous games."

"Untill I was sixty-six or sixty-seven I could make love two or three times a week." Now he complained that his brain was tired for three or four days after love, but he still went on, and he corresponded with three of his former mistresses.

When he was seventy Leautaud wrote, "I miss women and love terribly." He remembered how he used to make passionate love to the Scourge from the age of forty-seven to sixty-three, and then for two years with CN (another mistress).

"It was only three years ago that I noticed I was slowing down. I can still make love, and indeed I quite often feel sad at being deprived of it: though at the same time I tell myself that it is certainly much better for me to abstain."

At seventy-two he was still planning idylls that never came to anything, and he had erotic dreams that gave him an erection. "At night I still feel ready for anything." But that same year he observed that his sexual powers were declining. "It is no use giving yourself over to lovemaking when the physical side is dead or nearly so. Even the pleasure of seeing and fondling is soon over, and there is not the least eagerness to begin again. For a real appreciation of all these things, there must be the heat of physical passion." It is clear that Leautaud's greatest pleasure was visual. He retained it longer than any other form of sensual enjoyment and after the age of forty he prized it very highly indeed. When he lost it he considered that his sexual life was over. It is also clear how a man's image of himself is bound up with sexual activity. He was " in the depths of sorrow" when he could no longer experience these pleasures. Still, his narcissim did survive his sexual decline at least for some time.

The Feminine Disadvantage

Biologically women's sexuality is less affected by age then men's. Brantome bears this out in the chapter of his *Vies des dames galantes* that he dedicates to "certain old ladies who take as much pleasure in love as the young ones." Whereas a man of a certain age is no longer capable of erection, a woman "at no matter what age is endowed with as it were a furnace . . . all fire and fuel within." Popular tradition bears witness to this contrast. In one of the songs in the Merry Muses of Caledonia [2] an old woman laments her elderly husband's impotence. She longs for "the wild embraces of their younger days" that are now no more than a ghostly memory, since he no longer thinks of doing anything in bed except sleeping, while she is eaten up with desire. Today scientific research confirms the validity of this evidence. According to Kinsey, throughout their lives women are sexually more stable than men: when they are sixty their potential for pleasure and desire is the same as it was at thirty. According to Masters and Johnson, the strength of the sexual reaction diminishes with age: yet a woman can still reach orgasm, above all if she is regularly and property stimulated. Those who do not often have physical relations sometimes find coition painful, either during the act of or after, and sometimes suffer from dyspareunia, or dysuria: it is not known whether these troubles are physical or psychological in origin. I may add that a woman can take great pleasure in making love even though she may not reach orgasm. The "preliminary pleasures" count even more perhaps for her than they do for a man. She is usually less sensitive to the appearance of her partner and therefore less worried by his growing old. Even though her part in lovemaking is not as passive as people sometimes make out, she has no fear of a particular failure. There is nothing to prevent her from going on with her sexual activities until the end of her life.

Still, all research shows that women have a less active sexual life than men. Kinsey says that at fifty, 97 percent of men are still sexually active compared with 93 percent of women. At sixty it is 94 percent of men and only 80 percent of women. This comes from the fact that socially men, whatever their age, are subjects, and women are objects, relative beings. When she marries, a woman's future is determined by her husband's; he is usually about four years older than she, and his desire progressively lessens. Or if it does continue to exist; he takes to younger women. An old woman, on the other hand, finds it extremely difficult to have extramarital relations. She is even less attractive to men than old men are to women. And in her case gerontophilia does not exist. A young man may desire a woman

---

[2] Popular Scottish songs collected in the eighteenth century.

old enough to be his mother but not his grandmother. A woman of seventy is no longer regarded by anyone as an erotic object. Venal love is very difficult for her to find. It would be most exceptional for an old woman to have both the means and the opportunity of getting herself a partner: and then again shame and fear of what people might say would generally prevent her from doing so. This frustration is painful to many old women, for they are still tormented by desire. They usually find their relief in masturbation: a gynecologist told me of the case of one woman of seventy who begged him to cure her of this practice—she was indulging in it night and day.

When Andree Martinerie was conducting an inquiry for *Elle* magazine (March 1969) she gathered some interesting confidences from elderly women. Madame F., a rich middle-class sixty-eight-year-old, a militant Catholic, mother of five and grandmother of ten, told her, "I was already sixty-four. . . . Now just listen: four months after my husband's death I went down into the street just like someone who is going to commit suicide. I had made up my mind to give myself to the very first man who would have me. Nobody wanted me. So I went home again." When she was asked whether she had thought of remarrying, she answered, "That is all I ever do think of. If I dared I would put an advertisement in *Le Chasseur francais*. . . . I would rather have a decrepit invalid of a man than no man at all!" Talking of desire, Madame R., sixty years old and living with her sick husband, said, "It is quite true that you don't get over it." She sometimes felt like beating her head against the wall. A woman reader of this inquiry wrote to the magazine, "I must tell you that a woman remains a woman for a very long time in spite of growing older. I know what I am talking about, because I am seventy-one. I was a widow at sixty; my husband died suddenly and it took me at least two years to realize fully what had happened. Then I started to answer advertisements in the matrimonial column. I admit that I did miss having a man—or rather I should say I do miss it: this aimless existence is terrifying, without affection or any outlet for one's own feelings. I even began wondering whether I was quite normal. Your inquiry was a great relief. . . . "This correspondent speaks modestly of "affection," an "outlet for one's feelings." But the context shows that her frustration had a sexual dimension. The reaction of a young woman who wrote to *Elle* is typical: "In our group of young people we laughed heartily about the passionate widow (the member of the Action Catholique) who cannot 'get over it.' I wish you would now hold an inquiry on love as it appears to the fourth age of women, in other words those between eighty and a hundred and twenty." Young people are very shocked if the old, especially old women, are still sexually active.

A woman, then, continues in her state as erotic object right up to the end. Chastity is not imposed upon her by a physiological destiny but by her position as a relative being. Nevertheless it may happen that women condemn themselves to chastity because of "psychological barriers" that I have mentioned, which are even more inhibiting for them than for men. A woman is usually more narcissitic in love than a man; her narcissism is directed at her body as a whole. She has a delightful awareness of her body as something desirable, and this awareness comes to her through her partner's caresses and gaze. If he goes on desiring her she easily puts up with her body's aging. But at the first sign of coldness she feels her ugliness in all its horror; she is disgusted with her image and cannot bear to expose her poor person to others. This lack of assurance strengthens her fear of other people's opinions; she knows how censorious they are toward old women who do not play their proper role of serene and passion-free grandmothers.

Even if her husband wants to make love with her again later, a deeply rooted feeling of shame may make her refuse him. Women make less use of diversion than men. Those who enjoyed a very active and uninhibited sexual life before do sometimes compensate for their enforced abstinence by extreme freedom in conversation and the use of obscene words. They become something very like bawds, or at least they spy upon the sexual life of their young women friends with a most unhealthy curiosity, and do all they can to make them confide their secrets. But generally speaking their language is as repressed as their lovemaking. Elderly women like to appear as restrained in their conversation as they are in their way of life. Their sexuality now shows only in their dress, their jewelry and ornaments, and in the pleasure they take in male society. They like to flirt discreetly with men younger than themselves and they are touched by attentions that show they are still women in men's eyes.

However, it is clear from pathology that in women, too, the sexual drive is repressed but not extinguished. Psychiatrists have observed that in asylums female patients' eroticism often increases with age. Senile dementia brings with it a state of erotic delirium arising from lack of cerebral control. Repressions are also discarded in some other forms of psychosis. Dr. Geroges Mahe recorded twenty cases of extreme eroticism out of 110 sixty-year-old female patients in an institution: the symptoms included public masturbation, make-believe coition, obscene talk, and exhibitionism. Unfortunately he gives no idea of the meaning of these displays: he puts them into no context and we do not know who the patients were who indulged in these practices. Many of the inmates suffer from genital hallucinations such as rape and physical contact. Women of over seventy-one are convinced that they are pregnant. Madame C., seventy and a grandmother, sings barrackroom songs and walks about the hospital half-naked, looking for a man. Eroticism is the most important factor in many delirious states; it also triggers off some cases of melancholia. E. Gehu speaks of an eighty-three-year-old grandmother who was looked after in a convent. She was an exhibitionist, showing both homosexual and heterosexual tendencies. She fell upon the younger nuns who brought her meals: during these crises she was perfectly lucid. Later she became mentally confused. She ended up by regaining her mental health and behaving normally once more. Here again, we should like a more exact detailed account of her case. All the observations that I have just quoted are most inadequate: but at least they do show that old women are no more "purified of their bodies" than old men.

Neither history nor literature has left us any worthwhile evidence on the sexuality of old women. It is an even more strictly forbidden subject than the sexuality of old men.

There are many cases of the libido disappearing entirely in old people. Ought they to rejoice in it, as the moralists say? Nothing is less certain. It is a mutilation that brings other mutilations with it: sexuality, vitality, and activity are indissolubly linked. When desire is completely dead, emotional response itself may grow loose at its edges. At sixty-three Retif de La Bretonne wrote, "My heart died at the same time as my senses, and if sometimes a tender impulse stirs me, it is as erroneous as that of a savage or a eunuch: it leaves me with a profound feeling of sorrow." It seemed to Bernard Shaw that when he lost interest in women he lost interest in living. "I am ageing very quickly. I have lost all interest in women, and the interest they have in me is greater than ever and it bores me. The time has probably come for me to die."

Even Schopenhauer admitted, "It could be said that once the sexual urge is over life's true centre is burnt out, leaving a mere shell." Or again, "life is like a play acted at first by live actors and the finished by automata wearing the same costumes." Yet at the same time he says that the sexual instinct produces a "benign dementia." The only choice left to men is that between madness and sclerosis. In fact what he calls "dementia" is the spring of life itself. When it is broken or destroyed a man is no longer truly alive.

The link that exists between sexuality and creativity is striking: it is obvious in Hugo and Picasso and in many others. In order to create there must be some degree of aggression—"a certain readiness," says Flaubert and this aggressivity has its biological source in the libido. It is also necessary to feel united with the world by an emotional warmth: this disappears at the same time as carnal desire, as Gide understood very clearly when on April 10, 1942, he wrote. "There was a time when I was cruelly tormented, indeed obsessed by desire, and I prayed 'Oh let the moment come when my subjugated flesh will allow me to give myself entirely to. . . . 'But to what? To art? To pure thought? To God? How ignorant I was! How mad! It was the same as believing that the flame would burn brighter in a lamp with no oil left. If it were abstract, my thought would go out; even today it is my carnal self that feeds the flame and now I pray that I may retain carnal desire until I die."

It would not be truthful to state that sexual indifference necessarily brings inertia and impotence. There are many examples to prove the contrary. Let us merely say there is one dimension of life that disappears when there is no more carnal relationship with the world: those who keep this treasure to an advanced age are privileged indeed.

chapter 2
the social problems
of later life

Those working with or planning to work with older people should be aware of the many problems that confront individuals as they move into old age. To gain insight into these problems one must first delve into the factors that create them. Human services workers should understand the influence social attitudes have on the prevailing condition for older people in a society. Attitudes have a far-reaching effect on the status of the elderly, as they determine the magnitude of resources made available to people in this stage of life. In addition, they determine the resources available to human services workers who attempt to help older people with their problems. In this chapter we will discuss various cultural perspectives on aging and how the different views contribute to social conditions for older people. We will also review the major problems the elderly experience.

Old Age: A Time of
Growth and Wisdom

The history of human development has shown two dominant beliefs about old age (de Beauvoir, 1972). One belief is that old age is a time of growth and reflection; the other focuses on old age as a time of decline. Some social attitudes toward aging are deeply rooted in religious beliefs. For example, Confucius set forth the tenet of absolute obedience to the head of the household, and in pre-revolutionary China respect for the eldest male reached far beyond the limits of the family to embrace all the elderly of the community. In the intensive agrarian society of ancient China, experience and wisdom were seen as greater virtues than strength. Confucius provided a moral justification for the patriarchal system by giving old age and wisdom the same status:

At fifteen, I applied myself to the study of wisdom: At thirty, I grew stronger in it: At forty, I no longer have doubts: At sixty, there was nothing on earth that could shake me: At seventy I could follow the dictates of my heart without disobeying the moral law (Manney, 1975).

Another religion, Taoism, also depicted old age as a virtue. The doctrines of this religion set the age of 60 as the moment when a man can free himself from his body by esthetic experience and become a holy being. The "neotaoism" man's supreme aim was the quest for the long life. Accordingly, ecstasy could lead to a holiness that would protect the adept from death itself. Old age was therefore seen as life in its very highest form.

Because of Eastern culture's respect for old age, the elderly were given status and power of life and death over the young; perhaps old age was a better time of life than young adulthood. Many of these ancient values have transcended time and exist today in Eastern cultures, where the elderly are generally revered and, therefore, are well cared for by the society as a whole. Simone de Beauvoir (1972) maintains that in Chinese literature people may deplore the oppression of which they are the victims, but they never cry out against old age as a curse.

The Western Perspective:
The Old Gray Mare Syndrome

Reverence for old age does not exist in Western societies. One of the earliest Western writings depicts old age as a curse:

How hard and painful are the lonely days of an ancient man; he grows weaker every day; his eyes grow dim; his ears deaf; his strength fades; his heart knows peace no longer. . . . The power of his mind lessens and today he cannot remember what yesterday was like: All his bones hurt. . . . Old age is the worst misfortune that can afflict man (de Beauvoir, 1972).

This perspective continues throughout the history of Western civilization. It is called to mind by Michel Philibert (Manney, 1975), a French gerontologist and philosopher, in his characterization of the Western perspective on aging, which suggests that four main themes run through the Western attitudes. We will discuss these themes below.[1]

Aging Is Biological

In Western societies the biological concept of age governs our attitude toward what is clearly a complex and ambiguous collection of gains and losses. Our mental images of age are primarily images of unfavorable physical change. A problematic social institution such as mandatory retirement is justified as a necessary response to this biological decline. Old people's social isolation is similarly explained as an appropriate response to people whose physical conditions are rendering them so-cially, economically, and spiritually obsolete. The biological concept of aging even governs much of academic gerontology, which itself developed from the biological sciences. On the other hand, as we noted above, many historical non-Western and primitive cultures conceive of aging as a process in which biological, spiritual, and psychological forces have at least equal weight. For some, aging is a time of growth and learning, of continuing maturity, and of accomplishments.

---

[1] This material is excerpted from Manney, 1975.

Aging Is Unfavorable

The Western biological model of aging largely skirts the possibility of fulfillment in old age, a possibility that other cultures have allowed and enjoyed. If one conceives of aging as mainly a biological process, an unfavorable attitude is invariable in relation to this process, because the dominant physical experience in later life is one of loss and decline. However, a perspective on aging that foresees the possibility of spiritual growth outweighing physical decline is a more favorable view. All major cultures in history record examples of contempt for the old. However, past societies have tended to view this contempt as a feature of their own culture, usually one they perceive as inhumane. Our society views the devaluation of old age as a law of nature.

Aging Is Universal

Our biological perspectives, the social and economic isolation of the elderly, and their increased number combine to separate the old from everyone else. Since we believe aging is governed by irreversible biological processes, we perceive aging as happening the same way in all times and in all places, and our chronological age expectations govern social and economic isolation of the elderly. Although we must often think about the social problem of aging, we do so at the cost of obscuring the fact that aging is a differential and variable process.

Aging Is Unmanageable

The final aspect of the Western perspective as characterized by Philibert is ironic. We see aging as an essentially unmanageable process, precisely at the time when medical science has brought biological aging under control to a large degree. We isolate and worry about older people at a time when the number of older people is increasing, and they are much healthier and more alert than older people at any other time in history. Yet our conception of aging includes the notion that there is nothing we can do about this process.

These four aspects of the Western perspective on aging are somewhat loosely defined, but they exert a powerful influence on the way we view older people and treat them. These attitudes toward the elderly in our society also have an effect on how the elderly view themselves.

Society versus Older Adults

The most important indication of society's attitude toward older adults is how well it provides for them. One would assume that in a society of affluence all would benefit. In a capitalist society, however, the rules of the game are that you

35

b the system in the way of production. Consequently, for
____ d age is a tragedy, a period of quiet despair, deprivation,
desolation, and muted rage.

Such a fate can be the consequence of the kind of life a person led in younger years and of problems in relationships with others. There are also inevitable personal and physical losses to be sustained, some of which can become overwhelming and unbearable. But age is frequently a tragedy even when the early years have been fulfilling and people seemingly had everything. The American dream promises old people that if they work hard enough all their lives, things will turn out well for them. Today's older adults were brought up to believe in pride, self reliance, and independence. Many are tough, determined individuals who manage to survive against adversity, but even the toughest reach a point where they need help. Herein, maintains Dr. Robert Butler, Former Director of the National Institute on Aging, lies the tragedy of old age in the United States. The tragedy is not that each of us must grow old and die but that the process of doing so has been made unnecessarily, and at times excruciatingly, painful, humiliating, and debilitating.

The Economic Crisis of Old Age

Poverty

Poverty or dramatically lowered income and old age seem to go hand in hand. Elderly persons are more likely than other adults to be poor (Special Committee on Aging, 1986). Insufficient income is by far the most serious problem for most older people, for it affects every aspect of their lives. Financial needs can lead directly to serious medical and social problems. To conserve finances, old people may visit the doctor infrequently, permitting minor difficulties to develop into serious illnesses. They may sell their cars, shop less, eat starchy foods, see less of friends, and perhaps withdraw into a kind of aimless half-existence in order to conserve income so that there are sufficient funds to pay rent and utility bills. In an era when the annual rate of inflation has reached major proportions, few middle-aged workers can escape anxiety as they consider the prospects of possibly 20 years or more in retirement, even though public and private programs have substantially improved the financial situations of most older people.

It is generally well known that people who have been poor all their lives remain poor as they grow old, but what most of us do not realize is that these poor are joined by a multitude of others who became poor only upon growing old. When Social Security becomes the sole or primary source of income, it means a subsistence-level lifestyle. Recent increases in Social Security do not keep up with the soaring cost of living. Private pension plans often do not pay off, and pension payments that do come in are not tied to inflationary decreases in buying power. Savings can be wiped out by a single, unexpected catastrophic illness.

In 1980, there were 3.9 million older Americans, 15.7 percent of the total population, at the poverty level. The U.S. Census found that about 60 percent of elderly couples had incomes at the modest middle class level or higher, while only about 25 percent of unmarried older individuals had incomes at that level. About 21 percent of older couples and 55 percent of older unmarried people had incomes at or below the census-defined survival-only level (Atchley, 1985). These data show that many older couples can live comfortably, while the majority of elderly unmarried have financial difficulties.

In 1985, 12.6 percent of persons 65 and older had incomes below the poverty level, compared to 11.3 percent of those age 18 to 64 and 14.1 percent of all persons under age 65 (Special Committee on Aging, p. 35).

Certain groups of the elderly tend to be poorer than other groups (Cox, 1988). In 1984, one of every nine, 11 percent, of elderly white Americans was poor. During the same year, one of every three, 32 percent, of elderly blacks and about one out of every five, 21 percent, of elderly Hispanics were at the poverty level. Persons who are 85 years of age or older are likely to have much lower incomes than those 65 to 84 years of age. (Special Committee on Aging, 1986).

In his much acclaimed book of the 1960's, *The Other America*, Michael Harrington demonstrated that the millions of older people who live in poverty are the victims of a downward spiral. Poor people are ill more often than others because they live in unhealthy and poorly heated slum housing and feed themselves badly. The problem is circular, for they are too poor to take care of themselves, so their illnesses grow worse, preventing them from working and making their poverty even more acute. These older people are ashamed of their destitute conditions and may avoid all social contacts. They attempt to hide from others the fact that they live on public assistance and may deprive themselves of the little help available. One might say these elderly are the victims of a three-fold set of causes: bad health, poverty, and solitude. Some join the ranks of poverty after a relatively rewarding life. Their abilities diminish as they grow old: They can no longer find jobs because their techniques were out-of-date. For those who had earned a reasonable amount, retirement meant a precipitous drop in income.

But although it is apparent that older people are somewhat more likely than the general population to have incomes below the poverty line, the overall proportion of elderly within incomes below the poverty line has been decreasing. Twenty percent of the 65 and older group fell below the poverty line in 1966 compared to only 16 percent in 1979. In 1982, the U.S. Bureau of the Census reported that of those 60 and older only 13.6 percent fell below the poverty level. Fowles (1984) observes that the incomes of the elderly are continuing to improve and the number falling below poverty level is continuing to drop (Cox, 1988).

Unemployment

Major contributors to the economic and social plight of older people are mandatory retirement and discriminatory employment practices. Age discrimination in employment persists, taking the form of arbitrary retirement practices and biases against hiring older people. For a variety of reasons, unemployed workers over age 45 have difficulty reentering the work force. About 15 percent of all workers age 45 and over are unemployed at any one time. For many, early retirement means permanent unemployment. Along with the technological changes, factors contributing to this situation are the unwillingness of older workers to relocate, the concentration of older workers in dying industries such as railroad transportation, and age discrimination by employers. Chapter 12 describes employment programs for the elderly.

Retirement

Whether or not and when to retire is an issue that has many implications for human services workers who serve aging and elderly clients. Retirement in the United States is both a social and economic phenomenon. Some of the major economic issues and potential resources available for retirement are discussed in chapter 12. And, of course, counseling with the potential retiree requires one to help the client face both the economic and social consequences of the decision.

The various financial systems such as Social Security, private pensions, and tax-sheltered annuities, available for retirees need to be appraised and discussed with the person who is considering retiring. There is no perfect answer to the question of whether or not one can successfully retire at a given age.

Some people are quite successful in various financial enterprises and are, therefore, able to retire at early ages. Still others, however, are willing to accept major changes in their standards of living in order to be relieved of full-time employment. Low income people may never be able to comfortably retire.

Generally, the younger one retires, the less funds are available during the retirement years. Those who continue to work at their pre-senior year levels or who delay retirement as long as possible are able to maintain much higher standards of living for much longer periods of time.

In recent years, the mandatory retirement required by many public and private employers has been outlawed so that, with some exceptions such as various kinds of hazardous employment and in higher education, mandatory retirement no longer exists.

However, changes in health patterns, other interests, such as devoting one's time to a hobby or other recreational pursuits, mandatory layoffs of employees, especially in situations where corporations are encountering mergers or other major changes, and ill health, often lead to the retirement of many employees. In fact, some evidence indicates that in the 1980's and 1990's, the retirement age for most people was younger than it had been in an earlier time, when mandatory retirement was more common.

Many corporations also offer employees attractive early retirement programs as a means of reducing their work forces and saving money. Consequently, many people do formally retire from one job and either remain out of the work force, or, in some cases, assume a new job which they use their retirement funds to supplement.

The major issues around retirement, for many people, are more social than economic, however. Major issues for many people are how they will spend their time once they are retired; where they will live; what their relationships will be with spouses, children, and other family members; and, in general, what the retired life may be like. For those who have worked for many years, retirement without a relatively clear plan becomes less attractive after retirement than it seemed it might be before the change in employment status was made.

Some elderly people find retirement much less enjoyable than employment. Some families—including married couples—find themselves in conflict after retirement because of the extra hours and days together that they had not needed to occupy jointly in the past.

But the retirement decision is complex at any time for adults of any age. Assisting with the decision is a useful function of the human services worker with the elderly client. One of the issues that elderly retirees must consider is where to live once they are no longer employed. For many, there is an attraction to relocating to a more pleasant climate than the one in which they live and, perhaps, to an area in which various forms of recreation are more available than they were before retirement. However, it is often sound advice to help a retiree or potential retiree consider carefully the relocation decision. At times, individuals and couples want to move to a place where they have vacationed in the past. However, they sometimes find that they must confront the fact that the vacation community is not as attractive for the long-term as it was for short stays. A family that has gone to a beach or mountain resort for many years may find that, on a year-around basis, life is not as pleasant as it may seem. Medical facilities may be lacking, companionship may be in short supply, and other advantages to their current life style may be unavailable in a new setting. Some who find, for example, winters in Florida to be quite pleasant discover that the same areas during the summer are not nearly as attractive. The pitfalls of sudden relocations are many and most human services workers find it useful to spend time helping their clients clearly think through relocation decisions. There is no harm in waiting a few months or even a few years before moving from the home community—after one has a chance to see what that community is like without full-time employment. Moving costs may be higher or lower than one might have imagined, for example. And the current residence may prove to be more attractive, when time is available to enjoy it, than might have been imagined.

Depending upon the individuals involved, being near long-time friends, family members, and familiar surroundings, may outweigh the pleasures of recreational opportunities and a better climate.

In terms of retirement, one author, David Brown, (1987) discourages it. He devotes a chapter of his helpful and entertaining book to the subject, "Work Yourself to Death—It's the Only Way to Live." His effort is to explode the belief that early retirement—or retirement at any age—is the ideal solution for everyone.

Housing and Homelessness

One of the more critical problems faced by many older people is finding and maintaining a residence. Although all older people receive at least the amount of money made available through the Supplement Security Income program, even that ($340 per month for an individual and $510 per month for a couple) may not be sufficient to provide housing for older people in the United States. During the 1980's, there were major increases in the cost of housing. Property values, rents, and the like increased while other income factors such as the minimum wage did not increase. Furthermore, funds providing public housing and subsidized housing for low income people were reduced significantly during the Reagan presidency. Therefore, at a time when housing costs were rising, many people were unable to meet those rising costs. For a variety of reasons, including those economic factors, there was an unusual increase in the American phenomenon of homelessness, a problem more common in the Third World, developing nations. Homelessness among the aged is a long-term problem but it has grown significantly in recent years.

In a study of homelessness among older men, Cohen and Sokolovsky (1989) report on several studies that show many of the homeless are older men. One-fourth to one-third of the homeless appear to be over 50 years old. Although 50 is not generally considered aged in the United States, the homeless over 50 seem to be, in many ways, similar to people 10 and 20 years older. Some programs for the homeless report that half of their clients are over 50.

Although not all the homeless are mentally ill or substance abusers, many are. Alcohol is a problem of anywhere from 27 to 63 percent and drug abuse affects about one-fourth. As many as one-third are or have been mentally ill.

Many homeless older people are employed at least part time. Some beg for money from passersby. Many live on the streets or in parks. Others use shelters and flop houses. Still others rent rooms in single room occupancy hotels.

Many older homeless men live from their Supplemental Security Income checks and from Social Security, Veterans Benefits, or pensions (see chapter 12), not unlike their non-homeless peers.

According to Ginsberg (1988) and others, the rise in homelessness in the 1980's resulted from the deinstitutionalization of the mentally ill, the reduction in social welfare programs, and the decline in low cost housing. Cohen and Sokolovsky (1989) also cite the decline in and disruptions of the economy in the 1980's.

Cohen and Sokolovsky (1989) identify several themes that emerge about the homeless men in the Bowery area of New York:

1. A disruptive early family life.
2. Low-skilled employment with relatively poor education.
3. Some early exposure to the Bowery.
4. Moderate to heavy alcohol consumption.
5. Physical or psychological conditions that may have impaired work ability.
6. Turmoil over the loss of a wife or girlfriend.

Family conflicts and rejection of the homeless person by the family also seem to be characteristics.

Currently, many human services jobs are concerned with serving and overcoming the problems of the homeless, especially, it appears, older homeless persons.

Shelter

Housing is the number one expenditure for most older adults. The percentage of income spent on housing (excluding maintenance and repair) in 1983 was higher for older households than for younger households. Approximately 80 percent of the elderly own homes that are free and clear of mortgages. However, home ownership does not guarantee satisfaction and comfort. Rapidly rising property taxes and maintenance costs are driving some older people from their homes, yet suitable alternative rental quarters at prices they can afford are scarce or nonexistent. Since January 1969, property taxes have increased for most older people by 39 percent, and maintenance costs have jumped by one-third. The net impact is that millions of older people are finding themselves in a difficult situation.

The housing of the elderly is generally older and less adequate than the balance of the nation's housing. About 36 percent of homes owned by older persons in 1983 were built prior to 1940 (21 percent for younger owners), and 8 percent were classified as inadequate (6 percent for younger owners). While the age of a home does not necessarily determine the condition, it does indicate a relationship to size, functionality, and ease of maintenance. Many older persons live in homes that are too large for their current family size and need, and rarely do those with physical handicaps have the funds or services available to adapt older, larger homes to their physical needs.

According to the 1980 Annual Housing Survey, 10 percent of units headed by persons 65 years or older lived in housing with bedrooms that lacked privacy (25 percent of elderly owners and 62 percent of elderly renters). Smaller numbers of elderly persons lived in housing with flaws such as incomplete kitchen facilities (2 percent), open cracks or holes (4 percent), and incomplete plumbing facilities (3 percent) (Special Committee on Aging, U.S. Senate, 1986).

Another problem is that the supply of housing designed for older people is severely limited. In particular, there is very little group housing that can provide frail old people with an alternative to completely independent living or institutional placement in a nursing home or other long-term care facility.

Consequently, very few people are entirely free from at least some housing difficulty in later life. They are caught between a desire to stay where they are and the need to adjust to changing physical and social circumstances. Most older adults desire to live independently and have strong feelings against moving. Studies indicate that the factors reflecting a poor living situation, such as high living costs, loneliness, and distance from relatives and friends, are not likely to motivate older people to move unless their situation becomes very serious. Neither is the availability of good housing elsewhere likely to cause older people to look more favorably on relocation even though a move may be inevitable.

Most living arrangements become less adequate as people advance in age. House furnishings are incompatible with physical limitations. For example, high shelves, heavy doors, bathtubs and showers that are difficult to enter, and inadequate lighting all become troublesome and often quite hazardous for an older person. Children leave and spouses die, leaving the surviving old person with more house and more responsibility than is necessary or possible to maintain. The conflict between a desire to remain independent and the changing housing needs of older people places them under great tension.

A Crisis in Mobility

In studies conducted over the years it has been found that many older people identify transportation as their most serious problem after income and health, and a surprisingly large number name transportation as their number one problem. Without adequate transportation, many other problems of the elderly are intensified. Transportation, like income, is a compounding factor. If older people are mobile, they frequently find it easier to adjust to new problems that come with age; without mobility they are likely to experience a syndrome of deprivation.

The elderly with transportation problems fall into three groups: (1) those who could use existing public transportation but cannot afford it, (2) those who, for whatever reasons, need to be picked up from and returned directly to their homes, (3) those who live where there is no public transportation (Atchley, 1985). Although most of these older people usually manage to get to their market, doctor, or other health care services, they often are unable to do meaningful things such as visiting friends and relatives, or attend church or recreational activities (Atchley, 1985).

Private Car Economy

The root of the transportation problem for older people as well as for other groups is dominance in this country of the privately owned automobile. The automobile influences land use, zoning patterns, highway construction, and all but a small fraction of public transportation funds. Even traffic markings, street signs, and other pedestrian helpers are geared toward the smooth flow of automobile traffic, which is one reason older people constitute a disproportionate number of pedestrian fatalities. The private auto, with the economic and social change it has produced, has destroyed public transit systems in many cities. When people can afford cars they stop riding buses, reducing the income of transit systems. Fares go up to cover expenses, further discouraging additional riders. Routes are curtailed, quality of service declines, and equipment deteriorates. The poor, the young, and the old cannot support a transit system caught in this circular dilemma.

Cost

In 1895, 16 percent of the persons aged 65 and older were in families with incomes between the poverty level and one and one-half times the poverty level (Special Committee on Aging, U.S. Senate, 1986). They must spend most of their money on food, housing, and medical care, leaving little money for luxuries such as private cars, or even for public transportation. Those who drive must cope with an even greater problem because of the high cost of gasoline, insurance, and auto maintenance. Thus by virtue of their low incomes, older people have trouble obtaining any kind of transportation.

Access

Even if older people have enough money to use public transportation, services are usually only minimally available in the areas where they live. The private automobile rules supreme outside central cities, and the rural and suburban elderly are often totally without public transportation. Within cities, the public transportation system is geared to the rush-hour needs of commuters, not to the pace or needs of older residents.

Barriers to Use

Many older people cannot overcome physical and psychological barriers to the use of public transportation. Riding buses and subways requires speed, agility, and quick reaction. Despite some improvement in recent years, printed schedules are difficult to understand, and it is often impossible to obtain information over the telephone from transit companies. According to some studies, the most serious obstacle to better transportation for the elderly is their psychological reluctance. Older people are simply unwilling to face the uncertainty, terrors, and dangers of riding on public buses and subways. Muggings, purse snatchings, and pickpocketing are common crimes committed against the older people using public transit systems. These dangers are real; much of our public transportation seems to be designed for the strongest, heartiest, and most agile riders. High bus steps, hard-to-open exit doors, poorly placed hand rails, and open-air bus stops without benches constitutes formidable physical barriers for older people who must rely heavily on public transit. Recent adaptations in schedules and equipment itself, such as "kneeling" buses have helped with elderly transit.

Insufficient Support Services

Although inadequate income is the most serious problem confronting older people, we must keep in mind that many older individuals need certain support services as much as they need adequate income (Morris, 1970). In some cases, such as a friendly visiting service for the homebound, the service may be as important as money, because it enables the older person to remain in familiar surroundings rather than in an institution. The denial of services on the basis of age is common among both governmental and voluntary agencies and reflects institutional discrimination (Butler, 1975). The absence of services is a fundamental indicator of a general unwillingness to provide for the disadvantaged. Many of the old must become totally impoverished or so ill as to require hospitalization or institutionalization before they are regarded as eligible for even minimal services. They do not have access to preventive services, early diagnosis and treatment, or routine services that could prevent the emergence of new problems. In general, old people have had to wait for services essential to survival and imperative to a decent and pleasurable old age (Butler, 1975). They need facilities, programs, and services to enable them to survive short-term crises and meet long-term needs. Without these services many lose their capacity to live independently or semi-independently in their own homes. They often wait through agonizing intervals for the doctor to visit, the homemaker to come, and the Meals on Wheels to arrive. They also wait in vain for needed services that may be totally unavailable.

Health, Mental Health, and Security

Health Care for Older Adults

In our society those most in need of health care are least likely to have access to it. Health care for the elderly, because of the various chronic health problems characteristic of later life, represents about one-fourth of the expenditure for health services in the United States (Manney, 1975). Older adults frequently experience health problems such as malnutrition as a result of their inability to purchase food because of disability, loneliness, depression, and even fear of crime. Older people require more care, see doctors more frequently than people of other age groups, spend more time and longer periods in hospitals, and are more likely to need care upon release from the hospital. Older people consume approximately 25 percent of the medicine used in the United States.

Although older adults are major consumers of health ca
auxiliary health professions are often not sensitive to the ur
needs of this group. Older patients are viewed by some health professionals as
difficult and complaining; consideration is seldom given to the likely association
between mental and physical health problems. The plight of older people in the
United States with respect to health care seems almost insurmountable. Some of
the problems are discussed below.

The Dilemma of Chronic Illness

Management of older adults' chronic health problems presents a unique
challenge in the health-care field. The health-care professions are readily able to
deal with short-term or acute care problems. They clearly understand the cause
of and treatment for chronic medical conditions. But they have not yet effectively
dealt with the social and psychological ramifications of chronic illness on older
patients and their families.

Anselm Strauss (1973), maintains that the major concern of a chronically ill
person is not just to stay alive or keep the symptoms under control, but to live as
normally as possible despite symptoms and disease. Many older people have
evolved adaptive measures that enable them to cope effectively with the difficulties chronic illnesses present. Others, however, are not successful in carrying out
normal life functions. They experience diseases that are just too serious and demanding for a normal home environment. Older people very often find it impossible to manage a treatment plan; for example, they become confused about
medication and frequently either overmedicate or discontinue taking medicine
altogether. Many older people give in to the limitations of chronic illness because
they lack the necessary support to resist them. Without the assistance of trained
personnel or proper resources, many chronically ill individuals become depressed or isolated. Those who cannot live alone generally must enter nursing
homes or other institutions that provide care.

Very often children of chronically ill elderly attempt to care for them in the
home. Such efforts are often unsuccessful because of the psychological strains
created by the demands of the chronically ill patient. The dilemma of the chronically ill presents a challenge that demands social as well as medical considerations. This problem and its implications for human services workers are
discussed in chapter 13.

Crimes against Older Adults

Another stress that must be faced by older adults is the fear of victimization by
rapists and robbers (see "Prisoners of Fear," in chapter 10). In recent years individuals over 50 have been seen as easy targets for vandals and criminals. Because
of a dramatic increase in crimes against older people in many metropolitan areas,
they are often afraid to walk the streets alone. Television and newspaper stories

report that in these areas older people remain virtually barricaded within their own homes. They are afraid to answer the door or leave the security of the home for any reason.

In some low-income neighborhoods younger people, either as individuals or in groups, vandalize and even terrorize older citizens. Purse snatching and personal assaults are not uncommon. Property destruction, such as broken windows, torn-down fences, and trampled gardens, are frequent occurrences. Even the telephone and mail have been used as means of terrorizing or extorting older people.

In addition, in some areas the elderly are systematically preyed upon by thieves and con artists. High-pressure sales tactics are used to obtain signatures on contracts for nonexistent services. Many older people are subject to robberies that involve either forceful entry or breaking and entry. In addition, income checks are regularly stolen. Approximately 20,000 Social Security checks are stolen each year by direct looting of mailboxes (Butler, 1975). Besides the tremendous material loss, the psychological strain of living under these circumstances can affect physical health and result in driving older people deeper into a world of isolation.

Leisure Time

Besides the status problems retirement poses for older people, it also creates another difficulty: We have a whole generation of people with about 20 years of leisure time (Streib, 1970). The transition from work to retirement is one of the major changes occurring in the later years. Kalish (1975) reminds us that although in the past retirement has been primarily a concern for men, increasing numbers of women have entered the labor force during the past decade, and in the future, retirement will be a vital consideration for women as well.

Retirement is a new institution in our society. Until fairly recently the rich could retire, but others had to work until poor health and physical disabilities removed them from the labor force. In 1900, 68 percent of American men 65 years of age and older were working; by 1960 the proportion was reduced to 32 percent; and by 1975 it had dropped to 23 percent (Kalish, 1975). The percentage of older women who are working has remained roughly the same over the 60-year period, although the proportion of all adult women working increased substantially.

Leisure and Work

Like many concepts that defy precise definition, leisure and work can be approached in various ways. Kalish (1975) suggests that one possibility is to differentiate leisure and work activities by whether or not they are income producing; another consideration is whether or not the activity is sought for pleasure. On the whole, however, we need to recognize that the concepts are blurred. If a person dislikes gardening it becomes work, whereas it may be pleasurable for other people. Many older people find gardening very relaxing and seek the opportunity to garden many hours each week. If someone gardens for other people, should this be considered work? Is it work even if the individual thoroughly enjoys gardening and would rather be doing that than anything else?

Retirement and Use
of Leisure Time

The leisure activities of older Americans do not reflect great enthusiasm for the cultural opportunities of a leisure society. Manney (1975) reports the most popular leisure pursuit for old people, as for Americans of all ages, is watching television. On the average, retired people spend just under three hours a day in front of the television. The next most frequent activities are visiting, reading, gardening, walking, and handy work. Older people also spend some time just sitting, but pure idleness is not common until very advanced years. Older people do not frequently engage in creative activities, such as playing music, painting, sculpting, or writing. Neither do many attend concerts or plays.

In fact, patterns of leisure tend to remain extremely stable over the life span. While people will drop some interests, such as participating in sports, as they grow older, most retired people do the same thing for relaxation that they have done all their lives. Significant changes toward more effective use of leisure time will probably come slowly as young people learn the skills necessary for more creative activity. Whether this is happening yet is questionable. Social critics observe that mass higher education, including widespread exposure to liberal arts education, has not led to a wide range of leisure pursuits. Both college graduates and those with little education tend to pursue the same activities for relaxation—television foremost among them. Our educational system is still primarily oriented toward preparing young people to fill instrumental work roles not toward showing them how to enjoy themselves while not working. As Norman Cousins put it, "Science tends to lengthen life and education tends to shorten it. . . . Education has the effect of deflecting men from the enjoyment of living" (Manney, 1975).

Differential Concepts
of Leisure by Class

The low-income elderly men or women in the inner cities may spend much of their time sitting on a park bench visiting and talking with friends or neighbors (Kalish, 1975). This lifestyle may appear unsatisfactory or lonely, and indeed the old person may feel lonely and isolated. On the other hand, this behavior may represent the continuation of a lifelong pattern as a "loner."

Middle-income elderly couples living in suburban areas may be socially involved with friends, participating in political activities, doing volunteer work, or taking courses in painting or ceramics. Their lives may appear full and rich on the surface, but they also express feelings of loneliness, especially after a spouse dies.

Throughout life, time is structured for us by the various institutions of which we are a part. For example, when we work, our life is structured by a time clock; when we were children and went to school, our time was structured by the school bus and the school schedule. In retirement the days, the weeks, and the years may be without external structure, so individuals must structure their own time. The task of structuring one's own time can be very difficult, and very disconcerting for those who feel that time must be used in a constructive way, however that may be defined (Kalish, 1975). Others may take pleasure in unstructured time, whiling it away in casual pursuits. But in general, there are very few choices for how the older person can make use of leisure time. Many times individuals can use their leisure through volunteer activities, but on the whole they are left to their own resources to plan for how they spend the retirement years.

Summary

The problems discussed above are the types of difficulties experienced by older people that have called for the creation of many new service programs. Those working with older individuals must keep in mind that, at any given time, an elderly person is probably trying to cope with several of these problems simultaneously. Although we may first deal with an acute crisis, we must be sensitive to the fact that the difficulty may be accompanied or caused by several other underlying problems or conditions. The problems of older people are complex, and the solutions are complex as well. One of the most difficult aspects of helping older people deal with their problems and concerns is that there are many barriers preventing the helping person from providing the kind of assistance that is actually needed.

Social attitudes and prejudice toward the elderly in this society have created a world for them and those who attempt to help them that lacks adequate resources. This is not to say that what does exist is not good. But compared to other industrialized countries like England and Sweden, the United States allocates a small proportion of its resources to its elderly population.

READING 2.1

Growing Old in America / Grace Hechinger

Margaret Mead was an active participant in and observer of life. In the following interview she shared her reflections on American values and the status accorded older people.

Margaret Mead celebrates her 75th birthday this year. We went to see her in her office, tucked away in a Victorian turret of New York City's Museum of Natural History. It is the same place she began her work 50 years ago—cozy, comfortable and cluttered with books and memorabilia. To get there, we had to take a large museum elevator, walk down long, dimly lit corridors lined with fossil specimens and finally climb a tiny winding staircase. Few with her fame could resist the temptation to move to grander and more accessible quarters. But one secret of Margaret Mead's long and productive life is her ability to know instinctively what is right for her.

She has been acclaimed "one of the greatest women alive" and is known throughout the world as a pioneer in her chosen field of anthropology. She is the author of nearly two dozen books and countless articles on primitive peoples and all aspects of family life.

A petite and lively woman, she's seated behind her large desk, which overflows with papers and other evidence of work in progress, and beams her famous smile as she talks. Dr. Mead's energy and unflagging interest in life pervade her own unique and inspiring perspective on old age in America.

Family Circle: America has a bad reputation for our treatment of the elderly. Do you think it is warranted?

Dr. Mead: America is pretty negligent in this respect. As a nation of immigrants, we have always put a tremendous premium on youth. The young people, the first generation born here, understood American life better than their parents, who had come from other countries. In the more uprooted families, grandparents became a source of embarrassment. Though children whose grandparents were not English-speaking might learn to understand their grandparent's language, they would refuse to speak it.

But at least older people used to stay in the family. Homes were big, and there was room for extra aunts and grandparents. Families lived close together in communities. Today we have many more old people than in the past. And we have changed our whole life-style. The flight to the suburbs in the last 25 years has done a great deal of harm. In these age-segregated, class-segregated communities, there is no place for old people to live near the young people they care about. So the poor ones are stacked away in nursing homes, which are sometimes called "warehouses for the old." The more affluent ones move into golden ghettos or go to Florida, but they too are segregated and lonely.

FC: How were the elderly treated in some of the primitive cultures you have studied?

Dr. Mead: You don't find many early or primitive societies that treat old people as badly as the civilized societies do. The very earliest civilizations, of course, had to let their older people die, very often because they weren't strong enough to walk the necessary distance to find food. But as soon as there were ways of storing food, older people were looked after.

FC: Do you see any parallel in the way America treats its older people and the way we treat our children?

Dr. Mead: Our treatment of both reflects the value we place on independence and autonomy. We do our best to make our children independent from birth. We leave them all alone in rooms with the lights out and tell them, "Go to sleep by yourselves." And the old people we respect most are the ones who will fight for their independence, who would sooner starve to death than ask for help.

We in America have very little sense of interdependence. The real issue is whether a society keeps its older people close to children and young people. If old people are separated from family life, there is real tragedy both for them and the young.

FC: How could we structure our society to help bring older people back into the lives of their families?

Dr. Mead: It is primarily a question of replanning, of building communities where older people are welcome—not necessarily your own grandmother, but somebody's grandmother. Older people need to live within walking distance of shops and friends and family. They need younger people to help with the heavy chores, to shovel the snow and cut the grass so they can continue to live on their own.

FC: What do you think about the way we approach retirement?

Dr. Mead: The practice of early retirement is terribly wasteful. We are wasting millions of good years of good people by forcing them into retirement. The men especially suffer. Whether or not women work, they've always had to do the housekeeping and the shopping and the planning. So when they retire, they still have some continuity in their lives. But the men are admirals without a fleet. They don't know what else to do but die.

FC: What can we do to keep older people active in community life?

Dr. Mead: We can do many things. Some universities are building alumnae housing on campuses so that graduates will be able to move back near the universities. Some can teach, and all can enjoy the lectures, the intellectual stimulation and being near young people.

We shouldn't drop people from the PTA when their last child leaves school. We should have a grandparents' association that works for the local schools. At present, older people vote against school issues for schools their children once attended. They get selfish because they're no longer involved.

FC: It has been a fond American myth that in the good old days—whenever those were—we treated old people much better. Did the elderly really have fewer problems?

Dr. Mead: For one thing, there weren't a great many older people, and the ones that lived long lives were very, very tough.

Older people are more frail today. Many are the kind who would have died during infancy in earlier times and have had uncertain health all their lives. I had never seen an older person lying around like a vegetable, taking up the energy of doctors and nurses, until I was 28 years old. Every old person I knew as a child was somebody I could admire and listen to and enjoy.

When we're involved with old people whose hearing and eyesight go and who have to be cared for, we don't treat them like people, and that is frightening to old and young alike.

FC: When you were a child, grandparents had a much more active role in child-rearing than they do today. Do you believe that grandparents can educate their grandchildren?

Dr. Mead: If only today's grandparents would realize that they have seen more social change than any other generation in the history of the world! There is so much they could pass on!

In the small towns of earlier times, one good grandmother went a long way with her stories, her store of old-fashioned songs and her skills in the vanishing arts. From her, children absorbed a sense of the past and learned to measure time in meaningful biological terms—when grandmother was young, when mother was young, when I was young. Dates became real instead of mere numbers in a history book.

When my grandmother died in 1928 at the age of 82, she had seen the entire development of the horseless carriage, the flying machine, the telephone, the telegraph and Atlantic cables, radio and silent films.

Today, telephoning has largely replaced the family correspondence of two generations ago. I still treasure a letter that ends: "You are always in the thoughts of your grandmother by the sea. P.S. 'Apartment' is spelled with one 'P'."

FC: Was your grandmother very important to you when you were growing up?

Dr. Mead: One of my grandmothers, who always lived with us, was the most decisive influence on my life. She sat at the center of our household. Her room was the place we immediately went when we came home from school. We did our lessons on the cherry-wood table with which she had started housekeeping. Later it was my dining room table for 25 years.

I think my grandmother was the one who gave me my ease in being a woman. I had my father's mind, which he had inherited from her. Without my grandmother's presence—small, dainty and pretty—I might have thought having my father's mind would make me masculine. Though she was wholly without feminist leanings, she taught me that the mind is not sex-typed.

You know, one reason grandparents and grandchildren get along so well is that they can help each other out. First-person accounts of the parents when *they* were children reduces parental fury over disorders and fads of "the younger generation" and does away with such pronouncements as: "My father would never have permitted me to. . . . "

In small-town schools, there used to be teachers who taught two generations of children and mellowed in the process. They were there to remind the children that their parents had once been young, played hooky and passed forbidden notes in school. They were also able to moderate the zeal and balance the inexperience of young teachers.

FC: It is a popular belief that the way people were treated as children influences the way they treat older people. Do you agree?

Dr. Mead: There is a story that I like about a father bird who was carrying a little bird in its beak over the river. The little bird was completely in the power of the father bird. The older bird said, "My son, when I am old, will you care for me?"

The little bird said, "No, father, but I will care for my children the way you have cared for me."

The story shows something of the way affection is passed down through the generations. But it also reveals a fear of aging. In this country, some people start being miserable about growing old while they are still young, not even middle-aged. They buy cosmetics and clothes that promise them a young look.

A concomitance to the fear of aging is a fear of the aged. There are far too many children in America who are badly afraid of older people because they never see any. Old people are not a regular part of their everyday lives. Also, children are aware that their middle-aged parents cling to youth.

FC: It's true. We Americans are obsessed with staying young. There are not enough models like you, Dr. Mead, to show younger people goals to grow toward.

Dr. Mead: We have always had a good number of lively old people—it is just the proportions that are changing. We had Bernie Baruch sitting on his park bench, advising one president after another. We have many physicians who go on practicing late in life. Writers, too, and justices of the Supreme Court.

FC: How can middle-aged and young people lessen the fear of growing old?

Dr. Mead: It's very important to prepare yourself. One useful thing is to change all your doctors, opticians and dentists when you reach 50. You start out when you are young with everybody who looks after you older than you are. When you get to be 50, most of these people are 65 or older. Change them all and get young ones. Then, as you grow older, you'll have people who are still alive and active taking care of you. You won't be desolate because every one of your doctors is dead.

Another thing is to consider what you want to do later in life while you are still young. If you think of your whole life-span and what you are going to do at one stage and then at another, and incorporate these plans in your life picture, you can look forward confidently to old age. If you associate enough with older people who do enjoy their lives, who are not stored away in golden ghettos, you will gain a sense of continuity and of the possibilities for a full life.

FC: How did you plan for your life when you were young?

Dr. Mead: I went to work at the Museum of Natural History as a young girl, and of course I had no idea how long I'd stay. You don't when you are 24. Then I saw a doddering old man walking around the corridors, and I asked, "What is he doing here?" I was told, "He is working on a book. He retired 20 years ago." I discovered that at the Museum they keep you until you die. And so I decided to stay right there.

FC: How do you think people can learn to appreciate the past?

Dr. Mead: I frequently have my students interview older people. For the Bicentennial, we developed a model book called *How to Interview Your Grandfather.* It

is the reverse of a baby book. The students made up the questions simply by thinking of what they wanted to know about the past. The older people adore being
asked. They stop complaining that nobody is interested in them or that "nobody
listens to me anymore. . . . " And the young people find that what they have to say
is fascinating.

FC: It's so important for children to sense the treasure of memory, both personal and national.

Dr. Mead: Another thing we are doing with students is to tell them to write an
autobiography for their as-yet-unborn-grandchildren. What would you like your
grandson or granddaughter to know about you? Thinking like this gives young
people a new perspective about the future: They begin to realize that someday
they themselves will be old.

My mother was very fond of Robert Browning. She used to quote these lines
from Rabbi Ben Ezra. They are favorites of mine:

> Grow old along with me!
> The best is yet to be,
> The last of life, for which the first was made:
> Our times are in His hand
> Who saith 'A whole I planned,
> Youth shows but half; trust God; see all nor be afraid!'

cHAPTER 3
speciAL AGiNG
popuLATiONS:
miNORiTiES, offeNdERS,
RURAL, ANd WOMEN
AGed

We stated in chapter 1 that most older people experience similar processes of aging and many face the same kinds of problems. However, some special population groups such as members of ethnic and racial minority groups, women, offenders, and the rural elderly face worse and often more intense effects of growing older in the United States. Those who work with older people in such circumstances must be especially aware of some of those special problems and be prepared to help meet those needs when they help in planning and delivering human services.

The Minority Elderly

Minority groups are a major concern of human services programs and those who are employed within them because, for a variety of social and economic reasons, minorities, as a group, need more services than the majority population. That is because, in general, minority group members are more disadvantaged than their non-minority counterparts. Discrimination, long-term poverty, and lack of educational and employment opportunity often put the minority aging in a more difficult situation than other groups of older adults. Chapter 8 discusses some federal efforts for the minority aged.

The largest group of minority aged in the United States are blacks or, as the group name has evolved, African Americans. There are nearly 27 million blacks in the population, a proportion of 12.1 percent. Women in the black community outnumber men. Overall, the imbalance is about 1.4 million more women than men. Blacks are also a rapidly growing group. In the 1980's, the black population grew twice as fast as the non-black. Blacks are also a relatively young group, some six years younger in median age than whites. Black children constitute over 15 percent of all children, which reflects the higher birth rate and more rapidly growing population (McAdoo, 1987). About half of all blacks live in the South (Hopps, 1987).

The largest ethnic group, which is really a collection of several groups, is the Hispanic. According to McAdoo (1987), the U.S. Census Bureau counts blacks, whites, and other racial groups and then counts all the Hispanics from all the groups as an ethnic population. In any case, the Hispanic population is 15.4 million people and is growing faster than any other minority group. Hispanics generally live in the Southwest and West, although that generalization is not completely reflective of the reality of the situation because of special concentrations of Hispanics. For example, the Cuban population is largely settled in Florida. The Puerto Rican population is largely in New York and some of its bordering states. Chicanos, or Mexican Americans, are largely located in the Southwest.

Native Americans, who include American Indians and Alaska Natives, are another major minority group. They are also a very rapidly growing population group. There are now some 1.3 million, an increase of 72 percent since 1970. Again, Native Americans and Alaska Natives are concentrated in the Southwest and West. They constitute 16 percent of the population of Alaska and have concentrations of over 100,000 in California, Arizona, New Mexico, and Oklahoma, in descending order of population (Blanchard, 1987).

Asian Americans and Pacific Islanders are also a combined group that is growing rapidly, both through births and through immigration. In 1980, there were some 3 million in this group. The largest were the Chinese, with more than 800,000, followed by the Filipinos with 775,000, the Japanese, with 701,000, Koreans with 355,000, Vietnamese with 262,000, as well as 42,000 Samoans and 32,000 Guamanians (Kitano, 1987).

Hispanics and Asians are continuing to arrive in the United States—as they have for several decades—because of political issues in their nations of origin. The Vietnam war led to the arrival of many refugees from that part of the world. Political unrest in Nicaragua and El Salvador is causing current outmigrations to the United States, as did the Cuban Revolution in 1959 and later waves of departures from that island nation. There are, of course, many other smaller representations of minorities from all over the world.

Chapter 5 on working with the aging and their families discusses some of the issues in serving older people from ethnic minorities. Basically, however, the individual, group, and community approaches to serving the aged apply to all groups. It is important to know, though, that ethnic minority groups are often disproportionately in need of some kinds of help. Even that, however, is not universally true. For example, although there are low income Chinese elderly in some heavily concentrated Chinese population areas such as California, Asian Americans have, by and large, succeeded in their economic development. Even more recent arrivals such as Vietnamese families have become well-integrated into the economy. Other groups such as the Japanese and Koreans have also become economically powerful in many communities.

Although it is clear that blacks, Hispanics, and Native Americans, face more serious economic problems than many other peoples, that is still not an accurate portrayal of those populations. Cubans, for example, are among the most affluent of Florida residents. Many Native Americans and blacks have also become highly successful in business, the professions, and government positions.

The minority elderly tend to experience greater problems with health care. In fact, the life expectancy for the black and Hispanic population is generally much lower than for the white and Asian groups.

Because so many blacks, Hispanics, and Native Americans live in rural areas, they are victims of the lacks of services in those areas, as well as of the discrimination and deprivation often experienced by minorities. However, with the increases in population and the extension of the life span, which has affected older minority group members as much as those of the majority, the elderly population that is also minority has grown and presents a special target for services by human services agencies and their workers.

Ethnic-Group Elderly

A large segment of the elderly population is composed of individuals who immigrated to this country as children or young adults. The first-generation immigrants are now older adults, but many still practice old-world customs and beliefs. In many regions of the country there are enclaves of ethnic older Americans, for example, the French Canadians of New England. Many of our large metropolitan areas still have neighborhoods with strong ethnic identities, such as the North End of Boston. Those who came here as immigrants were a very independent and self-reliant breed. Because of the existence of ethnic neighborhoods and towns in this country, many found it unnecessary to learn English. Women who did not work outside the home relied upon their bilingual husbands and children to interact with the English-speaking community. In addition, these ethnic neighborhoods and towns had very strong informal social systems, including brothers, sisters, aunts, uncles, nieces, nephews, godparents, and friends, who would always come forth during any crisis. The existence of this system made it unnecessary to go outside the ethnic community for almost any type of service. Even social and recreational needs were met within the community through ethnic social clubs such as the Sons of Italy.

Many of these communities still exist in large cities. The non-English-speaking elderly in them often live alone but retain close ties with family and friends of similar ethnic origin. Because of their origin in this country, they are usually part of the "blue collar" culture and generally are not subject to extreme poverty. In some ethnic communities many of the elderly's needs are met through agencies set up by the ethnic community, for instance, Jewish homes for the elderly.

In some cases, however, out-migration of the middle aged and young have dissolved the ethnic community, and the non-English-speaking elderly who remain there may be subject to a form of cultural deprivation. The older immigrants' ethnic origins were kept alive in this country because they continued to practice old-world customs here. Marriages, christenings, and holiday celebra-tions were all occasions for continuing established old-world traditions.

Second- third-, and fourth-generation immigrant families are now assimi-lated into the American culture, and they neither speak a second language nor identify with ethnic origins. They do not carry out the old traditions of parents or grandparents. Very often old, non-English-speaking immigrants can rely only on other older individuals to help maintain ties with their ethnic origin. As the older immigrants' peers or cohorts die, however, they have fewer and fewer avenues through which to maintain these ties.

As it now stands, when older, non-English-speaking elderly find they need assistance, they must deal with an unfamiliar English-speaking world. Conse-quently, due to language barriers, the ethnic elderly often may not avail them-selves of much needed services. In addition, many service programs for older people do not take into consideration the dietary or religious traditions that are an integral part of the ethnic elderly person's life. Because of an earlier need to maintain ethnic ties, ethnic individuals frequently find themselves socially iso-lated in later life due to language barriers and others' lack of concern for their special needs.

Older Women

Some gerontologists suggest that the over 6 million older women in the United States constitute a technical minority group (Butler, 1975). Widows, sin-gle women, and female members of minority groups are often particularly disad-vantaged. Older women are among the poorest individuals in our society.

Women have an average life expectancy seven years longer than men and tend to marry men older than themselves. Consequently, 20 percent of American women are widowed by age 60, 50 percent by age 65, and about 67 percent by age 75. The income of a retired couple is generally based on the husband's work his-tory, and upon his death the wife's benefits are often reduced.

The older widow or single woman may also suffer from social ostracism. Older women do not have the same social prerogatives as older men to date and marry those who are younger. Since the ratio of older women to older men is three to one, the likelihood of remarrying is slim. Older women alone are subject to the prejudices that exist in this country against single and divorced individuals. The adult world of couples has little place for a single older woman.

The income levels of older working women are generally lower than those of men. This is due to employment practices that discriminate against women and the job opportunities available to women in the United States. It was not until World War II that employment in this country was seen as appropriate for women.

Because of the high proportion of older women in the elderly population, when we speak of the plight of the elderly, we are to a large degree speaking of the plight of the poor older woman. The social norms set for women by the society, which have been challenged only recently, are now taking their toll on older women. The woman who conformed to the norms of a male-dominated society and was economically totally dependent on her husband may pay tremendous social costs in old age.

The Rural Elderly

The rural elderly, for the most part, are older, more isolated, have greater transportation problems, live in the same places longer, have lower incomes, and reside in poorer houses for longer periods of time than do their urban counterparts (Auerbach, 1976). On the other hand, they appear to be healthier, live longer, complain less, and are freer from fear of crime and confusion of city streets. However, the attitude of the rural aged emphasizes the singularity, independence, isolation, xenophobia, and individualism that is a reflection of the psychology of rural living. Whatever the reason, rural aged are apt to be less knowledgeable about available social services, more indifferent or hostile to government-supported programs, more difficult to mobilize for participation in social programs, and less receptive to community action that supports social legislation.

The problems of growing old in the rural United States presents special and unique problems. Sheer distance between people and between people and services is the most obvious aspect in which rural areas differ from urban ones. Distance complicates the delivery of any services to rural older people; the expense of maintaining private cars and lack of public transportation bar older people from coming to the services. Many people in rural areas are isolated by a basic lack of roads.

One of the biggest problems of the rural elderly is that programs established to meet their needs are often not designed to fit their way of life. Most rural older people have been very self-reliant all their lives. They were their own mechanics, plumbers, carpenters, and doctors because often others were not available. When crises arose, neighbors quietly chipped in, often without being asked. Age has now stripped these people of all their resources but not their traditions. Many refuse to take advantage of the few services that are available because they don't know how to take the initiative in dealing with government officials, and they feel a strong sense of shame and failure if they must.

Programs for rural older people must be designed in a way that is not foreign to their lifestyle. Given that their needs are greater than those of their urban counterparts, greater energy should be used to help meet the rural elderly needs.

One of the best known writers on rural problems, Calvin L. Beale, found that older rural people are worse off than their metropolitan counterparts. He found that 20 percent of the rural aged were poor compared to 12 percent of the nonrural aged. He concluded that actually half the low income aged were people who live in rural and small towns.

Parenthetically, human services writers on rural areas are really distinguishing between metropolitan and non-metropolitan areas. A metropolitan area is one which has a population center of at least 50,000 people. Non-metropolitan areas lack such centers. The technical definition of a rural community is one with 2,500 or fewer people. It is sufficient, most writers on the subject find, to distinguish between metropolitan and non-metropolitan areas or between metropolitan areas and areas with only rural or small towns.

Health problems among the rural elderly are also more severe than among metropolitan dwellers. They make fewer visits to doctors but have higher rates of hospitalizations, for example. That results from the fact that because they cannot readily visit physicians when they are ill, their conditions are likely to deteriorate leading to the need for hospitalization. The lack of adequate transportation is an even more severe problem in small towns than it is in cities.

Housing also poses difficulties. In the late 1970's, it was found that four times as many rural elderly as metropolitan had incomplete plumbing.

Of course, rural life has its positive dimensions as well. The pace of life is slower and contacts with others are often more casual and more frequent. People often find it easier to obtain help, as well. The cost of living is also lower for rural than for metropolitan dwellers.

Older Offenders

One group that is often neglected in serving the aged is older prisoners. Both federal and state correctional institutions have relatively large numbers of older adults who are serving prison sentences, especially long sentences. Although many may have been convicted in their youths, if their crimes were serious they may have been sentenced to periods of many years or the balance of their lives.

There has been a tendency in recent social policy to extend prison sentences for a variety of crimes, especially those involving violence and drugs. Because of that, many people remain in prisons into their senior years.

Of course, older prisoners require special kinds of programs if they are to function satisfactorily in the prison system. In many cases, they must be segregated from younger offenders to prevent their exploitation. They may also, after serving long periods, lack any family or other personal contacts among family members and friends. Therefore, all of their social needs may be met in the institution. For those reasons, special social activities, education programs, and recreation, may be needed for this special population.

In many situations, older prisoners may make a special contribution to the prison population because of their special knowledge and experience. Effective human services workers in correctional facilities should make efforts to identify and use the talents of older inmates in the overall program of the prison.

There have been increases in crimes committed by older people, although they are still not a major group among offenders or prisoners. In 1965, some 0.5

percent of all crimes were committed by people over 65. By 1984, that figure was close to 1 percent (McCarthy and Langworthy, 1988). The crimes committed by the elderly are highest in the areas of larceny and theft, assault, embezzlement, fraud, and sex offenses other than prostitution. They are lowest in robbery, prostitution, and auto theft. In some studies, vagrancy, assaults not intended to kill or cause great bodily injury, and morals charges such as statutory rape were higher among older than younger offenders. Overall, however, younger offenders are more likely to be arrested than older (McCarthy and Langworthy, 1988). The nonviolent, perhaps "white collar" crimes are perhaps the most important of the offenses committed by older people.

In all cases, a variety of studies shows that older persons are becoming more and more common in the courts, are being placed on probation, and are being incarcerated. Because they are older, such offenders against the law and prisoners have the same kinds of health, economic, and social needs as other elderly people and skills extended by human services workers to other elderly must be applied to this very special and growing group.

Summary

In this chapter we have called to your attention the fact that programs and services developed for the elderly frequently do not take into consideration the special needs of the minority, ethnic, women, imprisoned and rural elderly. Consequently, these groups of individuals either cannot or do not receive services they need badly. Very often special outreach efforts must be conducted to locate these people and special assistance given to assure that they obtain services Furthermore, special consideration must be given to the way services are currently structured to assure that they do not inadvertently discriminate against these groups.

READING 3.1

A Miracle Story / Rosalie K. Jackson

Rosalie Jackson suggests that, considering the hardship, it is perhaps a miracle that any black person has managed to survive to old age. In this selection she creates a detailed background to a dynamic portrait of the black elderly.

I am going to talk about what I call a "miracle story." The fact that any black

From "New Ideas for Better Serving the Older Adult." Used by permission of the author.

person has survived in America (and I use the word "survive" advisedly) to live to the age of eighty or ninety years is indeed a miracle. What do I mean by a miracle? What are the implications of survival for the emotional needs in older black adults? Let's think about a black person who is eighty-eight years of age. That means he or she was born in 1886 in America. That's the reconstruction period. Reconstruction days for black people in America were difficult days. There was so much ambivalence—slaves, then freedom—they were working through a lot of things in those days. By the time this eighty-eight year old person was in his pre-teens America was in the Spanish-American war. This black person was a young adult around World War I in 1914-1918. Having come out of slavery, he was poorly educated. There were few jobs for any Americans, to say nothing about black ones; white men were marching off to war, becoming lieutenants and sergeants. The few black men who were conscripted or called up were the cooks, message boys, and a few of them served in regiments. But the majority served in menial jobs. Today this person is in a nursing home or a board and care home or in a ward. He is now eighty-eight in 1974.

Back in 1886 there were some positive things going for him mental health-wise. People had tight family ties; black Americans lived in extended family units. They were very religious. They had faith that things would be better and they really believed that God would take care of them. So they survived. These were positive aspects in those days. They knew nothing but hard work and hard times, but they possessed positive factors—the adaptive mechanisms prevalent in the black races—long muscles, diminished amount of skin fat, the ability to sweat and adapt to a climate—just as other races have adaptive mechanisms to stay alive. Blacks in America for their own mental health and survival took on the practices and the adaptive mechanisms to stay alive. Uncle Tomism was a survival technique.

Let's move to more recent times in America. When this eighty-eight year old black American was hitting middle-age there was the Great Depression. They were scrounging not only for the mental health but also for basic physical comforts. By World War II this person was over the age level to serve. He was fifty-five years old in 1941. The climate of the country which had contributed to poor mental health was shifting, was getting a bit more relaxed; jobs were opening up a bit, and the war brought great industrialization. I guess I am suggesting that in the majority culture mental health and physical comforts are tied in with economic state. The blacks had survival skills but not some of the creature comforts and job securities the rest of America had at that time. With World War II, our fifty-five year old black person migrated from the South to the city where there are factory jobs. For the first time he isn't chopping cotton and doing menial jobs. He is working in industry, in the shipyards, perhaps, and may be able to buy a piece of land and property and begin to get into the economic base of the nation. But he is fifty-five and at age forty-five, chronic diseases set in. The grim reaper takes its toll earlier with black Americans. So a good percent of blacks never become eighty-eight.

There has been some social legislation providing Social Security and some other benefits for all of the people and pension plans developed in some parts of the country. But remember, this black person, uneducated and unskilled, is still at the bottom of the ladder. This person can't move with the times. When the boys came marching home from war, the first fired were older people, and the older black in particular. If he managed to hold on to a job cleaning offices at night, that was at least a stable economic base. If they were lucky, the black people went back to menial jobs. I am leading up to how one develops status. We know that one of the tragedies of aging in the white American is to have been the president of a large firm, and to end up retired and occupying a chair on the board at eighty-eight. But that eighty-eight year old black American never had status, so therefore his mental health is slightly different.

With two-thirds of this man's life over, America is in good times; TV is becoming universal, and showing how everybody is living. But there is nothing on the screen that applies to anything that is happening to this group. Science and technocracy have come to the country, and the good times are rolling. One of the best things that happens to the older black American is things most people look down on. That would be the social programs . . . the things that guarantee you a little bit. For many black Americans the Social Security check is the biggest amount of money they ever had in their lives. When we think about the negative aspects of Welfare and how terrible it is we should remember that the little pittance everybody is getting, $167 or $121, is still more than many of the older generation has ever had or made. Medical care, the ability to go to the doctor and complain like everybody else, were things that were denied to poor people. But the adaptive mechanism of black Americans was herb medicine, to treat your own. These are the positive skills that people develop to survive and adapt. All this helps explain how a black person lives to be eighty-eight years old in 1974.

Hear now the story of Mrs. Blue, who is a 93-year old black. We know she is that old because of the events she can relate. She shares with us about herb medicine so if you try to give her your pills, you will be made to remember that she has been self-medicating all her life. How can you fight her? I can get knowledge from these old people about living and survival and about getting by. Mrs. Blue knows about the medicines. In an accident she burnt her foot badly and had to go to the hospital. They wanted to keep her there a long time. She said, "No. If I stay here longer, I'll die because you won't let me get up and walk on my foot." The doctor explained that his regimen would save her life. Nevertheless, every night she walked around that bed all night to keep her circulation going, to avoid pneumonia. She didn't know why she was doing it all, but she had a history of observing. And through her self-regimen she got out of the hospital sooner than they predicted.

I am sharing with you survival, and mental health practices, and common sense and things that have helped people to live to be eighty-eight and who now are in your care, under your jurisdiction. What I am suggesting is that you owe to that person some respect for his adjustment. If you managed to stay alive through this period (and I haven't mentioned discrimination, Ku-Klux-Klan, poor housing, or the whole gamut of destructive influences) then numerous obstacles had to be surmounted. Have respect for the old person's intellectual functioning, capabilities. In working with the older blacks, remember that little story about Mrs. Blue.

We should consider losses further. After forty-five, health begins to go, and chronic illnesses begin to set in. The implication here, it seems to me, is that you must listen all the more. Remember that the eighty-eight year old was never a master of the English language, so listening implies a deeper meaning. Help people with recalls, which sharpens what they want to say.

What about the implication in loss of family ties? Children of this eighty-eight year old black would be in their sixties, because they bred early, and many times they outlive their children, there may be only grandchildren left. We know great-grandchildren and grandchildren are very mobile; they have active lives and little time and even less living space to have extended family persons living with them. So the modern way of life has led to isolation of both black and white older Americans. What about the implications of loneliness? If the older person is isolated and separated, then TV is a form of involvement; it is something to listen to, and I suppose even talk to. TV still isn't enough, because people need to be touched; they need to be interacted with. The mental health implication for an old man having outlived all of his friends is that you listen to him, let him tell his stories and this enhances his status; it is important.

What about the implications in recognizing managerial skills? Managers are hard to find. We are used to so much incompetence that we are almost appalled if all goes well. Let's think of the managerial skills of older black Americans. What are the managerial skills of a woman who raised twelve children on next to nothing, who fed, clothed, housed them, disciplined them, and brought them up to standards that are mostly absent today? I am suggesting then, that a person who has managed a household has given reason for a status of respect and dignity.

And then there are the implications in de-emphasizing failures. I did a study in 1971 in Los Angeles with the Meals-on-Wheels program. I needed data for my study. These people are black and Mexican-American older citizens. We talked about lacks and about positive things. One woman said to me, "It sure is good to be free." She meant freedom from all the burdens and responsibilities she had as a manager. It is good, she was saying, to have no one but oneself to look after. So there are some positive aspects to aging. But she complained about lack of transportation. These are the trade-offs. Never having driven (black women were not that independent) it was transportation that they needed most of all. Of all the things that older black Americans need, transportation is the first. Eighty-eight percent of the people found transportation the number one problem. In the bus that picked them up for Meals-on-Wheels in Los Angeles they were trying to bribe the driver to take them other places but they didn't succeed.

The second thing I found in my study was that seventy percent of the people I asked, "How do you feel?" answered by saying, "I feel fine." Then I had another question later that asked, "Do you have any of the following illnesses?" Although five or six illnesses, such as heart trouble, hypertension, diabetes, etc., were cited repeatedly, they always presented themselves as "doing fine." I had a difficult time dealing with that. But compared to what they had been accustomed to, they *were* doing fine. When a person says he is doing poorly, talk with him about what that means; and if a person says he is doing fine, in comparison to what is he doing fine? You always have to put the answer in context as you seek the identity of that black American.

When I think of a mentally healthy person, I think of a person who has enough to make him happy, who wants to share, wants to give. We, as helpers, supply some of those things, and when we understand the background of this person, we can supply some of this status.

The older black American now is adaptable, but the new generation as it ages will have its own bitterness and frustrations that it will go through. The old ones worked through their bitterness a long time ago.

The last thing I want to talk about is the need of being touched, and the need for sensuality and sexuality. Remember also that the status of child bearing in this group is going to be different from the cohorts of today. Also a good deal of a persons's sexual identity for the cohorts of 1896, was evaluated on the basis of the number of children one produced. Another of the implications for mental health of older black Americans is the fact that for this group the idea of potency, of manhood and womanhood is tied up in the role of parent.

Individualize your clients; don't stereotype them; listen to them; put your client in proper context; learn about them, then relate to them appropriately.

READING 3.2

The Older Woman/Irene de Castillejo
Living to old age brings gains as well as losses. In this selection Irene de Castillejo eloquently presents some positive models of aging.

It would seem easy enough for me to write on "The Older Woman" since I am one, but perhaps it is for that reason I find it difficult. One can really only see situations clearly when one is outside them, not when one is in the middle of living them. However there is no help for it. When I have passed the stage of being an older woman I shall also be beyond writing at all.

It is obvious that there are two distinct classes of older women: the wife and

From *Knowing Woman* by Irene Claremont de Castillejo; copyright 1973 by the C. G. Jung Foundation for Analytical Psychology. Reprinted by permission.

the mother on the one hand, and the professional woman on the other, although today these two merge more and more. It is with the former that I am most familiar.

The fundamental truth to remember in thinking of woman irrespective of the role she plays, is that her life's curve, unlike that of man, is not a slow rising to the zenith of power followed by a gradual decline in the later years. The curve of a woman's life span follows more nearly the pattern of the seasons. She almost literally blossoms in the spring, but the long summer which follows is a very slow ripening with nothing much in the woman herself to show for it. If she lives a traditional family pattern she will be giving all the sap which rose so abundantly earlier to nourish her offspring, materially, emotionally and spiritually.

Then suddenly her children are all grown up, gone on their separate journeys, and she finds herself bereft. The apparent purpose of her life, for which she had strained every nerve, is snatched from her with the attainment of the goal. She feels stranded on the mud flats, while the river races by bearing away each new craft as it embarks, and she no part of the flowing waters. What then? What can happen then, with another thirty or forty years still to run and no one needing her? Even her husband has centered his life on his career and other interests apart from her while she was occupied with the growing family. At the best his need of her is not absorbing enough to assuage her aching emptiness.

What then? This is the crucial moment in the life of any wife and mother. It is then that she may notice, almost by accident, that from where the early blossoms fell fruit is hanging and almost ripe. Unsuspected fruit, fruit which has swelled and grown unheeded, is now ready and waiting to be plucked. The autumn of a woman's life is far richer than the spring if only she becomes aware in time, and harvests the ripening fruit before it falls and rots and is trampled underfoot. The winter which follows is not barren if the harvest has been stored, and the withdrawal of sap is only a prelude to a new spring elsewhere.

Conscious modern women of course know these things. They prepare for the autumn before the long dry summer is over. But far too many women still feel that life is finished at fifty and that vibrant loving ends with the menopause. This last bogie should be swept away at the outset. It is utterly untrue.

You may know some version of the famous story of the young man who asked his mother at what age women cease to be interested in sexual intercourse. "I do not know," she replied, "you had better ask your grandmother." "How should I know?" she answered gruffly. "Great Granny may be able to tell you." This is perhaps not as far-fetched as would appear.

It is true enough that some men cease to be interested sexually in women when their physical fertility is ended, causing their wives, who have a recrudescence of sexual interest at this time, great distress. Such a situation is the survival of an inherent primitive pattern where sexuality was for humanity, as it is for animals, only a matter of procreation.

Since the age of chivalry and the development of romantic love, sex has become very much more than that. And with the discovery and spread of contraceptives sex has entered a new phase. The contraceptive can certainly lead to irresponsibility, license and a devaluation of sexuality. In fact it often does so. But on the other hand it opens the door to immensely heightened emotional experience where sex ceases to be solely a biological function, and becomes an expression of love in its own right. In this context age with its absence of fertility is irrelevant.

This cultural achievement gives mankind a chance of healing the cleavage between body and spirit which has been fostered for centuries by the Church, and may enable us to weld once more the two together.

In this whole development the older woman is actually at a great advantage. She does not need the contraceptive, and I believe this is one reason why a woman's most profound and meaningful sex life often occurs after fifty when she is no longer caught in the biological net. For the first time she is able to give herself in the sex act completely free from fear of contraception, a fear which in countless women does still operate beneath the surface, even when reason and science assure them that they have taken the most complete precautions.

Moreover to a great many women contraceptives, though accepted intellectually, are still unaesthetic, and to a deep basic feminine morality they are wholly unacceptable, all of which inevitably causes inhibitions so long as they have to be used. When once a woman is free to use her body as an expression of deep feeling, without its becoming the impersonal vehicle of nature's insistent demand for life and yet more life, she can transcend her earlier inhibitions and attain physical expression of an emotional relationship beyond anything of which she had ever dreamed.

Do not misunderstand me. It is a grave mistake for a woman to look for some great spiritual experience in sex at any age, or even to assume that she ought to have such a thing. All assumptions about sex are disastrous. They tend to lead to disappointment and recriminations. To my mind most modern books on sex do more harm than good for this very reason: they fill women's heads with assumptions and expectations which actually prevent experience at its fullest. It is one's own personal experience that counts and it should not be measured up against any generalization. The statistical so-called normal man or woman does not in fact exist, and it is foolish to weigh our actual living experience against such a mythical figure.

Sex delight is like happiness. It does not come when sought. It is not until a woman ceases to strive for her own sensual satisfaction, but allows the voice of her heart to speak to her man through the medium of her body, that she finds that heart, spirit and body are all one.

Important as the heightening fulfillment of sex may be, it is none the less only a small part of the ripe autumnal fruit to which I have alluded. A woman's liberation from the service of nature's purposes frees an enormous amount of energy for something else. A man at fifty is probably at the height of his intellectual or administrative power. A family woman at the same age may be aware of an entirely new stirring. Latent possibilities dance before her unbelieving eyes.

I recall one such woman seated on the lawn of her house one summer evening holding forth to her family. I say holding forth but she was certainly not laying down the law. It was almost as though a dam had burst and a torrent of ideas came tumbling out to which she herself seemed to be listening with the same astonished amusement as were her hearers. She simply emanated vitality and I remember her ending up with the words: "I have no idea what is going to happen but I am quite sure something is." And as I watched and I listened so was I. She did in fact become a writer some ten years later.

The expression "change of life" exactly fits the situation. The menopause does not spell the end of life but a change of direction, not a living death but a change of life.

If this were more generally understood I am convinced that women's menopause problems would rapidly diminish. Glandular changes are inevitable but it is woman's own dread of this mysterious change in the whole tenor of her life which, I am sure, brings about the neurotic state she fears. No, change of life means an enormous release of energy for some new venture in a new direction.

The direction in which the newly released energy will flow depends of course entirely on the type of person and the particular gifts with which she has been endowed. Some may develop a latent talent, painting, writing or some such thing. Voluntary societies serving social, political and cultural causes of all kinds abound with such women. But these only cater for the more conscious and extroverted type of woman. There are innumerable others who can find no outlet. They suffer deeply, for energy which finds no channel in which to flow seeps into the ground and makes a marsh where nothing can be planted, where only slime and insects breed.

Women who find they are no longer vitally needed by their families yet have no other place where they can give themselves, sink into lassitude and finally fall ill. The magnates who organize society have hardly begun to notice this happening. The autumnal energy of countless older women escapes silently down the kitchen sink along with their tears.

Not only is the nation poorer for its loss, the wastage is double, for these women who could have been healthily active and useful become a wholly unnecessary burden upon the health services, while as likely as not their frustration poisons the atmosphere of the home. Swamps breed mosquitoes. Uncanalized, wasted energy breeds gloom and nagging.

Part-time work is at least one answer to this problem, but part-time work is not easy to find. Industry seems to frown upon it and our modern passion for degrees and paper diplomas shuts many a door. It is not sufficiently recognized that running a home can afford very valuable experience in organization, and particularly in handling other people with diverse temperaments. The mother of a family is generally adept at that very difficult accomplishment of attending to half a dozen things all at the same time, an asset by no means to be despised if diverted to other fields.

That society is gravely at fault in not providing outlets for the older woman's energy is unquestionably true. But her real problem is to discover in which direction her newly released libido wants to flow. Libido is like water, it always seeks its proper level. No amount of coercion can make it flow uphill.

So long as a woman is fulfilling her traditional role of bringing up a family, she is carried along by the stream of life. Indeed she has no alternative. She goes with the stream even though cooking and cleaning and changing diapers are not at all her ideal occupations. She has no real choice. But she herself develops as the family grows and she learns to meet the demands as they arise. Changing diapers gives way to helping with obstreperous homework and providing meals for expanding appetites in every field. But when all this is past and the river flows on without her, her own little stream of energy is dammed up. If she is fortunate the waters will rise till they are strong enough to burst out in a channel of their own.

What the channel will be depends on her concern. Even today, when education does its best to divert women's activity into every branch of industry and moneymaking, there are still older women who slide happily into the estate of grandmother because their children's children do in fact become the centre of their interest and their concern. Dedicated grandmothers who gladly put themselves at the service of the future generation without trying to run the show themselves are a boon to any family, but they are becoming increasingly rare. Like maiden aunts they are dying out, and the services which both maiden aunts and grandmothers used to give as a matter of course and with genuine devotion now frequently have to be bought with money. We all know what a poor substitute that is and how expensive.

The modern trend seems to be in the opposite direction. More and more mothers wait with impatience for their children to be grown and gone. Then at last they feel free to carry on with the career which family demands had forced them to abandon. These women are faced with relatively little conflict. They nearly always succeed in finding an outlet before the problem becomes acute. As the children grow they dovetail the new life into the old so that there is no traumatic moment when they feel deserted.

The ones who cannot look forward to any vibrant future or any sphere of usefulness to which they can give themselves, are those with whom I am particularly concerned here. For them especially is the surprise and delight of discovery. And for them above all is the paramount need to know what is and what is not their true concern.

. . . In the case of woman, the outstanding almost invariable object of her concern is, as we all know, the person or persons whom she loves. This is true right through her life. It is, I repeat, the essential ingredient of her nature. When she is true to herself love is her primal driving force. Love and the service of those she loves, I mean a wholly personal love, not the love of causes or of country. I believe this to be true for all the various ranks of women, and it is as true of professional women as of wives and mothers. It is not always apparent that this is so. We are all very good at covering up our mainspring. But I have yet to meet the woman who did not know in her heart that love is her main concern and that the secret of her success in any field was her personal love in the background.

Men really can give themselves to a cause, working wholeheartedly for it and inspired by it. Unless their ingredient of masculinity is very great, women cannot. If one is allowed to penetrate their secrets one finds beneath their apparent impersonal enthusiasms some very personal love, the existence of which makes them feel whole and gives them the energy which enables them to act.

The schoolgirl will work double for a teacher whom she loves. The career woman will either have a person who is the focus of her love at work who provides her dynamism, or some love outside which is her stimulus. It may be a lover in the background or children for whom she needs to earn.

Wherever I look I meet this incontrovertible fact that a woman always needs some person to do things for, even though to the outsider there is no apparent connection with the loved person and what she may be doing. We all know how difficult it is for a woman even to cook a meal for herself. She cannot be bothered. A bit of bread and cheese will do. But if there is someone to cook for she prepares quite elaborate dishes with delight.

The same prevails throughout. The work of a woman, whether factory hand or professional, will be quite different in quality if in some way she can connect it with her love. I have talked with women artists, painters, singers, actors. They all agree that art in itself is seldom quite enough. Beneath their devotion to their art is some person whom they love and for whom in some mysterious inner way they perfect their art. Even the nun, who is an extreme case of selfless devotion, is contained in and inspired by a very personal love of Christ. I suspect that men are far more singlemindedly purposeful.

The need to have someone to do things for comes out in most curious places. I recall a woman who was threatened with blindness which only an operation could prevent. Operations of any kind had always been anathema to her, and the thought of an eye operation was more than she could face. She raged internally at the meddlesomeness of doctors. Why couldn't she be allowed to go blind in peace? Then suddenly she realized what she might be doing to her children and grandchildren if she went blind. A blind old grandmother was the last thing she wanted to impose on them. Her torment ceased. She entered hospital without a further qualm. She had found someone to have her operation for.

This tendency only to be able to do things for someone whom one loves makes it difficult for a woman to know what she herself really wants. She is often accused naturally by men of futility or hypocrisy, because when asked what she wants to do, she replies "Whatever you like." But it is not hypocrisy. She really means that her desire is to do what he wants. It has not occurred to her to have any special preference. Even if she knew she wanted to dance it would give her no pleasure to do so if her lover was longing to watch a cricket match. This adaptability is not unselfishness and has no particular merit. It is the way a woman functions. Perhaps I am describing the last generation. I think it possible that the present generation of women not only know themselves better but are far more decisive than the last, thus changing their relationship with men. Whether the change is for the good, or rather a disaster, is still an open question. Perhaps it is both.

However this may be, the older woman's dilemma is precisely here. If no one whom she loves wants her services there is no one to do things for. There is in fact no reason for which to live. She is faced with an entirely new situation in which for the first time maybe she has to discover what are her own wishes, her own tastes and in which direction her energy, with no love focus to act as magnet, will consent to flow. It is fascinating to notice how a widow will sometimes reverse the habits of a married lifetime after her husband's death. The extent to which she does so is the measure of her earlier adaptability.

In the following poem I have tried to express an old woman's bewilderment. It is called "The Last Years."

> Now that my loves are dead
> On what shall my action ride?
>
> I will not make my children
> Lovers nor tune my time
> By footsteps of the young
> To ease my solitude;
>
> But sing of springs, forgotten
> In slow summer's tedium,
> And autumn ripe with fruit;
> Of winter branches, bare
>
> Beneath the storm bowed
> With weight of rain, and after,
> Lifting knotted fingers
> Towards a translucent sky;
>
> And wrest from the gathered sheaf
> Forgiveness, buried in the heart
> Of every grain, to knead
> My bread for sustenance.
>
> My action, sharing bread,
> Love becomes ability
> To bless, and be, in blessing,
> Blessed.

To go back and collect up one's past as his poem suggests, writing it down in poems or as good prose as one can achieve, has in itself a healing effect. I believe one has to return to one's past, not once but many times, in order to pick up all the threads one has let fall through carelessness or unobservance.

I believe above all one has to return again and again to weep the tears which are still unshed. We cannot feel all the grief of our many losses at the time we suffer them. That would be too crippling. But if we would really gather our whole lives into a single whole, no emotion that belongs to us should be left unfelt.

Moreover, the review of our lives enables us to notice the constant repetition of the same pattern of happening, met by the same pattern of behavior. Seeing this we cannot help being struck by the apparent purposefulness of every detail of our lives even though we do not like our fate. Those who do in fact gather up and write their story are enormously enriched. And women for whom nothing is worth the effort unless it is for the sake of someone they love, can write their outer or their inner story quite deliberately for their own grandchildren (if they have any) to read when they are grown up. If there are no grandchildren, most women will need to find someone else to write it for.

What fascinating pictures of antiquated ways of living we should have if this were done more often. Every single person has the material for at least one book. It is, I think, important that publication should not be the aim. Too many books are published already. Too many mediocre pictures are put upon the market. No, the aim is creativity for its own sake. The grandchildren or some other persons are merely the excuse which the aging woman needs to enable her to make the effort.

Creativity once begun goes on. Nothing is so satisfying to the human soul as creating something new. If the old can become creative in their own right they are lost no longer. We all long to see our works in print, I know, but this is not the point. It is the act of creation which counts. Every act of creation adds to the creativity in the world, and who knows if it has some similar effect as the ritual breathing toward the East at dawn of those primitive tribes who believe that their breath helps the sun to rise.

Unless some outer activity claims her, the family woman may make the discovery earlier than either men or professional women that libido changes its direction as old age approaches. It is a change that all must encounter sooner or later: at some time or other outer activities lose their glamour and the inner world demands attention. So strong is this demand that the old who refuse to turn their faces inwards, clinging desperately to outer values even though they watch them daily slipping from their grasp, are frequently made ill. Forced by illness or accident to be inactive, they are given the opportunity which they had been unable to take of their own free will, to ruminate and ponder and put forth new shoots in an unaccustomed inner world.

Illnesses at any time of life should not be merely cured, but utilized for growth in a hitherto unknown field. Particularly does this apply to the aging, whether man or woman.

If the old can become creative in their own right, they are, as I have said, lost no longer, but above all it is imperative that the older person should have a positive attitude towards death. The young can forget death with impunity. The old cannot. They are fortunate indeed who have faith that they will not be extinguished when they die, and can look forward to a new beginning in some other dimension or some other realm. But faith is a gift. Like love it comes by grace. No amount of thought or striving can achieve it: which paradoxically does not mean that there is no need to strive. We get from life in the measure with which we give to it, and our fundamental attitudes demand unceasing strife. But this is only preparing the soil. The actual planting of a spiritual seed like faith is beyond our control. It comes when it will.

To those who have been denied such faith I would ask, is it not a fact that the people who accept death most readily are the ones who have lived most fully? I do not mean necessarily the people who have done the most. Outer visible achievement is no criterion of living fully. The life of a great business magnate whose industry has erected huge buildings, set innumerable wheels whizzing and employs thousands of people, may have been so narrowly focused on the gain of material wealth that the riches of the spirit, art, music, literature and the warmth of human contacts, may have escaped him altogether. This is not full living.

At the opposite extreme I recall Spanish beggars seated on the cathedral steps, idly watching the passers by, receiving as though it were their lawful due occasional gifts of alms with a dignified "God bless you." How well the beggar must know those oft recurrent faces, nearly as constant in their daily presence as the stone saints and gargoyles behind him, the hourly chiming of the cathedral bells and the chant from within the church. What a setting in which to dwell and ponder! Does this man live fully? I do not know, but Unamuno, one of Spain's greatest writers, believed he did. Unamuno even declared that the most interesting philosopher he had ever met was a beggar, one of a long line of beggars.

I am not advocating beggary, but neither it nor visible achievement is any criterion of the quality of living. There is no yardstick for the surmounting of obstacles, the wrestling with angels and the transcending of suffering.

There is no yardstick for the measurement of others, but maybe for ourselves there is. One's yardstick is one's full capacity to be as complete a person as within one lies, and that includes becoming as conscious as it is possible for one to be in order to bring out and develop the buried talents with which one was born, and in order to realize one's own innate knowledge.

The more diverse the talents of any person, the more difficult may be the task. We only have a certain amount of psychic energy and throughout our lives we have to choose the road we will take, abandoning the fascinating paths in other directions. But the development of an ability to choose, and the consistent following of the path chosen, may be a large part of becoming as whole a person as one can be. So also is our flexibility a very real asset. The man or woman who has chosen the wrong path by mistake, and we all make mistakes, may need to retrace his steps and start again. This needs courage and should not be mistaken for the idle whim of the dilettante. Moreover, many people follow a vital thread towards a wholly invisible goal. We cannot possibly judge the value of their achievement.

To be conscious is not in itself a goal. It is possible to be a highly conscious person without one's character being influenced at all. Consciousness is not enough in itself. But one cannot develop a gift if one does not know that it is there, so to be conscious is indispensable. Many of us, through ignorance of our own capacities, only allow a small part of ourselves to flower. Neither can one lop off a branch that is marring the beauty of a tree if one has not noticed its presence and seen that its unbridled growth is spoiling the harmony of the whole. Or it may have to be sacrificed because it is impeding the growth of other plants.

Our individual psyche is very like a garden. The kind of garden will be determined by the nature of the soil, whether it is on a mountain slope or in a fertile valley. It will depend upon the climate. Green lawns flourish in England. In parts of Spain to sow a lawn is to make a present to the wind, for literally the seed is blown away.

Climate and geology are powers beyond our altering. They are the conditions we have been given to make the most of it, and for some the task is immensely harder than it is for others. The slopes of arid hills in Spain are a marvel of man's endeavour. Every inch is terraced with little walls of stones so that not a drop of the rare precious rain shall be lost in tumbling streams but held for the thirsty vines and olive trees. All honour to such gardeners. Some of us dwell in more temperate climes where the task is not so hard, but any gardener will know the unceasing vigilance which is needed to tend a garden, wherever it may be. Weeds are never eradicated once for all.

So, too, our psyches. They also can be invaded by pests from other gardens which have been neglected, making it harder to maintain the health of ours. Indeed, to maintain our psyche or our garden free of pests is a responsibility to our neighbours as well as to ourselves. Some gardens are more formal than others. Some have corners deliberately left wild, but a garden with no form and no order is not a garden at all but a wilderness.

The psyche which is a total wilderness ends in the asylum or burdens its family with unhealthy emanations. The well-tended but over conventional garden, on the other hand, may have no stamp of individuality upon it. It expresses the psyche of the mass man, and suburbia is full of them. The garden which is tended with care yet is not quite like any other garden for it conveys the psyche of an individual who has become a mature personality from where the scent of honeysuckle and roses and wild thyme will perfume the air for all around.

But gardens cannot grow without earth, and the loveliest flowers thrive on soil that is well manured and black. Dirt has been defined as matter in the wrong place. Manure is not dirt when dug into the borders. And rich emotional living in the right places is as indispensable for the flowering of wisdom in old age as the purity of the air and the brilliant sunlight of consciousness. No flower and no wisdom was ever reared on a ground of shiny white tiles washed daily with antiseptic.

It is the older person, whether man or woman, who has the need and the obligation to tend the garden of the psyche. The young are generally too immersed in active living; study, work, careers, and bringing up a family absorb all their energies. Indeed, a too early absorption with their own psyche may be an actual poison for the young. It may deprive them of the essential spontaneity which is needed for living. Actual experience can never be replaced by thinking about life or examining inner motives. To be ever conscious of the possible hazards before us snatches away our power to leap. We can only live fully by risking our lives over and over again.

It is in the latter part of life that people need to turn attention inwards. They need to do so because if their garden is as it should be they can die content, feeling that they have fulfilled their task of becoming the person they were born to be. But it is also an obligation to society. What a man or woman is within affects all those around. The old who are frustrated and resentful because they have omitted to become in life the persons they should have been, cause all in their vicinity to suffer.

Being is not the same as doing. Most people have had to sacrifice in some direction their capacity to do, but none are exempt from being to the full. There can be no limit to one's endeavour to become more and more aware of the depths of one's own psyche, discovering its lights and its shadows, its possibilities of unexpected vision as well as its dark regions.

The old woman, like the old man, needs to turn her natural receptivity towards the inner voices and inner whisperings, pondering on the new ideas which will come to her if she is attuned to her own inner self. Mrs. Moore, in E. M. Forster's *Passage to India*, was doing precisely this in her sudden and unexpected refusal to be drawn into the whirl of outer events. But we should not expect the insights of the very old to be revealed to the rest of us. There may be weeks and months or even years of slow, quiet gestation in the minds of quite old people. To speak of half-formed ideas is to destroy their growth as surely as to burn a seedling with the sun's rays shining through a magnifying glass. The very frailty of age guards its secrets.

Indeed, the insights of the very old may never quite reach the level of consciousness where they can be clothed in words. But this does not mean that they are not at work beneath the surface. The conscious mind is only a small part of our total psyche.

The very old, those who have given up all interest in the outer world even to the stage of being withdrawn from any point of contact, may still be receiving and quietly nurturing within themselves new insights which will enable them to meet the unknown future. One wonders sometimes what holds them here. Perhaps they are not ready. They cannot die till they are ready. I have often felt that modern medicine is very cruel to the old for it keeps them here when they are longing to be allowed to go.

But perhaps longing to go is not the same as being ready to meet the other side. I doubt if science could keep anyone alive if in this sense they were truly ready for their death.

It is a fallacy that the old are necessarily lonely when they are alone. Some are. But never those who are quietly pondering, preparing themselves, albeit without deliberate intention, for their coming death. They need long hours of solitude to round out their lives within, as they have earlier done without.

There is a lovely little book, *All Passion Spent*, by Victoria Sackville-West. She tells of an old lady after the death of her husband with whom she has shared a long life. Her children hold a family council. What can be done with mother? They plan it all out. She shall stay with them and their growing families in turn so they can share the burden of looking after her and keeping her from feeling lonely.

The plan is unfolded to the old lady who, to the amazement of her children, thanks them politely and declines their offer of hospitality. It transpires that for years she has been longing to have a little house of her own where she could live alone and undisturbed with her thoughts. Miraculously the chance had come and nothing should cheat her of it now.

This old woman had the good fortune to know her own mind, which many of us do not. Many old men and women are cheated of their essential solitude, and kept continually focused on outer things by the mistaken kindness of the young and their own unawareness of their need to be alone. We die alone. It is well to become accustomed to being alone before that moment comes.

Old age is the time of reckoning, our achievements balanced by our needless omissions and our mistakes. Some of our mistakes are hideous, but this is no reason for not facing them. Some we would never know if our children did not tell us the awful things we had done to them without realizing the dire effect of our advice, the example of our behavior or our condemnation.

The old are generally too much shielded. The next generation fears to hurt them. I say the next generation deliberately for it is seldom the young who over-shield the old. The vital calls to live of the young are more likely to make them callous, which is really far more healthy. It is those who are already advanced in middle age, often themselves already older women, who over-protect the very old. Nothing must be told to worry them. Frequently they are so pampered and humoured that they are turned into querulous children.

Indeed, it is more often than not our own dislike of feeling hard, rather than genuine affection, which makes us so falsely kind. Moreover there is no need for us to take upon ourselves the responsibility of sheltering the very old from worry. Griefs do not shatter them as they do the young. They have their own protection from those emotions which are more than they can bear. It is not our task to turn them into breathing fossils.

That is no kindness to the old. Rather it is cruelty because it deprives them of their power still to grow. It is an unpardonable belittling of the role of the aged, for it is they who, whether they can formulate it or not, are in fact the depositories of wisdom. Very often it is they who have lived more than those who shelter them. To the older woman who has the aged in her care I would say: Be careful not to spend more energy upon the very old than you can rightly afford to do. Your own life too makes claims. Deep thought and wise judgement are needed to give them libido where it is really due. If too much is given to the aged at the expense of the giver it will only breed bitterness, and that helps no one.

The care of the very old is a terribly difficult problem and every case has to be dealt with on its own merits. Many family women find an old parent a good substitute for the children who have grown and gone. Many others who have had no children turn the parent unwittingly into the child they have never had. In either case the old person is wrapped in cotton wool which he or she has not the strength to throw aside. They can very easily become victims, rather than grateful recipients, of our over-coddling.

And so they end their days either with a complacency to which they have no right, or in puzzled resentment that the young do not give them the love they thought they had deserved. There are no deserts in love. Greater outspokenness is better for everyone concerned, though the young might certainly temper their frankness with the constant remembrance that the old have done their best. Deliberate malice on the part of parents is, I believe, very rare. The vast majority of parents undoubtedly do the best they know. And as undoubtedly the next generation will have found it wrong, and rightly so. To be a parent is the most difficult task in the world. For a parent not to be understanding enough cripples. To be too understanding imprisons.

I have yet to meet the parents who have not made serious blunders with their children in one direction or the other. The childless in this are fortunate. The false steps they have taken in life are likely to have had less dire consequences on others.

I think it is important that mistakes should be brought out into the light of day, for how otherwise may they be forgiven? Forgiven by those sinned against but also forgiven by the sinner himself. This is something very different from complacency for it implies full consciousness and condemnation of the sin. To forgive oneself is a very difficult thing to do, but perhaps it is the last task demanded of us before we die. For the man or woman who can forgive him or herself can surely harbour no vestige of rancour against any other.

Impersonal forgiveness is very like love, but love on a higher plane than the personal love which women above all find so necessary. It is Agape as distinct from personal Eros. It is the charity spoken of by St. Paul. It is only possible for those who are completely on their own thread to God. No little isolated ego can forgive itself. In the last verses of the poem quoted the old woman found forgiveness of herself as well as others to be her inspiration and her goal.

And so, in the end, if endeavour is unceasing and the fates are kind, almost without noticing how it happened an old woman may find that love is still, as it always had been, the centre and the mainspring of her being, although, along with her years, the word has grown in meaning.

READING 3.3

The Elderly Prisoner

The special problems of elderly prisoners for both prison systems and the prisoners, themselves, are described in the following article from a South Carolina newspaper.* The requirements for different kinds of facilities, programs, and services, described are similar to those encountered throughout the United States as more and more prisoners are elderly. Most American corrections programs and facilities were constructed for younger people. The changes in prisoner age structures are requiring a reexamination of the ways in which such programs are operated.

They are career criminals like John Wesley Andrews, 69, who has been in and out of prison on various raps since he was 16.

They are old-timers like Gordon Cobb, 81, who has spent two-thirds of his life in prison for one crime.

They are "solid citizens" like Charles Missroon, 81, who had never been convicted of a crime until one day, 10 years ago, when he decided he was tired of his wife and shot her to death.

They are South Carolina's elderly prisoners, people with case histories as individual as the wrinkles on their faces.

And they are showing up in prison in increasing numbers—in South Carolina as well as in the rest of the country, bringing with them special health, social and residential needs that have to be considered.

During the last decade, the number of elderly inmates in South Carolina's prison population has grown almost as fast as the overall prison population, said Dr. Lorraine Fowler, who analyzes statistics for the S.C. Department of Corrections.

In 1979, South Carolina's inmate population of 7,691 included 376 inmates age 50 and older—the age at which state corrections officials begin to label inmates "geriatric."

Today's prison population of 13,270 includes 530 inmates 50 and older—504 men and 26 women. Of that, 119 inmates are in their 60s, 20 are in their 70s and four are in their 80s, according to the corrections department.

*Reprinted from *The State* (Columbia, S.C.)

The total over-50 inmate population, then, has risen 33 percent since 1979, while the total population has increased 42 percent.

Corrections experts say those numbers will only continue to go up, for a variety of reasons. One reason is natural: The prison population mirrors the outside population, and the outside population is aging at a rapid pace.

Beyond laws of nature are the laws of man—mandates such as South Carolina's 1986 Omnibus Crime Bill—that will force more criminals to grow old in prison. The crime bill cracked down on violent criminals, those convicted of rape, murder, first-degree arson, kidnapping and seven other crimes.

Violent criminals must serve more time than other inmates before they are eligible for parole. They don't get as many chances for parole. They must convince five, rather than four, of the state's seven parole board members that they are worthy of being paroled. Those convicted of two or more violent crimes cannot be paroled at all.

Violent criminals can't participate in "work credit"—a program that allows most inmates to decrease their sentences by working inside the prison.

Even without the omnibus Crime Bill, parole rates have been declining—possibly because the parole board is reflecting a get-tough attitude among the citizenry, said Judy Turnipseed of the S.C. Department of Probation, Parole and Pardon Services.

"There's no doubt a special population is building up" due to these factors, said William Leeke, state prisons commissioner from 1968 to 1987. "It's a new burden on the system. It's complicated."

It's complicated because the needs of the elderly are much different from those of other inmates, corrections experts say. South Carolina's typical inmate is male, 31 and spends one year and 10 months in prison, according to department statistics. He works in one of the prison industries and spends a lot of time being counseled about what he's going to do when he gets out.

Many elderly inmates, on the other hand, can't adjust to the unstable, noisy atmosphere found in most prisons, corrections officials say.

"You get somebody 75, 80, they're paralyzed or they've got a heart condition," Leeke said. "You can't just put them in the regular population. When you're that old, noise levels bother you. Plus, you've got the predator type in prison to bother you."

As do the aged in the outside world, elderly inmates often have chronic health problems.

They have recreational needs beyond the basketball courts and baseball diamonds most prisons provide for younger inmates.

And when it's time to get out, they sometimes have outlived their families and it's difficult to find a place for them to go.

Thirty years ago, none of these needs was taken into account. Elderly prisoners went to Central Correctional Institution along with everyone else. Those who were too frail to do tough jobs simply didn't work, and thus had little to keep them occupied.

Health care was at a minimum. In 1958, there was one part-time doctor for 1,800 inmates, according to Ellis MacDougall, who was deputy warden at CCI then.

As inmates began demanding their rights, corrections officials began taking a look at special needs groups.

In 1969, under Leeke's guidance, part of the new minimum-security Goodman Correctional Institution was devoted to the ailing elderly—and to the handicapped, whose special needs often parallel those of the elderly.

Ultimately, Goodman provided 88 beds for the minimum-security infirm.

But it wasn't until the early 1980s, as the waiting list for Goodman became longer and longer, that corrections officials really began taking a look at the elderly, said warden Judy Anderson, who was instrumental in bringing the aging population to the attention of corrections officials.

"That was when we really began noticing the graying of America," she said. "It was reflected in the facilities and on the street."

In 1984, the infirm were moved out of Goodman and into their own facility, State Park Correctional Institution. It was the state's old tuberculosis sanitorium, which had been renovated to provide 120 beds for minimum-security elderly and handicapped.

A wing at Kirkland Correctional Institution was set aside for maximum-security elderly and handicapped inmates until Broad River Correctional Institution opened this year with a special 48-bed wing for them.

Those infirm inmates who weren't a maximum security risk but who couldn't qualify for the open setting at State Park were sent to Stevenson Correctional Institution, where there were 32 beds set aside.

Today, even the most handicapped elderly inmate has an opportunity to learn a "cottage skill"—horticulture, basket-weaving or other craft work—so that all inmates can earn an income after prison.

Social workers are trained to deal with their special problems. They counsel them about possibly dying in prison or having no one to go to when they're released. They help them find some place to go—whether it's a nursing home or a community care home.

Today's health care system also is much improved over that of three decades ago. Corrections employs four psychiatrists, 15 doctors, nine dentists and 189 people in nursing positions, Hugh Riddle of the department's health services said. Critical care is now available at a 20-bed infirmary at Kirkland Correctional Institution.

The department spends an average of $1,436 a year on each inmate for health care, at an annual cost of $10.3 million, or 6 percent of corrections' overall $180 million budget.

A great deal of that budget is spent on the elderly, who are provided a continuum of care at the special institutions where they are housed.

Corrections experts who work with the elderly concur that the system has improved markedly, but they would like to see further changes.

The department's director of health services, Pat Satterfield, said there aren't enough nursing home beds available for those prisoners who need 24-hour medical care when they are released from prison. The corrections department is trying to contract with a nursing home so there will always be a bed for those types of inmates, she said.

Dr. Joann Morton, the department's director of special projects who has done extensive work toward improving prison life for the elderly, would like to see a larger institution built for minimum-security inmates.

Corrections Commissioner Parker Evatt acknowledges that the elderly population is an increasing concern and that construction of a new institution is probably imminent. He said the idea probably will be high on his list of priorities when the next bond issue comes up before the state Budget and Control Board, possibly in two years.

PART TWO

pROVidiNq diRECT SERViCES TO OldER AdulTS

Among the most important of the human services worker's skills is the provision of direct services to clients. These services are those which are designed to immediately benefit the client by counseling with him or her, by organizing and managing the overall services provided through "case management," by assisting with personal and psychological problems through services in groups, and by working with client families.

Many of the services most important to older adults are discussed in Part Two along with the means that many human services workers use to provide those services. Although the methods suggested are very complex and the subject of many books, themselves, these chapters provide an introduction to the worker who, by following the ideas carefully, will be able to skillfully assist many older people and their families through time.

Chapter 4
Reaching and Serving Older Adults: Interviewing, Case Management, and Follow-up Services

Those working in the field of aging have become aware that older people do not always receive services to which they are entitled. Over the years studies have shown that, as new programs for older people have been created, only a small fraction of those eligible actually make use of the services. Those providing the services have concluded that a major reason is that older people often do not know about the services or need assistance in obtaining them. In this chapter we will discuss how outreach services are conducted and how they can be used to enable older people to obtain the services they need. We will also cover the skills of interviewing, counseling, and directly helping older people with their problems.

The Need for Outreach Services

In the field of human services, providers generally assume that individuals in need of services voluntarily seek them out. We have become aware that many people do not know about the existence of service programs; consequently, we can no longer assume that potential clients know how or where to obtain services. This is particularly true for older people. Studies have shown that a great many older people are not receiving services that are available to them. There are several explanations. Today's older people were socialized throughout life to be self-sufficient and independent, and many find it difficult to seek assistance from social agencies. More important, perhaps, is the fact that many older people do not use services because they do not know about them, or, if they do know about them, are not able to obtain them.

Very often when services are initiated for the elderly, an agency or program is inclined to use mass media to solicit elderly participants or clients. However, mass media are often an ineffective means of reaching older people. Many older people do not use television or radios or receive daily newspapers. Even if they do have them, many, due to sensory losses characteristic of later life, do not use these resources. In addition, many older people are illiterate or do not speak English. Consequently, media are not effective in communicating with them.If programs are to be effective, special efforts must be made to inform the elderly about services and assistance that will enable them to make use of these programs.

The Purposes of Outreach

The basic function of an outreach service is to locate and inform older people of services that may be available to them. The specific purposes of an outreach program will vary, however. Sometimes outreach is conducted to provide older individuals information about special programs, such as nutrition programs, or it may have a more general purpose, for instance, as part of an information and referral service. In this instance, the purpose of outreach is to help with a specific problem by informing older people about the available services in the community. Outreach to older people has also been done on a national basis, for example, in the Supplementary Security Income Alert aimed at making people aware of a federal program to increase their income level and food outreach programs.

Some outreach programs are directed to the entire elderly population of a community, whereas others may be aimed at a subgroup or target population of the elderly, such as the poor, minorities, isolated, or handicapped. In recent years, for example, much of the emphasis has been focused on locating the isolated or "hidden elderly." Large numbers of older people have become withdrawn from the mainstream of society; they have lost contact with friends and neighbors and have infrequent contacts with others. The purpose of outreach is to attempt to get these elderly people back into the mainstream of life.

Providing Outreach Services

When outreach is offered as part of a program for older adults, it requires concerted efforts to actively seek out older people who may be in need of programs or services. Outreach service includes face-to-face contact with older individuals to make them aware of services. It will also involve helping individuals decide whether they want to receive services and then providing assistance so that they may obtain these services. Much time and planning is needed to successfully implement an outreach program.

Whatever the purpose or scope of an outreach program, there are four basic steps involved. First, the **target population** (the group to be served by the program) must be located. Second, the older person must be contacted and made aware of available services. Third, assistance must be provided to ensure that the older individual has access to services. Fourth, a follow-up contact should be made to ensure that the older person received the service. Each of these steps will be discussed in detail below.

*Locating and Identifying
the Target Population
of Older Adults*

Outreach services are unique in the realm of human services, as they involve provision of an unsolicited service. Consequently, a major function of an outreach service for the elderly is the location of older people in the community. The first step in most outreach efforts is to define the target population for whom the services are intended. For example, are you attempting to reach all people over 60 or 65 years of age, or are you looking for those who are isolated or low-income elderly? Once a target population has been defined, a systematic plan for locating individuals in the community is required.

One can begin outreach by attempting to get the names of older people from the many social service agencies that exist in the community. Much time and energy will be saved if these agencies are involved in efforts to identify members of the target population. Agencies that deal with elderly clients are public welfare or social service agencies, Social Security offices, public-health services, visiting nurse services, hospitals and medical institutions, the Red Cross, the Salvation Army, and community action programs.

Unfortunately, large numbers of the elderly population are not part of the existing service system, and consequently one cannot rely solely on this means of locating elderly people in the community. Moreover, it may be difficult to get such information from social agencies, for very often they are prohibited by agency or public policy from disclosing the names of individuals receiving their services. Sometimes, however, employees of these agencies will unofficially provide the names of older people or direct one to sources where they can be obtained.

A very important means of locating older people, particularly the hard-to-reach, will be through informal communications systems in the community. In small towns and rural areas it is particularly likely that people know each other or have indirect contacts with each other, for example, contacts through extended families. Very frequently in those areas, social contacts are interrelated and over-lapping; people in the community belong to the same clubs or go to the same churches. Very often if you make these in direct contacts aware of your purpose, they can be instrumental in helping locate older people in need of services.

In urban areas there are many individuals in the community who are not part of the social service system but who, by virtue of their positions or the nature of their employment, have frequent contacts with the elderly, usually consumer-provider contacts. Such people may be able to easily and quickly identify those elderly who may be potentially isolated or in need of services. Grocers, druggists, barbers or beauticians, and delivery people may have this kind of information. Very often delivery people are the only contacts that isolated elderly individuals have with the outside world. Other sources might be mail carriers, police officers, ministers, private physicians, local politicians, service organizations (such as American Legions, VFW, Elks, or Moose), public libraries, and bartenders. These sources should be explored in efforts to locate older people.

In other instances, the only means available to locate the target population will be through a door-to-door canvass of the community. This method is very time-consuming and requires careful planning. Very often, even with a door-to-door canvass, it is not productive to randomly search the entire community. It is generally more worthwhile to search those parts of the community where older people are more likely to live, such as the center or older neighborhoods in the city, resident hotels in center cities and in rural areas, isolated farms. Census tract data and city or county planning officials can help pinpoint where the older population of the community is concentrated. When one does a door-to-door canvass in large neighborhoods or communities, it may be helpful to subdivide the areas to be searched and start with the sections with the highest concentration of elderly and end with those with the lowest concentration.

Contacting and Informing
Older Adults about
Community Resources

Once having identified members of the target population of elderly and where to locate them, the next step in outreach is to make personal contact with individuals. The purpose of this contact is to provide information about service. Sometimes the information is general—about all services in the community; sometimes it is about a specific program for which you would like to recruit older adults. Even if the worker is making a contact to inform an older person about a specific service, having initiated the contact, the worker has the responsibility to obtain information about the individual's needs and to try to help with those needs even if they are not met by the worker's program.

Three major skills are needed to effectively carry out this phase of the outreach service. One is being able to identify social services in the community that are available for older people. This involves having specific information about services, including who provides them, who may receive them, and the steps an individual must take in order to obtain them. Another skill is gathering information; that is, being able to solicit pertinent information from the elderly person that will enable one to make some formulation about immediate problems or needs. The third skill is setting priorities. After helping the individual identify problems, the worker must help establish which needs should be dealt with first. Some problems can be dealt with immediately and quickly; others are more long-range in nature and will require a series of activities to be resolved. A good strategy is to begin by trying to help with those problems for which you can provide an immediate solution and then setting some time frame for those that may take a longer time to resolve.

In carrying out the contact and information phase of an outreach service, one should keep in mind that the first contact with the older person is a crucial step. It requires much skill, because it involves an effort to change the person's prevailing lifestyle from uninvolvement with social services to involvement through taking help. The worker will need to be tactful, as many older people are reluctant to let strangers into their homes or to share information with them. Often these concerns are realistic as many older people fear for their safety. Other older people have unrealistic fears, may be depressed, or feel rejected. Every effort should be made to avoid causing an already withdrawn older person undue concern or further reinforcing negative feelings about the outside world. Some things to keep in mind when making a first contact with the older client are as follows:

1. *Try not to appear at the home of an older person without some prior notice of your visit.* The best introduction is through someone the older person already knows and trusts. If this is not possible, the outreach worker should inform the older person of the impending visit either by letter or by phone. A letter should be short and simple. For example:

Dear Mr., Mrs., Ms., Miss _____ ,

The [name of agency or organization] is in the process of making contact with older individuals in the community in order to discuss the availability of social services with them.
Your name was given to us by _____ . I would like to visit you in your home and discuss our program with you. I will be in touch with you by phone in the next few days to set up a time when I might visit you.

Sincerely yours,

This letter will serve as an introduction when you phone or arrive at the older person's home. For example, you could begin such a visit by saying, "Hello. I'm Mrs. Jones. I mailed you a letter last week about our program. Could I talk to you further about it?" When approaching the home of an older person, the worker should have some form of identification verifying that he or she is a bona fide representative of a program in the community.

2. *When doing outreach, don't rush the visit.* Plan to spend more than 15 minutes with the older person. In addition, try to help the older person feel comfortable and relaxed with you. Be conversational. You might begin the conversation by talking about things of interest to the older person, such as the picture on the wall or the flowers in the yard, just to show that you are interested in the person as an individual. The contact that you make may be the first conversation this older person has had with another person in many weeks, or even months; you will need to be tolerant, for some older people

may take advantage of your presence and monopolize the conversation. If you sense that the individual has the need to talk, try to allow time for that.

3. *Don't pressure communication.* If the person prefers not to communicate, it may be best to reschedule the visit.

4. *Be a doer not just a talker.* In short, find a need the older person has right now and attempt to meet that need with a service. This is the most effective outreach tool of all. Simply by doing a small favor you will break down much suspicion and reluctance. You begin to become a friend—someone who helps by doing something rather than talking about it.

The major purpose of the outreach contact is to inform the older person of the various services available in the community. During the process of getting acquainted and talking about problems or needs, you will obtain information that should help you to identify a problem that is pressing. Your next step is to identify an agency or program in the community that may be able to help with the problem and to explain the services of that agency. In doing this, be sure you have current information about the service being provided and don't misinform the older person.

In addition, do not make promises you cannot keep. Don't guarantee that a person will receive a service, as many times technicalities may prevent that. You are discredited as a helper if you make promises you cannot keep. For example, if you identify as a potential need transportation services to a physician, then you should say that *you will attempt* to get the person connected with an agency that may be able to provide this service. In talking to older people about income programs or other programs where there may be eligibility requirements, you should say that the person *may be eligible* rather than stating emphatically that he or she is eligible for the service. Many times we think a person is eligible but when the circumstances are presented to the agency, it may determine otherwise. In order not to raise false hopes, make clear that this is a service for which eligibility must be determined.

Workers sometimes will find that even though older people need services, some may choose not to obtain them. You should explore the reasons for such a choice. Sometimes it's based on fear or misunderstanding. Once this has been explored and misgivings or misunderstanding dealt with, if the individual continues to refuse, this wish should be respected. The older person should be left with information (a card or phone number) on where to find the service in case of a later change of mind.

Providing Assistance to Older Clients

Once a worker has made the older person aware of services and he or she has agreed to obtain them, the next step in outreach is ensuring that the services are actually received. Very often such assistance requires the worker to make a referral for the older person. This may involve making a call to an agency and talking to a representative of the agency about the circumstances, or setting up an appointment for the older person to go to the agency or for a representative of the agency to come to the older person's home.

Once a referral has been made and an appointment set up, the worker may have to help the older person actually get to an agency. This may involve trying to locate a volunteer service in the community that provides transportation, or the outreach worker may have to take the individual to the agency.

Sometimes older individuals who have never been to social agencies feel more comfortable if someone goes along with them, so that here again the outreach worker may need to find a volunteer or accompany the older person. In this particular step, the outreach worker should examine with the older person any obstacles that may prevent use of services and try to help eliminate such barriers so that the older person can have access to the services.

Following Up on an Outreach Visit

The final function of outreach is to make sure that the client has actually received the service. This involves a contact a few days following the initial visit. The follow-up contact may be done in several ways. It can be done by telephone, that is, making a call to the older person's home or to the agency to make sure that the appointment was kept. It could also involve just dropping by the client's home, again on a social basis, to see how the older person is getting along and what happened with the agency. The major emphasis for follow-up is to make sure that nothing hindered the older person's receiving the service. If, for some reason, the older person or the agency did not follow through on the referral, then it is up to the outreach worker to determine the reason and to provide additional assistance, resources, or moral support to ensure that this does not happen again in the future.

If the agency fails to carry out its part once the outreach worker has made a referral, then it may be necessary to make a second contact with the agency. If the worker feels strongly enough about it, it may be necessary to inform the administrator of the agency about the situation.

Interviewing

Workers in human services agencies serving the elderly are often required to conduct interviews for a variety of purposes. This section offers concepts and methods for effectively conducting interviews with older people.

Purposes of Interviews

An interview is a purposeful and organized conversation. It is different from a chat or small talk because it always has a specific purpose. It has a particular form and usually includes a beginning, middle, and end, each of which is clearly defined.

Interviews with older people are conducted for many reasons. Perhaps the most important principle in interviewing is knowing why the interview is being held. Interviewing without a purpose usually misuses everyone's time—the service person's as well as the client's. The length, content, and format of the interview are determined by its objectives.

Some of the purposes for which human-service workers interview older people are:

1. *Providing information.* Workers sometimes conduct interviews with older people to explain the organization they represent. For example, someone who is interested in joining a community group for older people may want to know some facts about the program, such as the costs of belonging; the activities; when, where, and how often it meets; the names and interests of some of the other members; and the goals of the program. In such an interview, the worker explains the agency and its services to the older person while also learning something about the potential member's interests. The worker explains the purposes of the organization in terms of the client's needs and interest.

2. *Eliciting information.* The largest numbers of interviews are designed to learn something about the person being interviewed. Most human services agencies need information in order to effectively serve older people. In a public assistance program, for example, the worker needs to know about the older person's financial resources and social and economic requirements. In a mental health program the interview is designed to find out about the emotional problems facing the older person, and the interviewer will want the answers to such questions as: What are the older person's emotional problems? How long have they persisted? What possible solutions might there be for them? In what ways may the organization help the older person overcome them?

3. *Solving problems.* Sometimes the goal of the interview is to help older people resolve some of their social and emotional problems. Interviewers may try to help older people adjust to new life situations after they lose spouses or relocate in new communities. At other times, the interview is designed to help clients understand and deal more effectively with their feelings of depression, loneliness, or isolation or to help them find alternatives to their living situations through homes for the aged or other group programs. Therapeutic counseling and other change-oriented interviews fall into the category of problem solving.

Most interviews are conducted for one or a combination of the three broad purposes of providing information, eliciting information, or solving problems. It is critical for interviewers to understand their own purposes, the older person's objectives and reasons for participating in the interview, the goals of the organization or agency for the interview, and the potential results of this planned and purposeful conversation.

Some workers act as if it is always useful to gain information about older people for their organization's records, and so they question the older person extensively and prepare detailed records on their responses. However, it is often wiser to limit the amount of information one gathers from older people. Only that information necessary for the purposes of the organization and for providing effective services to the client should be sought. Effective workers gather as much of the information they need as possible-but no more. Revealing and interesting information is not always the information that should be pursued. Information becomes old quickly, and dated information loses its utility. In addition, most workers should not want to know about problems the client faces if they are not relevant. Information is best collected on a "need-to-know" basis. In other words, workers should find out what is needed, but they should not probe for the simply interesting and titillating.

The information gathered from people in interviews may be used to help the clients solve problems or for referrals to other programs and services, providing appropriate releases are obtained and confidentiality is observed.

Conducting an Interview

Length

Although there is no way to fix a proper length for all interviews, there are some helpful principles that interviewers can follow. One is that the time used for an interview ought to be variable. Some interviews can be satisfactorily conducted and concluded in ten minutes; others may require more than an hour. A useful guide is to ensure that the interview is not rushed and that the interviewee has ample opportunity to answer relevant questions. It is probably wise in most situations to allow 30 minutes to one hour for an interview. Spending less than 30 minutes with a client may insult some, but allowing more than an hour may encourage both the interviewer and the interviewee to engage in small talk or purposeless conversation. If there are limits to the time the interviewer will be available, those limits ought to be made clear to the interviewee at the beginning. Such information helps interviewees plan their time effectively and use interviews for dealing with their most pressing questions and issues.

Where to Interview

There is extensive discussion in the literature of counseling, social work, and psychology about the best places for conducting interviews. Some think the interviewee's home is the ideal place; others think that the worker's office is best; and still others choose neutral sites, such as restaurant tables, park benches, or special interview rooms in the agency's offices. In fact, there is no single best place for an interview. Each site produces different results, and the choice of the site depends on the purposes of the interview. If the interviewee is unusually anxious for the worker to see his or her home, if it is difficult for the interviewee to travel, or if the interviewer wants to observe or interview the whole family, then a home interview is ideal. However, if the older person wants to avoid interruptions from family members or if the subject of the interview is likely to be emotionally charged and confidential, then the worker's office or a neutral spot is best. If the interview is to inform the interviewee about the agency or institution, it may best be conducted on the site so that the worker can show the older person the facilities instead of simply talking about them. If the interviewee wants to talk to the worker but wants the family to remain unaware of the interview, a neutral site might be best.

How Many Interviews
Are Necessary?

The number of interviews depends on the purposes of each interview and the problems being addressed. There is no need for a series of interviews to introduce an older person free of emotional problems to an agency or institution's program if the person learns everything in one session. If the problem is continuing and unlikely to be resolved through one or two interviews, a series of eight or ten contacts may be necessary. But just as there is no reason to believe that every problem can be resolved in one conversation, neither is there reason to believe everyone who comes to a human services organization for help needs a lengthy series of meetings with a professional worker.

Ethical Foundations
of Interviewing

An ethical human services worker always remembers to follow two basic concepts of interviewing when working with older people as well as with clients of other ages. The first is the principle of **confidentiality**, which means the worker does not reveal information that is secured in the interview to outsiders. The material may be shared with other professionals, if the interviewee grants permission, but not with the general public unless the information is changed, omitting specific details such as the identity of the interviewee, address, age, and so forth. Then the information is shared only for educational purposes. Human services workers have ethical obligations and commitments similar to those of ministers, physicians, and attorneys when collecting information from clients. Frequently they do not have the same legal protections, however, and they must take special precautions to be clear about their ability to maintain confidentiality. Sometimes courts can force social workers and other human services workers to reveal information that they would rather maintain as confidential. It is unethical for clients to be told that anything they reveal will be protected when that is not true. The client decides how much to tell the worker, but the worker should promise no more confidentiality than it is possible to deliver.

A second ethical principle of interviewing is **self-determination.** It is the client who decides what to talk about, it is the client who decides how much to share with the interviewer, and it is the client who decides what to do next. Human services workers do not direct the lives of those they serve. Instead, they help them overcome their problems by offering information, providing opportunities to reach new decisions, and otherwise assisting their clients. Human services workers are ethically bound to help those they serve achieve the things they want in the ways they want to achieve them, so long as the client's goals do not violate the rights of others.

Interviewing Skills

A variety of skills are required for effective interviewing. Of course, each interviewer proceeds in a particular way, but effective interviewers tend to stick to a number of principles and exercise certain skills that enable them to be effective.

1. *Achieving a positive relationship between the interviewer and the interviewee.* The interviewer must communicate a concern about the interviewee's needs. The interviewer must accept the interviewee as a human being and treat the individual as one who is important and worth the interviewer's time and effort. Similarly, before effective interviewing can take place, the interviewee must accept the interviewer as someone who wants to and can help, and whose interests are similar to those of the elderly person.

2. *Defining or clarifying the problem.* With this skill the interviewer helps the client precisely define the problem that is faced. It may be as simple or fundamental as learning about the agency's services, or it may be a complex set of emotional concerns. This means the worker must take time to assist the elderly person in the clarification. Sometimes simply spelling out the issues resolves the problem immediately. Sometimes when people are helped to face matters directly and clearly, they realize their problems are not so difficult, and they feel better quickly. In any case, it is almost impossible to effectively help people who face what they perceive as a multitude of problems. The older person who is concerned about loneliness, rejection by children, finances, health, and many other problems cannot stop thinking about most of them long enough to resolve any one of them. That is why the third principle of interviewing is also significant in helping people solve their problems.

3. *Partializing.* The worker attempts to help the interviewee with **partialization,**

or cutting the problem into pieces in order to deal with its aspects one at a time. Again, simply being able to identify the elements of a problem and work on them as a series of concerns is often sufficient to overcome the difficulties. Many times, people are overwhelmed by problems hitting all at one time rather than about the specific problems themselves.

4. *Setting priorities, or distinguishing the order of importance of problems.* Once the client understands the problems in pieces in a series, the worker can be effective in helping the client set priorities for problem solving. Many people can be helped to determine what is most important so that they can work on solutions in an order of descending importance. Putting things in order and taking problem solving one step at a time is an important interviewing skill.

5. *Communicating effectively.* Competent interviewers speak loudly and clearly; avoid jargon; maintain eye contact with those who are being interviewed; and know when to be quiet so that the interviewee has an opportunity to participate, change the direction of the conversation, object to the subject being discussed, or otherwise maintain control over the interview. Older people frequently feel themselves inferior to professionals in human-service agencies when they are interviewed. Sometimes they suffer physical losses of hearing. Sometimes, also, generational differences make it difficult for old people and human-service workers to communicate in the same language, particularly when both use their own colloquial speech. For that reason effective interviewers pay careful attention to their skills in communication and adapt themselves to the needs and capacities of the older people with whom they are speaking. Figure 4-1 illustrates some of the principles of the communication process. The reading that follows this chapter, called "Guidelines for Interviewing Older Adults," stresses effective communication with the elderly.

6. *Summarizing.* An effective interviewer summarizes the interview and helps the client understand where the interview has gone, what conclusions have been reached, and what problems remain to be resolved. Again, simply pointing to the achievements of the interview and the solutions that have been reached in the conversation can be an important part of the resolution of the problems that the interviewee faces.

Recording Interviews

Working in a human services agency and conducting interviews often means that the worker must prepare a record of the interview. There are various forms for maintaining interview records, and they vary from agency to agency. The tra-

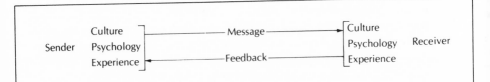

Communication takes place between two or more people who comprise two or more entities. The sender transmits a message to a receiver, and the receiver provides the sender with feedback. Messages are sent in terms of the sender's own culture, psychology, and experience. Senders say what they mean in accord with their understandings of the ideas and words. Receivers hear or understand messages in terms of their own culture, psychology, and experience. A sender must understand a receiver in order to communicate effectively. Feedback is the primary source of clear understanding.

Figure 4.1   A Simple Model of the Communication Process.

ditional practice in some human services programs has been to record almost verbatim or to maintain "process records." Detailed files are then constructed for each client or client family for the agency's archives. This kind of interviewing is generally avoided in modern human services programs. It is now more typical for interviewers to prepare organized summaries that aid the agency, cooperating human service workers, and subsequent workers, should the interviewer no longer be available to help the client. The focus is on maintaining sufficient information to ensure that the client's interests and needs are served but not so much that it will prevent the agency and other workers from ever looking back at the material. We would also like to point out that the amount of note taking done during the interview should be minimal. You may need to jot down dates, addresses, and names, but constant writing during an interview may denote to the older person lack of interest on your part.

Figures 4.2 and 4.3 are examples of formats that may be used in making records of interviews. Figure 4.2 is a sample interview face sheet. Most human services agencies try to maintain factual material on each individual, family, or group with whom they have contacts. Sometimes the face sheet is an index card, other times it is more detailed. The agency will want to record the names of the client or client family or group and the means for reaching them by telephone or mail; usually the names of the spouse, close relatives, or children of the client will also be recorded. It is occasionally useful to keep information on the problem or need that brought the client to the agency in the first place, and that may be briefly noted on the face sheet. Modern practice sometimes leads to a listing of the objectives or the service that is being provided by the agency.

Figure 4.3 is a form that may be used for individual interviews. It is not desirable, of course, for the interviewer to complete such a form during the interview

I.   Identifying Data:

          Name(s)   Telephone

          Address

          Alternate telephone and address (business, relative, home, etc.)

          Name of family members in client's household

II.   Presenting Problem, Concern, or Need That Brought the Client to the Agency

III.   Worker and Client-Determined Goals

Figure 4.2   Sample Interview Recording Format: Face Sheet.

Date of Interview_____ Time _____ Location _____

Client's name _____ Interview No._____

I.   Key Parts of Discussion in This Interview:

II. Worker and/or Client Evaluation of Progress toward Determined Goals or
     Modification of Goals:

III. Action Taken, Anticipated; Plans for Follow-Up, Subsequent Interviews,
     Referral to Other Resources:

Figure 4.3   Interview Form.

itself. The form is completed shortly after the interview with information from the interviewer's memory or from brief notes taken during contact with the client. The format is a simple one and suggests that the interviewer maintain information on the key points of discussion, progress toward meeting the goals of the relationship with the agency, modifications in those goals, and future action that is anticipated.

These are only sample forms; each agency develops its own, some of which are more complex and some simpler. The forms shown here may be adapted for individual, family, or other group interviews.

Some interviewers use automatic recording devices, such as audio or video tape recorders, which have the advantage of collecting very detailed and complete information, when they function correctly and are properly placed and employed. Our experience is that it is generally not useful to employ audio or video tape recorders when interviewing clients, because they tend to inhibit some people from communicating. Older clients particularly tend to resent taping. Recorders also may collect more information than necessary for effectively helping those who are served.

The exception to this general principle, in our experience at least, is the occasional use of audio or video taping to help clients see themselves as others might see them. If one wants to show clients how their depressed communications sound to others, an audio tape recorder can help. If one wants to show clients how they communicate with hostile facial expressions, videotaping them in an interview situation can be useful. Or if one wants to show a family what its interactions are really like, audio or video tape recording can be an aid. But for normal recording, brief notes or outline recordings are probably sufficient.

Family Interviews

Much of the discussion of interviewing implies that one human services worker meets with one other individual and conducts an interview. That is frequently the case, but increasingly interviews are conducted with larger groups of people. For example, many older people are interviewed as couples. In some circumstances one older person and a son or daughter are interviewed together. On occasion even larger family units are interviewed. Much depends on the circumstances, the needs of the clients, and the agency's goals. For example, if the interview is focused on helping an older person decide whether or not to enter a residential institution, it is sometimes useful for a child to join in the interview and participate in the discussion. The child may have financial obligations for the housing arrangement, but even if that is not true, many offspring still have feelings of guilt about their parents' entering a residential institution.

If the problems are emotional in nature, they may emanate from conflicts between the older person and other members of the family. When that is the case, many human services workers find it effective to talk to the older person along with other parties to the conflict in order to resolve the difficulties. Many older people are members of large constellations—for example, a grandfather, son, daughter-in-law, and grandchildren—all living together. In those cases, effective service can be provided with family interviews involving everyone. Human services workers must understand that interviews are not always events that involve only two people.

Effective family interviewing uses all the principles of interviewing already discussed, as well as some of the concepts of serving older people through groups, discussed in Chapter 5.

The following guidelines for interviewing older adults provide a summary of this section[1]

Guidelines for Interviewing Older Adults

1. In identifying the problem, get to know and understand the older person. What is his or her background—cultural, religious, financial? Will this affect how the person perceives the problem? Do you see the problem differently? Attempt to assess the strengths and weaknesses of the older person that will either delay or aid in solving the problem.

2. When determining what should be done, be aware of the available resources. Together with the client make a plan of action to resolve the problem, based on knowledge of the problem. Be sure the client is in agreement with the goals.

3. In implementing the plan, methods and techniques can be utilized effectively only after certain basic principles are understood and put into practice. Some of these principles are:

   a. Form a positive relationship. The older person's ability to accept help and to improve is dependent on the strength of the relationship with the helper. It may take more time for the older person to accept a new relationship. Understand this and be patient.

   b. Stimulate the client's motivation to accept help. Recognize the fact that an older person can change and utilize the client's strengths to help bring about change.

   c. Older people communicate in ways that are sometimes difficult for those younger to understand. The older adult may deny the need for help or for a helping relationship while discussing the situation but may reveal the opposite desire in behavior. Older people often speak and move more slowly and often need time to think things over; always remember this when speaking to them. Also, older adults may

---

[1] Adapted from material prepared by Anita Harbert for training human services workers.

show their acceptance and appreciation of the worker in less verbal ways. For example, appreciation may be expressed by a gift. The tendency for older people to reminisce may require more time and listening skill, but this is normal behavior for older people. Tolerance of such behavior is a means of building trust and confidence between you and the client.

Getting the older person to accept needed help will depend on your ability as a practitioner. The more knowledgeable about techniques, the more skillful you are, the more likely you are to succeed in your efforts as a helping person.

Techniques used to bring about change depend on the personality of the client and the particular goals. Some techniques that can be used are:

1. Always include the client and important other people in planning and establishing goals.

2. Let the client make his or her own decision.

3. Gather information about the problem accurately and try to assess implications of this information to the individual or group.

4. Obtain any additional information needed to understand the problem; speak to other people or groups when appropriate.

5. Explore possible alternatives for solution of the problem with the client or client group.

6. Explore with the client the consequences of the decision, and if a wrong choice is made, help the client with it.

7. Don't misrepresent things; don't give false assurance. For example, if you must send an elderly person to a state mental hospital, don't give a false impression of what it will be like. If you don't know what to tell the client, just say you don't know and deal with the client's having to leave home. Don't make an elderly person think he or she is going some place temporarily when you are making a permanent arrangement. It is hard to say to a weepy person, "Your family doesn't want you." But in the long run, it's less painful than the client's learning you were dishonest.

8. Don't imply you know all the answers and what is best. Listen to the individual; hear out the client's ideas and perceptions of the problem and its solution.

9. Reaching out is important to engage those older individuals who can't express their need for help, those who are too depressed and feel helpless, and those who don't know the available resources. This involves your being visible, flexible, creative, and sincere in your offer for help.

10. Work with groups of individuals when possible.

11. Obtain community involvement and community support for what you do.

12. Sometimes you will need to be an advocate or broker for the elderly; other times, a social activist.

13. The timing of what you say or do is of the utmost importance. Don't talk of relocation in a time of grief. Being prompt and keeping appointments is crucial. Some aged, like children, may tend to take what you say literally. I recall a situation when an older woman got up early and dressed every day for two months, because a relative said she would come and get her in a few days. She wanted to be ready, but the relative never came.

14. Follow through on referrals. Make sure your clients obtain the needed help or resources; don't let them get lost in the shuffle. Be certain the older person doesn't misunderstand directions.

    Some skills involved in implementing these techniques are:

1. Ask open-ended questions rather than ones producing yes or no answers. For example, "Have you thought about what you might like to do, and would you tell me about it?"

2. Try to guide the individual to a decision by making suggestions rather than giving advice. Bad advice discredits you as a helping person.

3. Don't take over! Give the client a chance to talk.

4. Convey concern, warmth, acceptance, and understanding, and learn to read between the lines of what is said; try to understand unspoken communication.

5. Instill trust and confidence in your relationship to clients or groups by being consistent, honest, and patient.

6. Keep in check your own feelings of anger and frustration toward the client.

7. Reserve judgments.

8. Don't impose your own values on the client.

9. Be realistic. Don't always be bright and cheerful. Don't be afraid to discuss unpleasant aspects of the client's life; you may be the only person who gives the client this opportunity.

10. Exercise judgment in determining if a plan is realistic in terms of resources and/or time. For example, some elderly like to postpone changes in their physical environment as long as possible. You must be the one to set a time limit or help the individual understand one already established. Although a building is to be demolished on July 2, Mrs. Jones may not want to move out until Septem-

ber, when she can go to live with her nephew. She must be helped to understand that this is not a satisfactory plan and something must be arranged temporarily. Similarly, patients who want to remain in the hospital when the physician wants to discharge them must be helped to accept the necessity of change.

11. Learn to assess whether the group or individual has the capacity to achieve the desired goal or will need outside assistance.

These are some skills and techniques you can employ in your helping role. There are others. Direct service will not of itself solve the problems of the aged, but if you can provide services effectively, it will at least help people deal with their difficulties.

As practitioners trying to help the elderly meet the problems of life, we have the responsibility to keep abreast of the needs and problems of the aged. We must keep in constant communication with those who best know these needs—elderly people themselves. We must not have a "communication gap" with them. In working with the aged, listen to what they say and to what they don't say. Frequently they will spell out their individual needs. Then, too, as you listen to more of the aged, you may find several older people with similar needs and no way to meet them. It is only with a clear understanding of such needs that we can best know how to help and the methods to obtain what is needed.

Case Management

One of the primary innovations in serving clients, including aging clients, is **case management**. Rubin (1987) defines it as " . . . an approach to service delivery that attempts to ensure that clients with complex, multiple problems and disabilities receive all the services they need in a timely and appropriate fashion."

Stated with regard to the function of the human services worker, case management is the system through which that worker helps make a variety of services available to the client and coordinates the delivery of those services. The worker also stays in touch with the agencies and services that are helping the client to make sure they are providing what is most appropriate or that when they have achieved the worker's objectives for the client, they are discontinued. The worker also stays in touch with the client to assess the ways in which the services are being used and the progress the client is making through the provision of those services. Under a case management philosophy, the worker is in charge of the case but does not, in any way, expect to provide all the services necessary to meet the client's needs. The worker becomes something of a broker of services and an organizer of help even more than a provider of help to the client.

For example, examine the case of Mr. Samuelson, a 64-year-old man who has worked all his life until two months ago when his diabetes and heart disease made it difficult for him to continue in retail sales—a field in which he had been working for 40 years. He has come to the senior citizen center in his suburban community for help. The worker assigned to him, Mr. Wyatt, makes an assessment of the client's needs. Together, they determine that Mr. Samuelson needs the help of a dietitian, regular medical follow-up from a home health agency, to monitor his diabetes and his coronary problems, as well as some retraining so the client may be able to obtain and use some new employment skills that will not be as demanding on his health. Mrs. Samuelson, meanwhile, is depressed because of the changes in the family's fortunes. She has not been employed since her youth. Mr. Wyatt arranges a single interview with a psychiatric social worker for the couple, principally to appraise Mrs. Samuelson's depression and to determine what additional services may be needed. The family also needs some information on financial help so Mr. Wyatt arranges for them to see and use the help of a retirement counselor.

After all the initial activities are begun, Mr. Wyatt checks with the Samuelsons as well as the various service providers to determine how the family is progressing. He also works with both providers and the client to determine which services, if any, should be continued and the level to which they should be pursued. After a month or two, the services may be changed significantly, maintained, and/or augmented by other forms of help.

Because of the complexity and extent of modern human services programs, no single worker or agency is likely to have everything available to help a client. For that reason, case management has emerged as one of the helping systems of choice in that it provides the client with both the continuing services of a human services worker who understands him or her and their needs as well as a connection to the large and diverse world of both voluntary and governmental human services programs, any or all of which may be needed to help a client deal with his or her own problems.

Today's human services workers must understand not only the services their agencies deliver but must also have strong knowledge of and access to a variety of other agencies. Help for the aged is fragmented in that some of it is provided by senior centers, other parts by federal agencies, and still other portions by state and local governments as well as related organizations including churches and educational institutions.

Human services workers must spend part of their time getting to know the agency structure and related employees in order to help clients. That kind of knowledge is often equally valuable as skill in reaching out to clients, interviewing clients, and advocating for them.

Treatment Services

The individual work that human services workers do with older people is sometimes perceived as "treatment." There are many kinds of treatment designed to help individuals and families overcome some of their personal problems. Some of them are discussed in other chapters, especially those on working with older adults and their families and on working with groups of older adults.

Among the many treatment approaches are the psychoanalytic, functional, and, behavior modification. All of these are used, from time-to-time, with people who are facing severe behavioral and emotional difficulties such as depression, disorientation, and interpersonal conflicts.

It is frequently the case, however, that the human services worker with the older adult does not directly provide these services but refers the older client to another individual or agency who provides them, such as a community mental health center or a family service agency. It is more commonly the role of the human services worker with older adults to make such referrals and to provide the kinds of case management described in this chapter. That is, the worker does not provide the services directly but, instead, tries to make sure that the direct services are provided by others and follows up with those others to assist in helping the client.

Of course, some human services workers who serve older adults work primarily in the field of direct practice designed to help alleviate or overcome the kinds of difficulties that have been described. That may particularly be true of those who serve older adults in mental health facilities such as mental hospitals and community mental health centers. It is always important, of course, that such help—which may be referred to by a variety of names such as counseling, social case work, or psychotherapy—be done by people well-educated in the methodologies being used. Direct intervention with clients on personal matters can be difficult for clients and can, under certain circumstances, exacerbate the problem rather than curing it. Therefore, it is important that such interventions into the lives of older adults be conducted with some caution and restraint.

Typically, the human services worker's contribution is with concrete forms of assistance and in the coordination of services by others. It is also important to understand that many older adults reject the kinds of treatment services discussed here. Unless people particularly ask for these kinds of help with their personal difficulties, they may not want them at all.

In many situations, group services, assistance to the family, and changes in the environmental circumstances of the client are more useful and less prone to be difficult than direct counseling or treatment. Of course, many of the kinds of services discussed here are therapeutic for clients.

Purposes

Perhaps the essential rule in all of this is that any form of work with older people, whether it is direct or indirect, must have a purpose and the worker must understand that purpose well. No efforts should be made with the client except in pursuit of those objectives.

Of course, the client is involved advantageously in the kinds of approaches suggested here. As has been emphasized many times in this book, when the client wants help and participates in choosing as well as using the help that is provided, the effort is more likely to have a satisfactory outcome than if a service is imposed upon the client.

Summary

This chapter has covered some of the most important functions of the human services worker with older adults—reaching out to potential older clients, interviewing clients, and providing case management services to older people in need of help.

It is most likely that human services workers employed in programs for the aging will initially and consistently participate in one or more of these three activities. They provide the core of services provided to people under the agencies that help older adults today. Therefore, it is important that the skills described in this chapter be understood and mastered. They are more likely than any others discussed in this text to be used by the human services worker.

CHAPTER 5
SERVING GROUPS of older adults

As earlier chapters have shown, growing old in the United States has many physical, psychological, and social consequences. One of the social results of aging for some people is the loss of familiar and pleasant group contacts, with loneliness as a result. This chapter discusses some of the group needs of older people and some of the programs human services agencies use to help older people replace former group associations with new ones. It also describes the ways human services workers may help older clients overcome a variety of social and emotional problems through group services.

Everyone has some concept of what a group is—it's simply people doing something together. However, as it is used in this chapter and in relation to human services in general, the term *group* means any association of three or more people that comes together to meet some of the needs of the participants. As we will explain, this coming together may be voluntary, or it may result from some efforts by a human services worker. The kinds of groups we are talking about specifically usually have no more than 25 or 35 members—more than that may be better described as a crowd.

Changes in Group Associations during the Later Years

Retirement has social as well as economic consequences for older workers. Thus older people who have been employed often miss their associates just as much as their pay checks after retirement.

The deaths of friends, colleagues, and relatives also signal the loss of group contacts for older people, as the social circle begins to narrow in the later years. Some older women who are housewives lose the close association of their children, who become adults and leave home to begin work or families of their own, although for some the families of their children create an ever-widening circle of associations. Some older women become very close to their married daughters, in contrast to the estrangement they might have experienced during their daughters' adolescence. Men, too, may find that their children's adult years provide them with new and different associations or loss of association.

Loss of association through widowhood is a common accompaniment of aging for both men and women, although many more women than men are widowed. In addition, the changes in mobility patterns mean that many older people find themselves either left alone in communities where they have spent most of their lives but from which most of their relatives and friends have departed, or, often equally difficult, in new residential areas or different parts of the nation, such as Arizona, California, and Florida, which tend to attract retired older people.

Another major cause of change in group associations for the aged results from people's becoming less mobile as a result of physical disability. They may be unable to enter and leave buses, go up and down stairs, or walk long distances. Some must give up driving because of hearing and vision losses.

In addition to the physical barriers, there are also social and psychological reasons for changes in group associations, as discussed in earlier chapters. Economic factors, such as insufficient funds for transportation, offering or repaying invitations, or dressing satisfactorily, also play a role in modifying the group associations of older people. Psychosocial limits, such as feeling one lacks adequate social skills or being unable to hear or see well enough to be an effective social companion, may also reduce social contacts.

For all of these reasons, aging often leads to major modifications in the group association patterns of older people. For many, the loss of associations with friends and families is the most difficult part of growing old. Finding new and satisfying relationships with others may be an older person's most important social need.

Individuals often take steps on their own to achieve solutions to their lack of group associations. Some join social, religious, and political groups; others become devoted to pets. Some are exploited by commercial enterprises, such as dance studios, which promise but often do not deliver social contacts. People who face emotional and physical problems because they are lonely may find that group associations go a long way toward helping them overcome their problems. Other older people have emotional and physical difficulties requiring socioemotional treatment, which often is best carried out in groups with the help of a human services worker.

Some Examples of Groups
for Older Adults

There is a wide variety of group activities for older adults sponsored by community centers, senior citizen centers, nursing homes, hospitals, and virtually every other kind of organization serving the elderly. The following are some examples of ways in which groups of senior citizens are served by human services agencies:

1. Three older women who live in the same section of a nursing home form a friendship group. A nurse or aide meets with them regularly and helps them plan activities, discuss current events, carry on arts and crafts activities, or simply share **reminiscences**.

2. Four older men who live in the same condominium in a large resort city play

cards together each afternoon. They are a close-knit group; the recreation director of their housing complex simply makes the facilities for their games available to them.

3. A social worker organizes a current events discussion group in a senior center that deals with different subjects each week, with each discussion led by a different group member or a guest.

4. Terminal cancer patients on a hospital ward meet for an hour and a half each day under the leadership of a nurse to talk about their anxieties, fears, and plans for their families.

5. A group of recovered alcoholic veterans meet daily in the hospital with their social worker, who helps them plan for departure from the hospital and return to their own homes.

6. Ten emotionally disturbed older men in a state mental hospital meet twice a week under the leadership of a psychologist, to learn to face reality.

Each of these is an example of a group meeting the needs of older adults. Some of the groups are natural, or organized by the members themselves; others are formed, organized by outside agents to meet one or several needs of the members through professional help. (The two types will be discussed in detail later in this chapter.) Whatever their origins, groups play an important part in the lives of older people. They are increasingly used to help older people deal with social problems, obtain information that they need, and enjoy the company of peers through activities. The variety of groups used by older people to help themselves is wide, and the purposes for groups organized under the auspices of human services programs are extensive—as extensive as the needs and problems of aging people discussed in this text.

Self-help groups are usually formed by and for their own members so people with similar problems can help one another overcome them. There are "Lost Chord" groups for laryngectomy patients, Alcoholics Anonymous groups for those who want to stop drinking, and varieties of other efforts to help people help themselves. Professionals may organize these groups, but the impetus is for those in need of help to help one another, rather than for someone who is free of the problem to help the victims.

A variety of self-help groups are used with and for older people. In addition to those suffering from the same illness such as stroke, cancer, or chronic heart disease, many also find it helpful to work with one another around social problems. The rejection many feel from their siblings and children is often the basis for the organization of a self-help group. People provide one another with support and encouragement in the face of a commonly shared problem. That is why groups such as these are sometimes called "support groups," in the human services field.

In this discussion we place emphasis on the ways workers may help older people resolve some of their needs and enhance their lives through group services. We stress the **formed group**, because that is characteristically the kind of group served by a professional worker. However, **natural groups** that are already organized often lay an excellent base for groups served by professionals. For example, look at the following situation:

George, the social worker in the Veterans Administration Hospital, noticed that Charlie, Jerry, Bill, and Bob usually ate together, shared cigarettes, played pool with one another, and spent their evenings together watching television. All were older veterans who had faced emotional crises that caused them to enter the hospital. Now they were no longer so upset that they had to remain in the hospital, but neither could they return to their families, who lacked room and the desire to house them. So George created a "discharge planning group" for the men to help them find ways to learn enough to leave the hospital. The patients talked about leaving the hospital, where they would go, how they would live, and how they would obtain services from social workers such as George. They met for an hour each day with the worker and practiced cooking, traveling by bus, visiting the bank, and other practical but critical activities for men who would live outside hospitals. After four months they all left the hospital for rooming houses, hotels, and apartments close to one another. They promised to get together often and did so, first with George's help but, as they became acclimated to their new environments, later on their own.

Thus the dichotomy between the natural and the formed group is often false. Sometimes the best formed group is one that begins "naturally."

Understanding Group Life

Before anything else, human services workers for the aging must understand the group lives and group needs of those they serve.

Effectiveness in working with older people in a variety of situations means that the worker, whether a gerontologist, nurse, social worker, recreation leader, occupational or physical therapist, or teacher, must become aware of the group dimensions of the aging person's lifestyle, problems, needs, and potential services.

Too often, directors of programs for the aging, arts and crafts personnel, homes for the aged staff members, and hospital employees think of clients or patients only as separate individuals. While it is true that each older person who participates in a program is an individual with special characteristics, needs, and potentials, there are profound effects from the groups with which each is involved.

Professionals trying to understand older people ask about their physical conditions, their emotions, and their incomes; they make socioeconomic diagnoses often without asking about group associations. However, group relationships may be the most significant part of life for some older people, and it may be those groups that they use for most of their emotional support. Therefore, fully understanding an older person requires knowing about that person's group associations as well as about his or her personal life.

The Dimensions of Group
Associations

Everyone has group associations, and for most of us they are numerous. With only a little imagination, you can think of at least half a dozen groups with which a typical older person might be associated. Family and neighbors constitute important associations. Most older people belong to at least one, and often more, organized social or service groups. Informal groups of friends and those with whom they worship are other examples. The loss of affiliation with or changes in these groups can have great impact on people of all ages; they can be especially difficult for older people, who have fewer opportunities to initiate new patterns of association and few outlets for building friendships.

Knowing about an older person's group life can often help a human services worker understand the client's physical and emotional needs more fully.

For example, an effective worker in an institution for older people will understand the residents and the context of the formal and informal groups with which they associate. The ward in a hospital, the wing in a home for the aged, the classes and other activity groups in institutions are all sources of group contact for those who are served by the institution, and they must be considered significant factors. Of course, informal group associations also should be studied. Group life analysts should look at the informal and voluntary groups created at mealtimes in institutions, at the groups of people who prefer to spend time with one another (as George found a group of friendly veterans) when they have free time, and at choices of friends within neighborhoods, centers, or institutions.

Some Purposes of Groups

The second step in providing services to people through groups is the development of group services with and for the older people who are being helped.

Knowing the group's goals is the first step in effective group work with older people. There must always be a set of specific objectives for the individuals in the group, for the group as a whole, or for both together. Although some human services workers act as though group involvement is always good, it is not true; groups are not always helpful. It is impossible to know whether or not groups aid the clients without also being clear about the goals they are aiming for.

Human services workers with groups should have specific goals for their groups that are within the context of the goals and objectives of the agency or association employing them. Workers must keep those goals in mind at all times when organizing and serving older people through groups.

There are many different types of group goals. For a friendship or social group of older people in a small community, the objective may simply be friendly and effective use of leisure time. For others, such as the recovered alcoholics in a hospital, the goal may be to help them leave the institution. The goals may be simple or complex, global or specific, but there ought always to be ends in mind when groups are begun.

There are many purposes for groups. In some institutional settings, groups may be used to improve the social skills of the members in order to help them find less intensive care. In an institution for convalescents, the staff may use groups to educate patients about how to overcome some of their health problems by using the medicine and other therapies prescribed for them. In these cases the goal is education, and the group members learn from one another as well as from staff members and others who may be brought to the group as advisors or resource people. The group solves the problems of some individual patients while also improving the operations of the institution.

In a home for the aged or a nursing home, group activities may be designed to provide members with self-directed and pleasant recreational, educational, and social activities to enrich their lives. In hospitals that serve the terminally ill, the groups may be designed to help older patients come to terms with their feelings about death.

Since the vast majority of older adults live outside institutions, it is the community group that is critical. As we have said, group programs may be organized in urban neighborhoods, rural senior centers, apartment houses, condominiums, churches and synagogues, and various other places that house or attract older adults. Often such programs are sponsored by service centers or senior service programs within their own facilities. At other times, they operate as extensions of senior programs sponsored by community centers, governmental recreation departments, or other human services organizations that are able to extend their efforts away from their own facilities.

In community programs for older adults, the goals may be social and recreational in nature. Some community groups are organized to achieve social action goals, such as developing better programs and services for aging people and their communities. Some programs organize groups of aging people who become lobbyists to work with state legislatures or city governments in defining and working to overcome the problems of older people as well as other groups in the community.

Goals and objectives are set for groups of older people that are in consonance with the purpose of the organization that sponsors the group and in line with the interests and wishes of the members of the group themselves. A crucial element in effective human services work with older people is the opportunity for the older people to set their own objectives, modify the objectives developed by the sponsoring organization, and control the operation of their programs.

Various Names for
Group Services

Through the years in the literature of the service professions, a variety of names have emerged for the kinds of activities this chapter describes. Some organizations and service programs call these activities *group therapy;* others use the term *social group work.* Others may refer to programs in terms of the specific method that is used, such as *Transactional Analysis, sensitivity training, Gestalt therapy,* and so on. We prefer to use a more general phrase, *working with groups,* as our way of describing all of those approaches to serving people through group methods.

The principles offered in this chapter are fundamental to all forms of group services. We think there are more similarities between the various methods than there are differences. It is important for knowledgeable workers in the service professions to avoid becoming committed to one approach to helping people through groups if that one approach excludes all others. It is better to know a range of group methods, from therapeutic intervention to recreational programs. Then the worker can use the system most appropriate to the group's needs. The key to providing services to groups is to provide the service that members need.

The needs of many older adults are frequently better served through recreational and social groups than through insight-oriented or treatment-directed group therapy programs. Although large numbers of older people face serious emotional problems, people who serve such clients ought to consider a range of means for aiding them. At times the support of friendly peers and participation in satisfying activities are sufficient to help older people overcome some of their depression and other problems.

For example, Mrs. Jones, a depressed 63-year-old woman, was referred by the community mental-health center to the community center for group activities. The worker had several groups in which he could place Mrs. Jones—one, an insight-oriented group for depressed widows, helping them to adjust to their loneliness and isolation. However, the worker chose to place her instead in an arts and crafts group that was in the process of learning pottery-making skills, an activity similar to others that had interested Mrs. Jones as a younger woman.

After six weeks of three sessions of pottery making per week, Mrs. Jones's depression abated. Although she did not confront her loneliness directly, she substituted for it group associations and an activity that interested her. Therefore, she became less lonely and, perhaps, had less reason to be depressed.

Of course, other people with emotional problems may want to talk them out and will need a therapy-type group. Many different kinds of groups can be effective in helping older people deal with their feelings and their problems.

Some Basic Concepts for
Working with Groups

Serving individuals effectively in groups requires that the human services worker understand and master a variety of concepts and skills. The following analytic approaches are fundamental in helping people through groups and are useful in informal education and recreation groups, hospitals, and institutions of all kinds.

Differentiating between Natural and Formed Groups

Earlier in this chapter we distinguished between natural and formed groups. However, workers must keep in mind that there is a continuity between them; many times formed groups are created over the base of a natural group. **Formed groups** are simply those that are organized by someone outside the group; they do not develop spontaneously. For example, therapy groups serving older people in community mental health centers, when those groups are selected by and organized by psychologists, social workers, or other therapists, are formed. So is the group of people living on the ward in a mental hospital, who are assigned there by some outside agent, such as the director of treatment services or the head nurse. A community senior center crafts group that is selected by the instructor is also formed.

Natural groups, on the other hand, are those that are constructed by the members of groups themselves. These are, for example, groups of older men who bowl with one another and who develop teams on their own. The groups of older women who hold weekly card games or regular morning conversations are also natural.

The key question is who organized the groups—the members or someone else. Those who work professionally with groups have different opinions about the value of working with formed or natural groups. Probably, the forming of a group ought to depend upon the purposes of that group. It is easier to form a group for specific objectives, because the worker then knows that the group will consist of individuals with similar needs or problems. Moreover, the group will be relatively homogeneous; for example, people who are physically handicapped, of a somewhat similar age, or of the same sex.

Natural groups are often divergent. However, natural groups often have the advantage of having already overcome the need to develop cohesion (see Figure 6.1) and, therefore, they may move more rapidly through group development processes than would the formed group. On the other hand, it is more difficult to develop specific objectives and methods for a natural group, since it will already have some of its own that may be different from or counter to those of the worker. For example, the discharge planning group in the Veterans Administration Hospital, mentioned above, might decide that they preferred to spend their time finding ways to avoid leaving the hospital, an objective directly counter to that of the social worker.

We have found that the best groups are those that are formed on the base of natural groups. The group's objectives are always a combination of those selected by the group members themselves, along with the human services worker. However, it is often difficult to find that kind of combination. In actuality, most groups are initiated by human-service workers.

Selection or Nonselection?

There is little conclusive research that guides the worker in the formation of groups. Much of the information is conflicting, and it is hard to know who to put into a group to achieve what results. We can observe groups and understand why they behave as they do, but it is almost impossible to predict how individuals will behave if we put them together in a group. It may be that human beings are too complicated, particularly when they interact with others, to make them behaviorally predictable. The outgoing individual may be stoic in the group; the shy person may assume leadership. The dynamics, or patterns of relationships, among as few as five or six group members are so varied and the potential numbers of relationships so great, that many group service specialists believe it is best to abandon any efforts to develop perfect combinations of group members and leave the development of groups to natural member choices or random selection. The late Dr. Eric Berne said, in his *Principles of Group Treatment* (1969), that he preferred and found greater success by randomly selecting members than by trying to choose the best people for a group.

So we believe that if, for example, you want to organize a group of older men for a current events discussion group at a senior center, you shouldn't try to construct the absolutely perfect group. Look instead for a number of men who want to spend their time together and enjoy each other's company, and work with them as a group. That would be a natural group building into one that is formed. Or select every tenth name from the center's card file and invite those people to join. You will save time and achieve results that will equal or better any efforts to design the perfect group.

Stages of Group Development

Virtually all observers of group behavior recognize that groups grow and develop through a series of stages. Various models have been developed to illustrate those stages.[1] Although these models differ in their descriptions of group development and in the number of stages through which groups grow, all students of the subject tend to agree on some core ideas. Figure 5.1 illustrates the fundamental idea of group development.

Stage 1. One of the core ideas is that groups begin with a quiet, cautious stage, in which the members do not want to make emotional commitments to other members or to the group itself, because they are busy solving some of their own emotional reactions to being in the group. Groups at the first, cautious, stage can-

---

[1] Faculty members at the schools of social work at the University of Michigan, Boston University, and Tulane University, among others, have developed and published theories of stages of group development. The material presented in this chapter was influenced most by the theories of the late Walter Kindelsperger of the Tulane University school of Social Work.

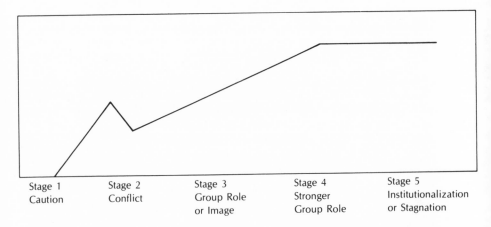

Stage 1	Stage 2	Stage 3	Stage 4	Stage 5
Caution	Conflict	Group Role or Image	Stronger Group Role	Institutionalization or Stagnation

Groups proceed through an uneven series of stages, from caution to stagnation. The line of development is not straight nor is it continuously upward, as the graph demonstrates. An upward line illustrates the development of greater group strength while a downward line indicates a retreat from group feeling.

Figure 5.1   Stages of Group Development.

not usually carry on concerted action. The group is so incohesive that it is best to treat any decisions it makes as only tentative. When the group "grows up," which means moving toward cohesion and group self-confidence, it may want to change those decisions. Therefore, those who work with groups have learned that it is best not to elect officers or develop rigid programs or constitutions and generally to avoid making many specific plans during the first stage.

Some older people remain at this cautious stage for a long time, and some groups of older people never move beyond it. When the group is heterogeneous, and people are uncertain about one another or suspicious, caution becomes the prevailing pattern.

Stage 2. Most observers of group behavior think that the first stage is followed by increasing **group cohesion** and group purpose. Some members, of course, remain cautious and uninvolved, but those who are most interested in the group's progress and growth and in reaching the group's objectives move toward closer relationships with one another and a more united spirit. However, that spirit is also characterized by a second level of **group conflict**. The conflict may be overtly expressed in shouting matches, schisms over decisions, and other differences of opinion. It may also be personal. In some groups of older adults, some members may want to remove others from the group, or they themselves may leave, if they are not satisfied with the officers who have been elected or with those who have taken leadership. In other cases, the conflict is covert and submerged, and the members may try to undermine one another outside meetings. Sometimes the conflict is not conflict at all but simply passive unwillingness to participate in the group's activities or a kind of negativism in reaction to the suggestions of the majority about what the group should do.

Conflict is a normal phase in group growth. It is not pleasant for either the worker or the members, and some groups fall apart over their conflict. Some groups even move back to the cautious first stage, because the conflict is so painful. Sometimes the conflict lasts for a long time, sometimes it is very brief. Groups that succeed have their conflicts, resolve them, and move ahead. In some cases groups of older people become fixed in a conflict stage and use the meetings for airing disagreements. Occasionally, group members enjoy the conflict, because they find that they are paid attention to when they argue. Some older people report that no one who is younger takes them seriously enough to argue with. The following example from a group of older adults illustrates the struggles that may arise at the second stage:

Seventeen men were present at the third meeting of the Friendship Club. Mr. Stein began the meeting by announcing to the group he was leaving for a six-month stay in Florida and that they would therefore have to choose a new vice president. The president, Mr. Bluestone, was present for the first time since the club opened for the year.

Mr. Bluestone sat next to the worker, and Mr. Stein sat next to Mr. Bluestone. Throughout the meeting there was an undercurrent of struggle between these two men, in terms of control of the group. On the whole, Mr. Bluestone appears to be more in control; he went so far as to tell the worker that the success of the club depended on the power wielded by the president.

Mr. Bluestone insisted that the group needed a treasurer and attempted to appoint one. Mr. Levinson declined, as did Mr. Steinberg. Finally, since no one would accept the position, Mr. Lieberman agreed. Actually, Mr. Lieberman is very unpopular with the men and strong feeling was expressed later by Mr. Kletz, Mr. Shiff, Mr. Steinberg and several others that the fact of Mr. Lieberman's being treasurer might prevent the club from getting new members. Mr. Lieberman and Mr. Shapiro are considered [misbehavers] in the group, but no action is taken against them, and a great many times it appears that the members give in to the whims of these two in order to get rid of them. Mr. Shapiro insisted that he wants to go to the old men's home to visit two former members of the club. Although someone had very recently made a visit to the home and had made a report Mr. Bluestone gave Mr. Shapiro seventy-five cents to cover expenses of a visit. [2]

Stage 3. As the group grows to greater cohesion and begins to resolve its conflicts, it reaches another stage, one of **group solidarity**, in which a **group role** or an

---

[2] Taken from *"The Friendship Club," Records of Social Group Work Practice,* Gertrude Wilson and Gladys Ryland.

image is developed. At this stage group members begin uniting in their desire to carry on a variety of activities. There are healthy debates about issues affecting the group, but they are carried on within the context of democratic decision making. The members may argue over issues, but they remain friends after decisions are reached. Sometimes group role behavior is demonstrated by the group's agreeing on a series of activities, a name for itself, or a service role in the community. At other times a group role is developed through the selection of leaders satisfactory to and in line with the needs of the whole group. In any case, the group's behavior and attitudes are much better spirited and more committed to a group purpose than in the first stage and not nearly as conflicting as in the second stage.

The most effective groups are those that have reached Stage 3. The group does not dominate the lives of the members, but it is sufficiently important to them for their activities to succeed. Groups in Stage 3 have good attendance, high degrees of camaraderie, and high degrees of satisfaction with participation in the group.

Stage 4. There are differences of opinion among analysts about the fourth stage of a group's behavior. Some define it as a time in which the group becomes so dominant for the members that it virtually takes over their lives. Others think that the dominance of the group over the lives of the members is only an advanced manifestation of the third stage of development. However they define the stage, most group experts agree there is a time when the group becomes too important, when members lose their individuality to the group, and when group decisions are made to preserve the group more than to carry on useful activities for the members.

Stage 5. The fifth stage of development is institutionalization, in which the members turn the group's program into ritualistic, repetitive activities. They resist adding new members and trying new things. The group is comfortable. It may continue indefinitely; many such groups persist for decades. The Wednesday night men's poker group is one example of an institutionalized group; weekly bingo games organized by older people are another. Such groups are not harmful, but the members do not learn from them or change through them.

The Human Services Worker
and the Various Stages
of Group Life

Human services workers who serve groups of older people must use everything they know about working with the needs and problems of older people to assist the group. They must assist at all stages in various ways.

In the first, or cautious, stage the worker helps the members overcome their suspicions of one another and helps them feel comfortable together. Sometimes the worker accomplishes this by introducing the people to one another by making name tags, serving refreshments, introducing activities that can interest the members in continuing with the group, and in other ways helping them feel less cautious and more confident with one another. The worker wants the members to become friends and makes every effort to move them in that direction.

At the second, or conflict, stage the worker can help the group express its conflicts and handle them in ways that do not destroy the group. He or she needs to understand the reasons for the conflict and may help the group understand that it is simply passing through a normal stage of development. The worker might minimize the conflict, suggest solutions to differences of opinion, and otherwise lead the group toward better and more productive behavior.

In the third stage the effective worker advises the group on increasing its efficiency by showing it how to choose activities and helping it develop means for carrying out those activities in useful ways. For instance, the worker might help the members plan a trip, a social activity, or a game night. In a therapy group the worker might introduce useful information that will help the members understand their feelings and discontents or suggest bringing an outside resource person to the group to help members deal with personal problems that are troubling them. One of the goals of the human services worker at the third stage is to help the group avoid entering institutionalized behavior by encouraging it to add new members, helping it to look for and carry out new activities, and helping it maintain some dynamism before its program becomes ritualized.

The worker's goal in the remaining stages is to help the group members continue to learn and continue to grow, because the human services worker with the aged believes that older people can continue to develop socially and emotionally, even though their physical circumstances are declining.

At the fourth stage of the group's development, the worker becomes more of a consultant to the members—particularly the leaders—and less a leader. Informal and formal training for the members may be offered directly or arranged through other resources. Ideas for programs may still be offered, but they are less important as the group more clearly becomes the members'. The worker also cautions the members about institutionalization and helps them develop the skills necessary for making their own group analyses and diagnoses. In this stage some workers drop out of active roles with groups and attend meetings only occasionally, when their help is needed.

If the group moves into the fifth, or institutionalized, stage, it probably will not make effective use of human services agencies or workers, since it simply does the same things over and over again.

Degree of Activity
of the Worker

Figure 5.2 illustrates how the degree of the worker's activity is related to the social health of the group members at each stage. This chart shows that the worker moves from being a controller with a group that is out of touch with real-

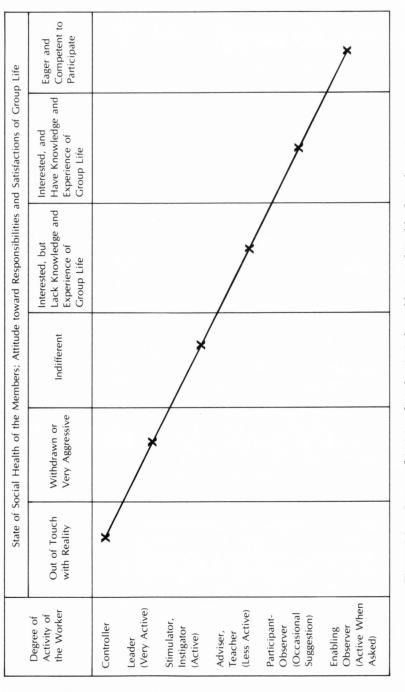

Figure 5.2 Degree of Activity of Worker As Indicated by Social Health of Members. (Source: Gertrude Wilson and Gladys Ryland, *Social Group Work Practice*, Houghton Mifflin, 1949. Reprinted by permission.).

ity to serving as an enabling observer with a Stage 3 group that is eager and competent to participate.

Many human services workers want to know more about how they can play their roles with groups. As Figure 5.2 indicates, it is not possible to give a single answer to that question—the worker's role varies from group to group and from time to time within the same group. When the group is new or when it is composed largely of people who cannot control their own activities, the worker is very much a "leader," someone who essentially directs the group's activities. With a group that is competent to meet its own objectives, the worker is simply a guide or advisor.

It is important to remember that not all groups pass through all these stages of development, although they do not skip any stages, either. Some groups remain fixed at the first or second stage. Other groups move ahead and then slip backward from cohesion and competence. Not all groups move through all the stages at the same speed. Some, when they are faced by external crises, move rapidly through all the stages. Others may require years to reach the third stage.

These stages of development are real; groups pass through them and observers of group behavior can see them as the group develops. On the other hand, they are metaphors for group behavior. There are no explicit demarcations between the stages. Neither is there always agreement by experts looking at the same group about when a group reaches a given stage. Human services workers should look at these stages as a guide for understanding and effectively working with groups rather than as a precise scale for defining social phenomena.

Some of the Dynamics of Groups

As we mentioned earlier, there are many ideas about the dynamics of groups. Some of the significant variables and knowledge about them are outlined here. Some are observable, some are speculative. An effective worker with groups needs extensive knowledge of the **group process** and group behavior in order to organize, understand, and help groups. Some of the suggested texts on services to groups in the bibliography may be of help to workers who are new to serving groups.

Size. Group size is one element that affects group behavior. Specialists who work with groups argue about the optimum number of participants. Some think that 10 is ideal, but 9 or 11 appear to work equally well; it is the approximate number of 10 that seems effective. Others say that a group ought to have an uneven number of participants—perhaps 7—so that there are no tie votes when the group makes a decision. But a group that votes four to three is a group that ought to discuss its differences some more; almost half its members are dissatisfied. Most observers of groups would define efforts to select the perfect group size as almost magical. They think no one can really say what is ideal, and trying to come up with the ideal number is almost impossible. But some principles of size seem to be agreed upon. For example, there are some practical issues. A group of older people must be small enough so all the members can hear and see one another well, which can be crucial problems for some groups. A group cannot be too large for the available meeting space.

The smaller the group, the stronger the impact the group has on the individual members. A very small group will put heavy pressure on individual members. This is particularly true with treatment groups. If the group's purposes are best served by a strong effect on the members—for example, a group designed to educate older people about medicine and to obtain agreement and compliance about their prescriptions—than a group of, say 3, 4, or 5 is ideal. On the other hand, if the purposes of the group are best served by reducing the pressure on individuals—for example, an informal group that anyone can attend and participate in modestly—then 12 or 15 could be better.

The optimum size for a group also depends on the social health of the members. People who feel comfortable in large groups and social situations will feel comfortable in groups as large as 50 or 100, a not unreasonable number for a drop-in, informal program in a senior center. Those who are intimidated by large groups and massive social situations may prefer and best be served by more moderate-sized groups of 6, 7, or 8.

Subgrouping. A normal occurrence in all group behavior is that of subgrouping, the phenomenon through which individuals organize themselves into fragments of the total group. In any group relationships among all the members are not as intense as they are between some of the members. Therefore, pairs, trios, and quartets of members may form themselves and become very important to the individual participants. Individuals in these situations deal with the total group through the small group with whom they happen to work. Most people cannot form close relationships with all the members of the group and, therefore, develop familiar and friendly contacts with much smaller units.

One of the things the human services worker must be careful to do is avoid the negative connotations and conflicts caused by cliques, which are a form of subgroup. The worker also must be careful to watch for isolates, individuals who are not participants in any subgroup, and help them find a place.

Conflict. As we discussed, differences of opinion and differences of choices are normal phenomena in any group. Conflict is necessary to help a group develop. A group does not survive to the third stage without engaging in some kinds of conflict. Conflict has the value of focusing issues, helping people align themselves with others in subgroups, and providing the basis for making decisions.

Leadership. Leadership is a complex phenomenon that is described and discussed in hundreds of volumes in the social and behavior sciences. Those who work with groups need to recognize leadership as an important phenomenon in the group. We are speaking here of member-based peer leadership—those members of the senior citizen group who are followed by other members, and whose suggestions and directions are followed by the group members. The human services worker or the employee of the sponsoring agency is a separate dynamic, whose task is to help peer leadership achieve some successes and to ensure that the leaders help the group in meeting its objectives.

The Human Services Worker. The human services worker constitutes a dynamic in the group's development, and the effectiveness of the worker has great impact on the success of the group. The effective worker carries out all the activities that have been described and uses all the skills of working with individuals, working with the community, and acting on his or her understanding of older people.

Program. Perhaps the most significant of all the dynamics is the program, or the activities in which the group engages. The group is always involved in some kind of program, whether it is group discussion, decision making, talking about problems of living, informal socializing, or more fully developed and planned activities. The worker with older people ought always to be aware of the program of the group, know what the group is doing, and be able to help the group define, plan, and carry out a clear, conscious program that meets its objectives.

A major principle of programming in working with groups is involvement of the members. The members should be involved to the fullest extent possible—in line with the social health of the group—in deciding what the group is going to do. The worker plays the role of an expert resource or consultant, helping the group choose alternatives, articulate its wishes, and channel its desires into specific program activities. The program of activities must be within the group's financial, social, and emotional capabilities, in consonance with the agency's objectives for the group, and in line with the objectives the group members have determined for themselves. Program activities may be divided into the following categories:

1. *Planning.* This is the opportunity for the members of the group to decide what they want to do, when they want to do it, and how they want to do it. The program may be as complex as a political campaign for new services to the aging or as simple as a trip to a neighboring city to visit another group of older people. The planning process itself is crucial, because it ensures that the members develop their own program and that the activities are pertinent to the needs, capabilities, and interests of the members.

2. *Games and Sports.* Group activities for people of all ages frequently revolve around games and sports. Many older adults enjoy such activities and join groups so they will have opportunities to participate. The human services

worker will often want to help the group engage in sports and games that are new to them rather then the more familiar kinds so that all the members will have a common base for participating and an equal chance to succeed and will engage in activities that are different and special for the group. The group may want to start with familiar activities in which members are already likely to participate, such as cards and bingo, which have value for older people because they are familiar. But even if the group sponsors these, the worker will want to be sure that the group moves ahead to other activities or at least will want to alternate the familiar with the new to help the group grow in their understanding of and exposure to activities. A "new" game for many older adult groups could be backgammon, which is ancient in its origins but still popular. Tripoley is a commercial game that combines a number of familiar card and dice games. Kickball is a gentler version of baseball. Long-distance running is one of the world's oldest forms of recreation, but it is again popular, particularly with older men.

3. *Music and Dance.* Music and dance activities have a number of possibilities for helping groups of older people. At times expert outside resources are needed to help with music, instruction, and other elements necessary for carrying out the activities. Sometimes musical activities in senior centers and other community-based programs for older people are almost infantile—group singing, for instance, is conducted in a style more appropriate to nursery-school-aged children than to groups of adults. There are adult ways to sing and adult ways to lead singing, and groups that can use such activities need help in adapting them to the characteristics of their members. Senior adults may prefer a wide-range of musical activities, from seminars on classical music to discussions with folk singers. Some groups seem to focus on choral singing and rhythm bands, which are all right in some ways but should not be the totality of the music program.

Older members of groups can learn square dancing, folk dancing, and modern dance, and they also can teach them. Culturally based dancing may be quite effective with groups of older people who represent a variety of ethnic communities. They may provide a channel for members to talk about and deal with their differences.

4. *Excursions.* Trips to both nearby and distant places have often been a part of programs designed for older adults. These are frequently effective, particularly when they introduce older people to new experiences and when they provide opportunities for travel outside the limits of possibilities for individuals. An excursion may be as simple as a field visit to a factory, a farm, or a park, or as complex as travel to foreign nations by ship or air. Senior groups both enjoy and learn from such programs. Of course, costs, safety, health services, special arrangements for physical disability, and proper supervision are important aspects of planning trips and excursions.

5. *Cultural Activities.* Many groups of older people enjoy current events discussions, book reviews, films and subsequent discussions about them, and dialogues with political figures. Opportunities to discuss, challenge, and learn are often welcomed by older people and ought to be considered part of the possible program for group activity.

6. *Arts and Crafts.* Some of the most successful programs for older adults provide them with opportunities to engage in arts and crafts activities. These might include painting, leather craft, ceramics, and weaving. The emphasis in a good program of arts and crafts should be on activities that provide the members with opportunities to learn from one another and to share in the development of the activities and the objects. Group art activities are often neglected but frequently are quite useful. For example, a group-created plaque for the agency might have more meaning for the group than ten keychains for the individual members.

7. *Therapy and Discussions.* For many groups the program needs to be dealing with the problems they face with loneliness, economic insufficiency, poor health, and emotional disturbances. In such cases the worker assists the members in coping with their problems constructively by helping them to clarify precisely what the problems are and what solutions there may be. At times the group provides an opportunity for members to simply get their problems on the table, which in itself can be very helpful.

Within each of these opportunities for programming, human services workers may want to call for advice and assistance upon experts, for instance, travel agents in the case of excursions; occupational therapists for arts, crafts, dance, and music programs; physical education teachers and physical therapists for sports and games; and any number of other people who have special knowledge. Psychiatrists and psychologists can sometimes give excellent help to treatment groups. The specialists can help the worker and the group determine the best activities and describe the resources that they might want to use.

Effective workers are willing to use specialists who can aid their groups; not every worker can be an expert in all of the activities suggested here. The human services worker who knows something about politics, dance, crafts, *and* therapy is rare. A group with a worker who is a specialist in music may have little need for musical activities but a great need for therapy. Therefore, a responsible worker should make sure the members have access to resource people who can assist them with activities that are designed to help them meet their needs.

Summary

This chapter has discussed the group needs of older people and has provided a brief review of concepts useful in serving people through group methods. The roles played by human services workers with groups of older people are covered, as is the range of activities that may be useful with groups of older adults. Group services are frequently an important part of the responsibility of the worker and of the organization serving older citizens. The concepts of working with groups specified in this chapter are applicable to group services with people of all ages, and can be applied to working with older people who have some of the specific problems discussed in Part Four.

READING 5.1

Peer Group Counseling for Older People / Elinor Waters, Sylvia Fink, and Betty White

Group work with the aged can take on many forms for a variety of purposes. In this article the authors give a detailed description of a group treatment program for the elderly they developed in Michigan. [3]

Group Counseling as a Treatment Modality

Although psychological help for the elderly can be offered in many ways, group counseling may be the treatment of choice for a variety of reasons. Certainly issues of loneliness and alienation can be meaningfully dealt with in a group situation where counselees have an opportunity both to realize that others share their concerns and to develop new and meaningful relationships with their peers. Additionally, group counseling offers the advantages of efficiency and economy.

A few attempts at providing such services have met with considerable success. Klein, et al. (1965), reporting on their use of discussion groups in centers for older people, wrote that members gained a more realistic view of their situation, increased their sense of inner resources, and added to their capacity to relate warmly to others. At the same time, the stress of loneliness and the sense of futility were relieved by identifying their strengths and focusing on the preservation of their existing health. In an earlier study, Kubie and Landau (1953) reported that through discussion groups elderly people were able to recognize and resolve their individual differences, share perspectives about public assistance, and talk about the problems of preventing deterioration. Similar good results were reported by Fast (1970), a chaplain in a church retirement home,

[3] From *Educational Gerontology*, Vol. 1, Issue 2, 1976. Reprinted by permission of Hemisphere Publishing Corporation, 1025 Vermont Avenue, N.W., Washington, D.C. 20005.

who formed small groups of the residents to enable them to share their sense of loss of usefulness, independence and self-esteem. Fast noted that the retirees had felt isolated from interpersonal experiences and that the small-group milieu afforded them the opportunity of sharing their philosophy of life with each other.

If Kahn's (1975) predictions are correct as to how mental health services will be provided for elderly people in the future, then the Continuum Center program described below may be a portent of things to come. It embodies many of Kahn's recommendations in that it is primarily a preventive program which focuses on the healthy, rather than the pathological, aspects of personality, and on the psychological and social factors in people's lives, rather than on their biological make-up. It also involves minimal interruptions by reaching people in familiar, non-medical settings in their own neighborhoods.

The Continuum Center's Approach to Group Counseling

Before describing the Continuum Center's work with older people, it may be helpful to give some background information. The Continuum Center of Oakland University is an adult counseling and leadership training center, designed to assist people of all ages and stages of life in self-exploration, planning and decision-making. The Continuum Center came into existence in the fall of 1965 as a women's center. Over the years it has diversified its clientele and operations so that it now serves men as well as women from young adulthood to old age. Most of the Continuum Center's counseling is done in small groups led by carefully selected and trained paraprofessionals working under the supervision of professionally trained staff members.

Since 1972, the Continuum Center has been offering time limited group counseling programs for older people affiliated with various community centers in the metropolitan Detroit area. Some of these centers have a religious affiliation, some are municipally funded, and others have labor union backing.

Each program consists of a series of seven two-hour sessions. During the first part of each session all clients meet in a large group of between 12 and 30 people in order to be introduced to a new exercise or approach to communications. Following this general presentation, participants join their small groups of five or six clients and two paraprofessional group leaders. Within these groups they have an opportunity to talk about their own needs, values, and problems as they relate to the materials introduced in the large group. We have found this combination of large and small group work to be particularly effective. The large groups are well suited to presenting information and the small groups to providing an opportunity for counselees to personalize the information which has been provided.

Perhaps this general statement will become clearer if we focus on some of the specific exercises and approaches used in the Continuum Center programs. A week before the program begins, an orientation session is held to acquaint potential group members with the operation of the program in order that they can decide if they wish to commit themselves to regular attendance. At this orientation session, a staff member explains the overall goals of the program and encourages potential participants to talk by asking each one to state "what this center means to me _____ ." The focus on listening to others is introduced by asking each member to repeat the statement made by the previous speaker before giving his/her own. This exercise encourages everyone's participation, fosters listening, and underlines the positive, important place the center has in the members' lives.

At the first regular session, participants are asked to join in a values clarification exercise, the forced-choice strategy adapted from Simon, et al. (1972). Group members must move to one side of the room or the other to indicate which of two words or phrases (e.g., Cadillac or Volkswagen, dancing shoes or house slippers, loner or grouper, bubbling brook or placid lake) they are most like. This activity not only serves to encourage self-exploration but also serves as an ice breaker and a vehicle for precipitating involvement.

At the next session, participants are asked to spend five minutes in the small group talking about people and experiences which have been most significant in their lives, ending with what is most important to them at the present time. This encourages participants to talk about themselves, to focus on strengths they have developed, and to look at and listen to each other. Throughout this exercise, group leaders model reflective listening.

Later sessions provide an opportunity for counselees to talk about helpful and unhelpful forms of interpersonal assistance, and to experience dependence upon and responsibility for others by going on a "trust walk" in which one member of a pair closes his/her eyes and is led by the other. Several other activities are included to heighten self-esteem. Each time the small group meets, a naming exercise is done to insure that everyone knows everyone else's name. This exercise usually proves to be reinforcing, as many group members who claim they are too old to learn find they are able to remember all the names. The sessions end with a Strength Bombardment activity, adapted from McHolland's (1972) Human Potential materials wherein each person lists their own strengths on a piece of paper and other group members add strengths they have observed during the program.

Follow-up Counseling

After each of the group counseling programs for older people, many members have expressed a desire to continue meeting. Since group discussions often bring personal issues to the surface we think it is important to provide people with opportunities to pursue these issues. Therefore we arrange for a Continuum Center counselor to be available for individual or small group counseling for a limited period after each program ends. Very few of the older people avail themselves of the opportunity for individual counseling but approximately one-third continue with small group work. This suggests that part of the oft-mentioned reluctance of older people to seek psychological help may be related to the form in which it has been available, that is, on an individual rather than group basis. The follow-up groups provide an opportunity for continued self-exploration and problem solving. Additionally some members' interpersonal communication skills develop to the extent that they gain the confidence necessary to enroll in the training program to become paraprofessional group counselors.

Program Evaluation

In assessing the impact of the counseling program we have had input from three different sources: (1) client written and verbal self-report data, (2) group leader reports on client behavior in the group counseling situation, and (3) observations from staff members of the host institution on behavioral changes they see in participants as they engage in other activities at the center. Let us deal with these sources one at a time.

Self-report data is obtained through feedback sheets collected at the end of each program as well as from verbal reports made on an on-going basis. General response to the program has been positive, as participants report increased self-confidence ("nothing has really changed but I feel better about myself" or "I've gained new courage"), feelings of warmth and closeness towards their fellow members and the community center in general "I've made a friend," "I feel closer to this group than to anyone I know"), and willingness to try new behaviors "who would have ever thought I would learn about myself at 69!").

At some of the programs for older people a ladder profile was administered at the first and last session. This profile, adapted from Saltz (1968) requires clients to indicate the rung of the ladder which best describes how they see themselves in the areas of general self-esteem, energy level, relationships with family and relationships with people outside the family. Among the older people, the area of greatest change seems to be that of relationships with family members, although the data here has been too sparse for statistical analysis. Our preliminary explanation is that older people who experience self-exploration and interpersonal communication activities learn in the program to express their positive and negative feelings. This practice enables them to speak more directly to their family members and to harbor fewer resentments, which results in generally improved relationships.

In our efforts to gather information about the effect of the program, we are trying to focus on observable behavior changes. At the end of each session group leaders rate participants on how often they speak during the session, show recognition of other group members, demonstrate interest in other group members' problems, respond in a helpful manner to others, volunteer information about themselves, and do not exhibit disruptive behavior. Group leaders also write reports on their clients at the end of the program and have noted many changes which do not lend themselves to statistical analysis. Many clients improve their physical appearance dramatically during the course of the program. One attractive 68-year-old woman who participated reluctantly at first and mentioned fears of touching, especially of men, later joined a square dance group. Some participants add new activities to their lives. One woman who was initially so shy that she looked down in her lap most of the time and never responded verbally to the group, began to write notes of her impressions to the group leader. After she had received several of these notes, the group leader asked for permission to read them to the group and the response was very positive. Toward the end of the program the leader asked the woman to read her own notes to the group, and this led to an increased interaction. The group feedback on her writing ability so encouraged her that she began writing a column for the community center newsletter of which she later became editor.

Clearly a goal of the program is to help participants increase their level of functioning outside of the counseling group as well as within it. In an effort to assess this at a relatively simple level we have devised a rating scale on which staff members of the community center, who are not involved in any way in the counseling program, are asked to rate participants before and after the program on their overall appearance, their level of social interaction, energy level, degree of optimism-pessimism, and level of self-esteem as indicated by the extent to which they speak highly of themselves. No statistical analysis is yet available on this data. There is, however, some impressionistic data which is encouraging. The director of one of the centers reported a "warmer atmosphere" in the center after the first Continuum Center program which manifested itself in more seemingly animated conversations in the lounge and more friendly greetings to newcomers. A librarian who periodically visits another of the centers with a bookmobile, and knew nothing of our program, asked the director what had happened because some center members had begun to ask for specific books, particularly psychology books.

An unexpected development was the presence and impact of handicapped persons in some of the programs. Recent participants have included people who are partially sighted, blind, stroke victims and arthritics, as well as people with cardiac problems and other disabling diseases. Severe hearing loss proved to be the greatest drawback to participation in the program because of the emphasis on verbal communication. Blind people were able to learn the names of their fellow participants, to identify who was speaking, to listen to others, and to be generally active in both large and small group activities. The presence of blind people who were leading active and relatively independent lives was reassuring and encouraging to others fearful of losing their eyesight.

The findings described here will meet few, if any, rigorous standards of research. They are, however, sufficiently encouraging that we want to continue with the programs and develop more systematic ways of assessing their impact.

Use of Paraprofessionals

As noted above, the Continuum Center small group counseling is provided by trained and supervised paraprofessional peer leaders. The value of peers as counselors has been demonstrated with varying populations, and may be especially important in dealing with older people. In a discussion of the need for counseling of the aged, Pressey and Pressey (1972) noted the value of using older counselors who have shared some of the same life experiences as their clients. In our work at the Continuum Center, we have found that the modeling effect of elderly group leaders is extremely valuable. It is difficult for clients to say that they are too old to learn when their group counselors range in age from 55 to 77, and are clearly launched in new directions.

Selection Procedure

Potential peer counselors are drawn from the pool of program participants. Group leaders and project staff look for the following indicators of group leadership potential: regular attendance; ability to learn and use the program material; willingness to self-disclose; ability to listen to, and empathize with, other group members; and a general emotional investment in the program. Project staff invite potential trainees to the follow-up counseling groups mentioned above, which provide an additional opportunity to assess their helping skills and group participation. If this assessment is satisfactory, the counselor invites the potential peer counselors to consider enrolling in the training program.

The final step in the selection procedure is an orientation session designed to familiarize trainees with each other, the trainers, and the training methods. As part of the orientation, trainees are asked to engage in videotape "mini" interviews which are then viewed and discussed in order to familiarize trainees with the use of videotape replay as a learning tool. At the end of the session trainees give brief statements of their learnings from day and make a final decision about participation in the training program.

Training Design

For those who agree to participate, the training program has several general objectives: (1) to reinforce in potential group counselors their already existing qualities of genuineness, empathy and nonpossessive warmth; (2) to develop their communication skills; (3) to help them become facilitators who can encourage their clients to think through alternatives; (4) to increase their self-awareness and self-confidence; and (5) to teach some principles of group dynamics.

The training program consists of ten five-hour sessions on a twice per week basis. Because of the highly personal nature of the training, participation is limited to between eight and twelve trainees. The program coordinator and counselors, who have previously worked extensively with the trainees when they were program participants, usually function as co-trainers. The training design combines didactic and experiential procedures. The approach is an eclectic one, drawing upon materials from adult education, group counseling, and humanistic psychology. Aside from the orientation session described above and the final session, which is devoted to trainee evaluation and assessment of readiness to group lead, the balance of the session follow a similar pattern.

Morning sessions are devoted to development of counseling skills using an adaptation of the Systematic Human Relations Training Model (Carkhuff, 1972). We lead our trainees through the steps of attending, observing and reporting of helpees' physical behavior, repeating helpee statements verbatim, identifying feelings and major content, and making responses which are action-oriented to encourage helpee growth steps. Throughout this skill training, trainees are encouraged to evaluate their own performance and are given feedback by the trainers and the other trainees, Skill practice during the eighth session varies somewhat, in that helping pairs are asked to have a five-minute interview, during which the helper attempts to use any of the full repertoire of interchangeable and action-oriented responses in "counseling" the helpee. This interchange is videotaped and critiqued by, first, the helper and then the trainers and other trainees.

Afternoon sessions are devoted to videotaped small group leadership practice sessions. This change from the structure of the morning underlines the importance of the specific helping skills learned, and increases the attention span by providing a change of pace, a particularly relevant issue with older people. Materials used are from the counseling program, as we think trainees can learn skills more easily using familiar materials.

At the end of the morning session trainers announce the names of the people who will be working as leaders that afternoon. Trainers then meet with the designated leaders in a mini-clinicing session to go over the rationale and approach to the exercise they will lead, and to encourage co-leaders to plan ways of working effectively together. This brief clinicing also serves as a model of the longer clinicing sessions for group leaders which precede all counseling programs and are a central part of our ongoing supervision of group leaders. Following the lunch break all other trainees have some common experience from the program agenda followed by a videotape discussion of their feelings about the experience in a small group. The entire videotape is then replayed and critiqued by trainers and trainees.

We have found that the opportunity to see and hear oneself is an invaluable learning tool as trainees can observe their responses, comment on their accuracy and effectiveness, and suggest alternative responses for themselves. They also get feedback from their peers, who have been members in the groups they led, and from the trainers on what they did and what else they might have done. Both trainers and trainees may stop the tape at any point to ask a question, to comment on verbal or non-verbal behavior, or to make a group process observation. This broad range critiquing of the tapes enables trainers and trainees to comment on issues of timing or pacing of responses, and to underline the importance of open-ended questions. Because of the value of positive reinforcement, trainers stop the tape and comment equally about good interventions and poor ones.

In addition to reinforcing constructive and effective counseling responses, trainers underline a variety of issues throughout the training program for older people. Since the trainees will work in group settings within the community centers and in the counseling program, trainers highlight group dynamics issues as they arise during the training. Sometimes trainers deviate from the agenda to comment on group norms, to identify the developmental stages of group process, and to focus on interpersonal group interactions. Trainers also emphasize the importance of co-leadership in group sessions and encourage effective cooperation through the use of specific step-by-step procedures.

Supervision and Inservice

The training program for older people is truly a preservice experience. Continued supervision and inservice programs are necessary for reinforcing basic helping skills and increasing trainees' level of function.

The clinicing sessions mentioned above provide the primary avenue for both supervision and inservice training. During these sessions, group leaders and staff consultants evaluate the effectiveness of the previous session, discuss any problems within the groups or between co-leaders,, and review the agenda for the day. Additionally, inexperienced group counselors are initially paired with experienced group counselors from other Continuum Center programs, prior to being paired with their own peers. Aside from the obvious on-the-job training implications, such exposure of younger men and women to their older peers affords several secondary gains. The older group counselors, and the group members as well, experience a young person who does not reject them for the usual age-biased reasons, while the younger person has the opportunity to work with older people who are dynamic, vital and striving for continued growth. Supervision is also provided in the feedback given to group counselors following site visits by the program coordinator and staff counselors to the small groups.

Special inservice workshops run by Continuum Center staff and outside consultants are offered to older group counselors on a regular basis. Recent sessions included a presentation of the communication model of Satir (1972) and a discussion of Transactional Analysis terminology and concepts.

Outcome for Group Leaders

As noted in the program evaluation section above, various informal measures seem to indicate that the counseling program has beneficial effects on the program participants. The same can be said for the effects of training and group leading on the older people who function as paraprofessional group counselors. In the most recent training program a checklist of behavioral observations was used to assess the impact of training. Trainer ratings were made after each session on the quantity and quality of group participation, level of counseling skills displayed, and ability to express feelings and to evaluate their own performance. Forward movement was shown on most measures. A few brief anecdotes will serve here as examples of the changes we see and as a wrap-up to this paper.

A retired 75-year-old English teacher had a difficult adjustment to retirement, hating the age-segregated housing for older people that isolated her from young people with whom she'd shared so much of her life. She recently negotiated a move back to an urban university neighborhood and thus increased the self-esteem and control over her life that has developed as she learned and used skills in her new role as group leader.

Another peer counselor entered the program after seeking help from an audiologist for a hearing problem. She had a slight hearing loss, but was suffering mostly from isolation and estrangement following a long illness. Initially quiet and shy, she gradually gained a feeling of confidence and excitement. She has recently become an ombudsman for Citizens for Better Care, and a resource person for Wayne State University classes on aging while continuing her group leading role. An initially quiet and unassuming woman recently modeled in a fashion show after complaining that clothes are always displayed by young, thin people.

A retired shipping clerk with only an elementary school education was the first older paraprofessional we trained. He has initiated several Continuum Center programs, provided out-reach counseling to widowers, and enrolled fellow retirees in college classes in the community center over which he has presided. He reports that his new learning and career have helped establish a deep bond with his adult children who are all professional people.

These individuals all express delight in finding a rich exciting part of themselves and amazement at being able to begin a new career that is helpful to others.

Bibliography

Carkhuff, R. R. 1972. *The Art of Helping.* Amherst: Human Resources Development Press.

Fast, Jay H. 1970. The Role of the Chaplain. *Guidelines for an Information and Counseling Service for Older Persons.* Durham: Duke University Center for the Study of Aging and Human Development.

Kahn, Robert L. 1975. The Mental Health System and the Future Aged. *The Gerontologist.* Vol. 15, No. 1, Part II, 24–31.

Klein, W. H., Le Shan, E. J., Furman, S. S. 1965. *Promoting Mental Health of Older People Through Group Methods: A Practical Guide.* New York: Mental Health Materials Center, Inc.

Kubie, Susan H. and Landau, Gertrude. 1953. *Group Work with the Aged.* New York: International Universities Press, Inc.

McHolland, James D. 1972. *Human Potential Seminars.* Evanston: James McHolland, Human Potential Seminars, Kendall College.

Pressey, Sidney L. and Pressey, Alice D. 1972. Major Neglected Need Opportunity: Old Age Counseling. *Journal of Counseling Psychology.* Vol. 19, No. 5, 362–366.

Saltz, Rosalyn. 1968. Foster Grandparents and Institutionalized Young Children: Two Years of a Foster-Grandparent Program. Unpublished report of the Foster-Grandparent Research Project, Merrill-Palmer Institute, Detroit, Michigan.

Satir, Virginia. 1972 *Peoplemaking.* Palo Alto, Calif.: Science & Behavior Books, Inc.

Simon, S. B., Howe, L. W. and Kirschenbaum, H. 1972. *Values Clarification: A Handbook of Practical Stratigies for Teachers and Students.* New York: Hart Publishing Co.

chapter 6
serving older adults
and their families

Thinking about the older client means thinking about the client's family too. For almost all older adults, the family is a crucial reference point. Many older people's lives have meaning primarily in the context of their families; failing to take the family of the older client into account may cause a human services worker to neglect the most important parts of that client's life. This chapter opens with a discussion of the older person and his or her family. The concepts in this chapter should be applied to all work with older people.

Families and the Aging

The family is the most important institution in American life. Although in recent years there has been extensive discussion of and reporting on the changes in the family system, those changes, though real, have not negated the importance of the family for most of us. Certainly, as the nation has changed from a rural to a metropolitan society, the *extended family* has become less pervasive; that is, the family that consists of several generations and several households with grandparents, grandchildren, parents, aunts, uncles, cousins closely involved. The *nuclear family*, which includes only the husband and wife and their children has become more pervasive. Yet many older clients grew up in a time when the extended family was the typical family of significance for all people. The extended family has disintegrated because of increasing population mobility with children leaving their birthplaces and, consequently, leaving the older adults behind. Maintaining connections with the family is an important part of the lives of older adults, no matter how frequently or infrequently there are actual contacts with that family. Even when there is minimal contact, reminiscence among the aged is often about their family lives.

Family Patterns

Of course, family has a variety of meanings for Americans. Family patterns may vary between rural and urban groups, among various ethnic groups, and among older people in the various regions of the country.

Generally, family life, particularly extended family life, is stronger in rural than in urban areas. Such secondary institutions as governments, social agencies, and civic clubs may have greater significance and impact on the lives of people in metropolitan areas than they do in rural areas, where the family sets behavioral norms for its members, where economic problems are resolved through borrowing and lend-ing among family members, where home may be the house where one grew up, and where face-to-face communications and contacts are regular, almost daily in some cases. In urban areas, family contacts and extended family influences may be less significant because of other types of relationships. Neighbors or business associates may play a more dominant role than family in urban areas.

Emerging Problems of Aging and the Family

Much of this book is focused upon several classic problems faced by older adults. All of them, such as economic support, health care, housing, transportation, and disabilities, remain the most serious concerns of the aged. Similarly, they are the kinds of problems most often encountered by human services workers as well as being the kinds of problems that most often require the assistance of counselors, social workers, and others.

However, as a result of the increasing population of older adults, the longer life span, and a variety of social and economic changes that have been discussed thus far, the aging are facing many new problems and conditions that increasingly require the attention and assistance of human services workers. These include intra-family conflict, conflict with the law, and homelessness.

Intra-Family Conflict

For several reasons, many older adults are now finding themselves alienated from and in conflict with their families. Whereas economic and social abandonment, abuse, and neglect, by the older person's family is not a new phenomenon, there may be a growing incidence of schisms—even when financial support or living arrangements are not issues—between the elderly and their children.

The reasons for these schisms are as diverse as the families affected by them. In some cases, they are about property disputes, with the elderly believing they have been financially mistreated in some business arrangement with their children or grandchildren. In other cases, the conflicts may result from disapproval either by the parents or their children of the other's marriages, divorces, child-rearing practices, career pursuits, smoking, alcohol and other substance abuse, religious choices—the lists are endless. It is possible that the incidence of such conflicts increases because individuals live longer, providing more time for occurrences that are sources of alienation. No longer are large numbers of children able to speak reverently of their long-deceased parents or grandparents. For many families, Dad, Mom, and the grandparents are ever-present sources of anger and distrust. Whatever the reasons and no matter how they may lead to interpersonal conflicts, alienation among the generations appears to be a fact for more and more families, regardless of socioeconomic status or geography.

Although formal, scientific studies of such behavior are rare, anecdotal evidence is great. Perhaps the most significant conflicts are those within the recent "ruling" families of the English-speaking world—former President Reagan and the royal family of the United Kingdom.

According to the popular press (Scott, 1988), Prince Charles does not get along very well with the Duke of Edinburgh. The Duke had bullied his son when the Prince was a child. That, coupled with different approaches to life—the duke is more aggressive, competitive, and physical than his son, who is oriented to more intellectual activities (Scott, 1988)—has led to some chilly relations between the two leading men of British royalty.

President Reagan, whose personal life is complicated by two marriages with children from each, and his second wife are viewed as being in conflict with or perhaps estranged from at least two of his children, both of whom wrote books purporting to describe their difficult family situations (Reagan, 1988; Davis, 1988). Such anecdotes are significant only as dramatic examples of a phenomenon that is shared with many—perhaps most—American families. Few families cannot share tales of less than close and cordial relationships among the generations.

With that reality complicating family life, human services workers need to understand the sensitivities associated with family life for many aged persons. As this book has made clear, many elderly people do not have regular contacts with their children. Financial support for living costs and health care is not necessarily available from children, even when those children may be well off. The distances between elderly parents and their children may be great, even when their residences are located in the same communities. The elderly are often not able to rely on their children for such help as transportation to medical appointments, social contacts, and the other needs of older adults.

Elderly parents are often the source of conflicts, as well, among siblings. The "good" child who is willing to support financially or house the elderly parent may earn the anger of a brother or sister who does not offer similar assistance. Wealthy families often conflict over the planned disposition of estates, bargaining or battling over who is recognized for how much in a parental will. Some parents are inclined, almost whimsically, to write one child or another into or out of an estate, leading to jealousy, competition, and conflict among the siblings. For reasons such as these, any relations or meetings among family members are complicated and, at times, impossible.

Human Services Work Implications

For the humans services worker, dealing with some of these kinds of intrafamily conflict poses special requirements and sensitivities. In many cases, they mean that the worker cannot automatically expect to use close family members as a resource for older adults who are in various kinds of need.

Further discussions of family conflicts follow in this chapter.

Ethnicity and Families

It is a general concept that the more ethnically identified a family, the closer the links among members of the family, including the extended family. For example, Italian, Polish, Jewish, and other ethnically identifiable families in urban and metropolitan areas who maintain strong ties with their ethnicity are likely to be more closely oriented to the extended family than people whose identities are less ethnically specific or who have assimilated into the broader culture of the United States. For an Italian-American family in an urban area, continued adherence to ethnically oriented diets, regular attendance at Roman Catholic services, attendance by children at parochial schools, and residence in neighborhoods that are largely Italian-American are signs of continuing identification with the ethnic group. Jewish families that continue to observe religious holidays, attend services regularly, and, in the case of Orthodox or Conservative Jews, maintain dietary laws, are likely to remain closely tied as well to the extended family.

Although the form of expressing ethnicity and concern for the extended family may vary, every ethnic group, whether Asian-American, black, Chicano, American Indian, and so on, may be characterized by strong interest in the family. It is often the older family members who hold the extended family together and who provide the basis for adherence to ethnic identifications. For instance, celebration of American Indian customs by families otherwise assimilated into the general culture are often maintained to satisfy and cater to grandparents. For some families, it is the older family members who hold everyone together by remembering and reminding young family members about birthdays, anniversaries, and other events that require acknowledgment or celebration, and which, in their turn, maintain family solidarity.

In the 1980's, there was something of an explosion of ethnic groups in the United States because of international developments and changes in immigration patterns. There are increasingly large numbers of people from many Asian nations such as Korea, the Pan Asian communities, which include Laos, Cambodia, Vietnam, Thailand, and other nations, as well as the large nations of China and Japan. As American trade becomes more extensive around the world and as more and more foreign nationals come to this country to produce and market goods and services, the populations from those nations increases. These populations often include older adults, who follow their children from their nations of origin for a variety of social, economic, and political reasons.

Many European countries also have increasingly large groups living and working in the United States. In addition, many African nations have large communities in this country and Middle Eastern countries such as Iran, Israel, and the Arab nations, have had significant amounts of immigration to the United States. The Caribbean countries such as Haiti and Jamaica as well as many Central and South American nations also have sizable communities here. Many immigrants are here as a consequence of political upheavals in their own nations, some of which have involved the United States.

Whatever the case, it is clear to most who work with the aging in America that ethnic identification is important and that each ethnic group has a life-style of its own. Effective human services workers must become familiar with and be ready to work with a variety of ethnic groups. It is impossible, in a text such as this, to define all of the characteristics of all of the ethnic groups that one may encounter. Each is quite different and fundamentally specific in religion, dietary practices, attitudes toward family, health, and recreation. The ethnically sensitive human services practitioner must become knowledgeable about the client and his or her family situation as well as ethnic identification—knowledge that may come in part from books but most commonly from informants among the client population. Getting to know ethnic group representatives and talking to them about all aspects of their lives is an effective way to learn about and to learn how to serve people who are different than oneself.

Socioeconomic Level
and Family Life

There is some evidence, too, that the lower the socioeconomic level, the more significant the extended family is. Daughters may use their mothers and grandmothers for information on appropriate child-rearing practices rather than texts by psychiatrists and pediatricians. Fathers and husbands may want to emulate their own fathers in recreation, employment, and family life patterns. The differences may result from differences in education or many other reasons on which one may speculate, but when encountering an older client from a lower- to lower-middle socioeconomic level, a worker may expect that the family will be of great importance. Since human services workers are more likely to come into contact with less affluent clients, recognizing the importance of and understanding the family in relation to the older person are crucial.

Changes in Family Life
Encountered by the Aging

Changes in family life during the older years are both positive and negative. Retired couples, for example, have more time to spend with each other and in leisure-time pursuits that appeal to them. Some of the more burdensome aspects of adult life, such as raising children, competing economically, and taking responsibility for community activities, are reduced during the senior years; for some older adults, those changes increase freedom.

The following discussion focuses on some of the problems reflected by changes in family life in the senior years and some of the ways human services workers aid older people and their families in overcoming those problems.

Leisure Time

Perhaps the best known characteristic of retirement is increased leisure time, which most recognize is both an advantage and a problem for retired older adults. Human services workers with the aged are often occupied in developing and organizing leisure-time programs for older people. Some of the principles of organizing those services and some discussion of the range of them are found in Chapter 14. In many ways the worker is most valuable by helping the senior adult identify and make use of leisure-time programs of a group or individual, formal or informal, structured or unstructured nature.

Marital Difficulties
and Retirement

Although they are less well known, marital problems resulting from retirement are encountered by many older adults. There is a variety of reasons for these difficulties, some of which are well understood and obvious. A typical situation might be seen in the following example:

Mr. Alexander retires at age 72 after 40 years of marriage to the same woman and an equal number of years of time-consuming work that kept him out of the house all day every day except Sunday afternoons, when he usually napped to rest from that morning's golf. His life with his wife was confined to dinner, after-dinner television, holiday activities, and an occasional Saturday night social event with friends or relatives. For all those 40 years Mrs. Alexander occupied herself with civic clubs, visits with her sisters, child rearing (her youngest daughter had left home 15 years earlier) and household management tasks. Now Mr. Alexander is home all day. He plays golf three times a week and bowls twice, but he can't bowl and play golf all day every day. He plays no musical instruments, rarely reads, and cares little for the company of the few men in his neighborhood who are also retired. He is at home with nothing to do, and his being there interferes directly and critically with Mrs. Alexander's routine. The result—bickering, mutual criticisms, or sullen stares—is unlike anything they had experienced in their previous years of marriage.

Retirement alone is not the cause of their problems. The two have also gone through some sex-role changes that almost guarantee a clash when they find themselves confronted with one another over long periods of time.

Sex-Role Reversals in the Later Years. Psychologist David Gutmann (1975) reports that as men age they become, in contrast to younger men, more interested in love than in conquest for power and more interested in communicating with others. They become less personally sensual and more generally loving. Young men are more interested in sex—even procreative sex—while older men become more interested in food, pleasant sights, sounds, and human associations.

Women move in the reverse direction. As they age, Gutmann says, women become more aggressive, less sentimental, and more domineering. In later years, "The older wife becomes something of an authority to the husband. . . . " According to Gutmann the relationship that began the marriage is almost completely reversed.

Sex. There are also distinct changes in the sexual inclinations and behavior of older people. Seymour Kornblum and Geraldine Lauter, two community center workers with the aged, report:

As a man grows older, certain physical-sexual changes become evident. The prostate gland often enlarges and its contractions during orgasm are weaker. The force of ejaculation weakens, and the seminal fluid is thinner and more scant. Orgasm is slower in coming and may not last as long as it once did. Erections are less vigorous and frequent, although the potential remains the same. The aging man may lose his erection rather rapidly after ejaculation and be unable to attain another for several hours, or even days. Studies of older men reveal that impotency increases steadily with age reaching 50 to 70 percent at age 75.

In contrast to men, women demonstrate few changes in the pattern of their sexual response as they grow older. . . . A woman's sexual desire ordinarily continues undiminished until she is 60 years or older, after which it declines very slowly, if a suitable outlet is available. . . . There is no time limit drawn by advancing years to female sexuality (Kornblum and Lauter, 1976).

Thus the retired couple may have significant psychosexual needs with which human services workers can help.

Working with the Retired Couple. The human services worker may help the couple become aware of and able to deal with some of their personal marital problems through some of the interviewing or counseling methods suggested in chapter 4, or through a group program for couples with similar characteristics and problems, such as those discussed in chapter 5. If leisure-time programs are indicated, the worker may help the couple make contact with them and may even lead the couple to them. Such programs may be recreational, educational, or oriented to political or social action.

The couple needs help in understanding the problems associated with their new relationship but, perhaps more important, they need help in adjusting to the changes in their circumstances. Certain kinds of marital and family counseling methods may prove helpful with retired couples. One approach that may help Mr. and Mrs. Alexander would be an opportunity to reminisce, with the help of the worker, on the reasons for their marriage in the first place. That may help them regain some understanding of why they have remained together as long as they have, what they have in common, and what they feel for one another.

Of course, all of their problems are not those of leisure-time or emotional difficulty. Perhaps a physician could help Mr. Alexander understand his waning sexual powers. Physicians with special knowledge may be able to help him restore his sexual functioning. Counselors on sexuality may be able to help the Alexanders find alternative ways for providing each other with sexual gratification.

New Relationships with Children

Aging makes for major differences in the relationships between parents and children. Some are obvious: Children grow up and leave. They become independent socially, economically, and geographically, with many relocating long distances from their parents. Outright estrangement is a common phenomenon in American families, with children and parents barely communicating by mail, telephone, or personal visits. There are also some less obvious changes that occur with the entry into the senior years by parents.

Closer Ties. For some older women relationships with their daughters become closer than during the daughter's adolescent and young adult years, when they themselves were younger. The grandmother has a useful contribution to make as a babysitter and a counselor. Daughters probably ask more advice about child rearing from their mothers than from any other source. The mother and her married daughter may also have more in common in the later years of their relationship. Both have husbands, both may have had children, both are or have been employed. There is a good bit to talk about and much to share. Some older women report that their daughters provide them, through the daughters' contemporaries, with an ever-widening circle of friends among both young and old women.

Men have similar positive changes in their relationships. Older fathers and their adult sons may share household chores, experiences in work and community affairs, and recreational activities such as hunting or fishing together. The tensions that may have existed between the father and his adolescent son may disappear when both become adults.

Such changes are generally pleasant for both parent and child and are not likely to come to the attention of human services workers. The family has found some satisfactions on its own and has developed a pleasant reaction to the later years without the intervention of any outside agency.

The Two-Way Guilt of Parents and Children. By contrast, for many families the later years are a source of increasing and unpleasant reminiscences about past unkindnesses perpetrated by children against their parents and parents against their children. The reminiscence, so characteristic of the later years, is a source of anxiety and tension rather than pleasant memories.

Although aging is the normal result of time passing, many children think they are responsible for the problems their parents face. The problems are physical and social results of growing old, but the children, nevertheless, feel guilt. In many cases, younger family members do not feel they are doing all they can for the older relative. Sometimes their resources or the availability of community resources are insufficient, and family members are burdened with the feeling that they have not satisfactorily aided their elders.

Older people often feel guilty, too, toward their children and other younger relatives. They dwell on the unkindnesses they have committed or imagine they have committed against the younger generation. Though it should be obvious that people cannot live together over decades without occasionally being less than kind, reminiscence about outbursts of emotion and denials of affection can lead to disabling feelings of guilt on the part of older people.

In many situations the human services worker's primary role with the family is to help the older and younger generations speak with one another about their feelings, particularly their guilt feelings. The human services worker may be able to arrange opportunities for the older and younger family members to confront one another directly and to explain why they do not want their older (or younger) counterparts to feel guilty.

For example: Mrs. Carter visits a human services worker in a family service or community mental health agency and talks about her overwhelming sense of guilt toward her son, William, whose career plans she criticized when he was a child and whom she rarely supported in his educational activities. When he married, she was critical of his choice of a spouse, and although she attended the wedding, she did not do so enthusiastically. In recent years, the families have been closer. Mrs. Carter has come to care deeply for her daughter-in-law and for the couple's children. She has helped when she could, and she has learned to be proud of her son's career. But she feels guilty about those earlier unkind and inaccurate judgments about her son, his career, and his wife.

The human services worker with Mrs. Carter could serve her best by bringing her together with her son and letting them talk things over. The son may deny having ever been disturbed by his mother's negative attitude. And the worker can be helpful to the client by helping her understand the normal reactions parents have toward their sons' departures from the home and selections of careers that may be unfamiliar to their parents.

Even more beneficial might be introducing Mrs. Carter into a group of women with similar concerns and backgrounds who can help her overcome her feeling of being unusual and unkind to her son and his family.

But the guilt associated with aging among family members goes in both directions. A typical case is: Mrs. Hellman develops cancer of the breast and requires surgery, long hospitalization, and extended care in a nursing home. Her small health and hospitalization insurance benefits run out quickly, and she is forced, before recovering, to obtain medical assistance from her state welfare department. Her daughter and son-in-law have a comfortable income but little more than enough to provide for food, clothing, and shelter for their own family of four. They feel guilty about their mother's seeking and obtaining public assistance, which is for some a demeaning course of action. (See chapter 12 for a more detailed discussion of financial assistance programs.)

In a case such as that of Mrs. Hellman, the social worker with the public welfare department would find it necessary and beneficial to the family to alleviate their guilt—to explain that, without drawing on financial assistance programs, many families would find themselves destitute and still unable to care for the health costs of a close family member.

In other cases, children feel guilty about the normal onset of aging in their parents, as if, by misbehavior as children or lack of attention as young adults, they caused the problems. Such families may be helped by conversations with a human services worker or by group sessions with other children of aging person.

Families Arriving for Service

One of the observations that many human services workers in health and welfare agencies make about older people and their families is that help is frequently sought not by an older individual alone but by an older adult and the total family.

Visit the waiting room of any large hospital, particularly one that cares for serious illnesses referred to it by family physicians, such as a university hospital, and you will find family groups waiting for an older person's appointment with a physician. Such hospitals frequently must build waiting rooms larger than usual, with seating for many more people than their patient load. That is because their patients may come with as many as five or six family members. Public welfare departments experience the same phenomenon and so, on occasion, do mental-health and family-service agencies.

At times there are practical reasons for the mass entry into the agency. The older person cannot drive, public transportation is inadequate, or the family wants to make sure that the older person can negotiate the complexities of entering and using a health or social service agency's programs.

Just as often, however, the reasons are emotional. The older person is afraid to go for help without the support of at least one, and probably more, family members, or the family members are unwilling to let the older person obtain the services without their presence. Family ties are so close, particularly in times of crisis when health or social services are needed, that the whole constellation is involved.

Situations such as these offer excellent opportunities for human services workers to meet and work with the total family around the social, cultural, and psychological problems associated with use of the service. Helping the family use the hospital properly, helping the family understand what is happening in the hospital, and helping the doctor understand the larger family constellation may have value in curing the patient of his or her problems.

Economic Insufficiency

As we have mentioned, economic need is one of the greatest problems of older adults. Chapter 12 discusses some of the programs established to help people overcome that need. However, beyond concrete financial assistance, there are service implications for helping older people and their families deal with the problems of economic need.

For example, education is one need. Frequently families with older adults will need help in finding ways to better use the money they have. Conserving resources by purchasing goods and services at the lowest possible cost is an important consideration for older people, who frequently find themselves short of funds for the first time in their memories.

Human services workers can aid older people and their families by informing them of consumer information and by helping them develop knowledge about the best places to shop, organizations that provide discounts to senior adults, and the principles of comparative purchasing. Many older widows, who have had little experience in handling finances, can dissipate their limited resources by bad choices of housing, clothing, or savings programs. Advice from consumer experts and the assistance of consumer advocates, which can be brought to the attention of older people and their families by human services workers, can make a significant difference.

Families and Institutionalization

The family problem of institutionalization is such that in 1988, a major national magazine's cover story was "A Home Not Her Own." (Tamarkin, 1988) It was the story of a 90-year-old woman who was being placed in a nursing home because she could not adequately care for herself. The cover of the magazine *People* carried a quote from the woman, "How could my son do this to me?" along with a picture of the patient crying.

Few issues cause as many feelings of guilt on the part of children or rejection on the part of older people as institutionalization in homes for the aging. The range of such institutions is great. Some are excellent, and some are scandalously inadequate as newspaper readers will testify.

The human services worker has a variety of roles to play working with the family around the need for and alternatives to institutionalization (see Chapter 13). For one thing, the worker must help the older person and the family decide whether or not institutionalization is absolutely necessary. If so, why? If not, what are the alternatives available and how realistic are they? Although unhappiness for both the family and the older person is a characteristic of the institutionalization progress, the worker can be helpful in minimizing the guilt felt by the family and the anger felt by the older person. Perhaps even better, the worker can be effective in locating an acceptable alternative to institutionalization, such as foster care, continued residence with the family, an apartment with associated assistance from a community agency, or relocation to another community with other family members. All may be realistic alternatives.

Emotional Problems

One of the key methods for helping older people and their families is family group therapy or family counseling.

Family methods are designed to solve the emotional, social, or, more generally, family problem that is being experienced by older people and those around them by dealing with the whole constellation that experiences the difficulty. Experts in family counseling believe it is better to help the whole family discuss a problem situation than to discuss it with only one or two family members, particularly when much of the conversation will be about others who are not present. Therefore, the human services worker enters into the family constellation and assists it in dealing with the problem.

Essentially, family therapy combines the techniques of interviewing with some of the understandings and methods of working with groups.

The methods for dealing with family problems through family therapy are several. They include those that have been developed by Nathan Ackerman, Virginia Satir, and many others.

Summary

Human services workers who hope to assist older people and their families in overcoming problems must understand the total family and the total family context in order to provide help to the family system.

This chapter has covered the various ways in which families function and has provided details on the reasons families play crucial roles in the lives of older people. Means for working with total families have been suggested. The subsequent chapters provide information on ways of working with older people through direct and organizational services and describe the service programs available for older people and the means for using them.

CHAPTER 7
WORKING WITH
TERMINALLY ILL AND
DYING OLDER ADULTS

One of the realities of working with older people is the fact that some will die during the course of a human services worker's contacts with them. Other older clients will be terminally ill over long periods of time while workers are in contact with them and their families. For those reasons, human services workers involved in helping the aging must become familiar with and capable of dealing with older clients who face terminal illness and death.

The taboos associated with terminal illness and dying are numerous. They are so strong that many social workers, physicians, nurses, and others who are required to become engaged with dying people actually do their best to avoid contact with the processes of death and with the dying. Studies in the social and behavioral sciences point to the difficulty professionals have in dealing with the issues surrounding the last stage of life.

The following excerpt is from David Sudnow's *Passing On: The Social Organization of Dying* (1967). Sudnow studied the way death was handled in two hospitals and described the ways in which health professionals handled dying patients:

Of the professions, clergymen and morticians work most directly and effectively with the realities of death. It is also they who are often most willing to deal directly with the families of the dead. However, dying people and their families need help from professionals in addition to clergymen and/or morticians. There may be times when those two groups are less well prepared to help the family with its needs than are others. However, for most people, including professionals in the fields of health, welfare, education, social work, and other human services, death is an issue that causes anxiety and fear.

One of the most comprehensive books ever written on the subject, Robert Kastenbaum and Ruth Aisenberg's *The Psychology of Death* (1972), includes some speculation about the reasons for the aversion to working with and dealing with death and dying.

First of all, human services professionals, particularly those in mental health, have the luxury of being able to avoid death, according to Kastenbaum and Aisenberg. Ministers, medical personnel, and morticians must deal with it.

Second, death is not an "interesting" intrapsychic problem. That is, it is a reality problem that cannot be cured through psychoanalysis, group discussion, psychotherapy, and the like. Feelings about it can be dealt with, and people can be prepared for its eventuality, perhaps, but it cannot be averted in those who are actually in the process of dying.

Third, death does not involve a common, mass ritual as it has at other times and in other cultures. The public funeral, the casket shop, and the deaths of people one knows throughout one's life are more common in less developed nations such as India and those of Latin America. Mass deaths caused by epidemics, natural disasters like floods and earthquakes, or war are not common in the United States, and neither is death among the young; therefore, people do not see death and can avoid it. Many American adults have never been to funerals and some people manage to avoid all funerals throughout their lives.

Fourth, the United States is an achieving society that focuses on making progress and on improvement. In such a context, there is little desire to talk about or deal with death. Death is unproductive, a sign of failure for some professionals. Some think that working with dying people who have emotional problems related to their death is obscene and disgusting.

Finally, death typically happens to people who are defined as relatively unimportant. That is, the old, who are often not considered important in this society. It is the old who usually die, and, therefore, little emphasis is put upon death.

Feelings about Death

Fear and Anxiety

There are differences in feelings about death, but it is not always easy to measure accurately people's attitudes toward it. Kastenbaum and Aisenberg report on a study by psychologists Irving Alexander and Arthur Adlerstein of the attitudes toward death of 50 male college students. They used a questionnaire, the Semantic Differential Technique, and a polygraph which measures psychogalvanic skin response.

In response to the questionnaire, most claimed that they had little anxiety about death and viewed it as the natural order of things and as God's will. However, in the Semantic Differential Technique, words that were related to death were evaluated as bad and potent by the subjects. And when terms associated with death were used, the psychogalvanic skin response of the participants was significantly different from the times words not usually associated with death were used.

It is possible that most people want others to believe they feel acceptance of death compared to fear of and anxiety about it, but they may not be responding with total honesty. However, a study of older people by J. M. A. Munnich (Kastenbaum and Aisenberg, 1972) found that two-thirds of older people felt acceptance of or acquiescence in thoughts of death. Kastenbaum and Weisman found apprehension about death minimal and found that there was much more apathy and acquiescence than anxiety.

Some studies have shown that those who live alone fear death more than those who live with families, friends, or in institutions.

Disengaging

Some older people recognize that they are dying, accept that fact, and begin to **disengage** from friends, relations, and regular activity. Others, although they may recognize that death is imminent, remain involved in daily activity.

There is some indication that personality characteristics, such as aggressiveness, irritability, and narcissism; the capacity to avoid acquiescence; and acceptance of life as it is can, in themselves, be deterrents to death. Morton A. Lieberman (Kastenbaum and Aisenberg, 1972), in a highly significant study, reports on people in nursing homes and public housing facilities and finds that those who coped with changes in their situations and with crises in aggressive, irritating, narcissistic, and demanding ways were those most likely to survive crisis. In other words, the more accepting, acquiescent, and tolerant were less likely to survive. Being pleasant and good seemed to be associated with earlier death.

Confronting Death

Although the intensity and nature of anxiety and fear of death differ from individual to individual, it is reasonable to assume that they are virtually universal phenomena. Human services workers who have difficulty confronting death or who fear dealing with it should not consider themselves either unusual or incapable of serving older adults who are terminally ill. Such workers are representative of the total population, which has characteristically feared the termination of life. Since fear of death is normal, human services workers should not be surprised about their fears; they should be capable of dealing with their reactions sufficiently to help the terminally ill and their families.

In reality, dying is no more difficult to handle than are other kinds of disabling, human, real problems that can arouse the anxiety of almost everyone, such as poverty, sexual dysfunction, and conflict with the law. Most human problems arouse anxiety in most people, which means only that workers frequently deal with problems that cause anxiety to them as well as to their clients.

Death is quite different from other crises in the life-span. The major difference is its finality. As individuals we cannot resolve this crisis. We can only choose whether or not to accept and prepare for it. It is universal—all people must anticipate it as their fate—and there are no personal witnesses to its exact nature. Although highly articulate professionals and others—Professor Lois Jaffe, a social worker who died of leukemia and wrote about her experiences, comes to mind—

can testify about the phenomenon of dying, no one can write about the realities of death.

Death Prevention

Human services professionals in such fields as health, welfare, and rehabilitation view death as a mortal enemy. Most such programs are directed toward the preservation of life. Therefore, social workers, physicians, nurses, rehabilitation counselors, and all others who serve the aging take, as their fundamental task, preventing the death of their clients.

Death prevention is accomplished in many ways by effective human services workers.

Some of the ways workers can assist the elderly in preventing early death are discussed in chapter 13.

Deteriorating Health Conditions

The aged are disproportionately affected by deteriorating health problems—the chronic illnesses that lead to death over long periods of time. According to the U.S. Bureau of the Census, (1984) in 1980, the leading cause of death among people over 65 was diseases of the heart. Malignant neoplasms, including cancers, were second. Cerebrovascular accidents or strokes were third. These three greatest killers of the aged—and of the total population, in part because the aged are such a large proportion of those who die each year—have long-term, lingering qualities in many cases. Most of the terminally ill older adults and their families with whom human services workers work suffer from such conditions. Atherosclerosis and Alzheimer's Disease are also major killers of the aged and also tend to involve lingering deaths, requiring long-term care, counseling, and other forms of human services assistance.Diseases of the lung, including pneumonia and influenza, are also major causes of death among the aged. At times, these are also lingering diseases and at other times they result from other conditions.

Accidents

Accidents are another significant cause of death among the aging. At times, they result from falls and other incidents that are not commonly fatal among younger people. Automobile accidents, which are a common cause of death among younger people, remain a cause of death among the aging.

The accidents of old age tend to result from failing faculties among older people—the deterioration of vision, hearing, and body flexibility. The loss of coordination and satisfactory mobility are also often causes of accidents. It is often the combination of aging with accidental events that causes the fatal event for the older person. What might be an annoying or even painful fall for a younger person can become a fatal or life-threatening event for the older adult. The fall may lead to a broken limb and the inactivity resulting from the broken limb can lead to a fatal case of pneumonia.

Accidents in the home are often an important cause of health problems for the aging. Helping older people arrange their residences to prevent accidents can be a life-saving act. Educating older people about home safety can also be an important way to preserve their lives.

Automobile accidents among aging persons are not only a source of death but also of public concern. Some states have initiated programs of retesting older people for drivers' licenses, although younger people may renew their licenses without examinations. There appear to be some contradictions in these policies. Although older people may encounter accidents with some higher degree of regularity because of slowed reaction times and other phenomena resulting from the aging process, the deaths among older drivers from accidents are less common than among younger people. That may result, in part, from older people actually driving more slowly than their younger counterparts. Insurance rates are not generally higher for older people. In fact they are often lower than those for younger drivers because of a lower rate of serious accidents. Some groups that work with and advocate for older people oppose these extra driving tests as discriminatory. Others support driver re-education programs for the aged in order to help older drivers both update their knowledge of driving practices and laws and to test their own skills to insure they will not be dangerous to themselves or others when operating motor vehicles.

Educational activities about accidents and accident prevention in the home and on the road may help prevent the deaths of some older people. Helping older people find alternative means of transportation, safer housing, and other preventive resources for avoiding accidents is a frequent and critical responsibility of many human service workers.

See chapter 13 for a discussion of health care for the aged.

Suicide

Suicide is a major cause of death among older people. In fact, the highest suicide rate for all age groups is 27.9 per 100,000, and this rate is for people 75–84 years of age.

The figures cited are for men and women combined. When they are separated, it is interesting to note that the male suicide rate at age 75–84 is 47.5 per 100,000, which represents a dramatic increase over suicides among men 55–74, which are approximately 37 per 100,000. For women, however, the suicide rate at ages 75–84 is 6.4 per 100,000, representing a decrease from those 55–74 years of age. In fact, the suicide rate for men moves steadily upward throughout the life-span, while for women it rises to approximately 10 per 100,000 in the middle years, 35–64, begins declining at age 65, and continues to decline for the balance of the senior years. Precisely why that is true is not absolutely known.

There is some disagreement about the reasons for such high suicide rates among people 75–84. Some have speculated that retirement and the associated loss of role and income that go with it cause people to terminate their lives. However, retirement usually comes much earlier than age 75.

Some theoreticians believe that all suicide among the elderly results from emotional illness and disturbance. Kastenbaum and Aisenberg report some belief that after age 60 the majority of suicide attempters are in a depressive stage of a manic-depressive psychosis, a few others have organic psychoses, and yet a few others a transient confusion that is organically based.

Those who terminate their own lives usually have one of the three elements delineated by Dr. Karl Menninger—the wish to kill, the wish to be killed, or the wish to die. Most believe that as age increases, the first two elements decline among those who commit suicide, while the third, the desire to die, increases.

Suicide prevention by human services workers includes a variety of steps, depending upon the kind of agency with which the worker is affiliated. This might include the telephone reassurance effort—trying to guarantee that contact is maintained with the older person as a means of helping the person overcome any fear, depressions, or desire for self-destruction. It can mean simply being available to talk over life and the future with older people and having time to talk to people who may be troubled. It may mean "crisis intervention" services—helping the person who is contemplating suicide avoid a positive decision to do so at an appropriate time, thus preventing the act from taking place.

Performing One's Job Well

Death prevention is perhaps best accomplished by simply doing one's job well. That is, the worker employed in a hospital or other health setting may prevent death by making certain that the client has all of the health resources, nutrition, medical care, and other physical elements necessary to remain healthy or to become restored to good health. Human services workers make major contributions toward curing individuals who are ill by serving as liaisons between the patients and other professionals and, at times, by serving as **advocates** for patients, ensuring that professionals know about and work to overcome the older clients' health problems.

In the field of recreation the human services worker may help prevent death and prolong life by assisting older people in finding pleasure in life through activity and companionship and otherwise finding and maintaining good reasons for living, which can, in many ways, contribute to the prolongation of life.

Social workers in mental-health programs may help maintain life through suicide prevention activities, such as those discussed above, and by helping older people overcome the socioemotional problems that may interfere with the maintenance of and continuation of life.

We may summarize by saying that death prevention is a major role of the human services worker with the aging and that effective performance of duties with one's client is a major way of preventing death.

Working with the Terminally Ill

Not all deaths can be prevented, and, the human services worker must come to terms with the fact that individual death is the fate of all of us. Dying is not an aberration; it is a normal state of life. It is more imminent for aging people, but it is the reality that must be faced by all. Therefore, patients and clients as well as workers in health settings, nursing homes, group projects, and all other service agencies must be aware of and deal realistically with the fact of death.

Effectively working with the terminally ill requires some understanding of the emotional processes of dying that are coming to be identified by students of the growing field of **thanatology**.

Perhaps the most widely studied and best-known student of death and dying is Dr. Elizabeth Kübler-Ross (1970), a European psychiatrist who has developed an international reputation as an expert on working with the dying. Kübler-Ross has identified five stages of dying, which are accepted by many professionals as those through which dying people pass. These stages are:

1. *Denial.* The person refuses to acknowledge the reality of impending death, whether he or she has learned about it accidentally or intuitively or has been told about it by a health professional.

2. *Anger.* The patient becomes a blamer—of physicians, the environment, the family, even God. The patient wants to know why he or she is dying and strikes out against the injustice of life and death.

3. *Bargaining.* Fate is offered a bargain. The patient essentially promises to lead a different or better life with the understanding that life will continue.

4. *Depression.* Denial no longer works, and it is replaced by fear, guilt, and feelings of unworthiness. Communication with the family and others begins to come to a halt.

5. *Acceptance.* The patient gives in to death. He or she is not happy with life's ending, but neither is there a willingness to fight death any longer.

Robert Kastenbaum suggests that one must understand these stages in relation to other phenomena. It is likely that people die differently from diseases and that the stages do not have the same effect for the cancer victim as they might for the victim of coronary disease, which is more crisis-oriented. Men and women may go through different stages on the way to death. Different ethnic groups may also experience different stages; just as funeral practices among various ethnic groups differ widely, so may the process of dying.

Furthermore, the personality of the dying person will affect the kind of death he or she experiences. The acquiescent personality will be likely to treat death differently than the battler. Kastenbaum says that the reflective person dies differently than the impulsive, the warm human differently than the aloof. In other words, personality has an effect on death.

Finally, the place of death has different effects. Whether one dies in a hospital, at home, or in a nursing home will have some impact.

In any case, the process of dying is, for many people, multifaceted. It passes through phases and it changes through time. The human services worker must be prepared to deal differently with different patients during the various stages of their dying.

The Hospice

Among the most important services for dying patients is the hospice. The hospice is a special institution or program for people who are terminally ill. It serves children and adults—not just the aging. However, because of the nature of death in the United States, the typical client is an aging person.

Hospices are organized in a variety of ways. The original versions developed in England provided residential facilities that were somewhere between nursing homes and hospitals in the intensity of the care they provided. In the United States, the hospice is more typically a program of services for dying people staffed by social workers, nurses, and other health care providers. The dying person lives in his or her own home and the services of the professional providers are taken to the person through periodic visits. Pain-reducing drugs may be used; assistance may be arranged for home maintenance, entertainment, and contact with family members; transfer to hospitals or other facilities that may be required can be arranged by the hospice staff.

The idea behind the hospice is to allow people to live and, ultimately, die in familiar surroundings among people, things, and pets, they may care about and that would not be available to them in the hospital or long-term care facility.

Many human services workers from all fields are intensely involved in hospices as providers of service, managers, counselors, and coordinators. There are many insurance programs and government health care assistance services that provide financial assistance to people who are using hospices.

Living Wills

Among the issues associated with dying is whether or not life should be prolonged for extensive periods of time through the use of "heroic" measures. Modern medicine has made it possible to maintain life through a variety of chemicals and mechanical devices. However, the person, though technically alive because he or she is not "brain dead," may be unconscious and nonresponsive. Because people may linger in that condition for months or years, many execute "living wills" while they are healthy. These wills usually provide those responsible for them as physicians or close family members to discontinue or avoid using these special measures, if their conditions seem irreversible. At the time such a decision must be made, the patient may be incapable of giving consent. However, previous consent may make it possible for the patient to avoid burdening the health facility and family members with extraordinary expenses and the pain of a lengthy death watch.

Dealing with the Practical Consequences of Death

Though death is not a problem like the adversities that happen by chance, since it is a natural stage of life, it poses crises for the dying patient and those around the patient. Therefore, there are practical, critical realities that human services workers with dying patients must help their clients manage.

Those who work with terminally ill people find that they have many concerns over and above their physical condition, comfort, and immediate health. Those with families will want to be assured that their spouses, children, or grandchildren will be cared for when they die. Others will be concerned about close friends or people with whom they have lived in recent years. Still others will want to have some assurance about the disposition of their financial resources. It often makes no difference how many or how few those resources are; the older person is concerned about them even if they are modest.

Funeral Planning

Some older people who are dying are deeply concerned about the disposition of their remains. They want to know where they will be buried and the kind of funeral they will have, and they will want to settle in advance other practical issues surrounding the physical fact of death.

It is often possible for the human services worker to help the aging and terminally ill client with these practical problems. The worker can help the client obtain information on funeral and burial plans and may help the client choose a grave site or mortuary.

Burial and funeral customs carry many cultural connotations that will be important to the dying client. Where the funeral will be held, what kind of clothing the body will carry, whether the casket will be open or closed, who will officiate, whether or not the body will be embalmed, and whether or not there will be an autopsy are issues that may make a great difference to the client.

Some ethnic groups think cremation is objectionable; other object strongly to concrete crypts and caskets; still others find the whole idea of burial distasteful. Clients divide along socioeconomic, cultural, and regional lines on these matters, wnicn maкe significant differences to dying people. The effective human services worker must be able to help the client make satisfactory decisions about them.

Legal Assistance

The human services worker may help the dying client obtain legal help for preparing a will, which is the usual means for guaranteeing that money and property will go where the client wants them to go. When such matters can be handled prior to death, it is often reassuring to the older person to know, with some security, what will happen to his or her resources after death.

Helping older people cope with the practical realities of death may, paradoxically, prolong life by reducing anxiety and helping the client feel mastery over the situation. If nothing else, the worker can assist the dying patient to feel in charge of his or her own life and the tasks at hand.

Psychological Assistance

Treating the Dying Person as a Whole Organism. Human services workers must understand that dying people are people first, and only secondarily dying. Those who are near death have the same sets of emotions, needs, and concerns that all human beings have. Therefore, human services workers must deal with terminally ill and dying people as those who are facing a special crisis but as individuals who have feelings; interests in other people; physical, emotional, and social needs; and who regard themselves as human beings with full identities—not as corpses. The perception of the client as a dying organism may exist more in the mind of the professional serving the person than in the mind of the dying patient. That is, Mr. Smith will think of himself as Mr. Smith not as a dying body.

With that in mind, effective human services workers deal with terminally ill and dying people through the same kinds of interventions and methods they might use with any other older person. These include interviewing individuals or families, doing group work with older clients, developing leisure-time activities, providing health services and mental health services, where those are indicated. Everything this volume says about serving older people applies to older people who are dying as much as to those who are not. After all, we are all dying—some perhaps more immediately than others.

Older people who are dying need some kinds of help that are different from that required by others. They may need to reminisce, and may need simply to be listened to and spoken with by human services professionals.

In some cases, the dying patient will have become physically less attractive than formerly. People who develop facial cancers may have only part of their faces, which may seem repugnant to some. It is critical that the human services worker not reject the client because of a poor appearance. Others may be bedridden and, in most cases of dying older patients, physical appearances are not pleasant. The worker must find opportunities to help the dying patient maintain some elements of a positive self-image through friendly contact with peers, group programs such as some of those described in Chapter 6, friendly conversations between the worker and the client, and positive relationships with family members.

Avoiding Somberness. An important principle in working with aging people is to avoid somberness or sadness when that is possible. Obviously, sadness surrounds the lives of people who face death as well as their families. One does not treat dying frivolously, because that would be cruel. On the other hand, treating dying people as if they had already died is even worse. That would involve never making jokes, never challenging, arguing with, or treating as viable organisms those for whom death is imminent. Dying people are not dead, and they want to be treated as whole human beings while they live. Therefore, it is inappropriate to continuously, consciously, and totally avoid laughter, disagreements, and other human responses that are normal with everyone else.

On the other hand, false cheerfulness is equally inappropriate and is best avoided. Sometimes false cheerfulness is in the face of terminal illness is more offensive than anything else. Being accepting, friendly, and responding to the human needs of the dying patient are some of the keys to effective human services work with clients.

Helping the Families of Terminally Ill, Dying, and Deceased Older Adults

Effective work with terminally ill and dying patients does not end with the patient; it extends to the family, which encounters problems with both practical and emotional elements surrounding the loss of a parent, sibling, or spouse.

Practical and Financial Problems

Some of the practical problems that cause concern for older people were discussed earlier. Matters such as burial and wills have their effects on family members also. The financial difficulties surrounding the care of a dying person whose life lingers is also of significance to a family. Some of the ways of handling such costs and obtaining extra resources to provide care are discussed in Chapter 12. Human services workers must be aware that long and lingering death may wipe out the financial resources of both the aging person and the family.

There has been extensive writing, research, and legislation on the "right to die," which deals with the power of an ill person to terminate his or her life if it is no more than a physical existence—if the person is terminally and irreversibly dying. Definitions of *life* and *death* are currently the subject of considerable legal dispute. Some states have absolved physicians of any criminal or civil responsibility for patients whose irreversible conditions are ended by the withdrawal of "life-support" systems such as respirators or other devices that artificially maintain heart function. Ordinarily these legal rulings make it possible for a person to be allowed to die if brain function has ceased. Counseling with patients or families about the patient's right to die will become an increasingly important role for human services workers.

Serving the Families of the Dead

Human services workers often find that their work goes on after the older person's death. There may be a need to counsel family members about their feelings toward the deceased parent, spouse, sibling, or other relative.

At some time in the dead person's life, some or all of those people probably treated the deceased with unkindness,, and the recollections of those unkindnesses may cause guilt feelings. Cases of depression among widows and widowers because of unkind actions—for which the deceased can no longer absolve them—are among the most significant causes of emotional breakdown among survivors. It is often the task of the human services worker to assist families and friends in handling their feeling about such matters.

There is also frequently a need to provide programs for survivors. Some community centers have provided outreach programs for widows and widowers that help them make the transition from marriage to single life, helping them to occupy their time and, at times, averting emotional or physical breakdowns. At other times, such outreach programs can help surviving family members cope with the financial difficulties associated with the death of a spouse or parent. One community center used a team of volunteer widows to locate and help other widows deal with the consequences of their widowhood, which seemed to have positive results for those who volunteered.

Summary

Dealing with death is one of the requirements of effective human services efforts with older people. It is a task that initially may seem unpleasant or undesirable to the worker. However, it is an essential element in serving the entire later stages in the life-span of the ways in which the human services worker intervenes.

READING 7.1

The Worker's Role / Leon H. Ginsberg

This article provides directions on the various ways social workers can assist clients or families of clients to cope with death and dying.

There is a dual reaction to death. On the one hand we may be astonished at how rapidly we forget those who have died and how rapidly others are likely to forget us. On the other hand dying and death itself have permanent effects—obviously on the person who dies but also on his or her family and others closely associated with the dying or dead person. The role the social worker plays in dealing with the dying and those affected by their deaths is the subject of this discussion.

It seems odd and perhaps anachronistic to discuss this topic. Although most social workers serve dying patients and their families in one way or another, it is clear that most would rather not. Like all the other human services professions (with the exception of funeral service) that ought to confront death and dying forcefully and directly—social work tends to avoid it. And that should not be considered unusual. Death may be viewed as the ultimate enemy of professions such as social work, nursing, and medicine. Admitting that it exists is a kind of insult.

Death does not fit the models for treating social problems most widely accepted in social work theory and practice today. The typical problems addressed by social workers are poverty, disease, crime, loneliness, and interpersonal conflicts—all of which may respond to strategies of elimination for amelioration, which are the usual goals of social workers when they confront social problems. Death, though it may be handled more intelligently and more humanely, is final, nonpreventable, universal, and irreversible. It requires a strategy of acceptance and adjustment. Death can be viewed as the ultimate defeat for a social work client, and it is not one taken lightly by the social workers who serve him. The client's defeat is also, in part, the worker's defeat.

There was a time in the development of social work strategies and philosophies when programs associated with death and dying could have been more in keeping with the established ways of thinking. That was during an era when social workers spoke about helping people to accept and adjust to certain conditions such as poverty, illness, and physical handicap. That is, social workers sought ways to enable people to function more effectively within the parameters of certain kinds of problems, among which dying might be included. But that attitude has changed, and social workers are now less willing to help people accept severe personal and social problems. Social workers believe that it is much better, in most cases, to help individuals and families change their situations. It is much more de-

From *Social Work with the Dying Patient and the Family*, edited by Elizabeth E. Prichard. New York: Columbia University Press 1977. Reprinted by permission.

sirable to change the facts of the society so that the situation no longer exists. Such a philosophy helps enormously when dealing with many phenomena. It sees to it that efforts will be made to create lasting changes and to ensure that problems will be finally overcome, not just for the individual but for society as a whole. But death is not one of those phenomena.

When I first studied social work in the late 1950s, we were still learning, in dealing with public assistance clients, to help them prepare reasonable budgets to live within very small monthly grants. But we changed that approach in the 1960s. Although I suspect there remain many workers in public assistance programs who help families with the realities of small welfare grants, the official strategy of professional social workers is to talk about the need for improving the system through programs such as guaranteed minimum incomes, better assistance grants, and social action activities designed to modify the distribution of wealth in the United States. Because of these changes and the new strategies of social change and social development, strategies aimed at helping people accept and live with problems are less well accepted than they once were.

Learning to accept and to deal with irreversible problems such as death and finding ways to make sad and difficult situations less so are essential in services to the dying and their families. For that reason it may be that most current social work problem-solving strategies do not fully lend themselves to this problem, although death and dying are among the most common phenomena with which professional social workers must deal.

It may also be true that social workers, like other health professionals, are psychologically set in a manner that makes it difficult for them to deal with the problems of death and dying, and they may be psychologically less adequately prepared for such problems than other professionals are. Social work may be the most optimistic and future oriented of the human services professions. Social workers seem to believe that improvement is possible, no matter how pervasive a problem might be; the notion that certain problems have always existed and will continue to exist is not acceptable. It is one of the lessons we have not wanted to learn from the sociologists and anthropologists who provide us with much of our theoretical background. I have encountered this nonacceptance of certain social problems as the normal state of affairs among social workers in this country, among social work Peace Corps volunteers overseas, and among social work educators. I remember my own experiences in East Africa early in this decade when I was enraged by the high infant mortality rate. I could not be comfortable in a situation that found the majority of children dying before they reached the age of five. A social worker who had spent many years in Africa responded to my rage by saying simply that one must learn that all people die, some young and some old, but they all die. For social workers all social problems are, by definition, phenomena to be battled and reduced, not facts to be accepted and dealt with as the realities of the situation. That may be more true for North American social workers than for others, but, of course, we are talking about social work in North America.

Death Prevention

Social workers can be and are effective professionals in death prevention. That is true within a number of institutional frameworks and could be true in many others. In the normal course of counseling and guiding, in helping people with emotional problems, through their work in mental health programs and family service programs, social workers can prevent suicide and the psychological depression that often leads to death from so-called normal causes.

Social workers also play active roles in suicide hotlines and suicide prevention centers. They take part in providing the 24-hour answering services, referral activities, and counseling programs designed to help those contemplating suicide and to prevent it. Such activities are in keeping with social work philosophy and typical social work practices.

Social workers are also effective in maternal and infant care programs, which also prevent death. They want to maintain life and have skill in doing so through the kinds of programs mentioned here.

Social workers also have a major role to play—and it has not been played so heavily as it might be in the United States—in the prevention of industrial deaths and accidental deaths in nonindustrial settings. It seems clear that accidental death, both on and off the job, has a high degree of social content. That is, death in industry, death on the highways, and all accidental deaths are frequently related to the emotional state of the persons who suffer the accidents, the other relationships among group members on the job, and the social structure of the place where the accidental death occurs.

This is not to deny that many deaths result from unsafe plant conditions in industries, from unsafe automobiles, and from the imprudent use of drugs and alcohol in connection with dangerous work and recreation. But each phenomenon has social components, and social workers can be effective in reducing the incidence of accidental death if their services are called upon.

In some countries large numbers of social workers are employed in accident prevention programs, particularly in industries, and provide major inputs in planning for industrial safety and preventing accidents.

Social workers can, I am suggesting, be highly effective in preventing accidental death within and outside industry.

The Social Worker with the Dying Person

Large numbers of social workers work in hospitals and outpatient programs helping patients with both physical and emotional problems. Many are highly effective, and more could be effective in serving the needs of dying persons, which implies a number of activities—among them the help with the acceptance of death mentioned earlier. That is, an effective social caseworker (or a group worker dealing with groups of dying persons) can help serve the needs of those who face lingering deaths. This service can include counseling that enables people to plan intelligently for the balance of their lives and for the lives of those around them, so that they can come to terms with death. It is possible and often desirable to use other resources, including religious resources, for those who need or can use such services.

There appear to be "stages" in the dying process. Kübler-Ross (1970) indicates that the stages—she identifies five—range from denial to acceptance. Anger, bargaining, and depression intervene between the two extremes. There is an obvious role for social work services at each of the stages, and it may be helpful, just as there are stages of development during the rest of the life span in which they are of service to individuals and their families.

The dying person has not stopped living. He or she often needs help in planning and coming to terms with reality just as other clients do. Social workers can provide this assistance.

Services to the Families and Other Significant Persons in the Lives of Dying Persons

Death has its personal elements but it is also a social phenomenon. That is, whereas it is an individual who dies, his or her death has its effects on family members, employees, employers, and friends. In many situations the needs of those around the dying person for the services of social workers may be as great as or greater than the needs of the dying person.

Again social workers can provide a variety of services, such as casework or counseling with individual family members about their own emotional reactions to the death of a family member, as well as help with practical matters such as future budgeting and living arrangements. Death often brings change in the lives of those around the person who dies. Social workers can provide guidance or at least someone to talk with about whether or not the living situation should be changed, whether or not the work situation should be changed, and the like.

In addition many individuals in the United States are employed by small, individually owned firms. The death of the owner or manager of a small firm creates significant needs on the part of his or her employees. Social workers can counsel and assist these employees, who are significant others in the lives of deceased employers.

In the other direction social workers can work with the employers of employees who are dying. Employers can be assisted in adjusting a dying person's work schedule and assignments as one means of helping him or her adapt to reduced health and the process of dying. The dying person may need vocational rehabilitation services, just as those who are temporarily ill or newly handicapped might.

In such roles social workers can be important mediators between employees and employers when death faces one or the other participant in an employment situation.

Services to the Families of Those Who Have Died

Social workers can also help the families of those who have died. The range of skills and of problems of this group may be larger than those of any of the other client systems social workers might serve in dealing with death and dying. For a variety of probably valid reasons, most discussions of death deal with older people or at least with adults. Of course, they constitute the "normal" dying population, but they are not the totality of that population. Infants, young children, adolescents, young adults die too—anyone may die at any time, an obvious statement but one we are reluctant to make and even more reluctant to accept.

It is likely that the extraordinary death causes the greatest social and emotional trauma to the significant others in the former life of the dead person. How many marriages terminate after the unexpected or accidental death of a young child? What happens to the parents of children who are believed to have committed suicide, an increasingly more common phenomenon and a leading cause of death among young people? How easy is it for them to escape the guilt that may be justified or unjustified but that must always exist? What happens to families who experience automobile accidents in which only some of the family members die? What are the emotional reactions of the surviving family members?

The trauma associated with the deaths of person who would not normally be expected to die is great and often demands the kinds of services that social workers can provide.

The same kinds of needs for counseling services exist with families of older persons who have died. A 60-year-old widow may face the same trauma at the loss of her husband as a 30-year-old widow would, and the same is true for widowers. Perhaps the shock and change are even greater because of the longer marriage and because of the long years of emotional and economic dependence.

There are also a number of practical matters that many families must face. For example, large numbers of families have virtually no savings to use in supporting themselves once the breadwinner has died. Social Security is not available to younger widows and older children, both of whom may have been supported nicely but precariously on the monthly income of the breadwinner. These great problems associated with economic and social changes may be reduced by the services of social workers, who can help families locate alternate financial resources or modify their living patterns to conform to reduced incomes.

The Social Worker as a Member of the Team

The best assistance social workers can provide to the dying is indirect. That is, they can serve the dying as members of teams of treatment specialists. While dying in itself is a physical phenomenon, it always has its social components. Physicians, nurses, psychologists, clergymen, and others dealing with the dying patient and his family, as well as the families of persons who have died, need to understand and work with these social components. Social workers can contribute to their knowledge as part of the team effort. Social workers can be an important part of the treatment team dealing with dying persons and with death.

Macroplanning

Much of the foregoing discussion has dealt with the microlevel aspects of death and dying, the ways social workers may serve individuals and their families when death and its consequences are being faced.

There are, however, macrolevel considerations as well. Probably not enough general programs dealing with death are available. Not enough services are designed to provide guidance in dealing with the problems of the dying and those who face the deaths of those around them. There are inadequate resources to which they may turn for assistance and guidance. We need more information on death—not just the simple demographic facts of death but the emotional phenomena and the social problems that arise because of it. There is a need for social research on death and dying and for programs in mental health and family service agencies dealing specifically with death. There could be groups of dying persons and of their family members receiving social work services. Groups of people who have recently experienced death in their own families might also be excellent vehicles for helping with the problems related to death. Broad educational programs on death might also meet major needs. Our social welfare services are willing to prepare parents, through family life education programs, for the births of their children, for the facts of marriage, and for retirement. But few educational programs deal with death and dying. Perhaps such programs of education and service in our communities are needed.

Conclusions

It is clear that social workers have many roles to play in death and dying—from counseling with dying persons to planning educational programs for the community.

It is also clear that more needs to be known to meet the needs of those who are dying and those who play other roles in the lives of the dying. Social workers now make and have additional contributions to make in these areas.

But we need to know and learn more about death and dying. We need to confront the phenomena of death and dying directly because they cannot be neglected in a profession that deals with the social components of human existence.

Reference

Kübler-Ross, E. 1970. On *Death and Dying*. New York: Macmillan Company.

READING 7.2

The Ritual Drama of Mutual Pretense / Barney G.
Glaser and Anselm L. Strauss "Make-believe" is a part of every child's life. In this selection Glaser and Strauss show that dying patients and hospital staff often co-operate in pretense that ignores the realities of dying and death.

When patient and staff both know that the patient is dying but pretend otherwise—when both agree to act as if he were going to live—then a context of mutual pretense exists. Either party can initiate his share of the context; it ends when one side cannot, or will not, sustain the pretense any longer.

The mutual-pretense awareness context is perhaps less visible, even to its participants, than the closed, open, and suspicion contexts, because the interaction involved tends to be more subtle. In some hospital services, however, it is the predominant context. One nurse who worked on an intensive care unit remarked about an unusual patient who had announced he was going to die: "I haven't had to cope with this very often. I may know they are going to die, and the patient knows it, but (usually) he's just not going to let you know that he knows."

Once we visited a small Catholic hospital where medical and nursing care for the many dying patients was efficiently organized. The staff members were supported in their difficult work by a powerful philosophy—that they were doing everything possible for the patient's comfort—but generally did not talk with patients about death. This setting brought about frequent mutual pretense. This awareness context is also predominant in such settings as country hospitals, where elderly patients of low socioeconomic status are sent to die; patient and staff are well aware of imminent death but each tends to go silently about his own business.[1] Yet, as we shall see, sometimes the mutual pretense context is neither silent nor unnegotiated.

The same kind of ritual pretense is enacted in many situations apart from illness. A charming example occurs when a child announces that he is now a storekeeper, and that his mother should buy something at this store. To carry out his

Reprinted by permission from Barney G. Glaser and Anselm L. Strauss, *Awareness of Dying* (Chicago: Aldine Publishing Company); copyright 1965 by Barney G. Glaser and Anselm L. Strauss.

[1] Robert Kastenbaum has reported that Cushing Hospital, "a Public Medical Institution for the care and custody of the elderly" in Framingham, Massachusetts, "patient and staff members frequently have an implicit mutual understanding with regard to death . . . institutional dynamics tend to operate against making death 'visible' and a subject of open communication. . . . Elderly patients often behave as though they appreciated the unspoken feelings of the staff members and were attempting to make their demise as acceptable and unthreatening as possible." This observation is noted in Robert Kastenbaum, "The Interpersonal Context of Death in a Geriatric Institution," abstract of paper presented at the Seventeenth Annual Scientific Meeting, Gerontological Society (Minneapolis: October 29–31, 1964).

fiction, delicately cooperative action is required. The mother must play seriously, and when the episode has run its natural course, the child will often close it himself with a rounding-off gesture, or it may be concluded by an intruding outside event or by the mother. Quick analysis of this little game of pretense suggests that either player can begin; that the other must then play properly; that realistic (nonfictional) action will destroy the illusion and end the game; that the specific action of the game must develop during interaction; and that eventually the make-believe ends or is ended. Little familial games or dramas of this kind tend to be continual, though each episode may be brief.

For contrast, here is another example that pertains to both children and adults. At the circus, when a clown appears, all but the youngest children know that the clown is not real. But both he and his audience must participate, if only symbolically, in the pretense that he is a clown. The onlookers need do no more than appreciate the clown's act, but if they remove themselves too far, by examining the clown's technique too closely, let us say, then the illusion will be shattered. The clown must also do his best to sustain the illusion by clever acting, by not playing too far "out of character." Ordinarily nobody addresses him as if he were other than the character he is pretending to be. That is, everybody takes him seriously, at face value. And unless particular members return to see the circus again, the clown's performance occurs only once, beginning and ending according to a prearranged schedule.

Our two simple examples of pretense suggest some important features of the particular awareness context to which we shall devote this [discussion]. The make-believe in which patient and hospital staff engage resembles the child's game much more than the clown's act. It has no institutionalized beginning and ending comparable to the entry and departure of the clown: either the patient or the staff must signal the beginning of their joint pretense. Both parties must act properly if the pretense is to be maintained, because, as in the child's game, the illusion created is fragile, and easily shattered by incongruous "realistic" acts. But if either party slips slightly, the other may pretend to ignore the slip.[2] Each episode between the patient and a staff member tends to be brief, but the mutual pretense is done with terrible seriousness, for the stakes are very high.[3]

---

[2] I. Bensman and I. Garver, "Crime and Punishment in the Factory," in A. Gouldner and H. Gouldner (eds.). Modern Society (New York: Harcourt, Brace and World, 1963), pp. 593–96.

[3] A German Communist, Alexander Weissberg, accused of spying during the great period of Soviet spy trials, has written a fascinating account of how he and many other persons collaborated with the Soviet government in an elaborate pretense, carried on for the benefit of the outside world. The stakes were high for the accused (their lives) as well as for the Soviet. Weissberg's narrative also illustrated how uninitiated interactants must be coached into their roles and how they must be cued into the existence of the pretense context where they do not recognize it. See Alexander Weissberg. The Accused (New York: Simon and Schuster, 1951).

Initiating the Pretense

This particular awareness context cannot exist, of course, unless both the patient and staff are aware that he is dying. Therefore all the structural conditions which contribute to the existence of open awareness (and which are absent in closed and suspicion awareness) contribute also to the existence of mutual pretense. In addition, at least one interactant must indicate a desire to pretend that the patient is not dying and the other must agree to the pretense, acting accordingly.

A prime structural condition in the existence and maintenance of mutual pretense is that unless the patient initiates conversation about his impending death, no staff member is required to talk about it with him. As typical Americans, they are unlikely to initiate such a conversation; and as professionals they have no rules commanding them to talk about death with the patient, unless he desires it. In turn, he may wish to initiate such conversation, but surely neither hospital rules nor common convention urges it upon him. Consequently, unless either the aware patient or the staff members breaks the silence by words or gestures, a mutual pretense rather than an open awareness context will exist: as, for example, when the physician does not care to talk about death, and the patient does not press the issue though he clearly does recognize his terminality.

The patient, of course, is more likely than the staff members to refer openly to his death, thereby inviting them, explicitly or implicitly, to respond in kind. If they seem unwilling, he may decide they do not wish to confront opening the fact of his death, and then he may, out of tact or genuine empathy for their embarrassment or distress, keep his silence. He may misinterpret their responses, of course, but . . . he probably has correctly read their reluctance to refer openly to his impending death.

Staff members, in turn, may give him opportunities to speak of his death, if they deem it wise, without their directly or obviously referring to the topic. But if he does not care to act or talk as if he were dying, then they will support his pretense. In doing so, they have in effect, accepted a complementary assignment of status— they will act with pretense toward his pretense. (If they have misinterpreted his reluctance to act openly, then they have assigned, rather than accepted, a complementary status.)

Two related professional rationales permit them to engage in the pretense. One is that if the patient wishes to pretend, it may well be best for his health, and if and when the pretense finally fails him, all concerned can act more realistically. A secondary rationale is that perhaps they can give him better medical and nursing care if they do not have to face him so openly. In addition . . . they can rely on common tact to justify their part in the pretense. Ordinarily, Americans believe that any individual may live—and die—as he chooses, so long as he does not interfere with others' activities, or, in this case, so long as proper care can be given him.

To illustrate the way these silent bargains are initiated and maintained, we quote from an interview with a special nurse. She had been assigned to a patient before he became terminal, and she was more apt than most personnel to encourage his talking openly, because as a graduate student in a nursing class that emphasized psychological care, she had more time to spend with her patient than a regular floor nurse. Here is the exchange between interviewer and nurse:

Interviewer: Did he talk about his cancer or his dying?

Nurse: Well, no, he never talked about it. I never heard him use the word cancer. . . .

Interviewer: Did he indicate that he knew he was dying?

Nurse: Well, I got that impression, yes. . . . It wasn't really openly, but I think the day that his roommate said he should get up and start walking, I felt that he was a little bit antagonistic. He said what his condition was, that he felt very, very ill that moment.

Interviewer: He never talked about leaving the hospital?

Nurse: Never.

Interviewer: Did he talk about his future at all?

Nurse: Not a thing. I never heard a word. . . .

Interviewer: You said yesterday that he was more or less isolated, because the nurses felt that he was hostile. But they have dealt with patients like this many times. You said they stayed away from him.

Nurse: Well, I think at the very end. You see, this is what I meant by isolation . . . we don't communicate with them. I didn't, except when I did things for him. I think you expect somebody to respond to, and if they're very ill we don't. . . . I talked it over with my instructor, mentioning things that I could probably have done; for instance, this isolation, I should have communicated with him. . . .

Interviewer: You think that since you knew he was going to die, and you half suspected that he knew it too, or more than half; do you think that his understanding grew between you in any way?

Nurse: I believe so. . . . I think it's kind of hard to say but when I came in the room, even when he was very ill, he'd rather look at me and try to give a smile, and gave me the impression that he accepted. . . . I think this is one reason why I feel I should have communicated with him . . . and this is why I feel he was rather isolated. . . .

From the nurse's account, it is difficult to tell whether the patient wished to talk openly about his death, but was rebuffed; or whether he initiated the pretense and the nurse accepted his decision. But it is remarkable how a patient can flash cues to the staff about his own dread knowledge, inviting the staff to talk about his destiny, while the nurses and physicians decide that it is better not to talk too openly with him about his condition lest he "go to pieces." The patient, as remarked earlier, picks up these signals of unwillingness, and the mutual pretense context has been initiated. A specific and obvious instance is this: an elderly patient, who had lived a full and satisfying life, wished to round it off by talking about his impending death. The nurses retreated before this prospect, as did his wife, reproving him, saying he should not think or talk about such morbid matters. A hospital chaplain finally intervened, first by listening to the patient himself, then by inducing the nurses and the wife to do likewise, or at least to acknowledge more openly that the man was dying. He was not successful with all the nurses.

The staff members are more likely to sanction a patient's pretense, than his family's. The implicit rule is that though the patient need not be forced to speak of his dying, or to act as if he were dying, his kin should face facts. After all, they will have to live with the facts after his death. Besides, staff members usually find it less difficult to talk about dying with the family. Family members are not inevitably drawn into open discussion, but the likelihood is high, particularly since they themselves are likely to initiate discussion or at least to make gestures of awareness.

Sometimes, however, pretense protects the family member temporarily against too much grief, and the staff members against too immediate a scene. This may occur when a relative has just learned about the impending death and the nurse controls the ensuing scene by initiating temporary pretense. The reverse situation also occurs: a newly arrived nurse discovers the patient's terminality, and the relative smooths over the nurse's distress by temporary pretense.

The Pretense Interaction

An intern whom we observed during our field work suspected that the patient he was examining had cancer, but he could not discover where it was located. The patient previously had been told that she probably had cancer, and she was now at this teaching hospital for that reason. The intern's examination went on for some time. Yet neither he nor she spoke about what he was searching for, nor in any way suggested that she might be dying. We mention this episode to contrast it with the more extended interactions. . . . These have an episodic quality—personnel enter and leave the patient's room, or he occasionally emerges and encounters them—but their extended duration means that special effort is required to prevent their breaking down, and that the interactants must work hard to construct and maintain their mutual pretense. By contrast, in a formally staged play, although the actors have to construct and maintain a performance, making it credible to their audience, they are not required to write the script themselves. The situation that involves a terminal patient is much more like a masquerade party, where one masked actor plays carefully to another as long as they are together, and the total drama actually emerges from their joint creative effort.

A masquerade, however, has more extensive resources to sustain it than those the hospital situation provides. Masqueraders wear masks, hiding their facial expressions: even if they "break up" with silent laughter (as a staff member may "break down" with sympathy), this fact is concealed. Also, according to the rules ordinarily governing masquerades, each actor chooses his own status, his "character," and this makes his role in the constructed drama somewhat easier to play. He may even have played similar parts before. But terminal patients usually have had no previous experience with their pretended status, and not all personnel have had much experience. In a masquerade, when the drama fails it can be broken off, each actor moving along to another partner: but in the hospital the pretenders (especially the patient) have few comparable opportunities.

Both situations share one feature—the extensive use of props for sustaining the crucial illusion. In the masquerade, the props include not only masks but clothes and other costuming, as well as the setting where the masquerade takes place. In the hospital interaction, props also abound. Patients dress for the part of not-dying patient, including careful attention to grooming, and to hair and makeup by female patients. The terminal patient may also fix up his room so that it looks and feels "just like home," an activity that supports his enactment of normalcy. Nurses may respond to these props with explicit appreciation—"how lovely your hair looks this morning"—or even help to establish them, as by doing the patient's hair. We remember one elaborate pretense ritual involving a husband and wife who had won the nurses' sympathy. The husband simply would not recognize that his already comatose wife was approaching death, so each morning the nurses carefully prepared her for his visit, dressing her for the occasion and making certain that she looked as beautiful as possible. The staff, of course, has its own props to support its ritual prediction that the patient is going to get well: thermometers, baths, fresh sheets, and meals on time! Each party utilizes these props as he sees fit, thereby helping to create the pretense anew. But when a patient wishes to demonstrate that he is finished with life, he may drive the nurses wild by refusing to cooperate in the daily routines of hospital life—that is, he refuses to allow the nurses to use their props. Conversely, when the personnel wish to indicate how things are with him, they may begin to omit some of those routines.

During the pretense episodes, both sides play according to the rules implicit in the interaction. Although neither the staff nor patient may recognize these rules as such, certain tactics are fashioned around them, and the action is partly constrained by them. One rule is that dangerous topics should generally be avoided. The most obviously dangerous topic is the patient's death; another is events that will happen afterwards. Of course, both parties to the pretense are supposed to follow the avoidance rule.

There is, however, a qualifying rule: Talk about dangerous topics is permissible as long as neither party breaks down. Thus, a patient refers to the distant future, as if it were his to talk about. He talks about his plans for his family, as if he would be there to share their consummation. He and the nurses discuss today's events— such as his treatments—as if they had implications for a real future, when he will have recovered from his illness. And some of his brave or foolhardy activities may signify a brave show of pretense, as when he bathes himself or insists on tottering to the toilet by himself. The staff in turn permits his activity. (Two days before he returned to the hospital to die, one patient insisted that his wife allow him to travel downtown to keep a speaking engagement, and to the last he kept up a lively conversation with a close friend about a book they were planning to write together.)

A third rule, complementing the first two, is that each actor should focus determinedly on appropriately safe topics. It is customary to talk about the daily routines—eating (the food was especially good or bad), and sleeping (whether one slept well or poorly last night). Complaints and their management help pass the time. So do minor personal confidences, and chatter about events on the ward. Talk about physical symptoms is safe enough if confined to the symptoms themselves, with no implied references to death. A terminal patient and a staff member may safely talk, and at length, about his disease so long as they skirt its fatal significance. And there are many genuinely safe topics having to do with movies and movie stars, politics, fashions—with everything, in short, that signifies that life is going on "as usual."

A fourth interactional rule is that when something happens, or is said, that tends to expose the fiction that both parties are attempting to sustain, then each must pretend that nothing has gone awry. Just as each has carefully avoided calling attention to the true situation, each now must avert his gaze from the unfortunate intrusion. Thus, a nurse may take special pains and announce herself before entering a patient's room so as not to surprise him at his crying. If she finds him crying, she may ignore it or convert it into an innocuous event with a skillful comment or gesture—much like the tactful gentleman who, having stumbled upon a woman in his bathtub, is said to have casually closed the bathroom door, murmuring "Pardon me, sir." The mutuality of the pretense is illustrated by the way a patient who cannot control a sudden expression of great pain will verbally discount its significance, while the nurse in turn goes along with his pretense. Or she may brush aside or totally ignore a major error in his portrayal, as when he refers spontaneously to his death. If he is tempted to admit impulsively his terminality, she may, again, ignore his impulsive remarks or obviously misinterpret them. Thus, pretense is piled upon pretense to conceal or minimize interactional slips.

Clearly then, each party to the ritual pretense shares responsibility for maintaining it. The major responsibility may be transferred back and forth, but each party must support the other's temporary dominance in his own action. This is true even when conversation is absolutely minimal, as in some hospitals where patients take no particular pains to signal awareness of their terminality, and the staff makes no special gestures to convey its own awareness. The pretense interaction in this case is greatly simplified, but it is still discernible. Whenever a staff member is so indelicate, or so straight-forward, as to act openly as if a terminal patient were dying, or if the patient does so himself, then the pretense vanishes. If neither wishes to destroy the fiction, however, then each must strive to keep the situation "normal."[4]

---

[4] A close reading of John Gunther's poignant account of his young son's last months

The Transition to Open Awareness

A mutual pretense context that is not sustained can only change to an open awareness context. (Either party, however, may again initiate the pretense context and sometimes get cooperation from the other.) The change can be sudden, when either patient or staff distinctly conveys that he has permanently abandoned the pretense. Or the change to the open context can be gradual: nurses, and relatives, too, are familiar with patients who admit to terminality more openly on some days than they do on other days, when pretense is dominant, until finally pretense vanishes altogether. Sometimes the physician skillfully paces his interaction with a patient, leading the patient finally to refer openly to his terminality and to leave behind the earlier phase of pretense.

Pretense generally collapses when certain conditions make its maintenance increasingly difficult. These conditions have been foreshadowed in our previous discussion. Thus, when the patient cannot keep from expressing his increasing pain, or his suffering grows to the point that he is kept under heavy sedation, then the enactment of pretense becomes more difficult, especially for him.

Again, neither patient nor staff may be able to avoid bringing impending death into the open if radical physical deterioration sets in, the staff because it has a tough job to do, and the patient for other reasons, including fright and panic. Sometimes a patient breaks his pretense for psychological reasons, as when he discovers that he cannot face death alone, or when a chaplain convinces him that it is better to bring things out into the open than to remain silent. (Sometimes, however, a patient may find such a sympathetic listener in the chaplain that he can continue his pretense with other personnel). Sometimes he breaks the pretense when it no longer makes sense in light of obvious physical deterioration.

Here is a poignant episode during which a patient dying with great pain and obvious bodily deterioration finally abandoned her pretense with a nurse:

There was a long silence. Then the patient asked, "After I get home from the nursing home will you visit me?" I asked if she wanted me to. "Yes, Mary, you know we could go on long drives together. . . . " She had a faraway look in her eyes as if daydreaming about all the places she would visit and all the things we could do together. This continued for some time. Then I asked, "Do you think you will be able to drive your car again?" She looked at me, "Mary, I know I'm daydreaming; I know I am going to die." Then she cried, and said, "This is terrible, I never thought it would be this way."

In short, when a patient finds it increasingly difficult to hang onto a semblance of his former healthy self and begins to become a person who is visibly dying, both he and the staff are increasingly prone to say so openly, whether by word or gesshows that the boy maintained a sustained and delicately balanced mutual pretense with his parents, physicians and nurses. John Gunther. Death, Be Not Proud (New York: Harper and Bros., 1949). Also see Bensman and Gaver, op. cit.

ture. Sometimes, however, a race occurs between a patient's persistent pretense and his becoming comatose or his actual death—a few more days of sentience or life, and either he or the staff would have dropped the pretense.

Yet, a contest may also ensue when only one side wishes to keep up the pretense. When a patient openly displays his awareness but shows it unacceptably, as by apathetically "giving up," the staff or family may try to reinstate the pretense. Usually the patient then insists on open recognition of his own impending death, but sometimes he is persuaded to return to the pretense. For instance, one patient finally wished to talk openly about death, but her husband argued against its probability, although he knew better: so after several attempts to talk openly, the patient obligingly gave up the contest. The reverse situation may also occur: the nurses begin to give the patient every opportunity to die with a maximum of comfort—as by cutting down on normal routines—thus signaling that he should no longer pretend, but the patient insists on putting up a brave show and so the nurses capitulate.

We would complicate our analysis unduly if we did more than suggest that, under such conditions, the pretense ritual sometimes resembles Ptolemy's cumbersomely patched astronomical system, with interactants pretending to pretend to pretend! We shall only add that when nurses attempt to change the pretense context into an open context, they generally do this "on their own" and not because of any calculated ward standards or specific orders from an attending physician. And the tactics they use to get the patient to refer openly to his terminality are less tried and true than the more customary tactics for forcing him to pretend.

Consequences of Mutual Pretense

For the patient, the pretense context can yield a measure of dignity and considerable privacy, though it may deny him the closer relationships with staff members and family members that sometimes occur when he allows them to participate in his open acceptance of death. And if they initiate and he accepts the pretense, he may have nobody with whom to talk although he might profit greatly from talk. (One terminal patient told a close friend, who told us, that when her family and husband insisted on pretending that she would recover, she suffered from the isolation, feeling as if she were trapped in cotton batting.) For the family—especially more distant kin—the pretense context can minimize embarrassment and other interactional strains: but for closer kin, franker concourse may have many advantages.

Oscillation between contexts of open awareness and mutual pretense can also cause interactional strains. We once observed a man persuading his mother to abandon her apathy—she had permanently closed her eyes, to the staff's great distress—and "try hard to live." She agreed finally to resume the pretense, but later relapsed into apathy. The series of episodes caused some anguish to both family and patient, as well as to the nurses. When the patient initiates the mutual pretense, staff members are likely to feel relieved. Yet the consequent stress of either maintaining the pretense or changing it to open awareness sometimes may be considerable. Again, both the relief and the stress affect nurses more than medical personnel, principally because the latter spend less time with patients.

But whether staff or patient initiates the ritual of pretense, maintaining it creates a characteristic ward mood of cautious serenity. A nurse once told us of a cancer hospital where each patient understood that everyone there had cancer, including himself, but the rules of tact, buttressed by staff silence, were so strong that few patients talked openly about anyone's condition. The consequent atmosphere was probably less serene than when only a few patients are engaged in mutual pretense, but even one such patient can affect the organizational mood, especially if the personnel become "involved"with him.

A persistent context of mutual pretense profoundly affects the more permanent aspects of hospital organization as well. (This often occurs at county and city hospitals.) Imagine what a hospital service would be like if all terminal patients were unacquainted with their terminality, of if all were perfectly open about their awareness—whether they accepted or rebelled against their fate. When closed awareness generally prevails the personnel must guard against disclosure, but they need not organize themselves as a team to handle continued pretense and its sometimes stressful breakdown. Also, a chief organizational consequence of the mutual pretense context is that it eliminates any possibility that staff members might "work with" patients psychologically, on a self-conscious professional basis. This consequence was strikingly evident at the small Catholic hospital referred to a few pages ago. It is also entirely possible that a ward mood of tension can be set when (as a former patient once told us) a number of elderly dying patients continually communicate to each other their willingness to die, but the staff members persistently insist on the pretense that the patients are going to recover. On the other hand, the prevailing ward mood accompanying mutual pretense tends to be more serene—or at least less obviously tense—than when open suspicion awareness is dominant.

part THREE

program planning and development for older adults

Human services workers learn quickly after they begin working with older adults that the kinds of direct services described in Part Two only deal with some of the problems and some of the solutions for the aging. Often more important are the programs that are planned and developed to cope with the difficulties of growing old in America.

Part Three describes some of the ways in which human services workers engage in planning and developing programs through voluntary and government organizations. It is these programs that provide the resources for helping older people. Among those resources are the workers who serve the elderly. Skill in helping older people through program planning is one of the more important of those that human services workers need to develop.

CHAPTER 8
THE OLDER AMERICANS ACT: THE STRUCTURE OF AGING SERVICES IN THE UNITED STATES

Most significant for older American services and programs is the Older Americans Act, first passed in 1966, which set up the whole national program for senior citizens. For the three decades, services were provided to the elderly with federal funds through the Social Security Act programs. However, the OAA for the first time gave a special emphasis to the aging and established the Federal Administration on Aging.

There is now a United States Commissioner on Aging who supervises and gives voice to the programs serving older people. Over $1 billion each year is appropriated under the Older Americans Act. With those funds, there are now 57 state agencies that deal with aging and these, in turn, finance and direct 660 area agencies on aging.

The Senior Center

The area agencies on aging supervise and finance thousands of senior centers and similar programs throughout the United States. These senior centers provide nutritional services, such as served meals, several times each week to those able to come to the centers and deliver meals to many who cannot.

In many cases, the local centers also have services that are directed to elderly persons who live in the area. These services, which are often referred to as "outreach," provide for human services workers to go into the homes of the elderly clients and determine what they need to maintain and enhance their health as well as their social and psychological functioning. They determine the economic well-being of the clients in order to know how much, if anything, the recipient of meals should pay for the served or home-delivered food. They also determine whether or not the client may need referral to or the assistance of other kinds of services such as mental health counseling, home health care, or any of the other kinds of help discussed in this book.

Within the senior centers, there is typically a high degree of activity for the participants. For example, the center, ideally located in the neighborhood of a large number of older people who need assistance from the program, may maintain a library, a program of current events discussions, arts and crafts activities, physical education services including exercise and some sports, games such as checkers, chess, and bingo, and periodic health-screening services such as blood pressure checks, for all the participants. Many of these kinds of services are discussed in chapter 5. In this case, the senior center is the location where those activities take place.

Advocacy

The Older Americans Act also helps make possible many of the advocacy activities discussed in chapter 11. Thanks to the national visibility given the problems of aging because of the Act and the programs and offices established under it, many elderly people are now assisted when they are faced with consumer affairs problems, abuse or neglect in their homes or in long term care facilities, by advocates for the elderly who are employed by the state agencies on aging or in local community senior adult programs or government bodies.

Research and Training

Studying about and finding ways to help overcome the problems and needs of older adults is also a function of the OAA. Colleges and universities as well as private research corporations are granted funds to study specific issues facing older people so that changes can be made in health and mental health practices and in policies governing programs for older people.

The OAA also makes funds available to educate and train human services workers with the aged so they can more effectively serve their clients. Many of those who have been and are being trained work in the senior centers. Others receive scholarships in order to complete degrees in fields such as gerontology, nursing, psychology, and social work, as a means of providing skilled professional workers to the agencies and organizations that work with older people.

Other Functions of the OAA

The Older Americans Act also helps arrange for commodity foods from the U.S. Department of Agriculture to reach older people through senior centers. That is the basis for the very low-cost daily meals available to senior citizens.

Transportation is also a typical program of the senior centers, made available through OAA funds. For many senior adults, the bus or van from their neighborhoods to the center make it possible for them to have a nutritious, hot meal at least once a day.

The OAA also makes money available to organize and operate employment programs for the elderly. One of the primary programs is subsidized community service employment. Those efforts provide senior citizen help for government and other community efforts to help children, other older people, and to assist with the regular functions of organizations such as professional services, clerical work, financial record-keeping, and maintenance. The OAA funds are targeted to keeping older people actively involved in their communities and to also help raise the level of services in those communities through the efforts of older people.

The federal aging program also takes responsibility for organizing and directing the White House Conferences on Aging, which occur every ten years. These conferences, which are held in Washington, D.C., have had a major impact on the President and the Congress. They involve thousands of older people as well as thousands of human services administrators and workers who serve the aging. These conferences study the problems faced by older people and make recommendations for overcoming them. Many observers believe that the White House conferences have led to the passage of many laws benefiting older people. Those conferences are one of the main reasons that older people now have Medicare, senior centers, advocacy services, transportation, employment programs, and much of the rest of the large additions to the well-being of older people that have developed in the past thirty years. The next White House Conference on Aging is scheduled for 1991. It should have some major impact on the future of aging services. (See the discussion later in this chapter.)

The following material on the development of the Older Americans Act is taken from a 1986 report of the United States Senate Special Committee on Aging, which was published in 1987. It details some of the ways in which the Act has helped older people and some of the hopes that the Senate Committee has for the future of aging programs in the United States.

OLDER AMERICANS ACT

OVERVIEW

Since its enactment, the OAA has evolved from a program of small grants and research projects to a network of 57 State Units of aging, over 660 area agencies on aging, and thousands of community organizations providing supportive social and nutritional services to older adults. At the same time, appropriations for programs under the act have increased from $6.5 million in fiscal year 1966 to $1.2 billion for fiscal year 1987.

Congress has reaffirmed its support for programs under the Older Americans Act on 11 occasions through passage of various amendments and reauthorization action. The most recent reauthorization of the act occurred during the 1984 fiscal year. Responding to time pressures prior to adjournment, as well as a pervasive feeling that Older Americans Act programs were operating effectively, Congress made only minor adjustments to the act. The new amendments in the act were signed into law by President Reagan on October 9, 1984 (Public Law 98-459). (For a full discussion of the 1984 amendments, see Developments in Aging: 1984, vol. 1.)

Fiscal year 1986 was legislatively uneventful for the Older Americans Act [OAA], but Congress began the 1987 reauthorization process with hearings in both the Senate and House. Congress continued to show its strong support of the OAA programs by reinstating the presequestration funding levels in the budget process, and by increasing appropriate levels for title III support and nutrition services programs.

There remains, however, growing concern from some OAA loyalists, both service providers and recipients, that deficit reduction actions are a sign that very few programs will escape the budget cutting ax in the months and years ahead. Program cuts could result in pressure to prioritize titles and programs within the OAA, and to target services. To date, the close link between OAA dollars and direct services that millions of older Americans receive appears to have helped to protect OAA funding.

A. BACKGROUND

1. History of the Older Americans Act

For the past 21 years, the Older Americans Act has served as the cornerstone of Federal involvement in a wide array of community services to older persons. Created during a time of rising societal concern for the needs of the poor, the act marked the beginning of a categorical approach to programs specifically designed to meet the social and human needs of the elderly. The act itself was one of a series of Federal initiatives that were part of President Johnson's Great Society programs. These legislative initiatives grew out of a concern for the large percentage of older Americans who were impoverished, and a belief that greater Federal involvement was needed beyond the income transfer and health programs. Although older persons could receive services under a multiplicity of other Federal programs, the act became the first major vehicle for the organization and delivery of community-based social services to the elderly.

The Older Americans Act followed on the heels of a similar but somewhat more expansive grouping of social service programs initiated under the Economic Opportunity Act of 1964. With a similar conceptual framework to that embodied in the Economic Opportunity Act, the Older Americans Act was established on the premise that decentralization of authority and the use of local control over policy and program decisions would create a more responsive service system at the community level.

When first enacted in 1965, the OAA established a series of broad policy objectives designed to meet the needs of older persons. These objectives, however, lacked both legislative authority and adequate appropriations to be truly effective. Despite its limited scope and funding—providing for a Federal Administration on Aging and making minimal grants to State units on aging—the act established a structure through which the Congress would later expand aging services.

Funding for the OAA grew slowly during the 1960's, but during the 1970's Congress followed up on improvements in income transfer programs with significant modifications in services to the elderly. In 1973, for instance, Congress enacted significant expansions in the services provided under the Older Americans Act to provide for the establishment of area agencies on aging, and in 1974 created the national nutrition program for the elderly. Fiscal years 1978 and 1980 saw further improvements in the level of financial support directed toward Older Americans Act programs, the development of the structures for providing community-based services [AAA's], and the added emphasis on the provisions of certain priority services—access, in-home and legal services.

This expansion trend continued until the early 1980's when, in response to the Reagan Administration's policies to cut the size and scope of many Federal programs, the growth of overall OAA spending was slowed and, for some programs, was reversed. Major budget cutting emphasis during this time, however, was placed on reductions in the income transfer and health programs (i.e., Medicare and Medicaid). The focus on the larger money items helped deflect budget cutting measures aimed at programs such as the Older Americans Act, although they were not entirely untouched. For example, between fiscal years 1981 and 1982, title IV funding for training, research, and discretionary programs in aging was reduced by approximately 50 percent. In addition, appropriations for title III, supportive services, and congregate and home-delivered meals (excluding the U.S. Department of Agriculture program), declined slightly from 1981 to 1982, from $624.7 million to $606.6 million. From 1983 through 1985 funding has increased at an annual rate less than the rate of inflation. The fiscal year 1987 appropriation is 6.4 percent higher than the fiscal year 1986 level, and the Congressional Budget Office forecast for the rate of inflation in 1987 is 4 percent. Widespread congressional support for other OAA programs, especially nutrition and senior employment, has served to protect them.

Congress has rejected some Reagan Administration proposals for reductions in Older Americans Act programs in various budget submissions since 1981, most notably the administration's attempt in fiscal year 1983 to eliminate the community service employment program under title V. Congress has also rejected administration proposals to consolidate appropriations for the supportive services, and congregate and home-delivered nutrition service components under title III, and to transfer the U.S. Department of Agriculture [USDA] commodity program from the Department of Agriculture to the Administration on Aging [AoA]. (The 1987 budget submission did not contain proposals to consolidate title III services or to transfer the commodity program to (AoA). With respect to the title IV research, training, and demonstration program, the administration's fiscal year

1987 budget reduction request of $12.5 million was a more moderate reduction request than in previous years. In fiscal years 1984 and 1985 the request for this program was $5 million.

Despite administration efforts, OAA programs have been spared funding reductions experienced by other social services programs. Table 1 shows that appropriations for the period fiscal year 1980 to fiscal year 1987 have increased from $993 million to $1.2 billion. This represents a 20-percent increase. The only funding decreases occurred from 1981 to 1982, and from 1983 through 1985 funding increased at an annual rate less than the rate of inflation. The fiscal year 1987 appropriation, however, is 6.4 percent higher than the fiscal year 1986 level. The decline in funding levels during the early 1980's was partially due to the rather substantial cuts in the title IV program for research, training, and demonstration projects. Title IV declined by some 59 percent during the 1980 to 1982 period. Title III supportive and nutrition services also declined slightly from 1981 to 1982.

Table 1.—*Older Americans Act Appropriations,[1] 1980-87*

Fiscal Year:	Millions
1980	$993
1981	1,040
1982	1,006
1983	1,098
1984	1,124
1985	[2]1,155
1986	1,165
1986 (after sequestration)	[2]1,117
1987 (administration's proposal)	1,147
1987	1,188

[1]Includes appropriations for all titles, except Section 311 USDA commodities program for which obligations of funds as shown in Budget Appendices are included.
[2]Includes fiscal year 1986 urgent supplemental funds for the USDA elderly commodity program.

Over the years, the essential mission of the Older Americans Act has remained very much the same: Provide a wide array of social and community services to those older persons in the greatest economic and social need in order to foster maximum independence. The key element in the program has been to help maintain and support older persons in their homes and communities to avoid unnecessary and costly institutionalization.

States and area agencies on aging constitute the administrative structure for programs under the act. In addition to funding specific services, they have broad responsibilities to act as advocates on behalf of older persons and to plan for the effective development of a service system that will best meet these needs. Beyond this mission, and as originally conceived by the Congress, this system was meant to encompass both services funded under the act, and services supported by other Federal, State, and local programs. The concept of resources mobilization and coordination was an important element in the early development of the act.

2. THE OLDER AMERICANS ACT AMENDMENTS OF 1984

The following is a brief description of each title of the Older Americans Act as amended in 1984.

(A) DECLARATION OF OBJECTIVES—TITLE I

Title I sets forth the national objectives for older Americans particularly for improving their income, health, housing, and community services opportunity.

(B) ADMINISTRATION ON AGING AND FEDERAL COUNCIL ON AGING—TITLE II

Title II establishes the Administration on Aging (AoA) within the Department of Health and Human Services (DHHS) and the Federal Council on Aging. The Council was first authorized in the 1973 amendments to the act. Federal Council appropriations reached their height in fiscal year 1976 and declined for most years since that time.

(C) GRANTS FOR STATE AND COMMUNITY PROGRAMS ON AGING— TITLE III

Title III authorizes grants to State agencies on aging to develop a comprehensive and coordinated delivery system for supportive services, nutrition services, and multipurpose senior centers for older persons. This system is intended to assist older persons attain maximum independence in a home environment, to remove individual and social barriers to economic and personal independence, and to provide services and care for the vulnerable elderly. Since original passage of the act in 1965, the title III program has evolved from simply a funding source for social service programs to a planning vehicle for the development of a comprehensive and coordinated service system for older persons. Significant amendments in 1969, 1973, and 1978 broadened the scope of operations and established the basis for a "network" on aging under the title III program umbrella.

The title III nutrition meals, is one of the most visible federally funded social service programs for older persons, and represents about 47 percent of total Older Americans Act funds in fiscal year 1987, including the elderly commodity program. The supportive service component, which funds a variety of social services, such as ombudsman, in-home, legal, and access services, represents about 23 percent of the act's total fiscal year 1987 funding.

Funds for State administration, supportive services, and senior centers, congregate and home-delivered nutrition services are allotted to State agencies on aging based on the State's share of the 60 and over population as compared to all States, with minimum amounts for the territories. State agencies, in turn, award funds to area agencies on aging for administration within specified planning and service areas. Area agencies provide funds to agencies and organizations for the delivery of a wide range of supportive services (with special emphasis on access, in-home, and legal services), and congregate and home-delivered nutrition services. The law requires that preference be given to serving older persons with the greatest social or economic needs with particular attention to low income minority older persons. Means tests as a criterion for participation are prohibited.

State agencies on aging also receive U.S. Department of Agriculture [USDA] commodities or cash in lieu of commodities, to supplement the costs of providing meals under title III. The law requires USDA to provide State agencies an annually programmed level of assistance that is based on the number of meals served with title III funds. The USDA reimbursement is provided on a per meal basis in an amount adjusted for inflation to reflect changes in the Consumer Price Index for food away from home. While the law provides for the distribution of commodities, most States have opted to receive a combination of cash in lieu of commodities as well as commodities to supplement meals provided under the title III program.

Appropriations for title III services and State administration increased by 25 percent for the period 1980-87 (including amounts for USDA commodities). (Excluding amounts for USDA commodities, the increase was 17 percent.) Although Congress appropriated specific amounts for supportive services, and congregate and home-delivered nutrition services, the act allows States to transfer funds between these separate categories. The 1984 amendments to the act increased the ability of States to transfer funds between these separate amounts. The 1984 amendments allow a State to transfer up to 30 percent in fiscal year 1987. In addition, the act allows States to transfer funds between the congregate and home-delivered nutrition service categories. In recent years States have increasingly shifted funds between these three separately appropriated amounts, with a notable shift of funds from the congregate nutrition program to other service components. For example, in fiscal year 1986, $47 million was transferred from the congregate nutrition appropriation to other title III services. The 1984 amendments also changed the manner in which funds for the State administration are made to States by consolidating funds for this purpose under the title III services amounts. Since fiscal year 1985, States do not receive a separate allocation of funds for State administration, but are allowed to use up to 5 percent of their allocation for title III services or $300,000, whichever is greater, for administration.

According to data reported by States to the AoA, the number of supportive service participants has remained virtually the same for the period 1980-85, at approximately 9 million participants each year. The number of meals served, supported by title III as well as other funds available under auspices of the program, increased 37 percent from 167 million in fiscal year 1980 to over 229 million in fiscal year 1986.

(D) TRAINING, RESEARCH, AND DISCRETIONARY PROJECTS AND PROGRAMS—TITLE IV

Title IV of the act authorizes appropriations for training, research, and demonstration programs in the field of aging. Under the training authority, the Commissioner on Aging is required to award grants or enter into contracts for activities related to the recruitment of personnel, in-service training for those employed in aging services, and technical assistance activities. It also authorized grants for multidisciplinary centers of gerontology.

Under the research authority, the Commissioner may support a wide range of projects related to the purpose of the act as well as conduct evaluation activities.

Under the demonstration authority, the Commissioner is authorized to conduct model projects to demonstrate methods of improving or expanding supportive or nutrition services or other services to promote the well-being of older persons. The Commissioner is required to give special consideration to certain projects such as those designed to meet the special needs of the rural elderly and supportive service needs of persons with Alzheimer's disease and other neurological and organic brain disorders.

The Commissioner is required to conduct demonstration projects relating to legal services for older persons. In addition, the Commissioner is authorized to conduct special demonstrations in comprehensive long-term care, projects which would relieve the excessive burdens of high utility and home heating costs, and other projects having national significance.

Appropriations for title IV reached their height in fiscal year 1980 at a level of $54.3 million. This program has experienced the greatest reduction of any Older Americans Act program in recent years, with a decline of 59 percent from the fiscal year 1980 level of $54.3 million to $22.2 million in fiscal year 1982. Appropriations remained at that level in fiscal year 1983 and fiscal year 1984, and increased slightly to $25 million in fiscal year 1985. The fiscal year 1986 funding level fell to $23.9 million as a result of the Gramm-Rudman-Hollings sequestration. The title IV fiscal year 1986 funding level represents about 2 percent of total Older Americans Act funds. In fiscal year 1985 the program supported 300 grants and contracts. An estimated 31,500 students were trained in academic aging programs and 241,000 State and area agency and service provider personnel received in-servicing training.

(E) COMMUNITY SERVICE EMPLOYMENT PROGRAM FOR OLDER AMERICANS—TITLE V

The program's purpose is to subsidize part-time community service jobs for unemployed persons aged 55 and over who have low incomes. The basis for the current program was a demonstration program created during the 1960's under the Economic Opportunity Act [EOA]. Modeled after operation mainstream, a pilot project authorized under title II of the EOA, it was first funded in 1965. In 1967, administrative responsibility for operation mainstream was transferred from the Office of Economic Opportunity to the Department of Labor [DOL] but funding authority continued under the EOA. In 1973 the program was given a statutory basis under the Older Americans Act amendments. The program continues to be administered by DOL, which awards funds to national organizations and to State agencies to operate the program.

Until 1984, the program had seen steady increases in funding and participant enrollment since its inception. In 1974, the first year the program received an appropriation under the Older Americans Act, participant enrollment was 3,800 with an appropriation of $10 million. Appropriations for fiscal year 1986 of $312 million are estimated to support about 61,000 employment positions (to cover the period July 1986-June 1987). (Note: the program is funded on a "forward-funded" basis; that is, funds appropriated for a given fiscal year are to be used beginning on July 1 of that fiscal year and ending on June 30 of the following year.)

Although persons 55 or older are eligible for the program, priority is to be given to placing persons 60 years or older in community service jobs. Their income must not exceed 125 percent of the poverty level guidelines issued by DHHS (in 1986, $6,875 for a 1-person household). Enrollees are paid no less than the Federal or State minimum wage or the local prevailing rate of pay for similar employment, whichever is higher. Participants may work up to 1,300 hours per year and average 20-25 hours per week. For the 1984-85 program year the average hourly wage paid to enrollees was $3.47. In addition to wages, enrollees receive annual physical examinations, personal and job-related counseling, and some job training.

Participants work in a wide variety of community service activities. In the 1984-85 program year, about 61 percent of job placements were in the services to the general community while over 39 percent were in services to the elderly. The program provides substantial support to nutrition programs for the elderly, primarily funded under title III of the Older Americans Act and administered by State and area agencies on aging. About 10.3 percent of the employment opportunities in title V aging services placements were in nutrition services. Other job areas in aging services were in recreation/senior centers and outreach and referral services. In services to the general community, enrollees were placed primarily in education and social service activities.

Funds are allocated to national organizations and to State agencies on aging. National organizations that receive funds are Green Thumb; American Association of Retired Persons; U.S. Department of Agriculture's Forest Service; National Caucus and Center on Black Aged, Inc., Association Nacional Pro Personas Mayores; and the National Urban League. In allotting funds DOL is required to reserve a "hold harmless" amount to enable the national organizations to maintain their 1978 level of activities. No more than 45 percent of funds exceeding the 1978 level of appropriations is to be awarded to national organizations and allocated among States according to a formula which takes into account the number of persons 55 years of age and over and per capita income. The remainder of funds in excess of the 1978 level of appropriations is to be distributed to State agencies on aging according to the same formula. In addition to this formula, appropriations legislation has, in the past, contained requirements regarding the distribution of funds to national organizations and States. Appropriations language has required that national organizations receive 78 percent of funds and State agencies receive 22 percent.

(F) GRANTS FOR INDIAN TRIBES—TITLE VI

The purpose of the title VI program is to promote the delivery of supportive and nutrition services to older Indians which are comparable to services offered to other older persons under title III. The program received its first appropriation in fiscal year 1980. In fiscal year 1986 awards were made to 133 tribal organizations.

(G) OLDER AMERICANS PERSONAL HEALTH EDUCATION AND TRAINING PROGRAM—TITLE VII

The 1984 amendments added a new title to the act which required the Secretary of Health and Human Services, through AoA, to award funds to institutions of higher education to design and implement standardized health education and training programs for older persons. No funds were appropriated for fiscal year 1985, requested for fiscal year 1986 or 1987, or appropriated for either of those years.

WHITE HOUSE CONFERENCE ON AGING—1991

Another issue with which Congress must grapple during the OAA reauthorization process is the future of White House Conferences on Aging. Aging advocates in Washington began to meet to consider the possibilities for a 1991 Conference during the 99th Congress. The reactions to the thought of holding another White House conference seem to be mixed. One of the primary issues to be considered is whether or not a conference would attempt to be all-encompassing or focus on one or more key dilemmas that the aging population will face in the coming decades. For example, should the conference deal primarily with the issue of providing long-term care for the elderly?

In addition, how much money should be dedicated to a conference in light of the budget deficit and the increasing demand for OAA services? Also, how can aging advocates ensure that the conference will not be used to misrepresent the political positions of the administration and to manipulate older Americans and press opportunities? These questions and others will most probably be considered during this year's reauthorization because funding for a 1991 White House Conference on Aging will be incorporated in the bill.

LONG-TERM CARE AND THE OAA

One issue that is bound to surface during the reauthorization process is how to focus more OAA resources on community-based long-term care services. And which community agency or service provider should have the responsibility to provide the necessary case management activities? Debate over the role that area agencies on aging play in case management will continue to cause some friction between OAA advocates.

In addition, the OAA ombudsman program, which is charged with investigating and resolving complaints made by or on behalf of elderly residents of nursing homes and other long-term care facilities is likely to be strengthened during the reauthorization process. Congress will need to sort through numerous bills and proposals that have been put forth during the last few years to improve the program.

MINORITY ELDERLY AND THE OAA

Recent criticism of the ability of the OAA to provide the needed services to many of the most needy minority older adults may help to focus the reauthorization process on the issue of minority group use of OAA funds. As mentioned earlier, there are advocates who believe strongly that the act should be better targeted to the most economically and socially needy older Americans. Declines in the number and proportion of older minority participants in OAA programs have caused concern and a desire to address this situation through legislative initiatives if possible.

Indian elders were the topic of two hearings during the 99th Congress conducted by the Senate Special Committee on Aging. Senator Nickles held a hearing in Oklahoma City which focused on the issue of access to services by older Indians, and the level of responsiveness to the title VI grantees by the Administration on Aging. The need for an Indian Desk at the AoA and the lack of availability of title III services for Indians was considered. Senator Bingaman held a hearing in Santa Fe titled "The Continuum of Health Care for Indian Elders." As the title suggests, the hearing covered a wide range of service delivery and availability issues. Witnesses revealed many of the gaps in crucial services which older Indians, often with few resources, must face. It is likely that legislative initiatives will result from these hearings, and that they may be incorporated in the reauthorization legislation this year.

In addition to the aforementioned issues, the upcoming 1987 reauthorization will probably encompass a review of many programmatic issues, including State and are agency on aging initiatives in community-based long-term care and new ways of handling the pressures created by the Medicare prospective reimbursement system. The case management systems (as defined in the 1984 reauthorization) will also be analyzed.

PROGNOSIS

Fiscal year 1986 marked the 21st anniversary of the Older Americans Act. With the exception of some 1981-82 program reductions, the act has consistently received increased appropriations despite the Reagan Administration's efforts to substantially reduce domestic spending.

The future funding of the Older Americans Act remains promising even in light of the Federal Government's current financial crisis and the corresponding budget-cutting mood in Congress. Although, the Title VII, Older Americans Personal Health Education and Training Program, has not been funded, the title III programs continue to receive small increases in appropriations. As appropriation levels continue to be high percentages of authorization levels, and 1987 brings a focus to the act's excellent accomplishments, it is very likely that reauthorization will expand the already broad-based support for the OAA. It will also give Congress a chance to put its money where its rhetoric is by increasing funding levels once again.

It is possible that many domestic programs will be further reduced between fiscal years 1988 and 1990, but the OAA appears to be safe at this time. If cuts were to be imposed, they would result in the provision of fewer services to the most rapidly growing segment of our population. Such cuts would magnify the claim by some that it is necessary to develop new ways to better focus resources while maintaining the integrity of the OAA approach.

The 100th Congress will almost certainly reauthorize the OAA during the first session. Several reauthorization hearings already took place during the 99th Congress, including a hearing conducted by the Senate Aging Subcommittee of Labor and Human Resources. That hearing, held on August 2, 1986, was designed to identify the main issues on which Congress should focus, and to measure the need for wide-ranging versus fine-tuning changes in the act. The type or scope of changes remain the major question for this year's reauthorization. The process, which could be over as early as late May, could be very exciting if the issues of targeting, use of commodities, the AoA proposal, and minority access to services are seriously considered, or it could be almost a formality if advocates and Congress feel content with the program's status quo.

In sum, the Older Americans Act, which has truly become a major social service initiative, has fared well during the past 11 years, and will continue to do so whether major modifications or fine-tuning proposals are adopted during its reauthorization process this year.

CHAPTER 9
PROGRAM PLANNING FOR OLdER AdULTS

Many programs and services needed by older adults are not part of the existing network of social services. To effectively serve the elderly, it may be necessary to create or develop resources, services, or programs. Program development generally involves **planning**, the systematic process of decision-making through which one makes rational choices among alternative problem solutions. The planning process enables the worker involved in program development to move through a series of steps leading to rational choices about the best way to meet the needs of the older adult. In this chapter we discuss the steps in the planning process—problem identification, problem analysis, involvement of vested interests, program implementation and evaluation—and how they are used in development of programs for the elderly.

Planning for Older Adults

Most of us engage in goal-directed behavior. We act in the present to secure desirable states of affairs in the future; that is planning. For example, many parents begin saving money when their children are infants to ensure their college education. These parents make decisions long before their children are of college age to achieve this goal; that is long-range planning. We also engage in goal-directed behavior on a day-to-day basis. For instance, you may plan at noon to attend a movie in the evening; that is short-range planning. Almost all processes of decision making can be considered a form of planning.

One way to define planning is as a relatively systematic method we use to solve problems. It is decision making that enables us to decide what is to be accomplished and that results in the identification of priorities for accomplishing our objective. It occurs through a series of logical steps or a process that enables us to identify and select among alternative problem solutions. Planning is a process for fully determining a preferred course for future action.

Planning is a useful tool in the development of programs for older people, for it increases common understanding of the issues in the community and facilitates communication, which, in turn, facilitates decision making. In addition, in any community there are limited resources available for aging programs and planning ensures that these are well used. Problems and conditions vary from community to community, making it impossible to devise a universal solution for the problems of older people. Planning permits the design of programs that best suit the needs of the specific elderly population we are concerned about.

When we engage in program development for older people, we attempt to find the best solution to an existing service need. For example, the director of a meals program, in looking through the agency files, may discover that a number of older people who would like to receive hot meals aren't able to, because they cannot get to the meals program. After discussing this matter, the director learns that other meals program directors have identified a similar problem. The director of the meals program may then make contact with service agencies in the community to determine if they provide transportation to older people. If they do not offer transportation services either, the program director will probably conclude that transportation is a problem not only for prospective participants of the meals program but for all the elderly of the community, and something should be done about it.

The "something to be done" may involve any of a number of solutions. For example, in the situation stated above, the need perceived by the meals program director is for transportation services. However, does this mean that older people need access to public transportation or financial aid in order to use transportation? If older people do not have access to public transportation, then the service needed is a transportation system. If, on the other hand, they do not have money to pay for public transportation, then the service needed may be an income subsidy to be used for public transportation. The planning process enables us to make the correct choices among the various alternatives available.

The Planning Process

The planning process involves a series of logical steps that should lead to an ultimate goal. Morris and Binstock (1966) have identified six major steps in the planning process. They are: (1) problem identification, (2) problem analysis, (3) involvement of interested people, (4) development of a plan of action, (5) program implementation, and (6) program evaluation. They maintain that these are the logical steps to follow in the planning process, and, if carried out conscientiously, they should lead to rational decisions about program development. Although we will discuss them sequentially, in reality they may occur out of sequence. Moreover, planning is a continuous process; the final step of the process, program evaluation, provides feedback that should reactivate the first step, problem identification. (See Figure 9.1.) In other words, in evaluating whether or not a planned program meets its objectives, we may learn that it does not, and this may motivate us to go back and reassess the problem. Or we may identify another problem that may reactivate the process. Planning is not static but a fluid process. Each step in the process is discussed below.

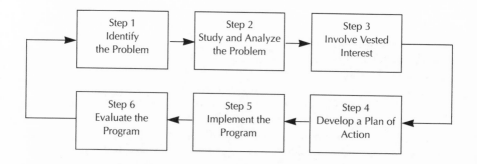

Figure 9.1   Steps in the Planning Process.

Problem or Need Identification

This step of the planning process helps to answer the question of what problems exist for the elderly. The problems addressed in program planning generally result from the elderly's having **unmet needs**. Needs for most older people are basic requirements for purposeful independent living, such as adequate housing, income, and basic material needs; psychological requirements, such as safety needs (need for protection against damage or deprivation); the need for social interaction (sharing love and social contact); the need to feel important or valued (achievement, accomplishment, and self-esteem); and the need for self-fulfillment (development of human potential).

In the planning process these problems or unmet needs are identified in many ways. Frequently they are observed by those attempting to provide services to older people, for example, the director of the meals program mentioned above. Another example of problem identification through service providers occurred in West Virginia. Welfare workers attempting to provide services to older people had begun to realize that many older people were forced into institutionalization, because resources were not available in the community to provide supportive services in the home. This was documented for a number of years by the welfare workers and finally resulted in the department's development of a homemakers' service for older people, which provided them with an alternative to institutional care.

Very often citizens in the community or national, state, and local government agencies will identify unmet needs of older people. Gerontologists and the elderly themselves may define problems. However the problem is identified, it is brought to a level of public awareness that prompts us to act to alleviate or resolve the problem.

Problem Analysis

This step in the planning process deals with the question of how pervasive the problem is in the community, what resources are available to respond to it, and where available services fall short in dealing with the problem. The purpose of this step is to identify priority unmet needs and to provide recommendations for how they can be met through program development. There are three tasks involved in this step: (1) assessing the needs of older people, (2) surveying available resources, and (3) establishing priorities and making recommendations.

Assessing Needs. We suggested above that the identification of problems and needs of older people can occur spontaneously as the consequence of observation made by an individual. They can also be identified through a more formal method of collecting information that permits a systematic analysis of the magnitude of the need, its frequency, and the perceived seriousness of the problem. This is done through an activity in planning called a **needs assessment**.

The needs assessment is a means of systematically collecting information about the problems and needs of older people, as well as their service utilization patterns. With this type of information at hand, a program developer may be able to assess the nature of the program actually needed to cope with the problems. For example, in the meals program problem discussed above, we need to know if transportation is needed only for older people who want to participate in the meals program or whether it is a more general need of older people in the community. Do older people also need transportation in order to get medical care, to get to the grocery store, and so on? The systematic collection of data through needs assessment should help answer such questions and provide a clearer definition of the transportation problem of the elderly.

Four methods suggested by Warheite, Bell, and Schwab (1974) can be used to obtain information about the needs of the elderly adult: (1) the knowledgeable person approach, (2) the public hearing approach, (3) the social indicators approach, and (4) the direct contact approach.

1. *The knowledgeable person approach*, involves obtaining information from those in the community who are in good positions to know about the needs of older people. The criteria for the selection of these individuals are logically based on the fact that they know about the community, older people and their needs, and patterns of services being received. Individuals who should be sought for such information are administrators and personnel of health and welfare agencies, aging-program directors and personnel, and the clergy. Both the public and private sectors should be used in trying to identify knowledgeable individuals. Information about the needs of older people can be obtained from these individuals through either mailed questionnaires or personal interviews.

    There are obvious advantages to the knowledgeable person approach. First, it is relatively simple and inexpensive; second, it permits the input and interaction of a great many different individuals, each with an individual perspective on the elderly's needs in the community. This approach is not the best, however, because it tends to be based entirely upon the perceptions of those providing services. There is thus a likelihood that an organizational perspective will be presented, which may not reflect fully and adequately the needs of older people.

2. *The public hearing approach* relies on the perspectives of individuals who are asked to assess the needs and service patterns of older adults in the community. It is similar to the knowledgeable person approach in that it is based on the views of individuals. However, some of the most serious disadvantages of the knowledgeable person approach are reduced by widening the circle of respondents to include the general population. Forums or hearings are planned around a series of public meetings to which all residents of the community are invited to come and express their beliefs about the needs and services for older people. This approach is flexible. It can be planned to elicit information from any member of the community willing to attend the meeting or it can be geared toward the elderly alone. If they are to be effective, public hearings must be well publicized. It will be necessary also to record the ideas, attitudes, and perceptions of those present.

Hearings are relatively easy to arrange and inexpensive to conduct. They provide an excellent opportunity for input from many segments of the community through a process that is very likely to bring into consciousness new ideas of previously unidentified needs of older people. They also aid in the identification of those citizens most interested in helping, who can be valuable resources for the later implementation of programs.

There are also shortcomings in this method. One of the most serious is the difficulty of obtaining representative attendance at public hearings. Only a partial view of the community's perception of needs and services will emerge unless the meetings are well attended by a broad cross-section of older people or knowledgeable citizens who are articulate in expressing their beliefs and in sharing their information. Still another disadvantage lies in the possibility that the meetings may heighten the expectations of those in the community in ways that cannot be met. Many of the factors associated with the problems of older people and the creation of programs to alleviate them are beyond the control of local agencies. Therefore, it is essential that expectations about what can be achieved be clearly spelled out to those attending.

The public hearings held prior to the 1971 White House Conference on Aging are an example of this method. The objective of the White House Conference and the general expectation of those who attended was to establish a national policy on aging. Public hearings were held all over the United States, and, on the basis of the information obtained and shared at the conference, recommendations for a national policy on aging were submitted to the president. The ultimate national policy never materialized, however, which may have been very disappointing to those who participated in the preconference activity and in the conference itself. Early in the public hearings sessions those who attended should have been made aware of what would be a realistic outcome.

3. *The social indicators approach* is based primarily on inferences of need drawn from descriptive statistics found in public records and reports. The underlying assumption of this approach is that it is possible to make useful estimates of the needs of older people by analyzing statistics on selected factors that have been found to be highly correlated with persons in need. Some of the factors commonly used as social indicators include the arrangement of the community's people and institutions; the social or demographic characteristics of the population, such as age, race, sex, and income; and the general social conditions in which people live. For example, substandard housing, overcrowding, inside plumbing, accessibility to service, transportation, and economic conditions are factors that can be used. When they are analyzed as a constellation, they can provide important information about a community and the needs of those who live there.

There are many advantages to using the social indicators approach. The most significant is that such approaches can be developed from vast information sources already existing in the public domain, such as census reports, governmental agency statistics, and the like. Such information can generally be secured at relatively low cost. However, one of the most serious shortcomings is the fact that many of the indicators are only indirect measures of need and may not be accurate.

4. *The direct contact approach* is based on the collection of information about older people in the community through either personal interviews or mailed questionnaires. This can be done by interviewing all the older people in the community or representative groups. The key to the success of this method is in obtaining pertinent information. The tendency is to ask a great many questions because they are interesting which so overburdens the older people with the demand for information that they may be uncooperative.

There are many advantages to using this approach. Properly conducted, this method of assessing need can provide the most valid and reliable information available about the needs and service utilization patterns of older people. On the other hand, it is costly and time-consuming. In addition, older people may be reluctant or refuse to participate in providing such information. Of the four approaches discussed, however, the direct contact approach is by far the best, for it provides information on needs as perceived by older individuals themselves. It should be used if at all possible.

Surveying Available Resources. A second type of information needed for a clearer understanding of the service needs of older people is an understanding of the current patterns of service provision in the community. A survey or overview of existing service patterns should provide information about the type of services available—for example, health, income, counseling, or recreation—and the pattern of utilization of these services by the elderly. Such a survey may provide a dual function, for in asking what types of services agencies provide to older people, we may also be enlightening them as to the needs of old people or helping them identify a potential client group.

Modification of the various needs assessment approaches can be used to obtain information about community services. The knowledgeable person approach would involve talking to those who know about agencies in the community; for example, the directors of the Council of Social Agencies of the United Way. Rather than a community forum, you may want to have an agency forum, with representatives of the various service agencies providing information about the services they provide to all those present.

Information on the availability of community services for the elderly can also be obtained from social services directories, information and referral agencies, social service councils, and even the phone book. By far the best method, however, is direct contact with the agency providing services, through either a mailed questionnaire or personal interview with the agency executive.

The type of information one may want to obtain when dealing directly with an agency in order to assess service gaps includes; (1) the formal objectives of the agency; (2) a brief listing of services currently provided; (3) staffing patterns; (4) facts about clients, for example, age, sex, income, and geographic distribution; (5) the types of problems people bring to the agency; (6) the types of referrals that are made by this agency to other agencies; and (7) service gaps identified by the agency.

Setting Priorities and Making Recommendations. The final aspect of needs assessment is an analysis of the information collected about the elderly and current services. On the basis of this analysis priorities should be developed for meeting the needs of older clients. The results of the needs assessment would generally reveal that older clients have many specific needs. Unmet needs typically far outreach resources available to respond, making it necessary to define priority of needs.

An effort should be made to rank needs from highest to lowest. For example, the most pressing transportation need may be travel for medical care; travel to a nutrition program may be needed but less pressing. The need most frequently expressed by older people can be given a rank of 1, the next highest, 2, and so on. Ranking will provide a perspective of which needs should be given priority in program development.

Although some needs are given higher ranking than others, those given the highest ranking may not be the needs given highest priority in program development. As part of the decision-making process involved in setting priorities, information about available services must also be taken into consideration.

Sometimes a needs assessment may indicate that rather than developing a new program, alterations in some existing program may be all that is required to meet a service need of the elderly. If an existing agency agrees to provide this service, a new program has not been created but a new service has, and the ultimate goal has been achieved.

In setting priorities, the worker may also find that some needs of older people cannot be resolved through program development. Resolution of some service needs for the elderly is beyond the realm of local resources. For example, a major need of older people is income. Very little can be done through local programs to deal with this problem, except perhaps something with regard to employment opportunities for the elderly. In setting priorities you should make a realistic assessment of whether the need can be dealt with at the local level.

In summary, priorities should reflect prevalence of unmet needs, perspective of citizens as to the hierarchy of need, and the program's potential available to respond. The product of this step in the planning process is generally a report that ends with recommendations about the kind of program or services that should be developed to resolve the problem. The report, with its recommendations, is generally prepared for a board, agency director, committee, or planning council. The report should be written in a way that enables those for whom it is prepared to understand clearly how priorities were established and how they relate to the recommendations.

Involvement of Interested People

The third step in the planning process addresses itself to the political aspects of program development. As stated above, resources for program development are generally limited, and gaining access to such resources may be highly competitive. In addition, just because a worker, agency, or board may think new programs or services for older people are needed in the community, others may not feel this way. Consequently, it is advisable to gain community sanction and support for what you are doing. This is done by bringing together people in the community who both support and oppose your goals.

This is one of the steps in the planning process that very often falls out of sequence. One may start the planning process by bringing together relevant interest groups of the community; it may be they who initiate the planning process in the first place. At what point relevant interests are involved will depend on the circumstances surrounding your specific planning process, but they must be involved at some point.

One should attempt to involve key people in the community who support the program's planning goals, as very often they can open doors that are generally closed and expedite matters. In addition, they may be crucial for obtaining the resources needed to implement the program. Very often it is advisable to seek counsel or sanction from older people in the community, city or county officials, key social agencies, and potential funding agencies. One way of involving others is to establish an advisory or planning committee that works throughout the planning process. We would like to emphasize that when you are developing programs for older people, it is always "good politics" to involve them as much as possible in the entire process.

Involving those who oppose your effort is crucial to its ultimate success. By involving them you put yourself in a position to overcome their resistance to what you are trying to achieve. We generally overcome resistance by a number of means: obligation, friendship, rational persuasion, selling, coercion, and inducement (Morris and Binstock, 1966). However, we must have access to the person or group in order to overcome the resistance. By involving them you or those who support your efforts will have an opportunity to influence their opinions about what you are attempting to do.

Development of a Plan of Action

Developing a plan of action involves designing a program or service that, one hopes, will alleviate the problem you are concerned about. The plan of action contains four major parts: (1) goals and objectives, (2) strategies, (3) work plan, and (4) the budget.

Goals and Objectives. **Goals** establish the direction of your plan of action. They state what will be accomplished over the long run. For example, the purpose of a transportation service may be to increase the general mobility of older people in the community or to enable them specifically to participate in the activities of a senior center.

Objectives also establish direction, but they are short-range and are always measurable. There are two types of objectives: **impact objectives**, which define outcomes in terms of change expected in project participants as a result of project activities; and **output objectives**, which define outcomes in terms of the expected level of services or activities of the project.

In development of a plan of action we are concerned with output objectives. Good output objectives generally answer the *what, where, who, how, how many,* and *how much* questions. More specifically they should include: (1) types of services or activities to be undertaken, (2) expected level of effort, (3) target groups for the effort, (4) time period for the effort, and (5) cost. For example, a transportation program may have the following output objectives: The program is to provide, through Title XX funds, a $40 monthly cash subsidy to each of 100 low-income elderly in the community in order to meet their transportation needs. Or the program is to provide private volunteer automobile transportation three days a week for the 200 older residents living in one area of the community.

Once objectives are developed, they should be assigned priorities. The following factors should be kept in mind in creating **priority objectives**: The priorities among unmet needs should serve as a guide by defining the immediacy of the unmet need; the ability to mobilize resources; and the overall feasibility, given constraints such as political situations, staff, and the like. Other factors include order dependency (what objectives must be attained before others can be initiated); viewpoint of the advisory board; and finally, short-term or long-term commitments implied.

Strategies. Objectives define what is to be accomplished; **strategy** defines how it will be accomplished, the approach to be used. There are two basic approaches to responses to unmet needs: (1) delivery of services by an existing program, or (2) using staff time to develop new resources or improving existing resources operated by other service programs. Developing a strategy involves developing alternative approaches to meeting the objectives. The selection of the most appropriate strategy involves deciding which alternative approach best meets the various objectives. There may be several alternatives that can be used to meet your objectives; these should be examined carefully and assessed in terms of projected costs. Often the ideal solution or the ideal program design or objective is most costly, and frequently less-then-ideal means must be used because of the scarcity of resources.

If a new program is to be created, a funding strategy should also be considered. In order to get funding for new programs, it often will be necessary to submit grant proposals to federal or state agencies. Funding may also be available by requesting money from the city government. Another alternative that should be explored is private funding sources, such as the United Way, private foundations, and corporations.

Work Plan. The **work plan** provides more detail to strategy and becomes a framework for action by those who would implement the program. The work plan makes operational the output objectives and milestone dates for accomplishing them or for implementing the design.

The work plan should spell out the major nonservice and service tasks that must be achieved in order to conduct the new program, and anticipated dates for project task completion. If you hope to begin implementing your new program at the end of one year of planning and development, then all necessary nonservice tasks and subtasks must be identified and the dates they will be completed indicated. Service tasks are related to actual service delivery. The work plan is a tool for the planner as well as a means of indicating to others how the objectives will be achieved.

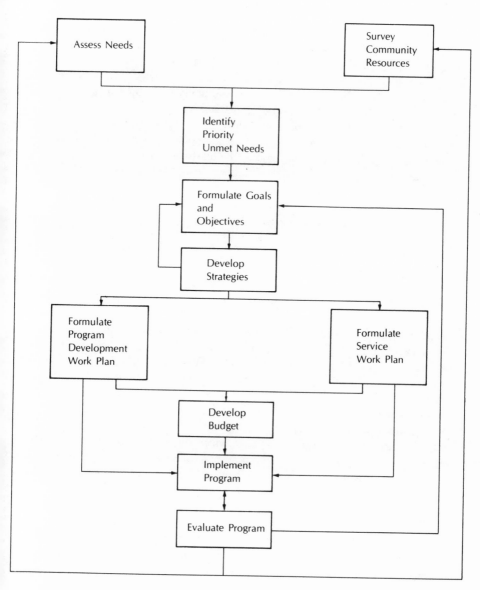

Figure 9.2   Relationships among Components of the Planning Process.

Work plans define, at a minimum, what will be done (tasks/services), how, when, where, and by whom. The work plan also provides the basis for developing a program budget.

The Budget. The final task in a plan of action is the development of a proposed budget. The **budget** should reflect as accurately as possible the amount of money that will be required to operate the program. In the planning process two budgets are needed. The first is an activities or service budget, which identified how much it costs to provide a given service. The second is a line item budget, which projects the expected costs by type of expense, such as personnel or staff, rental, travel, supplies, and so on.

All four parts of the plan of action—goals and objectives, strategies, the work plan, and the budget—serve as the foundation and the blueprint for the final phases of the planning process, program implementation and evaluation.

Program Implementation

The program implementation step of the planning process involves carrying out those activities necessary to prepare for actual provision of services to clients. The implementation step involves securing staff, facilities, equipment, and supplies—all things essential to the actual program operation—as well as establishing policies and procedures to structure the program. It may also involve the establishment of the policy-making body and an advisory board and developing relationships with other agencies. This step includes activities to inform older people about the program and, finally, actual provision of the service.

Program Evaluation

The final step in the planning process, evaluation, assures accountability and feedback as part of the process. The purpose of program evaluation is to determine if the program goals and objectives are actually achieved. This step may begin when the program begins, because evaluations are built into the program's implementation as data are collected from the onset of the program.

At some point established in the work plan, the data collected for the evaluation are studied to see if the program has accomplished its objectives. The information obtained in this step may be the basis for reactivating the planning process in order to achieve new goals or to modify the existing objectives.

Figure 9.2 shows how components of the planning process are interrelated.

Involving Older Adults in Program Planning and Development

There is a role for older adults in the planning process. They can be involved in several aspects of program development, beginning with voicing their own needs for services. The needs assessment phase of program development, inasmuch as possible, should include the direct input of older individuals; several of the methods suggested above for gathering information on needs call for their direct input. Since older people usually are not involved in program planning, it may take an overall educational effort to elicit help and to help them understand their role in the process and the need for their input in order for the program to succeed. To ensure participation it may be necessary to visit senior centers and other programs used by older people to explain the purpose of a needs assessment and encourage their participation. If mailed questionnaires are to be used, it may be useful to visit older people at agency programs or in their homes to explain the purpose of a needs survey and to solicit their support.

One way of assuring that old people will be involved in planning is by their participation on advisory and policy-making boards. Many federal programs for older people require that they be represented on such boards. To serve effectively as board members, the elderly may need some preparation, for many older people have not had such experience.

When older people become involved as board members, it will be necessary to provide them with an orientation to help them understand the purpose of the board, their role as board members, how the board is structured, how it will function, the nature of the service program, and the relationship of the board to program staff or a planner. If older people are being asked to serve on a policy-making board, it may also be useful to orient them to *Robert's Rules of Order.*

In developing an advisory board of older people, it will be helpful to have a board that is representative of a cross-section of the elderly population, including individuals with varied racial and socioeconomic backgrounds. You should probably seek out older individuals who are interested in such activities, will enjoy the experience, and have the stamina to carry out the responsibilities involved.

Summary

This chapter has provided some idea about the various tasks that must be undertaken to effectively develop programs for older people, with emphasis placed on involving older people themselves in the planning of programs for their benefit. In the next two chapters we discuss a number of programs that can be developed for older people.

chapter 10
support services for older adults

Many of the physical, psychological, and social conditions experienced by older people create barriers to their use of services and programs. Agencies must sometimes provide supportive services to guarantee that older adults are able to use their programs. The primary service provided by an agency must often be supplemented with support services in order for the agency to respond effectively to the needs of older clients. In this chapter we discuss various types of support services that might be needed by the elderly and suggest how such services might be established as part of an agency's program. Information and referral, telephone reassurance and friendly visiting, transportation, shopping assistance, escort service, legal services, and protective services are discussed.

Information and Referral Services

Older clients in the community may need aid in finding resources to help resolve the many problems confronting them. They may be plagued with a leaky faucet or frustrated because precious eyeglasses are broken. An information and referral service can provide assistance to older adults with such difficulties by helping them find people who can help deal with these difficulties.

Communities are dynamic places in which change and growth are constant, and the average person may find it difficult to keep abreast of all the changes in the service and business segments of the community. The major function of an information and referral service is to collect accurate and up-to-date information about all resources available in the community and to make this information easily available to the elderly. The foundation of a good information and referral service is the development and maintenance of an accurate community resources file.

The Community Resources File

To serve older people effectively through information and referral, a community resources file may be developed. The development of such a file entails a systematic survey of the community in order to identify the various resources available. The community survey can be done by either mailed questionnaires or personal interviews. A good resources file is not limited to information about social service agencies; information about resources available from civic groups and organizations and the business community should also be included. A community resources file should be a comprehensive statement of all services and resources available to the elderly.

Some resources are informal in nature, for instance, an individual who is willing to provide material or financial aid to those in need. Information about such people usually is available only by word-of-mouth. Much exploration may be required to identify these resources, but it is well worth the effort if it helps provide assistance to an older person in need.

To establish a useful resources file, the following information is needed: (1) The name, address, and phone number of the agency, business, or individual providing the service or the resource; (2) the nature, amount, and duration of the service or resource provided; (3) the conditions or criteria an individual must meet to receive assistance or the resource; (4) the name of a contact person within the agency or business.

In order to effectively and efficiently serve older people, the information obtained about community resources should be recorded on 3 x 5 cards and kept in a card file for easy access. The information in the file is generally organized by grouping together resources available for a specific problem area such as income, health, housing, clothing, transportation, and so on. If a specific resource is available for several of these areas, then duplicate cards will be required, and they should be filed under the appropriate problem category.

Once the resources file is created, the most challenging matter is keeping it up to date. This may require a periodic survey of resources, or perhaps arrangements for the information and referral service to be informed by a resource provider in the event of some change.

Information and referral services lend themselves nicely to the use of volunteers. Once a resources file is established, volunteers can be trained to use it.

Information Dissemination

Information and referral services are generally provided over the telephone. A "hot line," "need line," or other catchy name is often used to call attention to the service and to publicize its phone number. The phone number for the information and referral service should be announced in the newspaper and on radio and television. All service programs, hospitals, the police, and so on should have the number. Some information and referral services have developed decals that contain the information and referral service number, and these are posted in phone booths, public restrooms, grocery stores, and other public places.

The agency or individual providing the service must answer calls from clients who ask either about a specific service or where assistance can be obtained for a specific problem. The task of the information and referral worker is to attempt to identify, through the resources file, an agency, program, individual, or resource that can assist with the older person's problem and to share this information with the caller.

If resources are not available to deal with a problem presented by an older person, this fact should be noted, as it is a means of documenting the need for specific types of service in the community. Such information should be shared with appropriate individuals in the community concerned about such needs.

Telephone Reassurance and Friendly Visiting

Telephone reassurance and friendly visiting are two support services ideal for volunteers, particularly elderly volunteers. As we indicated in chapters 2 and 4, many older people live alone, and because of physical, social, or psychological barriers, they do not routinely have contact with others. Regular contact by an individual who is concerned about the well-being of the older person can be very helpful.

Rather than waiting for the older person to call and express a need, as is the case in the information and referral service, a telephone reassurance service is designed so that the volunteer calls an older individual on a regular basis. The purpose of the call is to check on the health and well-being of the older client, especially the semi-ambulatory elderly. In addition, if the older person called is in need of some type of service or resource, the volunteer will attempt to have this need met.

Generally the telephone reassurance worker arranges for the older person to call in and inform the volunteer if he or she does not plan to be at home at the time of the regular call. If the worker has not been prewarned that the client will not be at home at the time of the scheduled call, an unanswered telephone is an alert to the volunteer to have another person, such as a social worker, landlord, or neighbor, visit the residence to determine why the client was unable to answer the phone. Older people are prone to accidents in the home. Some are taken ill suddenly, and without such a service they may go many days without assistance. Most who live alone fear such events.

A friendly visiting service serves the same purpose as telephone reassurance but is accomplished by the volunteer's actually visiting the home of the older person. Often, in addition to visiting the home, a friendly visitor may also correspond with the older client or send greeting cards. A friendly visitor may also do small chores for the individual while in the home.

Transportation Services

Transportation is another support service that may be needed by older clients. Many older people do not use agency services because they are not mobile for any of the many reasons we have discussed earlier. Assistance by increasing the mobility of older people is quite beneficial from a social, psychological, and physical point of view.

Each community has its own transportation problems. In rural areas older people may have to travel many miles to get to services and programs, and public transit may be nonexistent; older people living in more populated areas may have to travel only a few blocks, but getting to the transit line may be treacherous because of hills or heavy traffic. Several types of services may be needed to assist with the mobility problems confronting older clients. (See also chapters 2 and 12.)

Pedestrian Travel

Very often accessibility to services and programs may involve the need to travel on foot only a few blocks, but this can present problems to some older individuals. Because of the physical changes that occur with age, some street curbs are too high, traffic lights too fast, and traffic signs unclear to the older pedestrian. The highest incidence of pedestrian death and accidents is among the elderly.

Government units should be made aware of these problems and encouraged to ensure safe travel by foot for older people by determining that: (1) they always have the right of way; (2) traffic lights are timed for their needs; (3) curbs are altered for the safety of elderly and handicapped individuals; (4) signs are placed or colored so that they are visible to older citizens; and (5) if at all possible patrols are posted at busy intersections and neighborhoods highly populated with older people.

If these options are not possible, then "people pools," "safety patrols," or escort services should be developed to assist older pedestrians move about.

Vehicular Travel

There are a number of ways assistance can be provided to older people who need to travel using vehicles. If public tranportation is available in a community, the transit authority might be persuaded to (1) reduce rates for older patrons; (2) establish bus stops near facilities, programs, and services frequented by older people; and (3) provide shelters and benches at bus stops used by the elderly; and (4) use buses that are easier to board.

If public transit is not available, volunteer transportation services may be organized. This would involve soliciting the services of private citizens using their own automobiles to transport older individuals to services they may need in the community. The responsibility of the agency with a volunteer transportation service would be to recruit volunteer drivers and coordinate the services of the driver with the needs of older clients.

Many community organizations, such as private or parochial school systems, churches, charity groups, sheltered workshops for the handicapped, and federally funded community programs, own vehicles for transporting their clients. It may be possible to get these groups to agree to provide transportation for older people when their vehicles are not being used for other purposes.

Still another option is organizing an effort to obtain a bus to provide transportation services for older people in the community. This may mean several years of fund raising or obtaining grants from federal or state agencies. (See chatper 8.)

Shopping Assistance

With the advent of the suburban supermarket and the demise of the neighborhood grocer, food purchasing has become a major problem for some elderly. Older individuals living in both cities and rural areas often experience difficulty. Because some older consumers are forced to use local grocers rather than chain stores, their food costs are often high. Shopping assistance to older people has several facets. The major problem for older clients is getting to the market or grocer, which may involve travel by bus or taxi or a long walk. Older people sometimes find it necessary to pay neighbors or acquaintances to transport them by private automobile. The reliance of the older person on any of these means of transportation increases their food costs. Some use home delivery which increases the cost of food.

Reliable and inexpensive means of transportation to the grocer sometimes can be dealt with through volunteers who will trasnport older shoppers. Some senior center programs operate mini-buses that transport older people to the market once or twice a week. In some metropolitan areas food store proprietors themselves operate such mini-buses. Store proprietors may be persuaded to reduce the cost of food for older shoppers to offset the cost of transportation.

Once in the store, an older shopper is confronted with another problem. How many older people need to purchase ten pounds of potatoes or a four-pound cut of meat. The tendency of markets to prepackage foods in quantities suitable for families of four creates a variety of problems for the elderly. First, having to buy quantities of food in excess of actual need increases the cost of the purchase. In addition, it creates difficulties in transporting purchases back to the place of residence. Because of diminishing physical strength an older individual may be forced to make several trips to the grocery store over a short period of time in order to obtain all of the necessary groceries. If the older person is paying someone for transportation to the store, he or she may shop for a month at a time and do without certain items until the next trip.

Food store managers should be made aware of the packaging needs of older consumers. For example, one or two potatoes in a package or a small quantity of meat are more suited to the needs of the older consumer. Some grocers have established senior citizen shopping days featuring discounts on food items, and some markets serve refreshments to older customers while they are in the store. The major task is to make the commercial businessperson aware of the needs of the elderly consumer group.

The inability to shop affects the eating patterns of older people and, ultimately, their basic health. Malnutrition is a serious problem among the elderly, and any assistance that can be provided in this area will assure better nutritional patterns in old age.

Escort Service

Escort service is another support program that may be needed by older clients. Many older people need to be accompanied by another person in order to get around, especially the elderly with physical impairments or language barriers. As we have seen, many elderly are homebound because they cannot cope with physical obstructions such as steps, curbs, or getting into and out of buses or automobiles. Other elderly persons may use prostheses, walkers, canes, and crutches. Many ethnic and minority elderly do not speak English and have limited mobility because of their inability to communicate. The availability of someone to accompany the older person and to provide assistance so that he or she can leave home without fear of feeling humiliation is very beneficial.

Through an escort service the older person with physical or language problems is provided assistance in leaving the home and getting to the desired destination. Sometimes the escort will provide transportation in a personal automobile or an agency's automobile; accompany the older person on a bus, train, or plane; or walk with the client to the destination. When immobility is created by a language barrier, the escort should be bilingual to act as an interpreter for the elderly client.

Escorts may accompany older clients to a variety of places such as the grocery store, department stores, physicians' offices, hospitals, and service agencies.

Legal Services

As individuals move into old age, they are confronted with a number of tasks that require legal counsel. Until a few years ago the legal needs of the elderly received little attention from the legal and other professions; however, this situation has started to change. Older people are beginning to be viewed as a distinct client group with its own set of problems, such as taxes, wills, pensions, Medicare, Medicaid, Social Security, nursing homes, and involuntary commitment. The poor elderly in particular have little knowledge of their legal rights and are timid about consulting attorneys. In addition, older clients often cannot afford to pay fees for legal advice charged by most private attorneys.

Although free legal-aid offices to serve the poor have been established throughout the country, these services have not been widely used by older people. Many older people whose income makes them ineligible to use public services are still too poor to afford an attorney, so they do without legal help. At this stage of life there is a need to put one's affairs in order, and access to legal counsel can greatly facilitate the process.

A number of ways are available to provide legal services to the elderly. The services of retired attorneys or volunteers obtained through the Bar Association can sometimes be obtained for a few days a month. A growing trend, however, is to use paralegals or legal advisors to provide this type of service. Paralegals work under the supervision of an attorney and provide assistance with a number of technical problems that may confront the elderly, such as eligibility for Social Security and Medicare. Older individuals themselves can be trained to serve as paralegals. Sometimes law students, with an attorney's supervision, can also be used to advise older clients. Agency staff members, such as caseworker, information and referral specialist, or outreach worker, may help older clients obtain assistance with their legal problems.

Legal services also play a role in advocacy, as discussed in chapter 11.

Protective Services

Older adults at times are unable to act in their own best interests, and it may become necessary for another individual to assist them with the administration of their personal affairs. There are times when, due to physical changes, mental functioning, and extreme stress, older adults may not be able to make decisions about their own well-being. There are some older people who cannot function adquately in the home and must be removed to another living situation. Older people may be abused by family members, or they may need to be removed from a nursing home for their own protection. There are instances where older people are harassed by salesmen and collection agencies. In all these instances court action may be necessary in order to protect the interests of the older person. In such a case the worker acts as an advocate and attempts to see that the older person's rights are not violated and that his or her interests protected.

Protective services are usually provided by workers of a social service agency. The worker must be able to assess whether an older person is capable of making decisions in his or her best interest. At times older people may not be able to function effectively, because they are demoralized by the seemingly endless circumstances that complicate their lives. At this point they are vulnerable and may agree to do things they will later regret and be unable to undo.

For effective protective services the worker may need to be able to demonstrate to the court or others in authority that the older person is not acting normally and is incapable at the time of exercising proper judgement. The older person may require commitment or someone to act in his or her behalf. Someone may need to be given the power of attorney for the older person. The worker in this service pleads the case of the older client in court. Very often in protective services it will become necessary to seek legal assistance in order to help the older person.

In many states, protective services for older people are required by law.

Summary

Many services can be made available to older people as a means of helping them cope with the complex matrix of problems confronting them. In this chapter we have discussed how several of the services, such as information and referral, telephone reassurances and friendly visiting, transportation, shopping assistance, escort service, legal services, and protective services can be provided to older clients.

The reading that follows illustrates problems confronting the elderly.

READING 10.1

The Elderly: Prisoners of Fear/*Time*

This article dramatizes one area of victimization in which the elderly are particularly vulnerable.

When they go out—if they go out—they listen anxiously for the sound of footsteps hurrying near, and they eye every approaching stranger with suspicion. As they walk, some may clutch a police whistle in their hands. More often, especially after the sun sets, they stay at home, their world reduced to the confines of apartments that they turn into fortresses with locks and bars on every window and door. They are the elderly who live in the slums of the nation's major cities. Many are poor. White or black, they share a common fear—that they will be attacked, tortured or murdered by the teen-age hoodlums who have cooly singled out old people as the easiest marks in town. Except in a few cases, police statisticians do not have a separate category for crimes against the elderly. But law-enforcement officials across the nation are afraid that such crimes may be growing in number and becoming more vicious in nature. *Time* correspondents surveyed the plight of the elderly in three cities.

New York: Charlie's Anguish. The couple inched painfully from Fordham Road into a wasteland of The Bronx. Clinging to each other for support, the old man and woman mounted a curb and struggled for a moment while she regained her balance. Then, slowly, they went on. Watching them shuffle into the shadows of late afternoon, Detective Donald Gaffney sighed heavily and said, "There goes prime meat."

In other rundown sections all over New York City, the elderly are indeed prime targets. Their chief tormentors are young thugs, who have even mugged a

103-year-old women, stealing from her a couple of dollars' worth of groceries. In Gaffney's district, about 97% of the offenders are black, and 95% of the victims are white women—usually Jews who have stubbornly stayed on in once comfortable apartments while the neighborhood deteriorated around them. "Fagin wouldn't last up here for half an hour," said Gaffney. "He'd be calling us."

The blacks prey primarily on the whites not for racial reasons but because they are convinced that the old people have money stashed away somewhere—hidden in old shoe boxes, tucked under mattresses. The young hoods operate in raiding teams of three or four, or as many as ten. Typically, they have a morning "shape-up" in a local schoolyard to plan what they call a "crib job," because it is as easy as taking money from a baby.

The team will send its youngest, most innocent-looking member, often an eleven- or twelve-year old, into a bank to spot a likely victim: a woman, say, who is cashing a money order or a Social Security check. When she leaves the building, only one member of the gang will follow her closely so as not to arouse her suspicions. The others trail far behind. When she gets into the elevator in her apartment house, two or three will catch up and board it with her and get off at the floor below hers. Then as she unlocks her door, they will suddenly appear in the corridor and shove her inside the apartment.

If threats do not succeed in producing valuables, one member of the gang will beat her—often someone under the age of 16 and thus a juvenile in the eyes of the law. The rights of juveniles are so well protected that it is next to impossible to send them away for any length of time. About 75% of the juveniles apprehended in The Bronx and brought into family court have been arrested before and let go, frequently several times over. Knowing how weak the laws are, many elderly victims refuse to prosecute their attackers, fearing that the hoodlums will soon be back on the street and might pay them a second and even more vicious call.

As a result, old people—black and white alike—live like prisoners in the decaying sections of the city. One woman was even afraid to put out her trash; she stuffed it in plastic bags, which she stored in a spare room. When one room would fill up, she would seal it off and start filling up another. At times she lived on candy bars, tossing coins out of a window to children who would go to the store for her. Visiting The Bronx, a reporter from the *New York Times* talked to Clara Engelmann, 64, who had moved her bed into the foyer of her apartment and slept fully dressed so she could dash out the door the next time someone tried to break into her bedroom—which had happened three times before. "They're not human," she cried. "They're not human."

To try to cope with the special problems of the elderly, New York police set up senior citizen robbery units in all five boroughs. One of the units' main jobs is to persuade old people to bring charges against their attackers. The police make special arrangements to eliminate the tedium and confusion of court appearances. Detectives also lecture groups of old people on how to survive in the city (e.g., don't go home if you think you're being followed—find a cop). In addition, the police have created a few "safe corridors" for the elderly: thoroughfares in shopping districts that are heavily patrolled. Civic-minded youths, mostly high school students, have helped further by volunteering to escort old people to stores and social clubs.

The police are convinced that some progress is being made; but it is painfully slow. So far this year, although some 600 apartment robberies have been investigated in The Bronx, only 82 arrests have been made. Voluntary agencies do what they can to ease the plight of the elderly, but the scope of the problem is overwhelming.

Time Correspondent Mary Cronin last week paid a visit to the victim of one of the hundreds of robberies that are still unsolved. Charles Bertsch, 87, is a huge, hearty man who lives with a dozen cats in a cluttered Bronx basement apartment that he has occupied since 1911. The once prosperous neighborhood is now an age-blackened slum of begrimed apartment buildings lining rubbish-choked streets.

One morning Bertsch opened the door to let out Peggy, his dog, for her regular 10 A.M. walk. Says he: "The next thing I knew, I was here on the floor. Eight Puerto Ricans piled in and started hitting me with broom handles. They hit poor Peggy on the head with a hammer. They picked through this drawer and found $60 worth of quarters. Then one of them bent over me with a knife, holding it to my throat. 'Shall I kill him now?' he asked another guy. And the other guy said, 'No, the boss doesn't want him hurt.' "

They left Bertsch on the floor, his cats meowing around him. "Peggy was washing my face with her tongue." he recalls. It was 6 P.M. before he was able to struggle to his feet.

Now Charlie Bertsch, no longer so hearty and outgoing, has turned his place into a fortress. The day after the attack, Detective Gaffney came over with a load of plywood and, at Bertsch's request, nailed up all the windows. "That'll keep people from throwing fire bombs in," said Bertsch. He rarely goes out, getting food deliveries from a delicatessen, paying by check. Next year, he says, he plans to move. "There is no law here," said Charlie Bertsch. "I'm even afraid for the police."

Chicago: "Where Can I Live?" On the South Side, old people in the ancient apartment buildings look out of their windows early in the month, when the Social Security checks are arriving, and see the knots of young toughs keeping watch. On the West Side, gatherings of the elderly break up by 4 P.M. so that everyone can get home before dark. Walter Bishop, 72, a retired dry-cleaning worker, remembers how "on nice days and nights we used to take strolls and walks and things. Now I wouldn't go anywhere without a car. And after dark I don't go any place."

According to a recent survey by the Chicago Planning Council on Aging, 41% of the city's 518,000 residents over 60 feel that crime is their most serious concern. "Statistically speaking," says Robert J. Ahrens, director of the Mayor's office for senior citizens, "the elderly aren't victims of crime more often than other age groups. But the effects are much more severe. If a young woman is knocked down during a purse snatching, she gets up with a few bruises. If an 80-year-old woman is knocked down, she could suffer a broken hip, have to enter a nursing home, and risk losing her independence."

That is exactly what happened to one 72-year-old woman. A year ago, neighbors found her lying in her bathtub, blood clotted on her head, a stocking twisted around her neck, and her arms trussed behind her. She had lain there for two days. The next day, the doctors amputated one arm; recently they had to remove the other.

Some elderly people fight back. Not long ago, Gertrude Booker, 75, wrestled a husky teen-age purse snatcher to the ground before she decided that her pocketbook, which contained only bus fare, really was not worth fighting for. Jane Gilbert, 70, has taken karate lessons, and is determined to go out after dark, although she has been held up twice.

The residents of a public-housing project in a decaying area known as "Uptown" live under siege. Like combat soldiers, they recount story after story of how their friends have fallen victim to attacks; a deaf woman in her 90's who was mugged and cut on her forehead, another neighbor who broke a hip when she was knocked to the ground. Ann Lewis, 77, a spirited white-haired widow, was recently knocked down right in front of the main entrance to the project by two twelve-year-olds and dragged by her purse strap. "The fright has gone to my stomach," she said. "I'm scared. But I can't afford to live any place else. Tell me, where can I go? Where can I live?"

Oakland: The 17¢ Slaying. At first glance, everything looks quite normal. The rows of frame or stucco houses are cheerfully painted, the hedges neatly trimmed, the yards well kept, the whole neighborhood clean and tidy in the warm afternoon sun. But where are all the people? The streets are virtually deserted, the blinds drawn, the casement windows fortified with heavy iron gates. The section is an enclave in the slums of East Oakland, and the houses, owned mostly be elderly retirees, are preyed upon by teen-age thugs.

There is no explaining the cruelty of some attacks. Hildur Archibald, 91, probably did not see well enough to identify the assailant who invaded her home in July, and she surely did not have enough strength to resist. She was found lying on the floor of her bedroom, dead of multiple knife wounds. Robbery was the apparent motive, yet police confess they are not sure what was taken.

Elsie McIntosh, 72, was walking beside her apartment building last month when a 16-year-old boy ran past and grabbed her purse. She was knocked to the ground, injuring her head. Four hours later she was dead. Her pocketbook had contained 17 cents.

By dogged work, Oakland Police have managed to put away a score of the members of one black gang, Wolfpack I, that sytematically terrorized East Oakland's residents last winter. But most of the dozen or so raiders who were under 18 when they were convicted will probably be back on the street within a few weeks, because of relatively light sentences.

"It's a sad commentary that the only way of stopping crime is locking up the offenders," says Howard Janssen, 33, a deputy district attorney of Alameda County. "But there are now only two solutions: letting them run wild and hurts more peple, or locking them up." Given that choice, the elderly in Oakland—and other major cities—would have no trouble picking the solution.

CHAPTER 11
AdvocAcy ANd
PROTECTION ON BEHAlf
of THE ELDERly

Since older people have low status in our society, frequently they do not receive a share of available community resources and services. Those working with older people and the elderly themselves must act to ensure that appropriate resources are allocated for them. This chapter examines the need to advocate with and on behalf of the elderly. The various ways those working with the elderly can advocate for older clients and ways older people can advocate in their own behalf are discussed.

Why the Elderly Need Advocacy and Protection

With the civil rights movement of the 1960s, we became keenly aware of the need to ensure that disadvantaged groups in our society are given fair and just treatment. Older people are often treated in a manner that violates their basic civil and human rights. Older adults are vulnerable, as they feel individually responsible for their status at this time in life and thus are not likely to challenge agencies or individuals that deal with them in an unjust or unfair manner. Therefore, in 1976 the Federal Council on the Aging reaffirmed, in a Bicentennial Charter for Older Americans, the following basic human rights for older Americans:

1. The right to freedom, independence and the free exercise of individual initiative. *This should encompass not only opportunities and resources for personal planning and managing one's life style but support systems for maximum growth and contributions by older persons to their community.*

2. The right to an income in retirement which would provide an adequate standard of living. *Such income must be sufficiently adequate to assure maintenance of mental and physical activities which delay deterioration and maximize individual potential for self-help and support. This right should be assured regardless of employment capability.*

3. The right to an opportunity for employment free from discriminatory practices because of age. *Such employment when desired should not exploit individuals because of age and should permit utilization of talents, skills and experience of older persons for the good of self and community. Compensation should be based on the prevailing wage scales of the community for comparable work.*

4. The right to an opportunity to participate in the widest range of meaningful civic, educational, recreational and cultural activities. *The varying interests and needs of older Americans require programs and activities sensitive to their rich and diverse heritage. There should be opportunities for involvement with persons of all ages in programs which are affordable and accessible.*

5. The right to suitable housing. *The widest choice of living arrangements should be available, designed and located with reference to special needs at costs which older persons can afford.*

6. The right to the best level of physical and mental health services needed. *Such services should include the latest knowledge and techniques science can make available without regard to economic status.*

7. The right to ready access to effective social services. *These services should enhance independence and well-being, yet provide protection and care as needed.*

8. The right to appropriate institutional care when required. *Care should provide full restorative services in a safe environment. This care should also promote and protect the dignity and rights of the individual along with family and community ties.*

9. The right to a life and death with dignity. *Regardless of age, society must assure individual citizens of the protection of their constitutional rights and opportunities for self respect, respect and acceptance from others, a sense of enrichment and contribution, and freedom from dependency. Dignity in dying includes the right of the individual to permit or deny the use of extraordinary life support systems.*

We pledge the resources of this nation to the ensuring of these rights for all older Americans regardless of race, color, creed, age, sex or national origin, with the caution that the complexities of our society be monitored to assure that the fulfillment of one right, does not nullify the benefits received as a result of another entitlement. We further dedicate the technology and human skill of this nation so that later life will be marked in liberty with the realization of the pursuit of happiness.

Those working with older people are frequently confronted with clear violations of their clients' basic rights. For example, older people may be denied services because they do not provide information requested by an agency, but at the same time they are not offered assistance in supplying the needed information. In nursing homes the elderly may be treated in an inhumane manner by personnel. They are also evicted at times without advance notice or due process. All these examples are incidents where the rights of the older person have been violated. In such cases, if the older person is unable to act in his or her own behalf, a worker must act as an advocate to protect the client's interests.

Moreover, lawmakers and public officials often forget the needs of older members of the population when proposing new programs and services for the community or state. They also lose sight of the fact that certain provisions or laws may have an adverse effect or create hardships for older citizens. Public officials must be reminded periodically of the needs of the older constituents in the community through advocacy by those acting for the elderly or by the elderly themselves.

Advocating for Older People

An **advocate** is one who defends, promotes, or pleads a cause. In this role the worker acts as a partisan in a social conflict and uses professional expertise in the interest of the older client. In the traditional advocate role the social worker acts as a representative for the individual client or family, fighting the client's battle with the agency. The ultimate goal, however, is that of showing the client how to fight the battles effectively.

Traditionally, advocacy has taken a personal approach, where the worker attempts to fight for relief of individual clients. In recent years the advocacy role has expanded so that the worker is one who also attempts to change the system. With the broader approach to advocacy, the individual's problem is seen in light of the social and political system that produced it, and in fighting for the cause that the individual client represents, the advocate takes on a prolonged, broader battle that may eventually lead to relief for many. Both approaches may be needed as you work with older people.

Understanding How to Act
as an Advocate

Advocating for older people involves a series of activities similar to those discussed in Chapter 4 as a problem-solving process: gathering information about the client's problem, making a decision about the type of assistance needed, determining how assistance will be provided, and providing the required assistance. The crucial aspect of the process for advocacy rests in the worker's ability to recognize a situation in which advocacy is required. To recognize such instances, the worker needs background in civil rights legislation, welfare laws, housing laws, mental-health law, and the like. The worker must understand that, in addition to denial of services or of due process, dehumanizing treatment, where agency employees tease, or humiliate through name-calling or derogatory remarks, also violates civil rights. Another type of inhumane treatment may involve cross-cultural misunderstandings, in which workers of a predominantly white culture ignore or deliberately misunderstand behavior of ethnic or minority elderly and belittle ethnic approaches.

Once a worker had identified a situation that may call for advocacy, a plan of action should be developed to deal with the problem. A crucial decision is determining the level at which one should intervene for or with the client. Sometimes the only action needed is to reprimand or remind the worker of the rights of the elderly client; in other instances it may be necessary to call the incident to the attention of the agency's administrator. If this is not effective, it may then be necessary to initiate agency grievance procedures or even legal action.

In dealing with individual advocacy situations, the worker must also determine whether the individual case has ramifications of a broader nature and whether the older person might be better served by tackling the broader issue. For example, insufficient income is a problem facing a large proportion of the elderly population. When confronted by older people with such a problem, workers frequently attempt to get temporary assistance. If an older person cannot pay for utilities, rent, or food, the worker may get some agency to pay the bill to relieve the immediate need. But the problem will remain the same next month and the next. Temporary assistance is a possible solution, but it is not a position of advocacy.

In a position of advocacy the worker should address the question of older people's being denied the right to overall well-being or a safe and secure life in old age. The worker must want to begin a concerted effort to lobby for higher income provisions for older people. Rather than dealing with an immediate problem, the worker is aiming for a long-range goal, which may involve legislative and policy change.

Developing a Strategy
for Advocacy

Development of a strategy or plan is essential to success for advocacy. The worker and everyone involved should have a clear understanding of the goal and the means through which the goal will be achieved. A strategy involves the selection of techniques to be used in the approach to advocacy. For example, in order to bring about change, an advocate may begin by using a case conference to demonstrate an unfair law or policy, then move in turn to an interagency committee, a coalition, direct contact with elected officials, and finally to demonstration and protest. The strategy is to gather a broader and broader base of support as one moves through the advocacy process. Very often it may not be necessary to use the final technique, but it should be made clear to all involved that the extreme may be necessary in order to bring about change.

The above plan suggests that time is on the side of the advocate. However, those attempting to help older people may learn at the last minute that a piece of legislation that is detrimental to the good of older people is being considered and will come up for a vote in a few days or even the next day. In this case, it may be necessary to employ dramatic or drastic action quickly to influence the legislative vote. Public outcry in the media and protest demonstrations may be the only way to deal with such a situation.

In developing a strategy the worker must be conscious of factors such as timing, the commitment of those involved, and the strength of the adversary. In attempting to serve as an advocate on behalf of older people, the worker should keep in mind the following:

1. *Make an accurate diagnosis of the problem and form an effective strategy.* Mobilize allies and check to make sure you are not duplicating efforts being made by others.

2. *Know the system you are dealing with.* For example, find out about the welfare laws, the ins and outs of the rent control office, and landlord-tenant laws.

3. *Locate resources.* For example, be cognizant of legal services, legislators, citizens' groups, and sympathetic individuals within the bureaucracy.

4. *Weigh the risks* to yourself, your agency, and the individual. Plan to protect the most vulnerable from paying too high a price for too small a gain.

5. *Work for cooperation and voluntary change but be prepared for confrontation* if this alternative becomes necessary. Learn to work constructively with anger, hostility, and resistance.

6. *Don't get discouraged.* Change takes time. As you think you are making progress, other events will precipitate even more crises. The only rationale for continuing is that there is value in the struggle, and the ultimate end is worth the struggle.

Techniques Available
to the Advocate

A wide variety of techniques are available to the worker who engages in advocacy. The selection of which specific technique to use in an advocacy situation is complex. Many factors should be considered, such as the nature of the problem, the objectives of the worker, the nature of the adversary, the degree of conflict in which the worker wants to become involved, and the effectiveness of the technique. It is generally possible to use more than one of the techniques identified by Panitch (1974) listed below to address a problem that requires advocacy:[1]

1. *Study and Survey.* The systematic gathering of information about the problem and sharing it with others is an important first step in advocacy for the

[1] Adapted from *Social Work*, vol. 19 (May 1974), pp. 330-331. Copyright 1974 National Association of Social Workers, Inc. Used by permission.

elderly. The information obtained from such studies is generally applicable to other techniques of advocacy, as well as for educational and publicity purposes.

2. *Expert testimony.* Social workers as professionals and as representatives of their agencies can testify at public hearings and in political arenas—for example, legislative sessions, committee meetings, or special sessions. Workers very often have pertinent information about the magnitude of the problem and the injustice existing in current laws and policies that affect older people.

3. *Case Conferences with Other Agencies.* If the worker learns that clients of a particular agency are being badly treated, a case conference with the worker, supervisor, and/or administrator of the agency can be requested to explain the problem. The goal of such a conference is to elicit information that may help clarify why the problem exists and to explore measures that can be taken to discontinue such treatment of clients.

4. *Interagency Committees.* This technique is similar to the case conference in that agencies may bring up specific cases that are indicative of problems entailed in services provided by an agency. One of the advantages of this technique is that such a committee can be influential through peer pressure in getting other agencies to alter practices that are harmful to clients. This technique also makes agencies aware of potential problem areas for clients.

5. *Education.* Public education through the media is another technique that can be used to aid older people. Consciousness raising through meetings, panels, exhibitions, and press conferences can make the general public aware of problems confronting older adults. This technique can also be used to educate a target segment of the population about the issues.

6. *Position Taking.* Taking a public stand on issues can have both internal and external advantages, as the worker or agency goes on record with regard to the issue. This technique also lets clients know where the agency stands on the issue and in effect, provides moral support for them. Very often such stands can be communicated without cost on the radio or television or they can go on public record at the meetings or in the agency's minutes.

7. *Appeal.* Most governmental units have procedures for reviewing decisions made by their representatives or employees. However, very often clients are not aware of such procedures, or they may be intimidated by testifying. With this technique the worker helps clients initiate an appeal and then acts as their advocate or defender at the actual hearing. If the appeals procedure does not satisfy the demands of the client and the worker, the next step may be to take the matter to court.

8. *Direct Contact with Officials and Legislators.* Many times agencies can provide information about community problems for public officials. Agencies

can have individual or group meetings with legislators on a regular basis in order to keep them abreast of current issues that affect agency clients. Individuals who serve in this capacity often are sought out by legislators when they have questions about upcoming laws and policies affecting older clients. In many cases these individuals have an indirect influence on bringing about change.

9. *Coalition Groups.* An agency may become part of a group committed to specific goals. The advantage of this technique is that it makes a specific agency less vulnerable to direct attack yet shows the community a cohesive group that supports a particular goal. Such coalition groups may become lobbying groups on behalf of the older client.

10. *Client Groups.* With this technique the agency or the worker helps the clients organize in order to fight their own battles and acts as a consultant to the group, providing them with technical assistance and expert knowledge. It is important that a leader be found among the elderly who can act as a spokesperson for the group. It may be helpful if the group identifies other client groups in the community with a similar cause and forms coalitions around common issues.

11. *Petitions.* Circulating a document within the community is a means of obtaining the supportive signatures of the general population. Petitions are a way of informing the general public about the issue and showing officials that there is public support for it. Often volunteer private citizens who believe in the cause will circulate such petitions. In addition, it may be advisable to publish such petitions in the local newspaper to call attention to the issue and to make the public at large aware of the stand of a number of citizens in the community.

12. *Persistent Demands.* This technique involves bombarding officials and legislators with letters, telephone calls, telegrams, and visits, and going beyond the usual channels of appeal. This tactic stays within the limits of the law, but it may verge on harassment or other extralegal means.

13. *Demonstrations and Protests.* Marches, sit-ins, vigils, picketing, and the like are forms of nonviolent direct action public demonstrations. This technique should only be used with the full sanction and support of the agency. Those participating should be aware of the potential consequences of being part of such activity such as lay-off, eviction, or arrest.

Preparing Older People to Act as Advocates

As stated above, in the traditional role of advocate the worker acts as a representative of the client, but the ultimate goal is to show clients how to fight their own battles. The civil rights movement of the early 1960s and the welfare rights movements of the late 1960s demonstrate that client groups can advocate effectively in their own behalf and sometimes are more effective than professionals in bringing about change.

Civil disobedience, demonstrations, and "challenging the system" were seen by some as activities of the younger generation. This is no longer true. Ralph Nader, the consumer advocate, maintains "all over the country, older people are beginning to question their powerlessness and their exclusions. Common grievances such as inflation, consumer fraud, unfair taxation and poor medical care are forging a common consciousness of how powerful they could be if they united around these causes" (1977).

Older people are beginning to organize, voice their own concerns, and take action aimed at changing the laws in their own behalf. A classic example of such activity is the Gray Panthers, founded by Maggie Kuhn, a national effort at advocacy for older people. Similar efforts are going on at the state and local levels.

Older people can become involved in advocacy in a number of ways. They can advocate in their own behalf, they can be trained to serve as advocates for other people, and, finally, they can become part of a coalition group whose goal is to influence legislators and other public officials in order to uphold and protect the rights of older citizens.

Organizing Older Adults

Older individuals may be brought together for the purpose of engaging in advocacy. The first step is to make them collectively aware of the need to become advocates through information calling this need to their attention. Older people can be informed through the media, town meetings, individual contacts, or talks given to organized groups of older people, such as senior centers, neighborhood centers, and religious groups. Activity of this nature serves two purposes. It informs older people of their right to advocate as citizens and makes them aware of the need to act as a group.

The next step is attempting to bring individual older people together to discuss the issue of advocacy, for example, at a general meeting held in the community. The time, place, and purpose of such a meeting can be announced in the newspaper or when effort is being made to make older people aware of their potential role as advocates. Another approach would be to work through an existing group of older adults or through a coalition of groups. One of these groups can sponsor a meeting, inviting nonmembers to come and discuss the issue of older people's becoming involved in advocacy.

Once the elderly are brought together as a group, efforts should be made to get their collective commitment to the cause or to an advocacy stance. Some older people may not agree with this type of activity, while others will be supportive. A consensus either for or against becoming advocates should be elicited from the group. If the consensus is against, then the group will probably disband. If the group is for such action, they must then begin to develop a formal structure with identified spokespersons or a leader. The group may decide to elect officers and establish a committee structure in order to function effectively.

From this point on, the function, purpose, and tasks of the group revolve around deciding on the issues or concerns for which they will advocate and the development of plans and strategies for making their positions heard.

Teaching Older People
How to Advocate

Once a group of older people have organized to become involved in advocacy, the worker's role becomes one of facilitator through consultation and teaching. The worker no longer advocates for the group but helps the group act in their own behalf. (See chapter 5.) However, the worker probably has special knowledge that will be of assistance to the group, and it should be shared with them through an educational or consultation process. If the worker does not have the expertise or knowledge required to educate older individuals about how to become advocates, then it is his or her responsibility to locate resource people within the community who can do this and to coordinate such activity.

Older adults participating in advocacy should have a clear understanding of their civil rights as citizens. They should also understand clearly the political structure of the state and national government and how contact can be made with legislators and other public officials. In addition, they need to know how to assess the strength of the opposition, how best to get their position heard, and how to apply pressure in order to obtain action.

As we have suggested, strategy is a key factor in bringing about change, and older advocates should be schooled in the art of strategy development. An effective way of teaching this skill is through simulation; that is, role-playing or acting out various strategies or approaches to problem resolution. If older people are to be successful as advocates, they need the kind of preparation that will enable them to succeed.

Older advocates must understand that success is not always possible when one enters the political arena. However, if they are well schooled, they should be able to gauge the likelihood of an activity's success or failure and weigh this in light of the long-term or short-term goals of the group. Success in bringing about changes is not always the measure of successful advocacy. Gains may be achieved even with failures, for, if nothing else, public officials and others are made aware of dissent or counteropinions of older voters. Such knowledge may be the foundation for future successes in attempting to effect change for the elderly.

Consumer Protection

Among the most serious problems facing older people are consumer frauds and mistreatments that may take their money. Many older people—especially surviving spouses who have not handled the family's finances while both were alive—may suddenly find themselves responsible for a number of financial activities as well as large amounts of money that comes from life insurance policies or other financial savings. Learning how to manage such funds and also meet responsibilities for home maintenance, charitable contributions, and investments, may require special assistance from the human services worker or an expert in financial planning. Generally, workers should encourage clients in such situations to be slow and cautious in making any large financial decisions. Mistakes with long-term repercussions can be made.

In addition, workers should also help the suddenly well-off older client protect against consumer frauds that often have an impact on such clients. For example, home improvement salespersons may read about the death of a spouse and make a quick visit to the surviving partner in order to sell aluminum or vinyl siding, persuade the person a new roof or furnace is needed, or otherwise attempt to make money from the survivor's lack of experience with such matters. There are thousands of cases each year of unnecessary and over-priced repairs being made to the houses of persons who are newly responsible, alone, for such work.

Similarly, financial instrument sales persons may also confront the older client and suggest some sort of scheme to invest their inheritances—often with much better financial results for the salesperson than for the customer.

Dealing with such matters is difficult for a client, alone, and human services workers often find it beneficial to assist in contacting and working with consumer advocate organizations. Almost every state and local community has a better business bureau, which is a voluntary organization of local businesses charged with responsibility for investigating and adjusting consumer complaints about businesses. In addition, many state and local governments have offices of consumer affairs or consumer advocates who are responsible for investigating and taking action against fraudulent business practices. Those who work with the aged often find it helpful to find out about and learn the procedures used by such organizations in protecting citizens from improper or unfair business practices. The worker can discharge his or her role as an advocate effectively by helping clients use such services.

Summary

One of the characteristics of aging is increased vulnerability. The older one becomes, the more one is at the mercy of organizations, individuals, businesses, and even one's own family and neighbors. Because of that increased vulnerability, human services practices and public laws have required advocacy and protection services. Protection of the older adult's person, property, and well-being often require human services workers to intervene on behalf of the client and take action to assist.

This chapter has described some of the ways these protection and advocacy services are provided to older adults by human services organizations as well as some of the ways in which human services workers provide them.

PART four

service programs for older people

The outcomes of planning and development activities are programs of service for older people. Many of the most important of those programs, especially those that deal with the economic and physical well-being of older people, are described in this part of the text.

It is important for human services workers to know about and be able to help their clients obtain and use these services. That kind of direct assistance is often the most pervasive part of the aid that human services workers are able to provide to their older clients. Helping them meet their financial, health care, and other practical as well as immediate needs is often at the top of the agenda of the older person.

These programs vary from state to state and also change over time. The descriptions contained here are basic and should provide a sound framework for the worker to use in helping clients.

CHAPTER 12
MEETING THE ECONOMIC NEEDS OF THE ELDERLY: FINANCIAL ASSISTANCE, HOUSING, TRANSPORTATION, EMPLOYMENT AND TRAINING

For much of the twentieth century, American social welfare policy efforts have focused on alleviating the economic problems of the aging. During the Great Depression of the 1930's, poverty among the elderly was a major social welfare and political issue. It was addressed by the passage of the Social Security Act of 1935, which provided social insurance for the elderly to protect them against the poverty associated with retirement as well as Old Age Assistance, a financial aid program for financially disadvantaged older people. However, by the 1970's, these programs had failed to keep pace with the increases in the cost of living to such an extent that aging was closely related to poverty. The older adult population was one of the largest impoverished groups in the country. "In 1959, when 22.4 percent of the general population had incomes below the official poverty threshold, over 35 percent of those over sixty-four years old were poor." (Aaron, Bosworth, and Burtless, 1989)

However, there were great changes in the 1970's that brought many of the elderly poor out of poverty. "By 1985, when the poverty rate for all Americans had fallen to 14.0 percent, the rate for older Americans had fallen to just 12.6 percent—1.4 points below the rate for the general population." (Aaron, Bosworth, and Burtless, 1989)

Although today's aging, as a group, no longer face the problems of poverty they might have encountered a decade earlier, it is only through the operation of various government programs that many older adults are able to meet their economic needs. For many older people, even the available programs do not move them above the poverty line. That is especially true for the "younger aged," who

228

Part 4 Service Programs for Older People

are in their late 50's or early 60's and, therefore, ineligible for some of the assistance programs covered in this chapter. In addition, those who encounter serious health problems also constitute an impoverished group of the elderly. No matter how high the income may be, long-term, disabling illness often leads to financial deprivation for many elderly people.

This chapter describes the current operations of the various programs and resources that help older adults deal with the problems of financial need.

Some Prototype Cases

There is a variety of typical cases one encounters among older people who face financial need. Although each case of need is unique to the individual, as are the individual reactions to the situations, such cases can be grouped into categories and generalized examples. The following are some fictional but not unusual examples of the kinds of financial need that human services workers who deal with the aging are likely to encounter.

Mrs. Baker, Too Young and Too Old

Mrs. Baker, age 58, was widowed recently. Her husband left little life insurance so her cash inheritance when he died was relatively small. She has not worked outside the home in the past 20 years and does not feel capable of being employed any longer. However, because of her age she is too young to collect Social Security. She has two children but hesitates in asking them for financial help. She is also not feeling well, herself, and has suffered from a variety of health problems in recent years.

Comment: This chapter includes discussions of the programs that might be applied to a case such as this one. However, helping Mrs. Baker would require a high degree of imagination and effort on the part of the worker. Mrs. Baker falls in the category sometimes flippantly called "Menopause to Medicare." That is, she is in an older age group and, because of recent limits in her life experiences, lacks the skills she might need for self-sufficiency. The programs that might help her, however, do not assist people of her age group. The years between her widowhood and her ability to rely on service programs are likely to be very difficult for her.

Mr. Epworth's Permanent Poverty

Mr. Epworth's financial situation has always been marginal. He has never earned a great deal and has had long periods of unemployment. Now that he is older, in his mid-60's, and unable to find or carry out employment, he has no personal financial resources on which to rely. Had he earned more money as a younger man, he might now have some savings, life insurance policies that could be converted to income, or securities such as stocks and bonds. However, few of his many jobs provided him with retirement plans and, for those that did, he took his contributions in the form of cash when he left.

Comment: As this chapter points out, income in the later years is often tied to one's earnings while employed. That is particularly true of Social Security. Those who earn low wages pay smaller amounts into Social Security and, when they retire, have smaller pensions. Supplemental Security Income is available for the low-income aged. It, too, is relatively modest. A person such as Mr. Epworth may encounter great financial need during his remaining years. He may become a homeless person or face other kinds of socio-economic deprivation which are related to his relatively poor financial status as a younger person.

Mrs. Digby's Illness

Mrs. Digby, age 67, inherited relatively large amounts of money from her husband when he died. He was well-covered by life insurance and also owned stocks and bonds that grew in value after he purchased them. She developed a brain tumor, however, one year after his death. The cost of her housing, uncovered health care, and postoperative nursing home care, have exhausted her inheritance. Her monthly Social Security payments have become the primary source of her discretionary income.

Comment: The financial coverage of health services is discussed in a subsequent chapter. However, there is a close relationship between health status and financial viability for many elderly people. Mrs. Digby is an example of the common problem older people face of becoming paupers because of health needs.

Programs of Financial Aid

The balance of this chapter describes the programs available for assistance to older people with economic problems and needs. Some of the ways in which human services workers help such individuals and their families through the use of public and private programs are discussed. The reader should keep in mind that all of the skills covered in this book are useful in assisting elderly people with economic problems. That is, assisting people in groups, direct counseling, and case management, as well as services such as leisure time activity, can assist people in practically and emotionally coping with debilitating problems such as these. This chapter is about programs that help. Much of the rest of the book is about ways in which human services workers help their clients use the help that is available.

Social Insurance

Social insurance is of help to many citizens but particularly the elderly. The United States has had social insurance, the largest program of which is called Social Security, since 1935 when the Social Security Act was passed. This act has been and continues to be amended by Congress so that the social insurance program is now much different from what it was originally. It is the most important piece of social legislation in United States history and is the basis for most of the human services, especially those for the elderly. It provides for retirement, survivors, and dependents insurance; the public assistance programs; health care payments for the elderly and the low-income; protective services for children; and financing for all the other kinds of social services offered to people.

The social insurance program is one of the primary components of Social Security. It is financed through contributions of employers and contributions from their employees in the form of wage deductions. The employer pays a specific amount and the employee pays the same into the federal Social Security program. Self-employed people pay a total amount. At the time this book was published, employers and employees were each expected to pay about 7.5 percent of the employee's wages for Social Security, including old age, survivors', disability insurance, and health insurance (Medicare), up to the first $48,600 of annual income. There were to be no payments on wages or earnings above $48,600. Self-employed people were to pay approximately the same total—about 15 percent of their first $48,600 of earnings. The estimates are those of Aaron, Bosworth, and Burtless in their 1989 book *Can Americans Afford to Grow Old?* These figures are adjusted periodically, so they will reflect increases in the cost of living and will allow people to receive enough money to stay at the same level of income.

Each participant in Social Security—which really means every person who is or has been employed—has a special account set up by the Social Security program. The Social Security number is the account number and any participant can, at any time, find out how much that account is worth to him or to her.

The fundamental idea of the social insurance plan is to provide a federal program through which citizens obtain low-cost, government-sponsored insurance against the common catastrophes all people face. Because the program is so large and is mandatory, the costs are relatively low. One author (Kingson, 1986) found that for a younger male worker with a wife and two young children, the value of private insurance to provide the same protection he had from Social Security would be close to $400,000. Paying for that insurance would cost a great deal more than such a man would spend each year on Social Security.

Under the current system, according to Aaron, Bosworth, and Burtless (1989), the 31 million beneficiaries of social insurance receive benefits based on a complex formula. The ingredients include the PIA or primary insurance amount, which is the amount of pension a worker would receive if he or she were single and retired at the age of 65. Aaron, Bosworth, and Burtless explain: "The PIA for any particular worker is based on the worker's average indexed monthly earnings (AIME) in employment covered by social security." That calculation is based on the worker's highest thirty-five years of earnings. Then the amounts are re-calculated based on wages in the total economy—to make sure the benefits stay current with inflation and other living cost factors.

As has been indicated, social insurance covers a number of catastrophes, some of which are more valuable to younger people than to the elderly. It may pay close to $2,000 per month for a typical family that has lost its breadwinner, to help support the surviving spouse and children until the children grow up, if that breadwinner has been paying the maximum in Social Security for a few years. It may also provide a sizable benefit to an individual or couple if the wage-earner has become handicapped. A retired individual or couple may also receive significant amounts of money in the form of a pension after the wage-earner retires in his or her 60's. In 1989 (AARP, December 1988) the *average* monthly payment for a retired worker was $537. The maximum for a worker who retired in 1988 at age 65 was $899 per month. The benefits change each year, depending upon changes in the cost of living in the United States.

The rules and regulations of Social Security's social insurance are very complicated, as has been noted, and change frequently. For example, people who retire early receive less than those who retire later. At later ages, Social Security recipients can work and earn income without the penalties they will encounter at earlier ages. The actual available benefits depend upon how long and how recently the beneficiary worker. Whether or not the Social Security benefit is taxed depends upon the extent of other earnings and the sources of those earnings.

Because of the program's complexity, it is difficult and probably impossible for a human services worker who is not a specialist in Social Security to be able to tell an older person how much he or she will receive in benefits upon retirement. The job of the human services worker in helping an older person who wants that kind of information is to help the person get in touch with the local Social Security office in person or by telephone. Those offices can give participants detailed and accurate information on their own accounts and the ways in which they might use them. Most Social Security matters can be handled by telephone or mail, which saves the older client the need to travel to an office. The human services worker can help the client understand the various options that are available and can also help the client plan his or her life after retirement. If the client is dissatisfied with the information received and thinks there might be a more favorable set of benefits, the worker can help the client with an appeal of the Social Security decision. But the essential role of the worker is in helping the client understand and use the Social Security system and the resources it offers.

One piece of guidance that workers can give social insurance beneficiaries is the value of directly depositing their monthly checks to a bank account. Social Security encourages them to do so. The protection against the loss or theft of checks through direct deposit is significant.

Social Security as a Partial Retirement Resource

Although Social Security has become much more generous in recent years, it is often not enough for people to maintain their previous standard of living.

Therefore, in helping people who are anticipating retirement with Social Security benefits, it is important to help them understand that they may need other resources, as well. Those might include the cash value of life insurance policies, retirement benefits from employment, annuity policies, the proceeds from investments, and savings. Social Security is only one part of the financial package needed by most people to become and remain solvent during their senior years. However, Social Security retirement, because it does not "run out" and is essentially available throughout the lifetime of the retiree, can be considered the cornerstone of a sound plan for retirement living.

Social Security Disability Payments

As has been indicated, retirement benefits are only one part of the Social Security package of insurance. Those who have become blind or physically or mentally disabled and were covered by Social Security at the time one of those occurrences changed their lives also receive monthly benefits. Therefore, a person who may be older but not old enough to receive retirement payments may be eligible for disability benefits if he or she is handicapped. In the disability program, it is often even more important than in retirement for older people to have some assistance in obtaining benefits from Social Security. Retirement benefits are based upon the age of the recipient, which is usually easy to document (although some retirees may need help in obtaining a birth certificate or other appropriate documentation of their ages). In some cases of disability, however, the determination of whether or not the client is truly disabled is a complex question. There are specific criteria used by Social Security for determining whether or not there is a real disability that entitles the applicant to benefits. There is also some discretion available to the specialists—including medical and other professionals—in making those decisions. Some applicants for help may need the assistance of attorneys and may want to appeal negative decisions. Human services workers can be helpful to their clients by helping them, again, make appeals and by putting them in touch with attorneys who understand and can help them deal with Social Security law, which is relatively complicated and which requires some special legal knowledge. Knowing the Social Security appeals process and being acquainted with lawyers or legal organizations that can help clients establish their eligibility is part of the skill of the human services worker, especially in cases of disability payments.

Supplemental Security Income

Mr. George, age 63, is a victim of a genetic condition that causes him to be classified as developmentally disabled. He is part of the estimated 1 percent of the population that is mentally retarded. He has been in special schools, sheltered workshops, and for a year during his childhood, in a state public institution for the mentally retarded. Now, however, he lives with two other mentally retarded clients in a supervised apartment that is organized and run by the local community mental health center.

As a disabled person, he would be entitled to social insurance payments. However, he has only worked episodically, part-time, and at relatively low wages. Therefore, he is entitled to little or no social insurance benefits. To care for him and for others in his circumstances, Social Security operates the Supplemental Security Income program, which makes payments each month to adults who are aged, blind, or disabled and who have low incomes. The SSI program, as it is commonly called, is not financed in the same way as Social Security, which depends upon contributions from employers and employees. Instead, SSI is financed by appropriations from the U.S. Government.

At the time of publication, SSI provided a maximum payment of approximately $4,000 per year, paid in monthly payments, to an eligible individual or about $6,000 for a couple. Those who are eligible but who have other income—from Social Security or trust funds or earnings and the like—receive only the difference between that other income and the SSI payments.

SSI, which is administered by the same Social Security offices that provide social insurance eligibility and payments, is especially helpful to older people who have not worked and earned very much under Social Security. Although the payments are not large, the SSI recipient is also entitled to a variety of other forms of assistance that are discussed in this book such as food stamps, in most cases, and Medicaid. In approximately half of the states, SSI recipients also receive a state-financed supplement to their SSI payments. The state government appropriates money for those supplements and sends the funds to the Social Security Administration which adds them to the checks of the recipients. Although only California regularly raises the supplements in line with changes in the cost of living (Center on Budget and Policy Priorities, 1988) many states periodically raise their supplements. The federal payments are only the basic help that is provided. When combined with state supplements, which range from as little as two dollars per month per individual to almost three hundred dollars (Center on Budget and Policy Priorities, 1988) the monthly checks for SSI recipients are relatively helpful in helping people meet their basic needs.

In reality, SSI is an assistance program for low-income people. However, it is probably more popularly accepted by the people of the nation—including those who receive the assistance—than the programs that preceded it, which were operated totally by the states with the use of both federal and state funds.

SSI is not paid to people who are residents of public institutions for the mentally ill, mentally retarded, or for other disabilities. Because it is for people who live outside institutions, it has helped in the process of "deinstitutionalizing" thousands of disabled people. It can be used to help pay the cost of boarding care or adult foster care, which are often used by disabled clients, as well as for living alone in their own houses or apartments.

Aid to Families with Dependent Children

The primary state government program for helping disadvantaged families is called Aid to Families with Dependent Children or AFDC. It is administered by the state agency that handles social services. In some states that agency is called the department of public welfare. In others it goes by the name of department of human services or social services or human resources. Virtually every county in the United States has a local office that provides those services. The state agency is mentioned in several other chapters because of the large number of services it provides to the elderly. Although it primarily serves younger people with children who are under eighteen years of age, AFDC is sometimes available to older people as well. When AFDC benefits are paid to a family with a dependent child, the total grant is based upon the total family, which may include an elderly parent, grandparent, or other relative. When that occurs, other sources of income such as social insurance or SSI are figured into the total family income. Depending on the state, AFDC may provide better benefits to the family than social insurance or SSI alone, might. The variations in AFDC benefits are great, according to a 1988 report by the Center on Budget and Policy Priorities. The lowest monthly payment for a family of three was about $120 in some Southern states. The highest was $749 per month in Alaska.

In 1988, the AFDC or "welfare" system, as it is commonly called, was changed with the Family Support Act. The new system, which was only beginning to be implemented at the time this book was completed, would place special emphasis on finding absent parents who should be but are not paying child support for their dependent children, and on requiring work and the training for work of some adult recipients of aid. Most elderly family members were to be excluded from the work requirements of the program, however.

Comparing the Programs

There are major differences among social insurance, SSI, and AFDC, both in terms of the levels of payment and in terms of the responses people have to them. Social insurance is viewed as a right or entitlement that has been paid for by the recipient just as any privately paid insurance is viewed by most people as their property. There is no **"means test"** for social insurance. A beneficiary can be very wealthy or very poor and still receive monthly benefits based upon age, past contributions, and other objective factors. For Supplemental Security Income and Aid to Families with Dependent Children, however, there is such a test. That is, the recipient individual or family must prove their low income status. For some people, SSI and AFDC seem to carry the stigma of poverty because of the requirement that one be in need to receive them. Such a stigma is often very difficult for older people who may have been fully employed for most of their lives but now find that the programs they must depend upon are not sufficient to meet their needs.

Some social welfare theorists believe that all programs ought to be "universal," as social insurance is. They think that all families ought to start with a guaranteed minimum income that they can supplement with work. For those who have good incomes, taxes can adjust their situations so they are not receiving more than is reasonable. But such a guarantee of income for all can help remove the stigma and the other forms of emotional distress that too often go with receiving public help in the United States.

Food Stamps

In addition to the cash assistance and support programs discussed already, there is another program that helps older people meet their basic needs. It is called food stamps and is usually administered by the public assistance agency, which also administers AFDC. Food stamps are given to those who qualify on the basis of income and assets, somewhat similar to the arrangements for AFDC. However, the food stamp program, which is administered by the U.S. Department of Agriculture, is basically the same throughout the nation. That is, a person or family entitled to food stamps in one state would be entitled to the same amounts in any other. In many states, the guidelines for food stamps are more generous than those for AFDC. That is, people can have more assets and income, if their expenses are great, than they can to receive AFDC.

Once the stamps are received, the family is able to use them in most food stores for purchasing food only (no cleaning supplies, paper products, and other non-food items can be purchased). Some states have special arrangements for providing food stamp assistance—such as giving the family some more money, instead of stamps, or electronic identification cards which can be used by the food store to charge the recipient's account.

Food stamps are very helpful to many older people with limited incomes because they allow the client or the family to use the money they have available to meet other financial needs such as housing, clothing, and utilities.

Fuel Assistance

The federal and state governments also aid low-income elderly people with a program of fuel or energy assistance to help them pay their utility costs during the colder winter months. Each state has its own program, based upon the number of cold days each year.

Some assistance is given directly to the utility, to pay the bill for the low-income person. In other cases, the money for the utility bill is given to the person or family to help them pay bills or to buy wood or coal for home heating purposes. Typically, this program is administered by the local senior center or other service center for the aging.

Not all of the assistance for fuel help is given directly. Some of the money, along with some special local programs, is provided in the form of "weaterization" assistance. In those cases, government money, sometimes connected with volunteer efforts, is used to help insulate and otherwise improve the client's home so that less fuel is needed to heat it.

In addition to government programs, many utility companies also provide assistance directly to low-income people—especially the elderly—from contributions made by their customers. Utility users are asked to contribute a sum of money every month or once a year that will be used to assist those in need with their utility payments. The utilities often work with the same agencies that administer government fuel assistance in helping those who require aid.

Fuel assistance is another of the major programs that help low-income elderly people survive financially.

Private Insurance and Savings

In helping a family or individual assess their financial resources, a human services worker will often want to consider their insurance and savings. Life insurance is often a resource that a person has purchased at an early age as a form of protection against economic need for his or her family. In the later years, that economic investment may have become an asset that can be used for retirement living. There are, of course, different kinds of insurance. *Term* insurance protects a family with large amounts of money at relatively low cost if the person who is insured dies. The younger the age of death, the greater the benefit because only a few years of coverage have been purchased. However, at the time of retirement, when children are perhaps independent and the insured person no longer needs to protect them, the insurance will have little or no "cash value." Other forms of life insurance, which are called *whole, ordinary,* or *universal life,* cost more in monthly or annual premiums for the amount of insurance purchased but, at later times, have built some "cash value" which can actually be converted into a retirement income or cash that can be used to pay for a house or to otherwise address the financial needs associated with the later years. The worker may find it helpful to discuss all of the clients' life insurance policies with him or her and to help in making decisions about how to use the value, if there is some, of those policies. In many cases, the client may be continuing to pay premiums on a policy that is already worth as much as it will every be— although the additional premiums may add up to something like a savings account. Deciding what to do about life insurance and how to do it is often a major issue for the aged person, and it is important to help with it.

In recent years, some insurance companies have begun selling policies that will allow an insured person to use cash value for care in a long-term facility such as a nursing home. The discussion of such facilities and the financing of them is in chapter 13. However, life insurance policies may be a resource for that service as well as others.

Many clients will have other forms of savings—certificates of deposit, passbook savings accounts, "tax-sheltered annuities" that allow people to buy insurance for retirement without paying taxes on the interest until they retire, Individual Retirement Accounts, which allow some people to save money and deduct those savings from their taxes along with the interest that accrues until they retire, and stocks and bonds of all kinds. Many times, because they are purchased either over a long period of time or were purchased by a deceased spouse for the later benefit of a survivor, the possessor of the financial instruments—insurance policies, stocks, bonds, and the like—may be essentially unfamiliar with them. Therefore, the human services worker can provide a valuable service by helping the client find all the instruments (in bank safe deposit boxes, in personal safes or strong boxes, or wherever important papers may be kept by the client) and by helping the client arrange for conferences with people such as insurance agents, attorneys, and bank officials about how to best handle them.

The worker also fills a useful function by helping the client plan for the use of those funds that are available. Many elderly clients, especially surviving spouses, do not know as much as they need to about planning for and managing their money. Simply helping design a plan for making the available money last for the time needed—when coupled with other money such as Social Security—is a function that the worker often provides or helps other professionals provide to elderly clients.

Employment and Training

For many elderly people, retirement from the labor force is not desirable or necessary. Some prefer entering the labor force for the first time or transferring to new employment after retiring from a job. In those cases, programs of job referral and training for the elderly come into effect. Certainly, employment is one of the ways in which elderly adults help meet their economic needs.

At the time this text was being written, there was heavy emphasis on the employment of older adults because of a labor shortage in the United States. Retail employers such as department stores and restaurants were calling upon the large numbers of retired people for both part and full-time work. Many older people have expressed enjoyment at being able to occupy part of their time in work. Others find that the economic supplement to their pension or social insurance is quite valuable. Many of those employers have carried out their own recruitment, training, and supervision program, so that older people are able to help them sell their products.

Some state employment programs find it relatively easy to identify work for their older clients. Therefore, human services workers who are serving those who would like to be employed often find that they can be helpful by referring their clients to employment security agencies in their home communities. Those agencies are usually a good place to start helping clients find work, when they want to. There are also a variety of programs funded by the federal, state, and local governments, and many of them have special services for older workers. Many senior centers are also often sources of referral for older people who are seeking employment.

A significant program in many communities is called Vocational Rehabilitation. It is administered by state agencies with some federal government help and is for the purpose of helping those who are physically or mentally handicapped to learn work skills that they can use to support themselves. In many cases, older people are eligible for such help, especially when they have become unemployed because of physical disabilities they have encountered in their later lives. Some older women have benefited from special programs referred to as "homemaker rehabilitation services" which are expressly designed to help them make the transition from working in the home to entering the labor force. Some program make it possible for homemakers to use their skills in the labor market. An article in a publication of the American Association of Retired Persons (Eastman, 1989) notes that the proprietary child care field is recruiting seniors to work in day care and other child care programs.

Older people who are changing jobs, relocating, or entering the work force for the first time can all benefit from the referral and counseling many workers provide on jobs and job training programs. Knowledge about those activities is important for the human services worker serving older clients.

Pension and Retirement Programs

For many elderly people, pensions and other retirement programs they have from their employment are the basic resource used in meeting the financial needs of the senior years. Human services workers need to help elderly clients appraise their pensions and determine how much support they will provide. In recent years, many pension programs have allowed for the "early retirement" of employees, in part as a means of reducing the work force.

In past years, pensions were not always correctly or sufficiently funded so that many elderly people who planned to live on them found that they were no longer available. That problem has largely been corrected because of legislation requiring that pensions be financed properly and protected from other uses that might have harmed the retirement planning of employees.

The changes in the use of private pension plans have been important. According to Aaron, Bosworth, Burtless (1989), "The number of beneficiaries under private pension plans has grown greatly in recent decades, rising from 1.8 million in 1960 to 9.1 million by 1980. Pension plans in 1985 provided incomes to nearly four of every ten household units with a member aged sixty-five or older and provided about 13 percent of the cash incomes received by these household units."

There are great variations among pension plans. Most governments, including the federal, state, and local levels, provide pension plans for their employees. Usually the employee and employer both contribute a portion of each salary payment to the pension fund. The collection of both principal and interest in the employee's account makes retirement possible.

Some pension plans are "vested" in the employee after a number of years or, in some cases, immediately. That means that the employee is entitled to all the

There is growing evidence that for the next decade, shelter will be a major public policy issue in the United States. As this article indicates, the issues of homelessness, deinstitutionalization, and the increasing costs of housing (which are significantly different than one another in terms of whom they affect and the possible solutions to them) are, when taken together, causing a widespread consensus about the need for public attention to helping the American people obtain and use adequate shelter. As this article suggests, some of those potential new public policies about shelter may be based upon models of adult foster care and community residential care. The significance of the emerging shelter problems and the perceived desires for policies to address them may have a major impact upon and expand the uses of programs of such forms of care.

The Nature and Scope of the Current Shelter Problem

There are several dimensions to the problem of shelter in the late 1980's. The most dramatic of these is homelessness, which has captured the attention of many popular publications and authors. For example, Kozol's *Rachel and Her Children* (1988) was first serialized in *The New Yorker* magazine (1988). It has also been reviewed in *Business Week* (1988) and *Time* (1988). The book, which is both a factual description and impassioned condemnation of policies that have led to homelessness, has the potential for developing an outraged public reaction to the problem of homelessness.

The popular media have reported homelessness on their own. *Time* (1987) described the special problems of those who are homeless because of economic difficulties. According to that magazine, 22% of the homeless hold full- or part-time jobs. They further report that one-third of the homeless are families with children. In addition, the average wait for subsidized housing, *Time* (1987) suggests, is 22 months.

A similar set of conclusions was published in *Parade Magazine* (Whittemore, 1988). An article in that publication about a homeless family was entitled "We Can't Pay the Rent." (p. 4) That article suggests that 40% of the homeless are families with dependent children and that such families constitute the fastest growing segment of the homeless population.

Public opinion about the problem of homelessness also appears to be strongly opposed to the development in the United States of a large homeless population. A survey of 818 persons of ages 18 to 44 by the Peter D. Hart Research Associates organization (Greider, 1988) found that 29% of those surveyed considered the provision of food and shelter for the homeless among the top one or two goals the next President of the United States should address. *Insight on the News* magazine (1988) reported that 82% of one thousand people surveyed in California would be willing to pay five dollars per year more in taxes to help the homeless and 72% of those same people said they would be willing to pay as much as $50 a year more in state income taxes for that purpose.

Although exact information on the actual extent of homelessness is difficult to obtain (Connell, 1987) it appears to be a growing problem. As Connell (1987) reports, the estimates range from 350,000 (according to the United States Department of Housing and Urban Development) to 2.5 million (according to the National Coalition for the Homeless). Kozol (1988) estimates that there are 500,000 homeless children.

Homelessness appears to be increasing for a variety of reasons discussed in this article. The factors that are contributing to increased homelessness also make affordable and adequate shelter beyond the reach of many groups of Americans. The homeless are simply the most obvious and dramatic example of the problems currently associated with the availability and affordability of shelter in the United States.

Deinstitutionalization

Some data indicate that the problem of homelessness is largely influenced by the population of deinstitutionalized mentally handicapped people of the United States. Connell (1987) reports that some studies show 50% of the homeless need patient care for mental illnesses. A report in the *Hunger Action Forum* (1988) quotes the author of a book to be published on the impact of the deinstitutionalization of the mentally ill as indicating that a large percentage of the homeless are mentally ill. The author quoted, E. Fuller Torrey, indicates that there are several reasons for the growth in the numbers of the homeless mentally ill including:

1. Legal changes made in the 1970's that make it difficult to involuntarily hospitalize or treat the mentally ill.

2. Inadequate community facilities for the discharged mentally ill.

3. The lack of provision of public housing for 433,503 individuals who reflect the decrease in the mental hospital population from 1955 to 1984 from 522,150 to 118,647.

4. Battles among the federal, state, and local governments over who will assume the role of caring for the mentally ill.

Although, as this article later indicates, some of the mentally ill have moved into adult foster care and other community residential facilities, the likelihood is that provisions were not made and are still not made for all the deinstitutionalized mentally disabled.

The deinstitutionalization of the mentally handicapped resulted from conscious policies, in part, that arose from legal and philosophical objections to the involuntary commitment of persons to mental hospitals. Szasz (1961, 1963), one of the leading figures in that critique of mental health policies, insisted that involuntary commitment violated civil liberties. Hollingshead and Redlich (1958) took a different approach and demonstrated that those viewed as suffering from the most severe mental illnesses were often from the lower socioeconomic classes. Ginsberg (1966, 1968, 1970) studied mental health and mental retardation commitment practices in Oklahoma and suggested that involuntary commitment was incompatible with the rights of individuals. He proposed ending that practice and relying on community mental health services for those who needed assistance in dealing with their mental handicaps.

Those who opposed involuntary commitment suggested that many of those who were defined as mentally ill or mentally retarded and institutionalized for those conditions were, in fact, not really victims of illnesses or disabling, diagnosable conditions. They were, instead, simply lacking in the motivation and resources to care for themselves or lacking in contacts with people who would help them with the personal—especially economic—problems (Okin, 1987).

A series of articles in a special section of *Hospital and Community Psychiatry* reviews the current state of involuntary commitment procedures and laws and suggests guidelines for commitment practices (Keilitz, 1988), describes some of the legal issues that are involved in those guidelines (Wexler, 1988), and evaluates those guidelines (Appelbaum & Roth, 1988).

In any case, the deinstitutionalized mentally handicapped appear to be one group that would benefit from improved shelter policies in the United States.

The Costs of Housing

The costs of housing appear to have increased beyond the means of many people. Locating an apartment or house for less than $150-$200 per month that is large enough for a family has become virtually impossible, according to some sources (Whittemore, 1988). Dluhy (1987) demonstrates that from 1970 until 1982, the median sales price of houses almost tripled. During the same period, he points out, median family income only doubled. Although many of the people for whom housing is a serious problem are not necessarily going to become homeowners, the cost of rent is directly influenced by the cost of purchase of housing. Therefore, rental costs have, one may assume, increased in a similar fashion. The U.S. minimum wage, however, has not changed in over a decade and remains $3.35 per hour.

The increased costs of housing are a concern of all income levels, it would appear. According to *Fortune Magazine* (1988), first-time home buyers find that the average cost of their purchases is $81,000 and that they must spend 44% of their incomes on rent and mortgage costs. Ten years ago, the magazine reports, the amount of income needed for mortgage costs was only 21%. Several corporations, they further report, are making housing assistance a fringe benefit for their personnel and are constructing houses for their employees.

As has been demonstrated, the issue of shelter is a major public concern in the late 1980's and likely to be of significance in the 1990's because of the shelter problems faced by three diverse groups—the homeless, the deinstitutionalized, and persons whose incomes are too low to afford the kinds of housing they want (the extreme examples of whom are homeless)—who are encountering dimensions of the same general shelter problems.

For these reasons, the issue of shelter has developed into what Meenaghan and Washington (1980) define as a public issue or a social problem as opposed to a "private trouble." These authors reference several sociologists (including C. Wright Mills) in defining a social problem which is paraphrased in the following:

1. The size and extent of the problem is such that it is shared by a considerable number of people. (As has been indicated, shelter problems affect, perhaps, at least a quarter million homeless, over 400,000 deinstitutionalized persons, and, it would appear, millions of lower and middle income persons who cannot afford the housing they need or want.)

2. The problem is endemic. (This discussion has identified the groups most significantly affected by the problem.)

3. The problem is relatively permanent. (Shelter problems became most severe, it would seem, in the 1970's and increased for several years thereafter.)

4. Institutions which should deal with the problem are malfunctioning. (The mental health system as well as several housing systems to be described in later sections of this article are not, it would appear, sufficiently resolving the shelter problems that are being faced in the United States.)

The Impact of Social Policy

Studies of the problems of shelter and housing indicate that a variety of social policies has helped cause the problem. Perhaps most significant of those social policies has been the retreat from federal policies supporting housing programs. Kozol (1988), for example, says that federal support for low-income housing dropped from $28 billion in 1981 to $9 billion in 1986. However, the federal argument and statistics are somewhat different. According to Dluhy (1987), there have been increases in federal housing support through tax breaks for home owners and owners of rental property, which are skewed toward higher-income households. There has not been an absolute drop in funds for housing but, Dluhy suggests (1987), the federal government subsidizes home owners—a relatively prosperous group—three and one-half times more than it does lower-income households. Dluhy (1987) also points out that of 91,561,000 housing units in the United States, only some 3.3 million units are assisted in some way by governmental programs although estimates indicate as many as 9 million units need assistance.

There are often proposals for reductions in housing assistance that affect those who need it, according to some sources. The American Association of Retired Persons (AARP, 1988) indicates that the Reagan administration has proposed a 38% reduction in the Section 202 Housing program for the 1989 fiscal year. That program provides housing for low-income elderly and handicapped persons.

Other policies and processes have also had an impact on the availability of shelter. In some earlier years, urban renewal projects and highway construction displaced many low-income households, including many single room occupancy hotels that had served and could continue to serve many of the homeless and deinstitutionalized (Dluhy, 1987). A current development is called "gentrification," which had led many people who had moved from central cities to return to them. A similar symptom of change in housing patterns is the conversion of former rental housing into cooperatives and condominiums, which are often beyond the economic reach of those who have shelter problems (Dluhy, 1987).

Utility costs have also been a factor in the increased costs of housing. Even being able to pay rent does not necessarily mean one is able to afford shelter that is heated and lighted. Federal programs have helped those who cannot afford utilities—especially the Low-Income Home Energy Assistance Program. (AARP, 1988) However, new proposals for 1988 include a federal reduction of $345 million in that program (AARP, 1988).

In some ways, general federal policy towards social programs and governmental intervention into social problems has changed in recent years (Ginsberg, 1987). The Reagan administration philosophically opposed domestic spending and, in some cases, reduced social expenditures, in others maintained them with no increases, and in still others, increased them less than might have been required for the programs to continue providing similar levels of services (Hopps and Pinderhughes, 1987). These policies, coupled with the market inflation in the costs of housing and other factors already discussed, appear to have contributed to the problem of shelter in the United States.

The Role of Adult Foster Care and Community Residential Facilities in Shelter

Among the potential solutions to the shelter problems identified in this article are the services known as adult foster care which may be considered as part of a larger network of community residential facilities. According to McCoin (1987):

An AFC home is essentially a privately owned home, usually owned by the manager, for the purpose of incorporating disabled and dependent adults for sustenance, shelter, protection, support, supervision and sometimes socialization. In exchange for these services the owner manager is financially compensated, usually through the resident's income (p. 24).

Community residential care facilities are a bit broader in scope, according to McCoin (1987) and "include all of the nonpublic residential facilities housing

adults with histories of mental retardation, mental illness, or dependent elderly"
(p. 22).

Oktay (1987) elaborates on the foster care services available to adults by saying they are provided in private homes small enough to provide a homelike atmosphere and in which the usually nonrelative primary caregiver resides;
residents are provided services such as supervision, provision of medicine, help
with the daily routine, and room and board, in return for financial remuneration;
and some supervision is provided by the staff of the agency that arranged the
placement.

These kinds of services aid many of the individuals who have difficulty with
shelter who are described here, especially those who have handicaps or are aged
among the homeless and the deinstitutionalized mentally ill. Oktay (1987) references McCoin in concluding that there are some 50,000 persons in state and local
programs plus 12,000 to 15,000 in programs of the Veterans Administration.

Adult foster care and community residential facilities are significant in a variety of ways, especially in the services they provide, because they fit the deinstitutionalization models discussed earlier that called for the removal of people from
involuntary settings such as mental hospitals and their relocation to community-
based residences.

Such community care is also significant in economic terms because it is often
used as an alternative to the typically more expensive long-term care provided in
nursing homes which, according to Kane (1987), quoting a U.S. Congress report
in 1985, cost private-pay patients between $12,000 and $50,000 per year. Although, as Kane (1987) points out, public payments for nursing home care may
be much lower than the fees paid by private patients, the range is still great and
may average $50 per patient per day or more, according to McCoin's (1987) refer-
ence from a 1984 study by Hauber, Bruininks, Hill, Lakin, and White. The same
study indicates that adult foster care cost $16.15 per day.

Financing Adult Foster Care

The payments for adult foster care, according to Oktay (1987) come from the
personal resources of the recipients such as Supplemental Security Income
grants, which are provided to the low-income aged and disabled as a kind of income maintenance service, veterans' pensions, Social Security benefits, and private insurance or pension funds, and an unknown number are private-paying
residents. In some cases, state mental health systems and other organized services make direct payments for adult foster care.

Despite the fact that adult foster care is less expensive than long-term care in
nursing homes, the two are hardly comparable in size. According to Kane (1987),
in 1984 1.4 million people lived in nursing homes, compared to the 50,000 in
adult foster care.

Among the reasons for these numerical disparities is the financial pattern followed in nursing home care. The largest funding source for long-term care is Medicaid, which is Title XIX of the Social Security Act (Kane, 1987). Medicaid serves the poor under the auspices of state government agencies that provide social welfare services. However, the financing of Medicaid is shared by the federal and state governments, the amount of the federal portion depending upon the state's per capita income (Ginsberg, 1983).

Medicare provides a smaller amount of support for nursing home care, usually for short stays in nursing homes (Kane, 1987).

Kane (1987) describes a variety of "waivers" that now allow some funds that might have been restricted to medical programs such as nursing home care to be used for community services such as adult foster care. For example, states may secure waivers of the rules on Title XX of the Social Security Act, which do not ordinarily allow for residential services, she says, so that Title XX funds, which come solely from the federal government in the form of block grants to the states, with no state matching required, may be used for adult foster care and community residential facilities.

It is also noted by Kane (1987) that both Medicare and Medicaid have allowed demonstration projects to permit those funds to be used for community care such as adult foster care. She also notes that Section 2176 of the 1981 Omnibus Reconciliation Act allows states to offer, without specially designated demonstration projects, community-based care.

Growth Patterns of Adult Foster Care and Community Residential Facilities

It would appear, to this writer at least, that community residential facilities and adult foster care should grow in scope for a variety of reasons identified thus far. The waivers, demonstrations, and experiments with different forms of caring for people who cannot fully care for themselves should tend to increase the funding for these services. Of course, the opening material of this article, which describes the large numbers of homeless and deinstitutionalized people in the nation, builds a case for the need for increasing facilities to house and care for those who cannot house and care for themselves. It should be clear, from the discussions of financing care, that adult foster care and community residential facilities offer a less expensive means of providing that help. Both are also more in tune with the legal and philosophical principles which led to deinstitutionalization. That is, these approaches offer less restrictive alternatives to caring for the disabled.

Conjecture About Future Expansion

The author of this article served for nearly eight years (1977–1984) as the chief executive officer of a state agency, the West Virginia Department of Human Services, that provided Medicaid and social services, as well as other forms of social and economic assistance, to the disadvantaged. The author worked closely with nursing home operators and associations, with adult foster care providers, with state institutions for the mentally ill and mentally retarded, as well as with the Veterans Administration, and became quite familiar with the issues of residential care programs.

In state government work, this author was held responsible for maintaining balanced budgets for Medicaid and Title XX services by the West Virginia Legislature and Governor as well as for providing shelter to the homeless as mandated by the State Supreme Court.

It was clear that it was impossible to provide all the services that were needed with the limited money that was available. The problem continued to expand for the reasons described earlier in this article—homelessness, deinstitutionalization, and the increased costs of housing, which caused many low-income people to become part of the needy and sometimes homeless families of the state. The following observations about ways in which adult foster care and other community residential facilities services models might usefully be expanded to deal with some of the problems raised thus far are based upon those experiences.

First, despite the increased costs of housing construction and rent, there are billions of square feet of unused real estate that could be used for solving the shelter problems many Americans are encountering. West Virginia alone had abandoned large parts of some state hospitals, as well as other hospitals, and youth corrections facilities (another result of legal requirements for deinstitutionalization). According to Kozol (1988), New York City owns 100,000 units of empty low-cost housing. Many communities have abandoned hospitals that could be converted to residences.

These available facilities could be used as the basis for a national shelter program that could house all the homeless, deinstitutionalized, and others unable to afford or use available shelter. It is realistic to assume, based upon some of the characteristics and needs of the homeless and deinstitutionalized described earlier in this article, that services would be needed to help those two groups with their daily living requirements. The kinds of services offered through adult foster care and other community residential facilities programs should be ideal for providing such assistance. Families could be provided housing and an income within such facilities in return for providing the kinds of aid adult foster care managers provide. It is possible that pooling the kinds of resources now used for homeless shelters and comparable services, along with the Supplemental Security Income, Social Security, and pensions mentioned earlier, could pay for such shelter.

For some families and individuals, only minimal services would be needed. Those who are homeless for economic reasons alone could reside in such facilities, maintain them, and only pay the kinds of modest rent typically charged for public and other subsidized housing. Some such families could, perhaps, be adult foster care providers themselves. The kinds of facilities that exist may lend themselves to becoming not only dormitory rooms for single individuals but also apartments for families.

It is likely that a cadre of new kinds of professional social workers might help develop the kinds of arrangements suggested here. They could range from community organizers and planners—who could bring together the various funds that might be available and help apply them to the effective use of the physical facilities. Many social workers already appear to be working in this general field (Connell, 1987). In addition, social workers who are prepared to provide direct services to those individuals and families who need them could be helpful in training and consulting with care providers, just as many social workers already do with the existing programs of adult foster care and community residential services. Others could provide services directly to the residents of these projected facilities.

It is possible that additional public funds would be needed to help pay for the costs of the facilities and the services provided within them. However, those costs may not be as great as attempting to start over with a national public housing program for all who need it and shelters for all the homeless who need those. In any case, as this article makes clear in its representation of strong public opinion about the need for shelter assistance and services, the nation will probably find it necessary to find some solutions to these problems. The solutions proposed here may be lower in cost than others that might be pursued.

Approaches such as these may be the beginning of a national policy that could eliminate the problem of homelessness, the problems faced by the deinstitutionalized, and the lack of affordable housing for low-income people.

Conclusion

This article has described the problems of shelter faced in the United States, particularly as those problems are being faced by three groups—the homeless, the deinstitutionalized, and low-income families who cannot afford housing. It proposes a partial solution that would bring together existing shelter facilities— abandoned public housing sites, unused public mental hospitals and correctional facilities, and closed general hospitals—with the adult foster care and other community residential facilities and services models in ways that would help alleviate the need for shelter of many Americans.

References

American Association of Retired Persons. (1988, April). *AARP news bulletin*, *29*, 7.

Appelbaum, P. Roth, L. (1988). Assessing the NSCC guidelines for involuntary civil commitment from the clinician's point of view. *Hospital and Community Psychiatry*, *39*, 409–410.

Business Week (1988, February 29). Land of the free—home of the homeless, 16–17.

Connell, S. (1987). Homelessness. *Eighteenth edition, encyclopedia of social work*. Silver Spring, MD: National Association of Social Workers.

Dluhy, M. (1987). Housing. *Eighteenth edition, encyclopedia of social work*. Silver Spring, MD: National Association of Social Workers.

Fortune (1988, March 28). Hot new employee benefit: A house, 8.

Ginsberg, L. (1966). Representation by counsel in Oklahoma mental health hearings. *The Oklahoma Bar Journal, 37*, 2061–2063.

Ginsberg, L. (1968). Civil rights of the mentally ill—a review of the issues. *Community Mental Health Journal, 4*,244–250.

Ginsberg, L. (1970). A radical view of social welfare and mental health. *Mental Hygiene, 54*, 44–49.

Ginsberg, L. (1983). *The practice of social work in public welfare*. NY: The Free Press.

Ginsberg, L. (1987). Economic, political, and social context. *Eighteenth edition, encyclopedia of social work*. Silver Spring, MD: National Association of Social Workers.

Greider, W. (1988, April 7). The rolling stone survey. *Rolling Stone, 523*, 34–61.

Hollingshead & Redlich (1958). *Social class and mental illness: a community study*. NY: John Wiley and Sons.

Hopps & Pinderhughes (1987). Profession of social work: contemporary characteristics. *Eighteenth edition, encyclopedia of social work*. Silver Spring, MD: National Association of Social Workers.

Hunger Action Forum. (1988, January). The grate society.

Insight on the News. (1988, April 25). 47.

Kane, R. (1987) Long Term Care. *Eighteenth edition, encyclopedia of social work*. Silver Spring, MD: National Association of Social Workers.

Keilitz, I. (1988, April). An introduction to the National Center for State Courts' guidelines for involuntary civil commitment. *Hospital and Community Psychiatry, 39*, 397.

Keilitz, I. (1988, April). NCSC guidelines for involuntary civil commitment: A workable framework for justice in practice. *Hospital and Community Psychiatry, 39*, 398–402.

Kozol, J. (1988). *Rachel and her children*. NY: Crown.

Kozol, J. (1988, January 25). The homeless and their children. Part I-reporter at large. *The New Yorker, 63*, 65–84.

Kozol, J. (1988, February 1). The homeless and their children. Part II-reporter at large. *The New Yorker, 63*, 36–58.

McCoin, J. (1987). Adult foster care: old wine in a new glass. *Adult Foster Care Journal, 1*, 21–41.

Meenaghan & Washington. (1980). *Social policy and social welfare: structure and applications.* NY: The Free Press.

Okin, R. (1987). The case for deinstitutionalization. *The Harvard Medical School Mental Health Letter, 4,* 5–7.

Oktay, J. (1987). Foster care for adults. *Eighteenth edition, encyclopedia of social work.* Silver Spring, MD: National Association of Social Workers.

Szasz, T. (1961). *The myth of mental illness.* NY: Hoeber-Harper, Inc.

Szasz, T. (1963). *Law, liberty, and psychiatry.* NY: Macmillan.

Time. (1987, December 28). A job but no place to live. 27.

Time. (1988, February 8). Not fair. 74.

Wexler, D. (1988, April). Reforming the law in action through empirically grounded civil commitment guidelines. *Hospital and Community Psychiatry, 39,* 402–405.

Whittemore, H. (1988, January 10). We can't pay the rent. *Parade,* 4–6.

CHAPTER 13
MEETING THE HEALTH NEEDS OF THE ELDERLY: physical health, MENTAL health, institutional care

A common denominator for almost all aging people is declining health. Longer life often means affliction with diseases that strike older people more often than the young, including the catastrophic illnesses and killers such as cancer, heart disease, and stroke. Many other diseases first strike people in their later years, including diabetes, kidney disease, arthritis, Alzheimer's disease, and rheumatism. Circulatory conditions such as hypertension (high blood pressure) and arteriosclerosis, are often characteristic of aging. In addition, there are the normal declines in vision and hearing. The physical process of growing old inevitably includes declines in health, as Chapter I explains more fully. Of course, the health problems of older people vary significantly among individuals. Some may be very healthy while others may be very ill. As people grow older, the variations also grow.

This chapter is about the health concerns of older people and the ways in which they are met. In addition, it offers some suggestions about things human services workers need to know and do about health in working with their older clients. Human services workers also need to know about the prevention of health problems inasmuch as more is now known than ever before about maintaining physical health throughout the entire life span. In fact, many older adults maintain good health until—although it may sound contradictory—their sudden deaths at advanced ages. Good health as long as one is living is an ambition that can be achieved.

Body and health preoccupation may become characteristic of some older people for physical, psychological, and social reasons. Physically, the deterioration is real. As some physicians put it, the "wear and tear" on the human body over the years leads to disabling and debilitating conditions for many. At times, body concerns may be more psychological than physical, however. It is almost a stereotype of the elderly that they are concerned about such things as bladder functions, bowel movements, digestion, and muscular pains. Sometimes they result from withdrawal into preoccupation with one's own body, especially when elderly people no longer need to be concerned about employment, recreation, families to rear, or other relatives to care for. Television and radio programs that are oriented to older audiences are often sponsored by over-the-counter remedies for muscle pain, constipation, and other conditions that appear to be associated—in the body or the mind—with aging.

There are some practical realities to the physical changes that come with age. David Brown, in his both humorous and serious guide for older people (1987) says:

The one thing you will do more of is go to the bathroom. Your plumbing system is aging and as prone to leaks and stoppages as the New York water system. I know the location of every men's room, and in fact, I can draw a map of their whereabouts in all major hotels, theaters, restaurants, and museums in the principal cities of the world, including a neat little facility in the Gobi Desert.

Because declining health is so closely related to aging, understanding health problems and the health services available to older people are important concerns. Everyone who works with the elderly must know something about the health problems facing those in their later years. Human services workers who serve the aged must be able to interview older people about their conditions, must be able to help them obtain services to alleviate their problems, and must be able to make effective referrals to health services and other agencies.

For all of these reasons, including the real declines in health faced by older people and the additional emphasis on their own bodily functions during the later years, health is a major concern of the aged and, therefore, of the human service workers who help them.

Health Programs for the Aging

Much of America's health care is paid for by "third parties." That is, the payment for care is not typically the sole responsibility of the patient and the patient does not typically pay the provider of services—the dentist, pharmacist, hospital, or physician—directly or ultimately. Instead, a complex combination of voluntary, private, and public programs step in to handle the financial aspects of much of the health care of the aging.

Private Health Insurance

A large portion of all the health care provided in the United States is paid for through private insurance programs. The most common of these are Blue Cross-Blue Shield, private profit-making insurance companies, and some self-insured or nonprofit insurance organizations. There are individual and group versions of each of these.

In the individual private insurance program, the client simply pays a specified amount to an insurance company and, in return, is provided coverage for all or a portion of the medical costs he or she may encounter. The benefits provided are most typically hospitalization and some forms of laboratory work and surgery. Depending upon the premium, the insured individual or family may be covered for as much as all the health care that might be needed such as physicians' office visit, prescription medicines, and equipment such as braces and bandages.

In the group insurance arrangement, the individual or family buys health insurance as part of an organization such as a fraternal order, a professional society, or a social club. Generally, the same insurance costs less for members of groups than it does for individuals who are purchasing coverage.

In many situations, the group through which the person or family is insured is an employment setting. The employer arranges for the group and the insured receives the coverage at some cost, in some situations, or as a fringe benefit of employment, in others. Most commonly, the cost of health insurance is shared by the employer and the employees in a group.

Private Practice Home and Health Assistance

In many communities with large older adult populations, private practice agencies are being developed which receive their financial support from older adults, government agencies, or family members. The financing may come from pension income, earnings of family members, or in the case of some health services, from Medicare. These agencies provide a range of services to older people such as occasional visiting, home health services, and counseling.

The authors encountered organizations such as these in the Miami, Florida, area, where large numbers of people retire. The children of the retirees often arrange for the services of these organizations or help their parents arrange for them as a means of replacing some of the help the family members may have received had they not relocated.

Such organizations are likely to grow dramatically during the coming years because of the increasing aging population, the frequent relocation of older people to warm climates such as Florida, and the greater availability of funds to retired people from earnings, savings, and government assistance programs such as some of those described in this chapter.

Government Financing Programs

Many of the aged benefit from the health care services financed for them by government programs. There are essentially two programs for assisting older people with paying for their health care—Medicare and Medicaid. Human services workers with the aged need to be aware of both programs and the ways in which they serve the elderly.

Medicare

By far the most important health care program for the aged is Medicare. It is available to all people over 65 years of age and is financed through the Social Security system. Because it is such a large program and because the aged constitute such a large portion of those who receive health care, it is probably the single most important factor in all health services in the United States. What Medicare does or fails to do has enormous influence on all other health services and programs.

Medicare has several parts and it has changed significantly in recent years. The newest program, which began in 1989, provided for unlimited hospital care under "Part A" of the program. That means that recipients would be covered for all of their needed hospital expenses, after they paid an annual deductible of about $560 per person. That is, Medicare would pay all of the hospital costs per aged person every year if they are above $560. Since $560 is less than the daily rate for hospital care in many places, Medicare recipients would receive virtually all of their hospital care without charge.

Under Medicare's "Part B," which pays for physicians' services and prescriptions, 80 percent of the physician costs are paid after the patient pays a deductible. However, no Medicare recipient would be required to pay more than $1,370 per year of the Medicare-covered physician bills. There is one exception. Medicare pays only a certain amount for each procedure or service provided by a physician. If the physician's charges are higher than Medicare pays, the patient has to pay the difference.

For prescriptions, beginning in 1991, Medicare will pay half the costs of all outpatient prescription drugs after a deductible of $600 per year. Through 1993, the deductible and the percentage Medicare pays will both increase.

These new benefits will also cause an increase in the amount that Medicare recipients must pay each year. In addition to a monthly premium that is deducted from social insurance benefits, those who have larger incomes will be taxed up to over $1,000 per year extra.

Despite its size, Medicare does not pay for all medical costs for the elderly. In particular, it does not pay for long-term care (except for short periods of time and under special circumstances) discussed later in this chapter, nor for the first $600 of prescription medicines and some other services.

As mentioned in this section, Medicare pays hospitals and physicians based upon a set amount for the services they provide. In recent years, the federal government instituted a complicated system of "Diagnostic Related Groups," which help determine exactly how much will be paid for a specific service or procedure. A specific kind of surgery will lead to a payment of a set amount, which varies with the complexity of the procedure and the condition of the patient. Similarly, Medicare policies allow a certain number of days to be paid for in the hospital—which also varies with the condition of the patient. These issues of hospital and physician payments are important for all the parties—the patients, the physicians, and the hospitals in which the care is given.

Medicaid

Low-income people in the United States are eligible for Medicaid, a program of benefits for those who cannot afford to pay for their own medical care. Low-income older adults are part of the group covered by Medicaid, which is paid for by federal and state taxes. It is similar to Aid to Families with Dependent Children in that it is based on a formula that takes into account the state's ability to pay. States pay no more than half the cost of Medicaid with the federal government paying the rest.

Since each state has a different program and pays different amounts for Medicaid services, it is difficult to generalize about it. However, it is important to note that in many ways it may be more beneficial than Medicare. In some states, for example, Medicaid pays the full cost of prescription medicines. It also pays the costs of long-term care in facilities such as nursing homes which Medicare only pays for in a few cases and for only limited periods of time. However, it often does not pay for as many days in the hospital or for as large a portion of physician fees as Medicare does.

Generally, the best arrangement for an older person is to be covered as fully as possible for Medicare and to also have Medicaid benefits, if he or she is of low income. The programs work together. Medicare and, for that matter, any other health insurance or financial asset, must be used before Medicaid will pay for health care costs.

It is also important to know that the costs of some forms of health care—especially long-term care—are so great that many older people of relatively good financial condition become poor enough to be eligible for Medicaid after they have spent their assets on nursing home care. (See the discussion of long-term care below.)

Developmental Disabilities

Developmental disabilities are those hereditary or birth conditions that cause physical or mental handicaps for many individuals every year. Although most of the attention is given to developmentally disabled younger people, particularly infants and young children, more and more developmentally disabled individuals are living into their senior years. Therefore, human services workers with the elderly are finding that in increasing numbers of cases they must work with mentally retarded, autistic, epileptic, and otherwise handicapped people.

There are a number of ways in which developmentally disabled older adults are served in the United States. In past times, there was an emphasis on institutional care of developmentally disabled people, particularly the mentally retarded. However, American values and social policy have moved in the direction of deinstitutionalization of disabled individuals. Therefore, there are fewer and fewer developmentally disabled in long-term public facilities. The tendency today is for developmentally disabled persons to live in apartments, as members of groups, in their own homes and with their own families, and, in some cases, in group or adult foster care homes. Adult foster care homes are those in which the owners of a residence provide care for people in return for pay. The home is non-medical in nature, although medical services can be arranged and made available to the residents. (See Reading 12.1.) Payments for care and boarding come from the Social Security or SSI or other funds available to the individual residence. Developmentally disabled persons who are physically unable to care for themselves or who are too handicapped to be cared for in a lower level of care such as an adult foster care home, are often placed in community nursing homes along with other elderly individuals.

It is important to note that the range and degree of developmental disabilities varies widely. Autistic and epileptic individuals, for example, can lead relatively normal lives with appropriate help and support. Mentally retarded individuals, depending upon the degree of impairment and the opportunities they have had to learn and develop, may also be able to lead normal to near-normal lives.

The human services workers has an obligation and a need to understand developmental disabilities and their manifestations. In addition, the worker needs to understand how to help developmentally disabled clients with practical arrangements for housing, food services, health care, and all the other daily living requirements older people, in general, face, but which are even more heavily required by the developmentally disabled.

Alzheimer's Disease

One of the most important medical discoveries in recent years has been Alzheimer's disease. That condition, which is closely associated with the aging process, leads to neurological debilitation. Its victims become forgetful and, ultimately, unable to function independently. The incidence is highest among the very old although there is some evidence that persons with specific genetic conditions such as Down's Syndrome contract it at a very large rate in their middle years (Karlinsky, 1986).

The disease, which is now much easier to identify and understand, although there is no specific biological test for it, has replaced, in the thinking of the medical community, a number of other conditions such as premature senility, hardening of the arteries or arteriosclerosis of the brain, and even senility, itself. The clear identification of the disease is possible primarily through autopsies but behavioral manifestations and assumptions about it are also becoming better indicators of the disease in living patients. Alzheimer's probably has a genetic base. That is, people probably are born with the likelihood of contracting the disease in their later years or at least the propensity to contract the disease.

Care of the Alzheimer's patient, some of whose behavior may mimic forms of mental illness, is primarily related to maintenance and living services including residential and custodial services. Many Alzheimer's patients can be cared for in their own homes, especially if a spouse or other relative is present. Many others must be cared for in group facilities such as nursing homes, adult foster care homes, and, in the case of terminally ill Alzheimer's patients with short life expectancies, through hospice programs.

The human services workers' efforts are typically required to be associated with helping the patient and his or her family make practical arrangements for care. Developing community resources so that more adequate care is available to Alzheimer's victims is a role of many human services planners and managers.

Case management services are also often important. They may imply helping the client receive health, financial assistance, residential, and other services from a variety of agencies, the combination of which is needed to help the Alzheimer's victim overcome his or her difficult living situation. Counseling of various kinds may also be indicated in some cases of Alzheimer's, especially counseling with family members who may believe that they are, somehow, at fault in the development of the patient's problems when, in fact, there is little or nothing that can be done to reverse the irreversible consequences of Alzheimer's disease.

Support groups for family members of Alzheimer's victims are another kind of service that many families find beneficial. Workers with these support groups often find that educating family members about the condition, helping members share information and ideas about their means of coping with the difficulties of the disease, and helping people find ways to alleviate some of the guilt they may feel, are among the methods used in serving victims' families. Some of the methods for assisitng people through groups outlined in chapter 5 can be applicable to the services of support groups suggested in this discussion of Alzheimer's.

Other Debilitating Conditions

Two other conditions are a disproportionately large cause of aging persons needing help with their physical care who might otherwise be able to live independently or with family members.

Incontinence

Some older adults lose the ability to control bowel and bladder functions. In some cases, those losses of control are consequences of aging itself. In other cases, the condition results from disease or injury. No matter what the reasons, incontinence creates a management problem for older persons and those who care for them. Many family members who might otherwise care for a bedridden older person find it too difficult to handle the care of an incontinent person. Therefore, many older adults must use alternative living arrangements or help from persons outside the family because neither they nor their relatives can cope with the problems associated with incontinence.

Fractured Hips

One of the more common causes of severe health problems among the elderly is a fractured hip. A fall or a wrenching body movement that may be only annoying for a younger person can cause a fracture because of the normal effects of aging or as a result of osteoporosis, a loss of bone tissue mass that often afflicts older women.

Fractured hips may be treated as other broken bones, and hips may also be replaced with prostheses. However, the lack of mobility arising from such fractures may result in fatalities from conditions such as pneumonia. Therefore, some older people who have suffered hip fractures must be placed in care facilities after hospitalization to treat the fracture because their conditions are too difficult to handle in a private home.

Maintaining the Health of the Aged

Providing medical services is, of course, only part of the problem of health care for the aged. More important, perhaps, is maintaining the kinds of conditions that make it possible for older people to satisfactorily survive and maintain high health standards. Occasionally, that means massive environmental efforts to eliminate air pollution, accidents, and inadequate nutrition, which can be the causes of ill health among older people and which can be eliminated. In other words, social efforts to eliminate or reduce illness can be more important than treating illnesses after they occur. The prevention of ill health becomes increasingly important for older people who are particularly susceptible to complications from respiratory illness, epidemics, and other infections.

Inadequate social conditions and inadequate opportunities for recreation and other kinds of growth often make life more hazardous. Poorly designed or poorly maintained intersections can result in traffic injuries or deaths that could be prevented if adequate crosswalks, signal lights, and other safeguards were provided. Insufficient recreational areas and facilities deny older people opportunities to exercise that might lead to illness or earlier death than normal. There is also some evidence that lack of social activities can lead to loneliness and, in turn, to depression, illness, and death. The relationship between an individual's health, the environment, and programs of illness and disease prevention are closely interrelated.

As was pointed out in Part One, people age at different rates. Some people are very old and very ill at age 50, while others regularly engage in sports at age 80. Therefore, we must be cognizant of and account for differential rates of aging and different kinds of health problems within the older population.

Health Education and Individual Responsibility

Many people of all ages do not have clear information on the differences between healthy and unhealthy living. In fact, many illnesses appear to be self-induced through overeating, excessive drinking, insufficient exercise, and other poor health habits. Human services workers and others involved in preventive health care need to assist older adults, who are more susceptible to illnesses resulting from improper self-care than are younger people, and to educate them about the practices that can lead to better physical health.

Sometimes in group service programs, senior center educational programs, and other opportunities for education, information about good health practices can be taught. Some current research (Kass, 1975) indicates that seven rules for good health can help people live longer. Those 75 years of age and over who followed the rules were as healthy as those 35-44 years of age who followed fewer than three. At age 45 a person who followed at least six of the seven rules had a life expectancy eleven years greater than someone who followed fewer than four. The rules are simple and reflect more common sense than medical science:

1. Don't smoke cigarettes.

2. Get seven hours of sleep.

3. Eat breakfast.

4. Keep your weight down.

5. Drink moderatley.

6. Exercise daily.

7. Don't eat between meals.

These rules appear to be more important than medical care and medicine in maintaining health and preventing illness. There is a special need for health services to reach out and provide direct services to older people, and, perhaps even more, to educate them in good health habits.

Humanizing Health Service

On occasion health service programs have to be humanized in order to make them effective and acceptable to older people. Older people are sometimes poorly treated in medical facilities. Some older people enter sophisiticated clinics and complex hospitals for the first time when they reach the senior years and may find them difficult to understand and deal with. Frequently these facilities are complex; require intricate registration procedures; necessitate writing; and involve tests, treatments, and other procedures that are frightening and seem foreign to the older patient.

Furthermore, although many of those who have the most severe health problems are older adults, and older adults are very heavy users of health services, there are few health programs genuinely geared to the needs of older people. Experts in working with and talking to older people are sometimes needed to adapt services to the requirements of senior citizens.

Many health programs increasingly are using human services employees to assist older patients with the health program. Sometimes human services workers in such positions sercv as guides and interpreters of the health program for older people. At times, the most important factor for older adults is some help in choosing medical care personnel. For a variety of reasons, some older adults are intimidated by physicians and other health care providers. However, it is often true that the best assurance of adequate health care is a second opinion from a qualified physician. Unnecessary and sometimes dangerous surgery may be avoided by seeking such an opinion. It is often the worker's role to help older clients use second opinions and to feel comfortable in rejecting the first medical advice and direction they receive.

Mental Health Services for Older Adults

The problems faced by older adults extend, of course, beyond physical ill health and physical declines. As Part One make clear, emotional problems are also part of the experiences of older people on American society. At times these emotional problems result from physical illnesses. Being sick or watching one's physical capacities decline often leads to depression and other kinds of emotional disturbances. The loneliness and isolation experienced by many older people are also sources of mental distress.

Emotional problems are also connected, in some cases, with physical disabilities themselves. For these reasons programs of service designed to assist older people in meeting their mental health needs and overcoming obstacles to adequate mental health are an important part of the human services system for older people.

The Comprehensive Community
Mental Health Center

Organizations called *comprehensive community mental health centers*, funded by a combination of local (county and city), state, and federal funds, are designed to provide access to mental health services to every citizen throughout the United States. The services provided include outpatient counseling, emergency care in general hospitals, day and night hospitalization, and, in some cases, halfway houses. Community mental health centers also often have contacts with mental hospitals or jails, where some communities keep mental patients while they are waiting for transfer to a mental hospital or other facility, and they generally serve as the major mental health program in the community. They provide educational and consultation activities to schools and other organizations. They often provide special programs for treating those addicted to alcohol and other drugs; direct or coordinate the efforts with sheltered workshops and other facilities for the mentally retarded or emotionally disturbed; and have close relations with employment services, welfare departments, rehabilitation programs, and a multitude of other services that can be helpful to older adults who face emotional problems.

The comprehensive community mental health center is such an important service that it is useful for anyone seeking information about or referral to mental health programs to contact the center first to find out the wisest course of action. Many times personnel at the center will ease the way for referrals of patients to special services or will be the provider of the services.

Mental Health Workers

A variety of professionals and nonprofessionals work in the mental health system in the United States. Some people believe that psychiatrists are the primary givers of mental health services, but, in fact, a whole team of people provide services to those who face emotional problems.

Psychiatrists provide many of the private services for those facing emotional problems who pay fees for professional help. However, private mental health services are only a small portion of the help provided, although psychiatrists are the most influential members of the mental health field.

Most of the medical people who provide services in mental health programs, for instance, mental hospitals, are physicians trained for general practice or for some speciality other than psychiatry. (A psychiatrist is a doctor of medicine who has completed a residency and other experiences in psychiatry and has been admitted for practice by the national certifying board in his or her specialization.) However, M.D.'s from all over the world, as well as doctors of osteopathic medicine, provide mental health services of all kinds.

In addition to the psychiatrists and nonpsychiatrist physicians who provide mental health services, nurses are also important deliverers of mental health help. All registered nurses have some preparation in work with the emotionally disturbed, and some have special preparation at the bachelor's or master's level in work with mental patients. Nurses who specialize in mental health work conduct counseling as well as providing nursing services to patients in mental hospitals.

Clinical psychologists are another important part of the mental health team. They conduct psychological counseling and psychological testing, the results of which are of use to other professionals.

Social workers constitute a large proportion of those who serve the mentally ill. Much of the direct individual and group work with patients in mental health programs is provided by graduates of social work programs with bachelor's or master's degrees.

The mental health service staff might also include rehabilitation counselors, occupational therapists, recreational therapists, licensed practical nurses, psychiatric aides, and outreach workers. These individuals have special roles to play and their impact on the patient may be most significant. In modern mental health practices all of these professionals and staff members coordinate with one another and work together as a team. The literature on the "team approach" to the provision of mental health services is extensive.

In any encounter with mental health services, the typical older patient is likely to be helped by several members of the team. That is why modern treatment approaches require that everyone associated with a mental health program be provided with training and guidance in working with the mentally ill. The switchboard receptionist can alienate an older patient to such an extent that the nurse, social worker, psychologist, or psychiatrist never sees the client. The cleaning crew in a mental hospital may so anger a patient that all the work done by professionals is immediately undone. That is why a close, team relationship among all the members of the staff in a program serving the mentally ill or emotionally disturbed is essential.

Special Services

Family Service Programs. Among the potential programs that can be of service to older people are those commonly designated as *family service programs*, many of which are affiliated with Family Service America. These programs provide a range of social services for families and help people of all ages. They can be particularly useful to older people in locating housing facilities, health care, leisure-time group activities, or other services. Family service programs offer the services of social workers who can provide counseling, referral, and information on health, mental health, and housing.

Alcholism and Drug Abuse. Older people may be addicted to alcohol and other drugs, such as barbiturates or even heroin. Although the emphasis has been on the drug problems of younger people, alcoholism frequently becomes most serious in later years. With the exception of homes for the aged, there are few areas as heavily populated by older men as the skid rows of American cities. Of course, alcoholism is the typical health problem of the skid row resident.

Alcoholism, which typically begins at a much earlier age—perhaps in the 20s or 30s, or even younger— can often have its greatest impact and be most severe in the later years. The man or woman who needs a drink every evening at age 40 may begin needing a drink in the afternoon by age 45, no later than lunch a couple of years later, and at breakfast time by age 60. Alcoholism may become more severe during the later years.

Alcoholism is not the only addicition faced by older people. Prescription drugs and dependence upon them—particularly amphetamines, barbiturates, and tranquilizers—may become a central part of the life of the aging person in efforts to overcome depression, loneliness, or physical pain.

Comprehensive community mental health centers, family service associations, mental hospitals, and some general hospitals have programs designed to help people with the problems of alcohol and drug abuse. But because the problems are widespread, difficult to treat, and poorly defined, there are many dilemmas for those who hope to provide services to those who face this set of difficulties.

Suicide Prevention. Among the most serious problems of older adults is suicide. A disproportionate number of the over 25,000 Amreicans who die from suicide each year are older. And the reported figures do not include suicides that are masked as deaths from other causes, such as single-car accidents. Therefore, the prevention of suicide is an important human-service for the elderly. Occasionally such services are provided through community mental health centers and mental hospitals. In other situations they are provided by general hospitals and, perhaps the most sophisticated example, through telephone "hot lines," which attempt to convince potential suicides to change their minds or at least to delay deciding.

The Continuum of Care

A current popular idea in health care of all kinds is the Continuum of Care, a plan whereby long-term case planning is done for the patient to insure that he or she is provided with the most necessary and appropriate care available. Patient progress is monitored by a continuum of care staff, which may be financed by government funds, to insure that persons are receiving no more and no less than they need. If they should be at home with some form of home health services meeting their needs, they should be removed from the hospital or nursing home. If home health services alone will not be sufficient, transport to a health center on several occasions each week or month can be used.

The idea of the continuum of care is that each patient should receive what he or she needs. That appropriate level of care requires careful evaluation and analysis to determine and it also requires constant monitoring by the continuum of care staff, which requires the services of many professionals in order to render an accurate and adequate social, medical, and nursing diagnosis. For that reason, many human services workers are employed in continuum of care programs to make social diagnoses and evaluations.

Long-Term Care

One of the common needs of the aging is long-term residential assistance for those who are unable to meet their basic living requirements. It is important to understand that long-term care is not the same as retirement living or residence in a senior housing program. Long-term care refers to a medical level of care that is only correctly used for people who cannot physically or mentally function without extensive help. Typically, the long-term care client is someone who cannot walk, dress, speak, eat, or get into bed, without assistance. In other words, the client is a patient who needs professional care—not just someone who is aged and who finds it difficult to take care of himself or herself without some assistance.

The typical long term care facility is popularly called a "nursing home," and provides some level of nursing care. In the provision of nursing home care, there are basically two levels—the skilled nursing facility and the intermediate nursing facility. The skilled facility has more intensive and professional services because it takes in and cares for people with more severe health problems. The intermediate facility also provides intensive care but people with somewhat less serious health problems can be cared for within them. Not all long-term care facility residents are aged. Some younger people who suffer from debilitating illnesses or the results of accidents also need such facilities. However, the predominant group of residents is aged. Some people confuse that reality with the real problems of the aging. Although the nursing home population is primarily aged, the aging, as a group, are not primarily in long-term care facilities. In fact, only 5 percent of the aged require long-term care service.

The cost of nursing home care is a serious problem for many people. The cost was, at the time this was written, more than $2,000 per month per person in most such homes, exceeding the retirement and social insurance income of most older people who require such care. Medicare, as has been indicated, pays for very little long-term care. Most of the long-term care provided to people who cannot pay for their own out of their own incomes comes from Medicaid. In many states, long term-care is the largest expenditure in the total Medicaid program, exceeding hospital payments, physicians' services, and prescription medicines.

In the 1980's, many insurance companies began selling individual and group long-term care insurance policies. Those are costly (the cost is less for people who purchase it early in their lives than for those who purchase it near their retirements) forms of coverage but many older people will have them in the future.

Paying for long-term care is a major preoccupation of many elderly people, particularly those who are of middle or higher socioeconomic status. There is a frequently expressed concern on the part of many that they "not be a burden" on anyone. For that reason, it is not unusual to encounter older people who have established and maintain savings accounts primarily for that purpose. The fear among older adults of losing their ability to care for themselves is a severe one that many human services workers may want to discuss with their clients. They may also be able to help those clients to establish and use a long-term care fund that is more financially advantageous than those the elderly clients might establish on their own. The alienation among the generations is such that many older people are concerned about not only becoming a burden but also about having anyone to care for them—physically and financially—as they reach their senior years.

Roles of Human Services Workers

Human services workers with the aged are involved in long-term care in many ways:

1. They counsel with and refer clients to long-term care facilities in order to facilitate placements.

2. Many work in long-term care facilities to help with the client contacts with their families; to assist with developing the social work program of the facility; to counsel with individuals and groups of clients; to help clients obtain and continue receiving financial assistance from public and private resources; and as consultants to facility directors and other staff about the program for the clients. Some social workers are directors of nursing homes, themselves, and others have organized and direct businesses that operate long-term care facilities.

3. Many work in state government agencies that monitor the quality of nursing homes and evaluate them for licenses.

4. Some human services workers serve as staff trainers and educators for those who are employed by long-term care facilities.

Long-Term Care Financing

The payment for nursing home care is a large and complex problem in the United States. It is one of the fastest growing expenditures of the people of the nation because of several factors such as people living longer, the mobility of the population, which causes people to be far removed from the children or siblings who might have cared for them at an earlier time, and the alienation among the generations, which leads to children actively avoiding caring for their aging parents. For all these reasons, nursing home care is increasingly necessary for older people and, therefore, is an increasing cost to the society upon which many older people become a responsibility. The costs are high because the long-term care facility is in the position of paying for services, twenty-four hours per day, seven days per week, that individuals and families provide for themselves and for one another without being paid. Essentially, the nursing home provides and pays for the services of those who prepare meals, clean, entertain, and otherwise operate a residence—services that are not paid for in a home.

Federal law requires that the public aid government agencies, which have often been discussed in this text, pay for Medicaid-sponsored nursing home care in very specific ways. Therefore, the states have established rather complicated rules and procedures for serving those who need long-term care:

1. Nursing homes must be paid on the basis of their costs. For instance, a home shows its property, professional services, food, and other costs, and is paid on that basis plus profit.

2. Admission to the nursing home, if it is to be paid by government funds, must be done on the basis of the need for care, and most states have established complex point systems that systematically define and evaluate the patient's need for care. If the patient does not meet the criteria, the government programs will not pay and other arrangements have to be made for serving the client.

3. There are periodic audits of the facility and its records to make certain that it is doing what it is supposed to do and is operating financially within the established rules.

4. Many states require nursing home advocates who visit the facilities and talk with the patients to be certain that they are not being mistreated. Because nursing home patients are typically elderly and ill and therefore unable to assert their own rights, governments establish advocates to secure their rights for them. Essentially, long-term care is one of the most important elements in the human services for older people. Human services workers play a large role within that field. Those who serve the aged find themselves either directly or indirectly involved with nursing homes in virtually any situation in which they are employed.

Other Long-Term Care

The Mental Hospital

Most casual observers of the mental health treatment services in the United States do not realize that a large and highly disproportionate number of those incarcerated in public mental hospitals are older adults. The normal process of aging leads to some conditions, already described, that may be classified as mental illnesses. Some mental hospital wards are almost totally devoted to older people, particularly those that deal with the physical problems of mentally ill patients.

Over the years, the American public has had a variety of reactions to and relationships with mental hospitals. Initially these institutions were considered humane alternatives to imprisonment or to isolation in the attics and cellars of private homes, which had often been the fate of older people with emotional problems. Recently, however, observers of practices in mental hospitals began to discover that such institutions were often cruel to inmates. Social scientists who studied institutional life began to report that *total institutions*, to use Erving Goffman's term, were inherently demeaning and that it was, in essence, impossible to improve institutional life. Therefore, the trend in the mental-health field has been to remove patients from institutions to a variety of other kinds of programs.

The Rights of Individuals in Mental Health Programs. One of the responsibilities of human services workers in institutions for the emotionally disturbed is to ensure that the legal rights of patients are upheld. There are examples of patients being physically beaten, having their personal property removed, being denied access to telephone and mail service, and being kept longer than either the courts require or their own conditions demand. It is crucial for mental health workers to understand the rights of individuals in mental health programs and ensure that these rights are upheld. Frequent Supreme Court decisions have added substantially to the civil rights of those whose freedom may have been denied for reasons of mental illness.

Older people in particular may find themselves incarcerated for long periods of time in mental hospitals, even though their only real problem is a lack of housing and an unwillingness on the part of their children to accept responsibility for them. The negative effects of mental hospitalization are so great that it is common to use all sorts of resources to avoid incarcerating a patient for any length of time. The process of "institutionalization" begins very early in the career of a mental hospital patient. Acclimating oneself to a mental hospital sometimes causes one to lose the abilities and social skills one has had in the past, and it is possible that before much time has elasped, the patient becomes capable of living only in an institution rather than in the free environment of the community. For that reason, in addition to trying to guarantee the civil rights of the patient, constant efforts are made to prevent and minimize mental hospitalization.

Alternatives to Institutionalization. One alternative to institutionalization is halfway houses, which are houses located in communities where mental patients can receive staff and other professional services after their departure from the mental hospital without the trauma of suddenly returning to their own homes. These institutions provide professional people to assist with counseling, food preparation, transportation, referral to education and employment, and other aids that can assist the older person in making the transition smoothly from the hospital to the community.

A similar set of arrangements is found in the *day hospital* and the *night hospital* programs. These kinds of services, which often are located in community hospitals or mental health centers, provide treatment and occasionally residences for half the time of the former or potential mental hospital patient. The day program may provide psychiatric treatment, occupational therapy, recreation, and education. Night hospitals provide residences for those who cannot live in their own homes; the patients work, study, or otherwise occupy themselves during the day.

These plans for partial hospitalization provide a compromise between complete residence in a mental institution and complete freedom, both of which may be impossible for some victims of emotional problems.

The *home for the aged* is an institutional living facility for people who have the need for group or institutional living arrangements. Medical and other health services are available but are provided only when they are needed by patients who are ill. Other services, such as barber and beauty shops, recreation, education, cultural arts, and counseling are also available. Residents of homes for the aged come and go as they please, take their meals in the home, and are sometimes provided transportation away from the home by the institution itself.

There is an increasing use of human services workers such as social workers in nursing homes and homes for the aged. Nursing specialists are almost always involved in both types of institution. The current trend is to provide personnel who can counsel with patients, organize group activities, and develop recreation and other leisure-time programs.

One of the key elements in providing satisfactory care to people in residential facilities is maintenance of contact between residents and their families. Frequently, it is the responsibility of the human services worker to encourage visiting in both directions—from the family homes to the residential facility and from the residential facility back to the homes of family members.

Increasingly, there are extensions of human services programs into the home, which make it possible for older adults to maintain their residences. Visiting nurse and visiting homemaker programs provide, respectively, skilled nursing care to older adults who need it and household assistance, such as cleaning and meal preparation.

Community and Foster Care

Among the most modern approaches to caring for physically and mentally disabled older adults are *foster care* and *community care*, through which older people who cannot live in their own homes or with their families can have adequate food, shelter, clothing, and social contacts in the homes of others. Many state mental hospitals, the Veterans Administration, and some public welfare departments pioneered these programs designed to provide living situations outside institutions for older people.

Those who house the older person provide food, including special diets when they are necessary, comfortable living arrangements, some recreation, and some transportation. In the Veterans Administration, the hospital that released the older person remains responsible for providing medical care, prescriptions, and other out-patient services. Social workers in the Veterans Administration recruit the community care homes and visit veterans in them regularly to supervise their situations and to satisfy themselves that the veterans are well cared for. Foster and community care provided by other agencies usually includes money to buy health care, medicines, and other unusual costs of maintaining the older person in the home.

Human services workers employed in community care need skills in recruiting homes, helping older people decide to enter those homes, and providing supervision to those who live in them.

Some older people live in homes for the aged as couples who are married; others—in fact, a great number of older people—live in small, low-cost hotels in center cities. The task of human servies agencies in those settings is to provide social services to people in their own neighborhoods, occasionally to find them alternative services and alternative housing, and sometimes to assure that they are referred to appropriate health, welfare, and mental health programs.

Summary

There are a variety of ways in which the physical and mental health needs of older people are met. Clearly, the range of needs of older people is great, and the range of services provided to them by human services workers and human services agencies is equally wide.

There are probably more opportunities for human services work aiding older people who face physical and emotional health problems than in any other area.

READING 13.1

Senility Is Not Always What It Seems To Be/Lawrence K. Altman, M.D.

The following reading was included in the first edition of this text and remains current and helpful in understanding the problem of mental deterioration among some older adults. In fact, there have been some changes. The term senile is not as commonly used as it was in the past and many cases of senility have now been narrowed down, as the author suggests they would be, to Alzheimer's Disease. Some evidence now exists to suggest that Alzheimer's is a very common disorder of aging and one that becomes more common as the person becomes older. As such, it needs to be better understood and addressed by the human services worker.

The brain of a young adult contains about 12 billion neurons, the cells that send nerve impulses through the body's most complex organ, and each day, as part of the aging process, the brain shrinks from the death of 100,000 neurons. After decades of losing these irreplaceable cells in an uneven pattern through the brain, the mind of the older individual may wander and he may no longer be able to care for himself. In a word, he becomes senile.

Lapses of memory are common, and when an older person forgets an appointment or name, he is naturally inclined to ask, "Am I getting senile?" In most cases, the answer is in the negative because humans are fallible at all ages, and most older people are not senile.

Nevertheless, the problem of senility is becoming increasingly important. Sometimes, the problem comes to dramatic public attention as it did last week when a California Supreme Court justice was ordered to retire because of senility. But the case of hundreds of thousands of other senile people who manage to carry out their jobs and daily household activities with varying degrees of success receive far less publicity despite the magnitude of the affliction.

Geriatric specialists estimate that 15 percent of people 65 to 75 years old and 25 percent of those 75 and older are senile, a total of about four million. The National Institutes of Health say that 60 percent of the 950,000 nursing home patients over the age of 65 are senile. No accurate statistics exist to know if a larger percentage of older people are getting senile or if there are more senile people because there are more older people. But some geriatricians express the belief that for unknown reasons senility is truly increasing.

Nor do doctors know the cause of senility. It appears to be more than just the loss of neurons, because many older people who have shrunken brains maintain keen minds, and some senile people do not have unusually small brains. And doctors do not know if senility is a disease or a natural aging condition that would affect everyone who lived long enough.

For unknown reasons, the loss of neurons occurs unevenly in the brain seemingly affecting the frontal and temporal lobes (which among other things play key roles in verbalization and hearing) more than other areas of the organ.

Doctors who have studied senile changes have often found it difficult to pinpoint the exact nature of the anatomical brain changes and even more difficult to correlate such changes with the patient's symptoms.

Senility—the word is derived from the Latin word meaning old—is a condition

generally characterized by memory loss, particularly for recent events, loss of ability to do simple arithmetic problems, and disorientation to time and place. It is a
diagnosis doctors must make by impression, primarily by a bedside examination,
because they have no specific diagnostic laboratory test such as a high blood sugar
to confirm diabetes.

The computerized axial tomogram, a new x-ray technique that has revolutionized neurology, has helped diagnose senility in more people by showing a
shrunken brain on x-ray. To get the same information in the past, doctors had to
inject air into the brain, which involved not only pain but some risk to the patient.
Because it is so new, the tomogram technique's usefulness in senility has not been
fully explored. At present it can support the doctor's bedside impression, but it is
not considered a specific diagnostic test.

Many conditions can produce symptoms that mimic senility, and many people
are falsely labelled senile when their symptoms are due to depression, a thyroid
gland abnormality, pernicious anemia, effects of drugs like bromides, or a variety
of other conditions that can be effectively treated, if not cured by psychotherapy
or drugs.

But at most 20 percent of senility cases have a treatable cause. This situation
has raised questions in the minds of some budget-conscious officials about the
cost-effectiveness of spending up to $500 just for extensive series of diagnostic
laboratory tests on all senile patients when they have but a few years to live.

However, the overwhelming majority of physicians would agree with Dr. Leslie Libow, chief of geriatric medicine at the Jewish Institute for Geriatric Care in
New Hyde Park, who said:

"Senility is one of the most serious medical diagnoses that can be given to a
patient because the prognosis is so serious and the effectiveness of treatment is not
clear. If we value our older people, how can anyone seriously argue that every
physician should not do the tests to make sure a treatable cause has not been
overlooked?"

The older population's growing political influence has led government officials to devote more attention to their medical troubles. Next month, for example,
the National Institute of Aging, the newest unit of the Federal National Institutes of
Health in Bethesda, Md., will hold one of the larger scientific meetings on senility.

One impetus for the meeting is the recognition from research studies during
the last five years that arteriosclerosis, or hardening of the arteries, plays less of a
role in senility than doctors previously believed. Senility on the basis of arteriosclerosis tends to produce worsening symptoms on an episodic basis. Now, geriatricians believe the bulk of cases are due to senile dementia, a disease of unknown
cause that occurs more commonly in women and that is characterized by the gradual, unrelenting, irreversible deterioration of the mind. The process can occur so
slowly and subtly as to escape attention until the affected person shocks his family
by wandering away from home, failing to recognize an old friend, or squandering
money on a worthless cause.

When senility develops in a 40- or 50-year-old individual—it is then called pre-senile dementia—doctors generally suspect a wide variety of conditions but two in particular, Alzheimer's Disease and Pick's Disease. In Alzheimer's Disease, the shrinkage occurs throughout the brain, whereas the Pick's Disease the changes are more localized. Anatomically, Alzheimer's Disease is indistinguishable from the shrunken, senile brain to the pathologist, raising questions whether Alzheimer's might be the early onset of the more common form of senility.

The main thrust of the meeting will be to explore the various avenues of research through which the mystery of senility might be solved. Among the current areas of focus:

Epidemiology—What clues can be picked up by examining the differences in incidence among various populations that could not be detected by laboratory studies?

Viral—Can viruses that take years to incubate and produce damage be an important cause of senility?

Hereditary—Is there a genetic defect that predisposes some individuals to senility? If so, what is it?

Metabolic—Is there a biochemical abnormality that leads to senility?

The answers to these and other questions could lead to effective therapies and preventions for one of society's more costly troubles.

READING 13.2

Nursing Home Reform and the Politics of Long-Term Care/Catherine Hawes

The following article is taken from P.S., a journal published by the American Political Science Association. It deals with nursing home issues and long-term care policies.

Nursing home care has been described as the most troubled and troublesome segment of the American health care system. Despite the annual expenditure of billions of dollars, extensive regulation, and the emergence of an increasingly sophisticated and concentrated industry, significant problems persist. Inadequate quality of care continues to be a serious and pervasive problem. Discrimination against patients whose care is paid for by Medicaid and Medicare, as well as

Catherine Hawes is a Senior Policy Analyst at Research Triangle Institute (RTI). Reprinted with permission of the author and the American Political Science Association.

against those with "heavy care" or extensive needs, is rampant. Costs have escalated at a phenomenal rate and continue to represent a substantial fiscal burden,
causing one state Medicaid director to refer to nursing home payments as "the
black hole of state budgets."

These circumstances are neither new nor surprising. They are, in fact, the result of rather startling failures in the public sector that are rooted in the special
nature of the politics of long-term care. This article discusses the history of public
policy toward nursing homes and the politics of long-term care, emphasizing
problems in assuring acceptable quality of care. It also addresses the possibilities
for reform during the next two years, particularly in light of new patient advocate
and nursing home reform coalitions that promise to change the face of long-term
care politics.

Public Policy and Nursing Homes

Public policy virtually created the nursing home industry; however, much of
nursing home policy has been the product of a series of after-thoughts. It is a "program" shaped largely by the unintended consequences and side-effects of policies
aimed at other sectors of the economy and health care system (Vladeck, 1980). As
a result, nursing home policy is a schizophrenic combination of mental health,
welfare, housing, acute care and social service policies in what has become a
nearly uncontrollable amalgam of increasing costs and continuing concerns about
quality and access.

Most observers view the creation of the nursing home industry as an out-
growth of the passage of Medicare and Medicaid legislation in 1965. But its roots
are older and more complex and it is as much an heir to the English Poor Laws and
"indoor relief" as to health policy. The industry has grown as a result of a multiplicity of factors, including the infusion of public dollars through Old Age Assistance
and Social Security, Kerr-Mills, and finally Medicare and Medicaid. Demographic
trends (the aging of America as well as the growth in the"very old old" and shifting
morbidity patterns toward chronic diseases have also contributed to increased demand and a growing industry.

In addition, the nursing home industry has grown as a result of the interplay of
health and welfare policies aimed at almshouses, mental institutions, and acute
care hospitals, policies that have moved older persons out of other institutions and
into nursing homes. Finally the industry grew and changed as a result of regulatory
policy. In general, government agencies adopted a strict regulatory approach on
building and fire safety standards but a lenient one on health and psychosocial
care issues. This contributed to the demise of much of the original industry, particularly small facilities, and the emergence of the modern nursing home industry.

As a result of this potpourri of policies, the nursing home industry has grown
larger while its ownership structure has changed. It has moved away from an industry defined by the church-related homes and the mom-and-pop owners of

small proprietary facilities to one dominated by for-profit owners and multi-state, multi-facility chains whose stock is traded on the major stock exchanges (Hawes and Phillips, 1986). In effect, public policy has created a new industry, one that has grown and become profitable largely by providing services to the infirm and disabled elderly who are what I call the "nouveau poor." [1]

Public policy also structured the political dynamics in this area. The 1950 amendments to the Social Security Act authorized the states to make direct payments to nursing homes for care provided to Old Age Assistance program recipients. This vendor payment system was carried on through Kerr-Mills and is the system through which Medicaid currently assists in paying for nearly 70% of all nursing home residents. This system has one important characteristic that has significant implications for the politics of long-term care. The vendor payment method removed the consumers of care—nursing home patients—from the payment process, one of the most fundamental exchanges. It gave shape to a system in which decisions concerning the cost of care, as well as the quality and level of services to be provided, are made in a set of transactions between providers and the state—transactions in which patients are not even participants.

Since its inception, long-term care policy has been shaped in a political environment dominated by nursing home owners. Their fundamental goal has been to minimize regulation and maximize reimbursement from Medicare and Medicaid. And they have been remarkably successful. While extensive regulation exists on paper, and while several agencies inspect nursing homes, the regulations and enforcement systems are weak and remarkably ineffective in dealing with violators (see, e.g., U.S. Senate, Aging, 1975; IOM, 1986). The result has been a history of poor, though improving, quality.

Current Problems in Quality

Certainly, quality of care in nursing homes has improved over the last three decades. As a result of government regulation and increased professionalism in the industry, many of the appallingly bad living conditions in nursing homes have improved quite substantially, particularly in the areas of fire safety and building code compliance (Vladeck, 1980). Indeed, many facilities now provide quite good care and are developing innovative programs (e.g., for patients with Alzheimer's disease) and internal quality assurance systems (IOM, 1986). Nevertheless, one of the

---

[1] On any given day most of the residents of nursing homes are long-stay patients, who will reside in the facility an average of 2.5 years, often longer. Because of the high cost of nursing home care and because private insurance and Medicare pay basically only for short, rehabilitative care stays (or 2% of all dollars spent on nursing home care), 67% of all patients exhaust their savings in paying for care, usually within the first 18 months (U.S. Senate, Aging, 1985). As a result, most become recipients of Medicaid. Although Medicaid is thought of as a program for AFDC recipients, approximately half the dollars are spent on nursing home care.

most common findings of studies is tremendous variation in the quality of care from facility to facility (Kane et al., 1979; Ohio, 1979; Mech, 1980). It varies from excellent in a growing but still relatively small proportion of homes to seriously substandard in perhaps as many as 10 to 20% of facilities nationwide, with the majority of homes in some states having notably poor records.

Most homes provide care that is in substantial compliance with existing state licensure laws and federal certification standards for Medicare and Medicaid. But the minimum standards are inadequate, and some serious violations of even these regulations persist. The most common include misadministration of medications, overuse of psychotropic drugs, overuse of physical restraints, failure to provide needed therapies and restorative nursing care, failure to treat depression and other mental problems, and inadequate attention to residents' rights and to their social and activity needs (e.g., Ray et al., 1980; Kane et al., 1979; Hawes, 1987; IOM, 1986). Scandals about insufficient food, unsafe and unsanitary conditions, physical and verbal abuse and poor medical and nursing care are now less common but still occur with troubling frequency (Williams, 1986; Pope, Smith and Romano, 1986).

Failure of the Regulatory System

These problems are the product of many factors and persist despite extensive regulation by states and the federal government. States license all facilities providing nursing care. In addition, any home wishing to receive reimbursement through Medicare or Medicaid for program beneficiaries must be inspected and certified as meeting federal health and safety standards. More than 80% of all nursing homes participate in one or both of these programs. Thus, every nursing home must meet state licensure standards, and the vast majority must also meet federal regulations.

Unfortunately, the history of nursing home regulation in action reads like the reports on the Nuclear Regulatory Commission and Three Mile Island: inadequate standards; an inspection system that focuses on the records provided by the regulated entity and measures only "paper compliance" with regulations; and an enforcement system that relies on consultation and persuasion rather than meaningful sanctions when violations are detected.

The federal standards are often viewed as superior to licensure laws in most states, but they have also been widely criticized. When originally drafted, the federal standards were based on an assumption (since proved incorrect) that most patients in nursing homes would be there for short, recuperative stays. As a result, the nursing home standards, modeled along those for hospitals, concentrated on patients' presumed medical needs. The needs of patients with chronic diseases and disabilities who reside in the facility for more than 2.5 years were neither anticipated nor adequately addressed in the federal standards. As a result, the standards are criticized for being inappropriately focused on only the medical needs of patients while giving too little attention to patients' mental and emotional needs, their desire and need for meaningful activities, and their civil rights. The standards are also criticized for representing bare minimums rather than desirable standards of quality.

Another problematic characteristic of the regulations is their focus on structural standards of care. In general, the regulations specify inputs, such as door widths and suggested staffing patterns. Because these structural standards set the framework for inspections, the focus of the inspections is on whether the faciltiy meets these input standards, measuring its "capacity" to provide care rather than observing some measures of its performance (e.g., DHEW, 1975).

Thus, the inspections focus on reviews of the facility's records and its reported compliance with the structural standards. Of the several hundred items on the annual survey instrument for Medicaid and Medicare certification, all but a handful can be answered in the administrator's office and through reviews of the facility's records. A surveyor could conceivably "inspect" a nursing home and not even see a patient. In effect, the regulatory agency infers that the facility's performance—the quality of care it provides—is acceptable if the facility can demonstrate its capacity to provide adequate care. As a result, facilities may be in "paper" compliance, even while they provide inadequate patient care (e.g., DHEW, 1975; IOM, 1986).

Even if the standards were ideal, most observers believe the inspection system would not reveal violations for other reasons. For example, in most states and for Medicare and Medicaid, the inspections are scheduled to occur once annually. Thus, even when the inspection's dates are not announced in advance by the agency, which has been common practice, the timing of annual inspections is easily predicted by the facility. As a result, many observers believe the inspections fail to provide an accurate picture of the facility's day-to-day performance and compliance with even structural and input standards (e.g., Ohio, 1979; Illinois, 1984).

Finally, regulatory agencies are criticized for their position that inspectors need find facilities to be only in "substantial" rather than full compliance with minimum health and safety standards. As with hospitals seeking to participate in Medicare, this policy position was initially adopted because of concern that few facilities could meet even minimal federal certification standards and that, as a result, program beneficiaries would not have access to needed care if full compliance were demanded (Feder, 1979; Vladeck, 1980).

As a result of this concern, the federal government chose to allow facilities to participate in Medicare and Medicaid if they were in "substantial" compliance with standards and promised to correct the deficiencies over a specified period of time. However, the policy has persisted for nearly 20 years. Many homes continue to operate and are reimbursed without meeting minimum standards. Some facilities have plans for correcting the deficiencies but never actually do so—or do so only for the short period of time it takes for the certification survey inspectors to note the compliance (Ohio, 1979).

Even if there were model standards and these problems in the inspections system were corrected, enforcement problems make quality assurance difficult. Enforcement rests largely on two similar but unworkable mechanisms: revocation of the operating license by the state and/or termination of the facility from participation in Medicaid and Medicare. Either, if imposed, results in the closure of the facility.

Sometimes referred to as the atom bomb approach to enforcement, this type of penalty is too harsh for many types of violations and is seldom used even for serious and continuing violations. Such sanctions are also troubling because they can impose substantial burdens on patients and may be difficult for a state to impose, particularly when, due to state health planning decisions, nursing home occupancy rates in most states exceed 95%. Moving large numbers of nursing home residents, most of them quite frail, and finding beds in or near their home community is clearly problematic. Thus only the most serious, life-threatening conditions lead to the impositon of such penalties (e.g., Butler, 1979; California, 1983; New York, 1975).

Even in states with a wider range of sanctions, such as fines, penalties are seldom invoked (IOM, 1986). Regulatory agencies resist the notion that they are police and have the ability (much less the responsibility) to take miscreants to court. Instead they rely on consultation and attempts to educate and persuade providers to correct violations. For chronic violators, such an enforcement posture by the states and federal government represents a financial bonanza. They continue operating and receiving public dollars while in violation of minimum standards—without incurring either the cost of correcting the deficiencies or of penalties (e.g., Ohio, 1979).

This sorry state of affairs derives from several factors, including the existence of what are often conflicting policy goals: cost containment, high quality care, and access. At the outset, the main concern of policymakers was not quality of care. They felt the most immediate problem was securing the widespread participation of health care providers in Medicare and Medicaid (Feder, 1979). As noted, they feared that the imposition of strict quality and safety standards on health care institutions would restrict program beneficiaries' access to care. They decided to opt for the goal of access over that of insuring uniformly high quality of care.

A second factor that explains the failure of policy to address quality issues adequately lies in the genesis of government regulations. Government-mandated health and safety standards initially emerged in programs that provided funding to institutions that cared for children. The evolution of nursing home standards at the federal level followed much the same pattern, emerging in conjuction with Medicare and Medicaid funding. In effect, the standards represent "minimums," seeking less to define and assure high quality of care and life for insitutional residents than to ensure that government funds are not expended for obviously substandard care.

A third factor that explains inadequate attention to quality assurance rests with the nature of bureaucracy and interest group politics. The regulatory agencies are poorly equipped, both in terms of legal staffing and attitudes, to pursue stringent enforcement. Moreover, they seldom receive much support for such activities, particularly from legislators who receive campaign funds from the increasingly active groups representing providers' interests (e.g., New York, 1975). The combination of generally low enthusiasm for aggressive regulatory activity with well-organized and financed interest groups representing the nursing home industry, and resource-poor consumers makes for a weak regulatory system. The result can be seen in inadequate standards, ineffective inspections, unworkable enforcement mechanisms, and, not surprisingly, poor quality of care.

A final factor that helps explain quality problems is policymakers' fundamental concern with the cost of nursing home care. In the past ten to fifteen years, expenditures on nursing home care have escalated at an astounding rate, outstripping even inflation in hospital costs. This rapid rise in expenditures has stretched the Medicaid budget, which pays nearly half of all dollars spent on nursing home care. States, which match federal Medicaid dollars, have been particularly hard pressed since the imposition of caps on the federal share of increases in Medicaid expenditures. As a result, both state and federal policymakers are reluctant to implement any changes in nursing home policy that may result in higher expenditures.

Prospects for Reform

Despite this litany of problems, the potential for reform exists. Indeed, within the next two years, reform is likely as a result of three factors—a law suit by Colorado nursing home patients, a study and set of recommendations on nursing home regulation by the National Academy of Sciences Institue of Medicine, and a new reform-minded coalition of patient advocates, senior citizen groups, and professional organizations.

In the past, nursing home reform has been the product of scandals, a nearly textbook example of what Anthony Down (1972) called the "issue-attention cycle." The consumers of care, 1.2 million nursing home patients, suffer from an array of physical and mental impairments. Most have become impoverished in payng for care. Thus, most patients lack both the ability and resources to be politically active. The providers, an even smaller minority, are well-organized and politically astute. Many benefit financially from the very conditions and policies that result in increasing costs, discrimination and poor quality. Moreover, the price of substantial reform is high—perhaps less in terms of money, though that too, than in terms of political "will" by regulators and policymakers.

In past years, the precipitators of reform were events that temporarily captured media space, public concern, and politicians' limited attention—a series of tragic fire deaths in nursing homes, a well-publicized congressional investigation, massive fraud and despicable care by New York nursing home operator Bernard Bergman, muliple food poisoning deaths, and reports by state investigatory commissions and newspaper series of dire conditions and provider fraud. Yet even with these, the scope of reform was limited and often cosmetic (Vladeck, 1980; Mendelson, 1974).

For decades, the political process has been dominated by fairly well-organized industry interest groups, particularly proprietary providers who constitue nearly 80% of the operators of nursing homes. Regulatory and reimbursement policies have been the product of negotiation between legislators, bureaucrats, and providers, a process in which patients, the consumers of care, have had virtually no voice. Patients' main contribution to reform has come not through voting or lobbying, but through needless suffering and tragic deaths.

Recently, a more diverse set of players has emerged on the policymaking scene, altering the politics of long-term care by challenging the political dominance of the providers. For example in Ohio, a powerful coalition advocating nursing home reform formed during 1978-1979. The coalition formed around a nucleus of players from the state chapter of the American Association of Retired Persons (AARP), the Ohio AFL-CIO, and the United Auto Workers (UAW). Initially, representatives of these groups met at the instigation of the legislators and staff of the Ohio Nursing Home Commission. During the first meeting, the labor union participants made a point of criticizing AARP for its early (1960-61) position on Medicare. But once old grievances were aired, the members struck an agreement on what needed to be done—how would they arrive at positions on Commission recommendations, what lobbying was needed, who else should be invited to join the coalition, and who would take responsibility for the various legislative/lobbying tasks.

AARP, with 600,000 members in Ohio, was especially effective discussing the reform bills with Republican legislators and in turning out hundreds, sometimes thousands of letters to legislators on a particular bill. AARP contributed both the support of its state membership and the time and skills of state legislation staff from national headquarters. The Ohio AFL-CIO was the cornerstone of the lobbying effort and contributed the extraordinary services of their chief lobbyist on social welfare and health issues to the task of passing nursing home reform legislation. They also took responsibility for coordinating the activities of the other coalition members, working closely with the Commission's legislative members and staff. The UAW, though not nearly as active as the AFL-CIO, nevertheless voted as a group to support the reform legislation, let legislators know of their support, and sent some of its retired members to legislative hearings.

In addition to the three core organizational member of the coalition, groups representing patients' interests were active in the coalition. While their activities were formally limited by law to exclude lobbying, nursing home ombudsmen were helpful in clarifying and explaining problems and potential reforms to some legislators. Similarly, a statewide patient advocate group, though not lobbying directly, provided information to legislators.

Other less active but still critical members of the coalition include the American Federation of State, County and Municipal Employees (AFSCME), who with the Ohio NAACP lobbied the black legislative caucus very effectively. The associations representing registered nurses, hospital discharge planners, social workers, and a few other welfare advocacy groups were also active, writing letters, attending hearings, and buttonholing important legislators for discussions of nursing home reform. Finally, the coalition and members and staff of the Nursing Home Commission were able to structure the debate and focus some of the legislative proposals so as to pick up the support of one of the industry interest groups, Association of Ohio Philanthropic Homes for the Aging (AOPHA).

This coalition was successful in passing two substantial reforms in Ohio; however, when the Commission disbanded at the end of its legislatively authorized term, there was no one to give the time and care required to maintain the coalition. As a result, the coalition split, initially over some relatively small disagreements over compromises on another major reform bill and then through the force of fundamental differences in membership, strategy, and major legislative goals and interests.

At the federal level, new coalitions are also emerging, altering the nature of the politics of long-term care. But the most notable reform to date is the product of a successful class action lawsuit by Colorado nursing home patients against the U.S. Department of Health and Human Services (*Smith v. Heckler*, 747 F.2d 583 [10th Cir. 1984]). This suit, which began nearly a decade ago, engendered cooperation between legal aid attorneys, patient advocate groups, and policy analysts, as well as some providers, and has resulted in a proposed new inspection/survey system, the Patient Care and Services (PACS) survey that focuses on the quality of care actually received by nursing home residents.

While PACS is a vast improvement over the previous inspection process, it does have some problems (IOM, 1986), and the plaintiffs in *Smith v. Heckler* are unwilling to accept what the Administration proposed as of February, 1987. Thus, addiitonal policy changes may emerge from this lawsuit. But even if the major problems with PACS were corrected, the inadequacies of the standards and enforcement system would still allow poor care.

A more comprehensive set of reforms was recently proposed by the National Academy of Sciences Institute of Medicine (IOM, 1986). The IOM conducted a two-year study of nursing home regulation between 1984 and 1986 and issued a report calling for substantial new regulatory standards, an improved inspection system, and a more effective range of sanctions. The sanctions include both penalties for nursing homes violating state and federal law and for states failing to enforce the standards.

The IOM study resulted from congressional rejection of the Reagan Administration's plans in 1980-81 to reduce nursing home regulation. This congressional opposition was engendered in large measure by the National Citizens' Coalition for Nursing Home Reform (NCCNHR) and patient ombudsman and advocacy groups around the country. Congress then prohibited the Administration from enacting its proposals and persuaded the Administration to fund the IOM study. As a result, there is substantial interest in both the House and Senate in the IOM Committee's recommendations, and in 1986, reform bills incorporating many of the IOM recommendations were introduced by Sen. John Heinz (R-PA), Rep. Henry Waxman (D-CA) and Rep. Claude Pepper (D-FL).

A group similar to the one in Ohio coalesced at the national level around the issue of nursing home reform and the implementation of the IOM recommendations. Largely spearheaded by NCCNHR and AARP, a large group of interested parties formed to discuss the recommendations and draft position papers. The group included the National Gray Panthers, the National Council of Senior Citizens, the National Association of State Long-Term Care Ombudsmen Programs, the Villers Advocacy Associates, the National Council on Aging, the National Association of Area Agencies on Aging, the American Psychological Association, and the National Committee to Preserve Social Security and Medicare. Other organization members included the AFL-CIO, AFSCME, the Service Employees International Union (SEIU), the National Association of Social Workers, the American Nurses Association, the Association of Occupational Therapists, the Association of Activities Directors, and the Association of Directors of Licensure and Certification. Also part of the group were representatives from the two major trade associations representing nursing home operators, the American Association of Homes and Services for the Aging (usually known as AAHA) representing the voluntary providers, and the American Health Care Association (AHCA), representing the proprietary providers.

The focus of this group was on identifying specific legislative proposals emerging from the IOM recommendations and, when possible, on working out language that would satisfy all members of the coalition. Last year, the coalition fragmented when the National Citizens Coalition for Nursing Home Reform made a separate agreement with the proprietaries' interest group (AHCA) to support legislation that excluded major IOM recommendations on sanctions, some nurse staffing requirements, and a prohibition against Medicaid discrimination (IOM, 1986). The Citizens Coalition felt that this agreement was necessary for the passage of any legislation last year, maintaining that without the support of AHCA no bill would pass.

Whether or not this assessment of AHCA's strength was correct, the political fallout accompanying the agreement precluded the passage of any reform legislation last year. Congressional staffers whose members had introduced reform legislation were surprised that the Citizens Coalition agreed with AHCA to a compromise that asked for less than influential members of the House and Senate were willing to introduce and strongly support. Members of the original reform coalition disagreed with the Citizens Coalition position, arguing that the excluded recommendations were central to any meaningful reform. As a result, the reform coalition fragmented, with some members withdrawing support for any of the proposed legislation, preferring to wait for the next congressional session and the potential for a more comprehensive package. This splintering of the reform coalition, combined with the pressure of other congressional business, effectively killed the bills introduced last session.

This circumstance underlines the fragility of such coalitions, each member of which has different views on what reforms are essential, the degree to which accommodation with the industry is necessary, and legislative tactics. Moreover, for most of the coalition members—with the exception of the Citizens Coalition and the two industry groups—nursing home reform is not the number one legislative priority. Thus, the coalition for nursing home reform is unstable, as theories of interest group politics would predict.

This year, the Citizens Coalition has taken a stronger stand on the reforms proposed by the IOM, and the loose coalition of interested groups has been reconstituted. However, in a departure from last year, the group has agreed to disagree with the providers' representatives on enforcement and antidiscrimination provisions. Members of the group have met with key congressional staff, and bills will probably be introduced in both the House and Senate, with some real prospect for passage of improved federal regulations on nursing home standards, inspections and a range of enforcement remedies.

Continued opposition by AHCA to sanctions and antidiscrimination rules make passage of those provisions somewhat questionable; however, significant reform is possible for three reasons. First, the reform coalition is working smoothly, with the citizens' advocacy groups working more closely with AARP, the country's largest organization representing senior citizens, and with the unions. Thus, the reform coalition seems less likely to fragment during this congressional session.

Second, the industry interest groups seem more committed to supporting many of the reforms. AAHA and the voluntary providers, particularly church-related homes, and some individual proprietary providers have begun to see substantial regulatory and reimbursement reform as both necessary and beneficial to their interests. At the national level, AHCA also seems willing to discuss and perhaps support some patient-oriented reforms. Finally, quality of care is the "buzz word" on Capitol Hill. The mounting concern over the impact of Medicare's prospective payment system (PPS/DRGs) on the quality of care provided by hospitals is carrying over to concern about nursing home quality of care.

Advocates' hopes are high. Policymakers, however, face an unhappy task of meeting potentially conflicting demands for more and better services, both institutional and community-based, improved access for patients who rely on Medicaid and Medicare and for those who have "heavy care" needs, and cost containment. The task is further complicated by remaining disagreements between patient advocates and providers over how to improve the quality of nursing home care. However, this is the most impressive and cohesive coalition to have formed around nursing home reform, and each organization seems to place this reform high on its list of priorities. In addition, the convergence of congressional concern over quality with the issuance of the IOM report—which offers potential solutions—seems extraordinarily serendipitous.

Thus, this congressional session is likely to see not only attention to but action on nursing home reform and a fundamental shift in the politics of long-term care.

References

Butler, P. 1980. Nursing Home Quality of Care Enforcement: Part II: State Agency Enforcement Remedies. *Clearinghouse Review*, 665-701.

Commission on California State Government Organization and Economy. 1983. *The Bureaucracy of Care: Continued Policy Issues for Nursing Home Services and Regulation*. Sacramento, CA.

Feder, J. 1979. *The Politics of Federal Hospital Insurance*. Lexington, MA: Lexington Books.

Hawes, C. 1987. Quality Assurance in Long-Term Care for Patients with Dementia. In R. Cook-Deegan, ed., *Losing a Million Minds: The Tragedy of Alzheimer's Disease and Other Dementias*. Washington, DC: U.S. Congress, Office of Technology Assessment.

Hawes, C. and C. Phillips. 1986. The Changing Structure of the Nursing Home Industry and the Impact of Ownership on Quality, Cost and Access. In B. Gray, ed., *For-Profit Enterprise in Health Care*. Washington, DC: National Academy Press.

Illinois Legislative Investigating Commission. 1984. *Regulation and Funding of Illinois Nursing Homes*. Springfield, IL: Illinois Legislature.

Institute of Medicine. 1986. *Improving the Quality of Care in Nursing Homes*. Washington, DC: National Academy Press.

Kane, R. et al. 1979. *The PSRO and the Nursing Home: Volume I: An Assessment of PSRO Long-Term Care Review*. Santa Monica, CA: Rand Corporation.

Mech, A. 1980. Evaluating the Process of Nursing Care in Long-Term Care Facilities. *Quality Review Bulletin*, 6:24-30.

Mendelson, M. 1974. *Tender Loving Greed*. New York: Vintage.

New York State Moreland Act Commission on Nursing Homes and Residential Facilities. 1975. *Regulating Nursing Homes: The Paper Tigers*.

Ohio Nursing Home Commission. 1979. *A Program in Crisis: Blueprint for Action*. Columbus, OH: Ohio General Assembly.

Pope, E. et al. 1986. Nursing Home Horrors Persist after Decade of Reform. *San Jose Mercury News*, San Jose, CA.

Ray, W. 1980. A Study of Antipsychotic Drug Use in Nursing Homes: Epidemiological Evidence Suggesting Misuse. *American Journal of Public Health*, 70:485-491.

U.S. Department of Health, Education and Welfare. 1975. *Long-Term Care Facility Improvement Study*. Washington, DC: GPO.

U.S. Senate Special Committee on Aging, Subcommittee on Long-Term Care. 1975 *Nursing Home Care in the United States: Failure in Public Policy*. Washington, DC: GPO.

Vladeck, B. 1980. *Unloving Care: The Nursing Home Tragedy*. New York: Basic Books.

Williams, W. 1986. Patients Lose as Columbia Grows. Also State Nursing Home Policy Flawed. *Cape Cod Times* (September 28-30).

READING 13.3

Older—but Coming on Strong

The following reading on the health of older Americans was taken from Time Magazine's special story on aging.

Doctors who specialize in treating old people delight in telling the story of a 90-year-old man named Morris who has a complaint about his left knee. Says his exasperated physician: "For heaven's sake, at your age what do you expect?" Rejoins Morris feistily: "Now look here, Doc, my right knee is also 90, and it doesn't hurt." It is an apocryphal tale with a pointed message. As long as anyone can remember, old age and disability have been paired as naturally and inevitably as the horse and carriage or death and taxes. After all, advancing years have been seen by most people as an inexorable slide into illness, impotence and immobility.

No longer. Nowadays America's seniors are giving the lie to that grim vision. Fully half of all people now 75 to 84 are free of health problems that require special care or that curb their activities, according to surveys. Says Sociologist Bernice Neugarten of Northwestern University: "Even in the very oldest group, those above 85, more than one-third report no limitation due to health." Declares Dr. Richard Besdine, director of the aging center at the University of Connecticut: "Aging doesn't necessarily mean a life that is sick, senile, sexless, spent or sessile."

That more cheerful view of growing old is gaining currency mainly because of the rapidly expanding scientific discipline of gerontology. Modern studies of the aging process involve everyone from laboratory researchers examining brain tissue to nutritionists interviewing nonagenarians to physicians specializing in treating the elderly. The goal of gerontology is not to extend the upper limit of human life—now about 115 to 120 years of age—but to make the lives of the elderly less burdensome physically and more rewarding emotionally. "The new focus," says Dr. John Rowe, director of the division on aging at Harvard Medical School, "is not on life-span but on health-span." Although still in its infancy, gerontology has produced major revisions in doctors' understanding of how people grow old. Explains Dr. T. Franklin Williams, director of the National Institute on Aging: "It's the diseases that we acquire in later years that really cause the deterioration of functions." Or, as Dr. Robert Butler of Mount Sinai School of Medicine in New York City puts it, "Disease, not age, is the villain." The good news is that in many instances, physical disorders that afflict the aging can be effectively treated. Today even multiple afflictions do not necessarily incapacitate a person. Citing the case of a man of 75 who has diabetes, heart disease and a history of cancer, Rowe points out, "You can't tell me whether that man is in a nursing home or sitting on the Supreme Court."

How long and how well one lives, of course, depend in part on heredity. The chances of blowing out 85 candles go up 5% with each parent or grandparent who has passed that milestone. A family history of certian ailments, such as breast or colon cancer, heart disease, depression or alcoholism, extends the risk of developing such problems. Increasingly, though, researchers believe personal habits and environmental influences may hold the key to why some people are more "successful" at aging than are others. "You find a tremendous variability between individuals," observes Rowe. "The older people become, the less alike they become."

Many of the fears people have about aging are greatly exaggerated. Senility is probably the most dreaded of all debilities, yet only about 15% of those over 65 suffer serious mental impairment. Alzheimer's disease, now considered the scourge of old age, accounts for more than half that total. For much of the remainder, mental impairment from conditions such as heart disease, liver or thyroid trouble and dietary deficiency is either reversible or preventable.

Another frequently overlooked culprit: overmedication. Nearly 80% of people 65 and older have at least one chronic condition (top four: arthritis, high blood pressure, hearing impairment, heart disease); about one-third have three or more. To combat their problems, they rely on a battery of over-the-counter and prescription drugs. The majority of people in this age group use more than five medications, and 10% take more than twelve. Interactions among drugs, as well as too much of some drugs, can cause a host of complications, from mental confusion to slowed blood clotting to disturbance of the heart's rhythm.

Depression, often mistaken for senility, or dementia, is by far the single most ignored disorder among the elderly. About 15% of older people suffer from the condition, double the figure for the the general population; the elderly have the highest suicide rate of any age group. Drugs account for some of the high incidence of depression. But the old are also more vulnerable because they have suffered more major stresses, including the deaths of spouses or friends, living alone, retirement from a job, serious illness. The classic symptoms of depression—guilt, hopelessness, sleeplessness, lack of appetite, and suicidal thoughts—are more likely to be noticed in younger people because they are so out of character. But families and doctors too often overlook depression in the elderly. The warning signs may sometimes be subtle: headaches, stomach ailments, vague complaints of not feeling right. And there is always the tendency to dismiss the signals as normal aging, just old folks' crankiness. When depression is recognized, counseling and drugs successfully treat three-quarters of the cases.

Flagging libido and sexual ability have also been wrongly equated with advancing years. Women supposedly lose interest in sex after menopause; in fact desire normally remains strong throughout life. The dampening of sexual urges often results from physical problems, such as hot flashes and vaginal dryness, which may be alleviated by estrogen therapy, lubricants and attention to nutrition and exercise. Older men, for their part, routinely accept continued impotence as normal. It is not. As a man ages, he does need more time to achieve an erection. But almost all impotence, whether psychological or physical, is reversible. Among the common physical causes: diabetes, heart disease and chronic alcohol abuse.

Yet another widely held fear is that wear and tear on the joints inevitably leads to painful and immobilizing arthritis. Yes, there is a wearing down of the cartilage pads that cushion bones, but less than half of those over 65 whose X rays show degenerative arthritic changes suffer symptoms. Many of the aches and pains attributed to acute arthritis, doctors say, have more to do with weakening muscles than creaky joints. People with some joint damage fare better when they engage in regular moderate exercise, such as walking or swimming.

Aging, however, is hardly a benign process. Acknowledges Dr. Christine Cassel of the University of Chicago: "By and large, the chances are decremental. Every organ is losing reserve capacity." That means a decline in the ability to recover from physical stresses. A 60-year-old and a 20-year-old who race around the block may start out with the same pulse rate, notes Vincent Cristofalo, director of University of Pennsylvania's center for the study of aging. "Even when they stop," he notes, "their pulses may be only a little different. The big difference will be in how long it takes for each person's pulse rate to return to normal."

Slowed recovery has a profound impact when it comes to illness. With advancing years, bones take longer to knit, wounds to heal and infections to clear up. Ultimately, says Cassel, the difference is that a "healthy young person can lose a lung, a kidney and do fine. And so too an old person can be doing fine, but then he has a stroke, a heart attack, whatever. Because of the stress, it's much more likely that all the major organs will go one after the other."

There are some striking physiological changes that accompany age. Among them:

▶ The immune system starts to decline at around age 30. For instance, white blood cells that fight off invaders, such as viruses and bacteria, lose their effectiveness as a person gets older. The gradual weakening of the immune system makes it harder to stave off illness.

▶ Metabolism begins to slow at around age 25. For each decade thereafter, the number of calories required to maintain one's weight drops by at least 2%. Muscle mass gradually shrinks. As a result, people tend to get fatter. Kidneys may lose up to 50% of their efficiency between ages 30 and 80. Some of the liver's functions may decline. Thus alcohol remains in the body longer. So do drugs, a fact doctors are beginning to consider in deciding on dosages for older patients.

▶ Lungs lose on the average 30% to 50% of their maximum breathing capacity between ages 30 and 80. Blood vessels lose elasticity, though the heart stays astonishingly well preserved. Notes Cardiologist Jerome Fleg of the National Institute on Aging: "The heart of normal 80-year-old can pump blood as effectively under stress as that of a normal 30-year-old."

▶ Bone mass reaches its peak in the 30s for both men and women, then begins to drop by about 1% a year. In women the rate surges for a few years after menopause. About 24 million Americans, the vast majority of them women, develop osteoporosis, a condition in which the bones become dangerously thin and fragile. Brittle bones are the major cause of the fractures, particularly of the hip, that cripple many of the elderly. Alcohol and tobacco use accelerates bone thinning. Another reason to stop smoking: women who use tobacco reach menopause about two years earlier than women who do not.

▶ The senses flag. Taste diminishes as the nose loses its sense of smell (odor accounts for about 80% of overall flavor sensation). The loss of taste can lead to lack of appetite and sometimes to serious nutritional deficiencies. Hearing fades, particularly in the high-freguency range, and processing of information slows. Vision begins deteriorating at about 40. The pupil shrinks reducing the amount of light reaching the retina. An 80-year-old's retina receives only about a sixth of the light that a 20-year-old's does. The lens hardens and clouds. More than half of those 60 and older have some cataract formation.

▶Changes occur in the skin. The topmost layer, or epidermis, becomes dry and blemished. The middle layer, or dermis, thins dramatically, making the skin seem translucent, and becomes much less elastic and supportive. These changes, along with loss of fat from the underlying subcutaneous layer, cause the skin to sag and wrinkle. Drinking, smoking and suntanning speed up these processes. With less fat and a decline in the activity of sweat glands, the skin becomes a less efficient regulator of body temperature. The result: older people have a harder time staying warm and cooling off. Protective pigment-forming cells that absorb the sun's harmful rays are reduced by 10% to 20% for each decade of life, thus increasing susceptibility to skin cancers.

▶ The need for sleep gradually diminishes. Newborns sleep 16 to 18 hours a day; by age 65, three to six hours a night, perhaps with a nap during the day, is typically all that is necessary. The quality of sleep changes, becoming lighter and more fitful. Shorter, restless nights lead many who recall the easy slumber of youth to complain of insomnia. As a result, half of elderly women and one-quarter of elderly men take largely unneeded sleeping pills.

▶ The brain loses an average of about 20% of its weight, but as Neurologist

David Drachman of the University of Massachusetts points out, "there is redundancy in the brain. It's like the lights in Times Square. Suppose you turn off 20% of the bulbs: you'll still get the message." Speed of recall and mental performance slow, but essential skills remain intact. Researchers speculate that memory loss among the elderly may be something of a self-fulfilling prophecy. Old people are supposed to have memory problems, so they may be more aware of, and bothered by, occasional lapses than are younger people.

So far, gerontologists have no surefire prescription for staying healthy longer, but they do make some strong recommendations: stay out of the sun, cut back on drinking and stop smoking. They stress that it is never too late to adopt better habits. A person of 70 who stops smoking immediately reduces the risk of developing heart disease. The elderly should follow general principles of a sound diet: avoid foods rich in cholesterol or saturated fat, such as eggs and beef, and eat more chicken and fish. Seniors should stress high-fiber foods, including whole-grain cereals and many fruits, and items rich in vitamins A and C, such as broccoli and cantaloupe.

Though some vitamin or mineral supplements may be beneficial, experts warn that taking excessive doses of nutrients is dangerous. Moreover, the combination of too much of a supplement and certain medications can cause trouble. For example, excessive vitamin E by itself can lead to diarrhea and skin rashes. Taken with certin blood-thinning drugs, large doses of vitamin E can trigger severe internal bleeding.

Exercise, at least half an hour three times a week, is an important aid to controlling weight, keeping bones strong, building muscle strength, conditioning the heart and lungs and relieving stress. Declares Physiologist William Evans of the U.S. Department of Agricultrue-Tufts University center on aging: "There is no group in our population that can benefit more from exercise than senior citizens. For a young person, exercise can increase physical function by perhaps 10%. But in an old person you can increase it by 50%." The advice is catching on: a Gallup poll taken at the end of last year found that 47% of those 65 and older regularly engage in some form of exercise.

Such seniors are living proof that aging is not synonymous with illness, that increasing years do not necessarily lessen desires or capabilities. That is a welcome surprise, particularly to the old. Muses Margaret Strothers Thomas, 72, a retired teacher from Philadelphia: "As a child I used to look at older people, and they were bent over, stooped and complaining. I can't believe that when you reach the age that you've feared you feel great." Achieving better health for longer requires a continual alertness to false assumptions about old age, whether they come from family, friends, doctors or the old. Declares Thomas: "I have lived so many years, but I'm not old. I have a very positive outlook on life."

More of such moxie is in order. Resignation exacts as heavy a toll on the road to old age as disease or poor habits, warn gerontologists, who stress the importance of cultivating new interests and staying mentally engaged. That view is shared by no less an authority than Comedian George Burns. "People practice to get old," he avers. "The minute they get to be 65 or 70, they sit down slow, they get into a car with trouble. They start taking small steps." Burns stays young by taking fearless strides. He plans to play the London Palladium on his 100th birthday— eight years from now. —**By Anastasia Toufexis. Reported by J. Madeleine Nash/ Chicago and Dick Thompson/Washington**

CHAPTER 14 MEETING THE LEISURE-TIME NEEDS OF THE ELDERLY: RECREATION, VOLUNTEER, AND SELF-HELP PROGRAMS

When they retire, many older adults find they have leisure time available for the first time in their memories. Their loss of traditional roles as parents, workers, and, in some cases, spouses, which is characteristic of the later stages of life, creates major problems for some. American society has few ways of preparing individuals for the changes in their lifestyles and the increased leisure resulting from retirement. Emotional problems may result for many older adults who cannot cope with leisure time, although others thrive on their freedom to try new activities.

This chapter discusses some of the programs, services, and activities available to help older adults use their leisure time. We consider various types of recreation programs and volunteer, self-help, and political programs, which are service-oriented and can aid the older adult in making effective use of free time.

Leisure Time and the Elderly

Leisure time, especially for adults, is one of many issues some Americans have failed to handle with skill. Only in relatively recent years have appropriate use of leisure and forms of recreation become subjects of public interest. In fact, only recently have many Americans become sufficiently affluent to be able to afford structured leisure-time activities, so that extensive resources and facilities have developed.

There are many reasons for the American ambivalence toward and lack of attention to leisure-time programs.

First, the nation was founded by followers of self-sacrificing, puritanical religious groups, and they influenced the lives and philosophies of the nation from its beginnings. More Americans have been inclined to believe that "the devil has work for idle hands" than have believed people need structured and effective leisure-time activities.

Many of the nation's most recently-arrived ethnic minority groups share the devotion to work and disdain for leisure time that have long characterized the United States. For a variety of practical economic and ideological reasons, many of those who have emigrated from various parts of Asia are much more strongly oriented to work than to free-time pursuits.

Second, for most of the nation's history, life has been difficult. Simply earning enough money for food, clothing, shelter, and education has taken all the available time and energy. That was true of the earliest settlers, and it remained true for the later immigrants, most of whom had been poor in their nations of origin and who had little reason to be concerned about the effective use of their leisure time. Today's older people were raised in an atmosphere of scarcity and hard work geared to overcoming that scarcity or to earning sufficient money to survive. Leisure has traditionally been viewed as an evil at worst and a luxury at best. Although the traditions are changing, today's cohort of elderly people grew up in a society that placed low priority on adult leisure-time and recreational activities.

Third, many Americans believe that play is for children; adults are supposed to work. Play is appropriate for the young; as one becomes older, it becomes less and less socially acceptable to engage in organized leisure-time programs. The suggestion of the need for leisure-time services is viewed by some older people as patronizing and insulting.

As is true in many other circumstances, American attitudes toward leisure are contradictory. There is public acceptance and high status accorded to adults using vacation and resort activities. Few question the need for vacations, golf, tennis, bowling, and other commercial activities for men and women. However, the conventional view of those activities is that they are releases and relaxations from work. In other words, it is acceptable to engage in recreational activities if they are designed to make one a more efficient worker. Valuing leisure-time activities for themselves is an idea that has not yet gained wide popular acceptance.

Lack of Models

One of the problems in providing effective leisure-time and recreation services for older people is that most of the models for leisure-time programs come from recreation work with children. Recreation workers may have studied theories of recreation for children and practiced recreational activities with children. At times they may be bound by that experience and, at best, may work to adapt their knowledge of recreational programs for children to the needs of older people. In the worst cases some recreation workers use children's activities as if they were appropriate for groups of older people.

A relatively new development in recreation has been therapeutic recreation which focuses on services to physically and emotionally handicapped persons, including older adults.

Involving Older People in
Planning Leisure-Time
Programs

Acceptable and useful programs for older people may arise from careful involvement of the participants in planning their own programs. Involving people
in planning for their services makes a difference in every area of human services
work; it makes a crucial difference in the quality of recreation and leisure-time
programs for the elderly. Planning *for* older people implies they cannot plan for
themselves. However, most who serve older people know that the elderly themselves usually best understand what they want and need, and recreation workers
need to develop programs that are planned *with* older adults. That does not imply
older adults want no help in developing their own activities. In many cases they
very much want assistance in planning programs.

The specific kinds of programs developed are less important than the process
used in choosing the programs and the involvement of older people themselves in
the selection and planning of their leisure-time activities.

Methods of Planning with Older
People in Community Programs

Many recreation and leisure-time activities develop from groups of older
people in senior centers and other kinds of community programs. Human services workers who are staff members in such centers may expedite the planning by
organizing meetings with the members. Sometimes a committee of older people
elected by the total membership develops recreation and leisure-time activities
for the whole center. At other times the staff members meet informally with everyone actively or potentially involved to solicit ideas for activities.

The key to involving members in planning and carrying out their own activities includes knowing how detailed the members want their involvement to be.
Some want specific consultation on every element of the activities. Others will
want the right to advise and the power to veto plans that staff members develop. It
is an error for a worker to force the style of member involvement in planning. The
activities belong to the members, and they decide how and to what extent they
want to participate.

The more involved the older people are in the program and the more
strongly they view it as their own, the more demands they will make for control over the activities. But members come to the point of involvement and
control over their programs through several stages of participation. Human
services workers who are effective help their members find levels of involvement that are comfortable and reasonable. Some groups begin with the staff
planning most of the activities, using only occasional advice from the older

members. After a time those efforts may evolve into elected advisory committees of older members. Ultimately planning might include the members' controlling the group, with only some advice from staff members—a reversal of authority and roles. Pertinent here is Figure 5.2 (chapter 5), which defines the degree of activity of a worker in line with the social health of a group of members. The process of working with elderly people in planning recreation requires the skills of working with groups that are discussed and delineated in chapter 5.

The process of involvement and the relative roles of the staff member and the group members are subtle. For example, The Old Timers' Club in a medium-sized community senior center had been operating for five years. It met once each week and chose as its programs a lunch prepared by the members; some remarks from one of the local Protestant ministers; bingo after lunch once each month, with prizes donated by local merchants; a recipe-swapping session once a month; a lecture, frequently on health or social service problems, at another monthly meeting; and group singing at the fourth meeting of each month. The men in the group stayed away from the recipe-swaps and the group singing. The women were inclined to attend every week.

When the recreation worker with the group met with his supervisor, who asked why the group did the same things every month, every year, the worker replied that he was simply letting the group do what they wanted to do. The supervisor suggested that the worker propose something new to the group—an all-day excursion in the spring to a park and museum within easy bus transportation distance, followed by a picnic lunch, a brief hike, and some free time to feed the tame deer that abounded in the park.

When the worker proposed the idea, the members were thrilled with the opportunity to try something different and said that they needed suggestions and encouragement from the worker. The program was held in good weather and led to a series of similar programs as well as other new approaches to their weekly sessions.

Of course, it is also possible to overdo the innovations: The Golden Years Senior Adults Club had been meeting regularly for nearly a year in a metropolitan area community center. A new worker was assigned to the group to help them plan and carry out their program of recreation and leisure-time activities. The worker was full of ideas—an excursion next week, a musicale the following week, attending a movie and discussing it three weeks from now—an idea for every meeting. After six weeks the members approached the worker and said, "We got together after last week's meeting and decided to propose a plan to you. How would it be if you planned the program for the odd weeks of each month and let us decide what we want to do on the even weeks?"

The worker realized his suggestions had been too numerous and that he had been too aggressive with the members, which led to a discussion of how he might help them without taking over their club.

The Worker's Skills

No matter what the level of functioning of the group or its degree of participation, human-service professionals working with the aged need knowledge of potential leisure-time and recreation activities. An effective worker develops lists of possible programs, resource files, guides of places to visit in the community, games, musical activities, dances, and a whole range of educational programs. Workers may find such resources in books, in conversations with other workers carrying on similar activities, from supervisors, and from observing and listening to the members themselves.

Comprehensive Planning for Recreation

Chapter 6 discussed some of the ways in which group services are applied to the recreational interests and needs of older adults through group processes. While the emphasis in working with groups is on helping the members grow and develop through group activities, recreation and leisure-time activities are employed for their inherent value and potential for giving pleasure to the members.

Perhaps the most important principle for human services workers with older people is that a wide range of activities is needed, because older adults constitute a varied population. For example, some older people will have extensive experience and sophisticated skills in the arts; others may have only limited exposure to such activities. Some older adults may want to participate actively in a wide range of programs—they will be eager to try anything—while others may have no interest in or an aversion to anything new. Older people who consider themselves "clumsy," as well as those who have physical handicaps, may be reluctant to engage in dance. Some older people may associate music with unpleasant experiences from their youth, perhaps unsuccessful school years or association with religious institutions. Therefore, the effective worker will help develop a recreation and leisure-time program that meets needs in many ways.

Some of the principles to follow in organizing and planning recreational programs are the following:

1. *Variety.* There should be a rich and broad opportunity for recreational activity geared to older people. The group's recreation program should not be limited to one kind of activity, for instance, card games, ceramics, or current events discussions, although all three, plus others, might constitute a well-balanced and popular program. A variety of recreational activities ensures each member the opportunity to find something interesting within the group and provides members with new experiences, rather than a repetition of those they have had in the past. We do not propose that programs simply permit older adults to carry on their own activities in isolation from one another. Effective recreation programs should enable each older person to find

something in which he or she can excel while fostering interaction between the members of the group. Mr. Brown, who may be a fine painter, may take great satisfaction in helping Mrs. Green or Mr. Blue paint a landscape. He has an opportunity to participate in an activity that pleases him and offers him an opportunity to excel while he develops his personal skills in helping others. Mrs. Green may have the same opportunity through organizing a chess tournament, and Mr. Blue may be a gourmet cook who can achieve similar gratification through organizing a cooking lesson.

2. *Development.* Recreational activities should progress. It is usually inadvisable to use the same activities all the time, because they tend to institutionalize the group (see chapter 6) and because they become monotonous. Activities ought to develop. For example, if a crafts group begins with paperfolding, there ought to be provisions for that activity to grow into other experiences. Perhaps leather work, copper enameling, and other more advanced crafts such as pottery can be introduced to the group and build upon the base that was established with paper work. Participants in recreation programs need to be stimulated and "stretched" through activities. It is often an objective of recreation programs to help people improve skills they already have and to learn new skills. This principle can apply, for example, to dance activities, which might begin with simple movements, similar to calisthenics. Such activities, which are useful in themselves, may provide a base for more complex activities such as ballroom and folk dancing, which have additional physical and social advantages for the members.

3. *Flexibility.* Though members might usefully be "stretched" in their activities, they ought also to be permitted, if they choose, to remain where they are. Some participants in older adult recreation programs may want to spend years playing checkers and never move to backgammon or chess. Of course, that is their right, and one must assume they are benefiting from the activity if it provides them with personal satisfaction. Similarly, a current events group might, under the developmental principle, grow from newspaper discussions to conversations dealing with more advanced theoretical works on political, historical, and social subjects. On the other hand, some members may want to discuss newspapers alone, without any additional growth. Others may want to reminisce about the past and focus on almost personal histories rather than the present or future. There ought to be provisions for people to follow these inclinations, if they choose to do so. The principle of flexibility can be established and implemented through such means as having a variety of groups within the program; organizing some recreational activity on an individual rather than a group basis; or providing participants with materials and resources for recreational activities with a minimum of direction.

4. *Degree of Structure.* The concept of flexibility suggests that activities need to

be both structured and unstructured. In terms of structure, there ought to be set times and places when activities are provided. For example, a drama club meeting every Saturday from 3–5 P.M. provides the members with information on when they should come and, in essence, guarantees them compatriots who will join them in dramatic activities. However, a program ought also to have time for relatively unstructured activities, such as "Senior Lounge" from 10–12, Monday, Wednesday, and Friday, which might be an opportunity for members to join in games, crafts, and other activities they choose at the time. Members should be able to remain affiliated with the program without being involved in structured activity at all times.

5. *Attendance.* Recreation programs for adults have a history of successful participation. However, numbers do not always mean the program is what it ought to be. For example, in one community several senior centers, churches, and other groups sponsor senior recreation programs on different days of the week. On Monday it is the Senior Center; on Tuesday the Presbyterian Church sponsors a drop-in lounge for older people; on Wednesday it's the Roman Catholic Church; on Thursday, the Jewish Community Center; and on Friday, the Kiwanis Club. One day at a community meeting on aging programs, staff from all three programs meet. After they talk for a while, it quickly becomes clear virtually the same people rotate among these programs each week! The programs assumed they were serving a half-dozen special interest groups, but they were all serving the same single group. In many communities older adults are so hungry for leisure-time activities that they will attend and participate no matter what the quality of the activity or its sponsorship. Therefore, human services workers must carefully evaluate programs with their participants to ensure they are genuinely popular and in line with the needs and interests of the participants. The simple fact that people come does not mean they are getting what they can and should be able to handle.

6. *Costs.* Workers helping plan leisure-time activities with older adults should ensure that the costs of the activity are within the means of the members. Cost can be an important factor for the members of the group, as lack of money is a pervasive problem for older Americans. When shortages of funds are the problem, costs may be the most significant factor in deciding what to do. It may mean that the worker has to help the group choose a program that is relatively inexpensive and located, perhaps, within the facilities of the agency sponsoring the group. Or, if it is at all possible, the worker may want to find a way to raise funds through contributions or grants to support a particularly expensive activity, such as a trip to a distant community. Or the agency may have a budget that will provide support for more costly programs. In any case, cost is a consideration that cannot be overlooked. The evaluation of activities by senior adults may be centered upon how much they cost, more than anything else.

7. *Specialists.* Activities also frequently require special skills and special in-struction, which may be available from part-time specialist staff members within or outside the agency sponsoring the group. Recreational therapists, occupational therapists, physical education teachers, dance instructors, and many other people may be available to provide the necessary instruction or supervision for the members. In all cases the use of outside experts and re-source people must be taken into consideration when the worker is not equipped to handle the activity with the group members.

It is not enough, we stress, for the members to participate in and seem to enjoy programs. Even more important is that the members reach their maximum level of functioning in recreation and leisure-time programs through the efforts of the human services worker.

As Part One makes clear, older adults have a range of capabilities. They may move more slowly, respond more slowly, and appear to be less competent than younger people, but those characteristics are more appearances than reality. With proper time, help, and resources, most older people can do all or most of the things younger adults can.

Workers serving groups for recreational purposes should reach beyond the apparent and the simple in developing programs. They should help their mem-bers maximize the level and quality of their participation and the quality of their activities.

Agencies That Sponsor Recreation and Leisure-Time Programs

There are many organizations that sponsor recreation and leisure-time programs for older adults. Senior centers funded through state, local, and fed-eral funds are best known. In addition, many sectarian human-service organi-zations provide programs for older citizens. These include the YMCAs and YWCAs, Jewish Community Centers, and church-related settlement houses. These organizations usually receive their funds through voluntary contribu-tions and through allocations from local United Funds and community charita-ble groups. Although they may be identified with sectarian objectives, they are generally nonsectarian in their programs. That is, participants need not be af-filiated with the religious group sponsoring the program in order to participate as a member. Sectarian organizations may be devoted to preserving the heri-tage of the sponsoring group or to serving members of that group. However, they accept for membership people who want to affiliate with their activities. At times recreational facilities provided by a religious group different from that of the older person may still meet the individual's needs; location may be a more important criterion for the older person than the specific cultural or religious affiliation of the facility. A Roman Catholic older adult may find usefulness in the senior adult program of a nearby Jewish community center. So might an older Jewish person find that a neighborhood Presbyterian settlement house has a good bit to offer.

Public Recreation Programs

City and county recreation programs frequently sponsor leisure-time activities for older adults. These are diverse and vary in quality from community to community. Many will have the whole range of activities for senior adults suggested in chapter 6; others may be more limited. The majority of recreation and leisure-time programs financed by tax funds include some degree of activity for older people.

Religious Organizations

Churches, synagogues, and other religious organizations frequently sponsor special programs for older adults, particularly their own members. In fact, religious institutions of all kinds probably have the greatest success in attracting and maintaining the interest of older adults.

The programs for older members are not always recreational. Many are based upon religious activity, the degree of which varies from congregation to congregation. Bible study groups, worship services, language instruction (in the cases of Greek Orthodox, Jewish, and other churches that worship in a language other than English), as well as volunteer service activities, such as visiting the sick, preparing meals in order to raise funds, maintaining church facilities, and generally supporting the religious institution, are among the activities that engage the time and efforts of older adults.

Civic Clubs

Some civic clubs serve older adults through recreation and leisure-time programs. Many also involve older adults as local and regional leaders, since they are likely to have extensive experience in the organization as well as sufficient free time to provide it with help. Civic clubs include Kiwanis, Lions, Rotary, Optimists, and various women's organizations either affiliated with these men's groups or independent, such as the American Association of University Women. Fraternal organizations, such as the various Masonic groups, the Elks, Moose, Eagles, and others, also carry on social, recreational, and service activities for older people.

Other civic organizations attract and serve sectarian and ethnically supported groups, including B'nai B'rith, which is primarily for Jewish men and women, the Knights of Columbus, for Roman Catholic men, and various smaller organizations for almost every ethnic group. One of the ways ethnic groups maintain their identity is through such organizations. There are social and civic groups serving blacks, others with a predominantly Hispanic membership, and still others for Asian-American men and women.

Veterans Organizations

Veterans organizations are among the most important of those groups serving older adults. The American Legion, Veterans of Foreign Wars, Disabled American Veterans, Jewish War Veterans, and many other smaller organizations are sponsors of leisure-time services for older adults, many of whom may be members of the organizations.

The significance, configuration, and roles and status of these groups will vary from community to community. An effective worker with and for older adults must become aware of the various groups that develop and sponsor programs of recreation and leisure-time activities for older people. Coming to know the range and limits of these activities is an important part of the orientation to the community for workers in older adult programs.

Self-Help Groups

Among the more significant developments in recent years for older adults have been self-help groups through which older people become engaged in programs designed to help them deal with their problems, interests, or concerns.

The self-help group is an important vehicle for older people in identifying and dealing with problems. Such groups follow a long American tradition of people organizing themselves to work toward overcoming their problems. The labor union movement, the ethnic minority groups, the civil rights movement, the National Welfare Rights Organization, neighborhood groups, and thousands of others in American history have organized themselves to take action that will benefit them.

Perhaps the best known of the self-help groups for older adults is the 80,000-member Gray Panthers, founded by Maggie Kuhn, a retired human services worker. (See chapter 11.) The core of the membership is older adults, and the group works to define and overcome problems of the aging, particularly in the localities of the various chapters around the country. Although they are nonpartisan, the Gray Panthers' efforts are to influence local, state, and national governments in ways that will benefit older people. Members work with legislatures, city governments, law enforcement organizations, public and private social welfare programs, and many other organizations whose programs affect the welfare of the elderly.

The Gray Panthers are a prototype of the legislative and governmentally oriented self-help group. They discovered, as did other groups for older people, that modest changes in administrative regulations and legislation affecting Social Security, Medicare, and other economic aid programs, such as those described in Chapter 12, could be of major benefit to older people.

Political Action

There is a long tradition of older people's participating in political groups, frequently as individuals but more frequently in recent years as representatives of their age group.

In addition to groups such as the Gray Panthers, there are local, regional, and national groups of older people who work for the development of service programs as well as legislation to benefit their population. In West Virginia there is a statewide organization called the Council of Senior West Virginians. It, in turn, has helped create the Coalition on Legislation for the Aged, which includes a variety of groups concerned about the problems of the elderly. The Coalition lobbies intensively each year in the halls of the state legislature.

The extent of such nonpartisan political activity by older people is not known but it is clearly growing along with the aged population. The American Association of Retired Persons, with some 28 million members, is an influential voice for older people.

Because the AARP is so large and well-organized, it serves a variety of functions for older people. As indicated, it provides chances for older citizens to be actively involved in the political process. The officers and board members of AARP on the local, state, and national levels, exercise a significant amount of influence over legislative and administrative decisions. There are so many AARP members (persons as young as 50 may join the association for five dollars annual dues) that when their representatives speak to legislators or a governor or the President, they may be representing a population that is larger than that of most countries. Therefore, they are likely to have a better chance than most groups of getting what they want from government. Because many older people have the time to spend pressing their legislative priorities, the AARP positions also have a strong possibility for approval because those who make decisions hear regularly and intensely from those who care about senior citizen issues. In addition, the justice of the senior citizen issues is also persuasive. Treating older adults in any way other than very well is not popular with political figures or the larger publics they represent.

AARP is wealthy in money in addition to its wealth in large numbers. Because it earns income from the life, accident, and drivers' insurance it sells, as well as from its mail order prescriptions, and advertising in its magazines and newsletters, the Association has enough money to print materials and otherwise influence American politics and legislation.

The smaller but also very active and aggressive National Council on Aging is also an important factor in American self-help and legislative activities. Thousands of older adults and those who work with them are involved in the NCOA's programs of research, education, and social action.

Among the many other organizations that deal with aging is the Gerontological Society of America, which has headquarters in Washington, D.C. It has a membership of some 5,700 professionals who work with older people from fields such as medicine, biology, and the behavioral and social sciences.

Older adults are also active in local, state, and national political committees and campaigns for individual candidates. In some political jurisdictions, the aged are a crucial voting bloc that can swing an election in one direction or another. The aged in Florida and California are particularly important and aged populations in all states will continue to become active and articulate participants in all political activity.

For a variety of reasons, older people are likely to be effective participants in political campaigns and in efforts to influence government agencies as well as state legislatures. They may function as an active and effective lobbying group in Congress. Some of the reasons are discussed in the section of this chapter dealing with volunteer roles for older people, since political volunteering is one of the main forms of free-time activity engaged in by older citizens.

The self-help group focusing on public policy developments and the needs and rights of older people constitute a significant form of self-help group.

Therapeutic Self-Help Groups

Some older adults are organized into different kinds of self-help groups focused less on changing the larger society than toward helping the individual members overcome specific personal, emotional, or health problems. (Also see chapter 5.)

The typical personal change-oriented self-help group is Alcoholics Anonymous, which includes many older members. Alcoholics Anonymous accepts no funds from any outside source whatsoever. Rather, they support all of their activities through their own contributions and through the sales of their educational materials. Instead of using professional staff to help them with their problem, alcoholism, the members help themselves and each other through group programs.

There are dozens of similar organizations operated in several problem areas. The Lost Chord group helps those who have had laryngectomies, for example. There is a local self-help group for almost every kind of problem in one part of the United States or another. Such groups require that their members face their problems themselves; they prefer not using professional staff, and they work to be totally self-supporting. One example of a self-help group organized by a human services worker is the following:

The worker discovered that in her recreation group of 45 older men, some 20 had experienced problems with heart disease or had been warned that they could develop heart disease problems if they failed to care for themselves properly. The worker called these 20 members together and suggested that they might want to organize a self-help group. She offered to help them find an appropriate meeting place, agreed to provide them with some suggestions on how they might organize their program, and offered to provide consultation on a regular basis but also to stay out of the members' activities if they preferred not having her participate.

The men joined together and organized a weekly group meeting, calling themselves "The Powerful Pump Club." They took turns reporting on ways to reduce the risk of heart disease, monitored each other's diets and weight, talked about ways of avoiding anger, and began a program of exercise in the group that could be continued through walking and jogging on their own. When they wanted the worker's help, they asked for it, and they gave her credit for helping them begin. They occasionally called on experts from outside their group, such as physicians, psychologists, and social workers. But it was their group, and they used it well. Over a period of two years, none of the members had any problems with heart disease, and they attributed their good fortune to the activities of the club.

Education

Informal and formal education are among the important self-help and self-improvement activities available to older adults. Colleges and universities are frequently open to older adults on the same bases they are available to younger people. Some institutions of higher education cater to older citizens by reducing or waiving tuition for them. Participation by older adults in higher education is of benefit to the institutions as well as the older participants, because the colleges and universities are able to make their classes more heterogeneous through the introduction of people with life experiences to share with younger students and faculty members. Many sponsor "Elderhostel" programs for seniors.

Vocational schools have some classes in auto mechanics and other trades for senior citizens. Continuing education programs sponsored by community centers, YMCAs, YWCAs, and community colleges offer short courses and workshops that may have special interest for older learners on subjects as diverse as creative writing, history, consumer safety, drama, and so on.

Public libraries are important leisure-time resources for some older adults, and occasionally libraries sponsor programs geared to help older adults select and make the best use of books and periodicals.

Of course, the continuing education of older adults is not limited to reading. Some theaters, both live and motion picture, sponsor senior citizen matinees or discount programs to make it easier and financially feasible for older adults to attend.

Miscellaneous Activities

There are many other activities that lie somewhere between simple recreation and creative use of leisure through self-help programs. These include gardening programs, camping, and the whole range of sports. Virtually anything pleasurable for people of all ages can be adapted to the needs of older adults. For instance, many communities have "Master's" long-distance running groups that include men and women in the senior years. There are national competitions for older runners. Some of the sturdiest long-distance runners in the United States are older adults; many are able to outdistance men and women who are much younger.

American Health magazine (Greengard, 1988) reports that thousands of people are walking daily in shopping malls. Some mall managements have posted mile markers, organized competitions and other events, and established exercise stations for the walkers. They also report that one company is marketing a special shoe for walking in malls and that some clubs for mall walkers have thousands of members.

Volunteer Programs
for Older Adults

Volunteering to serve others is one of the ways older adults occupy their leisure time. In recent years, volunteer programs for older adults have been developed by the federal government as well as by many states and cities. Volunteer programs for the total population also have attracted many volunteers from the ranks of the elderly.

Federal programs include the retired senior volunteer program (RSVP), Senior Companion Program, and Foster Grandparents Program; the Peace Corps; and Volunteers in Service to America (VISTA).

The Peace Corps recruits and trains volunteers to serve in technical and human services positions overseas. The cost of their maintenance, travel, and work are borne by the United States government; the nation that receives the volunteers contributes some technical assistance and other kinds of help, along with the development of assignments for them. VISTA does something similar in selected communities in the United States, usually communities that have high needs for human services specialists in fields such as mental health, community development, youth work, and, of course, services to older adults.

RSVP is a federally funded program that provides for the development of senior volunteer programs in local communities that apply for and receive grants to develop and operate such programs. The range of services provided by the senior volunteers is enormous. Many engage in social service projects, others work in hospitals and correctional institutions. Many of the RSVP programs are sponsored by local senior centers that develop plans and programs in consonance with the needs of the local community and the potential interests of senior citizens in it.

Volunteers in Human Services
Agencies

For a variety of reasons, many human services agencies engage volunteers to carry out their programs. It is a common practice for departments of public welfare, family service agencies, community mental health centers, and many other programs to rely heavily on volunteers.

Older Adults and
Youth Services

Voluntary youth organizations operate almost totally through the efforts of volunteers. This is especially true of the Boy Scouts, Girl Scouts, and Campfire Girls, which are the three largest voluntary youth organizations. Older people provide an excellent and frequently untapped resource for volunteer leaders of those youth groups. Even when they are unable to provide assistance to the program as scoutmasters, den mothers, or group leaders of other designations, they may be able to supplement the efforts of other volunteers by assisting them or by providing specialized help with camping, crafts, or educational activities.

There are a number of ways for older adults to be of service in such groups. In one community center older men played the role of "den grandads" to a Cub Scout den. The community center decided that the youngsters needed contact with men, particularly with older men, since many of the youngsters did not live in the same city as their grandfathers. These den grandads fulfilled important functions for youngsters in their community.

Other Sources for
Volunteer Activity

Many communities have volunteer bureaus, voluntary action centers, and other organizations designed to bring together groups that are seeking voluntary assistance and those who are looking for voluntary activities in which they might be helpful.

At times volunteers supplement the activities of an agency by extending the service the agency can provide to its clientele. In other situations volunteers help the agency develop connections with the larger community. They bring their own knowledge of the community to the agency and provide service to their own special communities on behalf of the agency. Many volunteers serve the functions of relating the agency to the larger community by serving on the board of directors as policy makers, helping the agency develop policies that are in line with community norms while interjecting the interests and concerns of the community they represent. At other times, they provide help to the agency by soliciting funds in the community. Much of the fund raising done on behalf of social agencies is carried out through the efforts of older volunteers. Some people retire from their work with the full intention of devoting all or most of their free time to human services agencies in the community.

In other cases agencies use older volunteers to help them with new and specialized activities they may not be able to develop on their own. For example, retired music teachers may organize choral groups, artists may develop painting projects or sculptures, and physical educators can introduce sports programs. Retired psychologists and psychiatrists can bolster the mental health program of counseling agencies. Older adults contribute voluntarily some of the kinds of professional services that the agency might not be able to afford.

Most large hospitals, both psychiatric and general, have large volunteer departments. In some major hospitals, gift shops, visitor food services, information desks, and other crucial parts of the health care program are directed by volunteers.

*Voluntary Political
Participation*

Among the most significant voluntary activities of older people is political participation. Both of the major parties and many others use large numbers of older volunteers to help them in their programs. Older people are among the most active workers in local and state political committees and campaigns. There are many reasons why older people can be effective participants in political activity. For one, they are a large and active group. When they are organized, they represent a bloc of voters that is impressive for any political aspirant. When they battle for programs geared to improving their lives, their case tends to be persuasive for members of state legislatures, the Congress, and administrators at all levels.

Available leisure time, which may seem disadvantageous and problematic for many older people, is a significant advantage in political activity. Older people have the time to prepare and process mailings or to visit with individual voters to convince them to support candidates, and often they are able to help transport voters to the polls. Much of politics involves hours, days, and months of repetitive, difficult work. Older people, more than any other group in American society, have the time for such activity and, for that reason, they are a respected and highly valued resource in many political campaigns.

In addition, older people are often more politically knowledgeable and responsive than the general population. They tend to vote, attend rallies, and, when possible, contribute to campaigns. Moreover, they do not pose a threat to candidates. It is rare for a 70-year-old volunteer to become the candidate's opponent in the next election, but not so rare for a younger supporter to do so.

For all these reasons, voluntary participation in politics is a major opportunity for many older people and one that ought to be considered in the analysis of and development of any leisure-time program for older adults.

The Dual Advantages of
Volunteer Programs

Clearly, older adult volunteers help others of all ages and all situations in many ways. Volunteering is also of value to the older adults themselves. Those who are otherwise unemployed add significance to their lives by helping young people, the handicapped, other older adults, institutionalized people, and others through volunteer programs. Many psychologists would agree that we help ourselves by helping others—that we build our self-esteem when we improve the lives of other people. In addition, people who are occupied with positive activities may improve their mental health through activity.

Summary

The sudden availability of leisure time is one of the obvious attributes of aging in the United States. This chapter has explored some of the consequences of the increased availability of leisure time for old people and outlined some of the problems and opportunities associated with that change in the life-style and patterns of the older person.

Some of the ways in which older people may use leisure time were outlined, including recreation programs, self-help programs, and volunteer programs in many kinds of organizations and institutions.

Increased leisure constitutes one of the more complex problems of older people and from it arise some of the most important needs older adults have and some of the most important contributions human services workers with the aging may make to their clients. Helping older people find effective ways to use their leisure time that are compatible with their health, interests, and financial resources is one of the most important ways professionals help older clients.

READING 14.1

Teaching Old Folks Is An Art/Robert Coles
This review of Kenneth Koch's I Never Told Anybody . . . Teaching Poetry Writing in a Nursing Home *demonstrates that physical incapacity need not be a hindrance to successful elderly participation in leisure-time activities.*

In a letter to a young admirer, William Carlos Williams once had this to say: "I hear lines of poetry every day from my patients. They sometimes say what they see and feel in interesting ways. In my car, later in the day, I hear their words." Kenneth Koch has had the same willingness to pay close heed to the lyrical possibilities that many ordinary human beings possess, and even demonstrate rather impressively, given any encouragement at all. His book *Wishes, Lies, and Dreams* told of his work with children, who ache at times to use their imaginations and stretch the bounds of language, only to be put down repeatedly by various literal-minded, sadly restrictive adults. The boys and girls he came to know eventually produced strongly worded, suggestive, eye-opening poems. Now he has taken his thoughtful, giving, resourceful and patient spirit to quite elderly and often infirm men and women, in obvious hopes of finding among them a similar responsiveness of mind and heart. If anything, the result is a more poignant and dramatic victory, because many old people have learned only too well that even their prose statements, never mind any written poems they may come up with, are of scant interest to others.

The American Nursing Home (no less) is located on the Lower East Side of Manhattan—not far from the Catholic Workers' St. Joseph House. It was there, with about 25 men and women, that Koch tried to teach poetry. "The students were all incapacitated in some way, by illness or old age," he tells us. He is brief and matter-of-fact with specifics, his purpose being educational and literary, rather than sociological: "Most were in their seventies, eighties, and nineties. Most were from the working class and had a limited education. They had worked as dry cleaners, messengers, short-order cooks, domestic servants." To a significant degree they had given up on life; it was enough to stay alive, be fed and cared for. Needless to say, they did not write poems. Yet one day Kenneth Koch and another poet, Kate Farrell, showed up and began to talk about poems, to read them and to suggest that they were not only the creations (or property) of a lucky, privileged few, but also that they could begin to take shape in the thoughts of ordinary people, and be acknowledged, shared, enjoyed by them.

Koch had not romanticized his students. He knew that they were tired, hurt, ailing. Some were blind or hard of hearing. They all had serious complaints, and a number were in constant pain. As he took the measure of the class, he observed the serious initial obstacles of memory loss and rambling speech among many men and women. But he was not there to dwell on negatives. He began by asking the people to think of a sentence or two. He had modest, concrete suggestions: choose a color, say something about it, then something else, then something else again, using the name of the color. He received gratifying responses. Mary Tkalek, for instance offered this: "I like green; I used to see so many greens on the farm/I used to wear green, and sometimes my mother couldn't find me/Because I was green in the green."

The teacher became bolder. He asked his students to imagine themselves the ocean, or holding a conversation with the moon, the stars. He suggested that they recall especially quiet moments, or make particular comparisons or hark back to one or another time—the end of World War II, for instance. He read to them. He singled out, to start, the verse of Walt Whitman. D. H. Lawrence and William Carlos Williams. He never looked down on his students; he regarded them as quite able to write poetry, given encouragement and provocative hints about what tack they might take. He did not want to blur the difference between the dead poets he cherished (and in a way was calling upon for assistance) and the members of the rather unusual writing class he had chosen to teach. He knew that, finally, he could only count on this from a given student: "The music of ordinary speech and the memories and feelings his long life had given him."

Over the weeks they learned to summon and repeat words joyfully, to exaggerate enthusiastically, to celebrate contrasts, to become immersed in nature, to imagine all sorts of places, to put themselves into many different kinds of shoes. Most of them were wheeled in; some arrived in walkers, and only a few came to class on their own—yet they reached out for the sky, crossed the seas, fashioned their own time-machines and used them gladly, at times wantonly. And their teacher, clearly, loved what happened. He praised them; fed them more and more of his ideas, received back increasingly intricate, dramatic and subtle poems. "Poetry is like being in Inner Space," William Ross decided, early on. "Your leaves sound different," Nadya Catalfano told the season, autumn, one day: "I couldn't understand why/The leaves at that time of year/Had a rustle about them/And they would drop/At the least little thing/And I would listen/And pick up some of them."

The students were encouraged both to speak and write their poems. They were treated to jazz, to readings of Keats as well as more contemporary poets, and as their blood stirred they were asked to talk about their past lives. Their teacher was not, however, interested in becoming yet another of America's flourishing breed of psychological counselors. He makes an important clarification: "I don't think I would like to adjust to a life without imagination or accomplishment, and I don't believe my students wanted to either. It is in that sense, perhaps, that it can best be understood why it is better to teach poetry writing as an art than to teach it—well, not really teach it but use it—as some form of distracting or consoling therapy." And a little later on, referring to one of his students: "We were never contemplating Mary L. Jackson, she and I, but the things she said and wrote." He never expected too little of her—that curious condescension that is masked as compassion: "One trouble with a kind of falsely therapeutic and always reassuring attitude that it is easy to fall into with old people is the tendency to be satisfied with too little."

And so those men and women, nearer death than most of us, worked hard and became in their spirits lively, attentive, dedicated. "I'd like to write the book of my life/I've started it already," Mary L. Jackson observed. Their enthusiasm, their bursts of memory, reflection, fantasy were matched by the evident satisfaction of their teacher. In this book he tells others how they, too, might work with elderly people. He shows us that in Iowa (he spent time at the Lutheran Old Age Home in Cedar Falls), as well as in New York, apparently apathetic, even dazed men and women can suddenly begin to sing with their own words. And with a sentence here and there, he gives us textbooks of psychology and sociology: "Many had spent most of their adult lives at jobs like housework, steam-pressing, being a short-order cook. They had unusual (for poetry) lives and were looking at them now in an unusual time." But he is not one to argue with others or to come up with pompous generalizations: he merely implies with a casual, personal thought the significant difference between his way of regarding people and that of others—with their talk of "cultural disadvantage" and whatever: "I did think sometimes, too, what a marvelous thing it was for someone, for instance, to be writing poetry, and loving it, who had kept through decades of hard domestic work, a fine and delicate sensibility that she could now express with eloquence in words."

Mostly Koch encouraged in his students what he calls "unrhymed, nonmetrical, fairly unliterary poetry"; it was an easier kind for beginning students to approach. But they enjoyed hearing and occasionally trying to write a more formal and intricate language. They would, no doubt, recognize a familiar spirit at play in the pages of "The Duplications." Their teacher has completed a long poem, somewhat arbitrarily divided in half by an autobiographical section. Using mostly rhymed octets, he sets out to abolish space, time, and historical experience in order to create exuberant images that entertain, and occasionally (though with a light hand) instruct. The narrator is a rather sensuous, symbol-prone itinerant, at once rhapsodic and skeptical. He clearly sympathizes with those "Students dreaming up some pure Havanas/Where love would govern all, not francs or dollars"; but he worries that new tyrannies, announced with messianic slogans, keep replacing their predecessors—one of the "duplications" intended by his title, which more broadly refers to the cyclic rhythms of life. He is, always, very much an individual—someone who might not bother Fidel Castro, but who certainly would arouse the suspicions of his bureaucratic henchmen: "O Liberty, you are the only word at/Which the heart of man leaps automatically."

Koch has a delicious sense of ironic detachment running through his rather lyrical, if not ecstatic, celebrations of the flesh. On a Greek island, contemplating the serene beauty of the Aegean, he thinks of the life underneath: " . . . Fish are nice/In being, though we eat them, not revengeful/I think that we would probably be meaner/To those who washed us down with their retsina!" It is an observation utterly worthy of Pueblo or Hopi children, who, like Emerson or Thoreau—speaking of duplications—are not especially inclined to what in the 19th century was called "human vainglory." He is especially wry and touching when he tells of his struggles to write while living in Ireland. He had finished part of the poem, put it aside for other interests (teaching children or the elderly how to write poetry?) and had come back to himself, his mind's (the writer's) self-centeredness. Ought he to go on, "Continue my narration of the fallacy/We find by being born into this galaxy"? His answer is characteristically lacking in egoistic justifications, or sly academic boasting. He simply wants to reach others; maybe make them feel like singing, or smile in recognition of a particular vision, suggestion, anecdote. Of

course, he cannot resist, occasionally, tucking into his narrative a bit of philosophical speculation or moral concern.

His is a wanderer's unyielding struggle for life: " . . . Take that, you/Dull insect
Death! . . . " His is a naturalist's pantheistic, humorous advocacy: "Now turtles
have on Mount Olympus landed/With numerous troops, and pistols, flags, and
bells/And hostile mottoes painted on their shells/DOWN WITH OLYMPUS! WHY
SHOULD WE ENDURE/AN ALIEN RULE? LET TURTLES REIGN O'ER TURTLES!/
AND GODS GO HOME! THE VERY AIR IS PURE/WE TURTLES BREATHE. WE DO
NOT NEED MYRTLES,/THE OAK, THE BAY, THE SHINING SINECURE!/GIVE US
OUR LIVES TO LIVE IN OUR HARD GIRDLES!" It is a point of view one can imagine
the old ones in the American Nursing Home of New York's Lower East Side taking
to rather heartily: their good, dear friend Kenneth Koch doing some of his marvel-
ously entertaining and sometimes unnerving acrobatic stunts.

SElECTEd U.S. STATiSTiCS ON AGiNG*

The U.S. Aged Population

Ages 65-84, 1985	25.8 million
Ages 65-84, 2020	44.3 million
Over 85, 1985	2.7 million
Over 85, 2020	7.1 million
Life expectancy, 1985	
men	71.2 years
women	78.2 years
black men and women	69.5 years
white men and women	75.3 years
Number of men per 100 women	
at ages 65-69	81
at ages 85-89	43

*Compiled from Aaron, Bosworth and Burtless, 1989; Bird, 1988–1989; Bureau of the Census, 1983 and 1984; Gibbs, 1988; Kingson, Hirshorn, and Cornman, 1986; Shapiro and Greenstein, 1988; Toufexis 1988.

Social Security and Medicare
  Surplus, 1988 $50 billion
  Projected surplus, 2030 $2 trillion
  Tax in 1990   15.3%**
  Benefits in 1990 $252 billion

Recipients in 1987   31.4 million
  Federal revenues from Social Security   34%

Income and Poverty
  Poor over 64
    1959   35%
    1985   12.6%
  Estimates of very low income renter   12.7 million
households, 1983
  Households receiving federal housing   4.2 million
assistance, 1987
  Persons over 65 living alone, 1982   40%
    men   7.7
    women   31.9
  States that supplement SSI payments   27
  Range of supplement values   From $2 per
                                   month, Ore-
                                   gon, to $292,
                                   Alaska

  Beneficiaries of private pensions
    1960   1.8 million
    1980   9.1 million
  Median annual income of couples $22,000
over 65, 1987
  Elderly Blacks with incomes less than   33%
$5300
  Black women living alone with less   55%
than $5300

Political Activity
  American Association of Retired Per-   28 million
sons membership, 1989
  Persons over 65
    registered to vote, 1982   75%
    voted, 1982   60%

**Half from employer, half from employee on earnings up to $48,000

Health Status and Problems
Cost of health care for aged, 1981	$50 billion
Projected cost of health care for the aged, 2000	$200 billion
Nursing homes needed to be opened between 1988 and 2000 to meet projected demands	One every day
States with a program for medically needy aged and disabled	34
States that *do not* automatically provide Medicaid to SSI recipients	14
Elderly poor covered by Medicaid	34%

Deaths per 100,000
men 65 and over, 1980	6,388
women 65 and over, 1980	4,484

Causes of deaths
Heart disease, men	2,779
Heart disease, women	2,028
Malignant neoplasms (cancers)	
men	1,372
women	768
Cerebrovascular diseases (stroke)	
men	557
women	584
Accidents	
men	124
women	79
Suicide	
men	35
white men	38
black men	11
all women	6
Hours of sleep needed by those over 65	3–6 per night
People over 65 who regularly exercise	47%
Health improvement elderly receive from regular exercise	50%
Persons out of 1,000 over 65 with chronic health problems	
Arthritis	495

Hypertension	390
Hearing loss	300
Heart disease	257

Work and Work Attitudes
  Average earnings of older employed

| women | $6,650 |
| men | $9,100 |

  Men over 64 working

1960	34%
1985	16%
Percent of employed over 55 who are women	41%

Reasons workers over 55 give for
continuing to work

Money	46%
Like working	15%
Keep busy	14%
To be with people	9%
Help others	4%
Other	12%

How they feel about their jobs

Love it	57%
Like it well enough	35%
Don't like it much	6%
Hate it	1%

What they specifically like

People	38%
Work itself	33%
Challenge	20%
Work environment	13%
Schedule	11%
Pay or benefits	11%

Their work problems

No problems	67%
Age discrimination	15%
Finding work	13%
Pay	9%
Social Security Limitation	7%
Other	13%

Age they plan to quit working

55–59	1%
60–64	18%
65–69	19%
70–74	8%
74–79	4%
80+	4%
Never	17%
Don't know	29%

qlossARy

Adult foster care: Lodging, some personal care, and nutrition provided in the home of a nonrelative for a fee paid by the adult resident or by a human services agency. Does not apply to nursing homes and other long-term care medically oriented facilities.

Adult residential care: Another name for adult foster care.

Advocate: One who defends or promotes a cause and the subsequent pleading of that cause.

Age-grading: Attributing or classifying types of human behavior as appropriate or inappropriate for specific age groups in society such as the young and old.

Age norms: Socially defined expected behaviors for people at any given age.

Alzheimer's disease: A neurological condition associated with aging that causes mental deterioration, memory loss, and other irreversible handicaps. In advanced cases, constant supervision and personal care is needed by the patient.

Budget: A financial tool, used as part of planning, to allocate available resources to anticipated expenditures.

Case management: The arrangement of several services for a recipient of human services and the follow-up and monitoring of those services while they are being provided. Services are augmented, discontinued, and otherwise changed through the case management process.

confidentiality: Principle that the worker does not reveal information secured from clients.

Consumer protection: Programs organized by governments and private organizations such as Better Business Bureaus to help those who purchase goods and services avoid being exploited. Consumer protection programs help people gain refunds, replacements of products, and other restitution when they have been mistreated by a vendor, as well as serving as a repository of information, in some cases, about businesses with bad business practice records.

Demographics: Descriptive information about a population or group based on vital and/or social statistics.
Disengage: To voluntarily disassociate oneself from social contact.

Formed group: A group organized by an outside agent.

Goal: A broad statement of what is to be achieved over time by a program.
Group cohesion: A united group spirit.
Group conflict: Disunited group spirit.
Group process: The stages of dynamic interactions in the development of groups.
Group role: A specific position or set of behaviors assumed by individual group members as part of the interaction of the group as a whole.
Group solidarity: A group's total agreement and presentation of solid front.

Hospice: A service or facility that provides various kinds of assistance and support to dying persons. Designed to avoid the necessity of hospitalization and to enable people to die with dignity.

Impact objectives: Outcomes expected in project participation as a result of project activities.
Interviewing: The process of gathering information from and counseling with a client. Serves as the basis for direct assistance to those who use human services help.

Later maturity: A phase of the life cycle, including the years 60–74.
Legal services: Assistance of attorneys and other persons, sometimes in offices of public defenders or legal aid societies, to help those who cannot afford private help to be represented in judicial actions or to resolve legal disputes.
Life cycle: Stages of development in an individual's life span.
Life expectancy: Total number of years an individual can expect to survive at birth.

Means test: Requirement that recipients of aid programs prove their poverty in order to be eligible.
Middle age: A phase of the life cycle, including the years 40–59.
Minority elderly: Subgroups within the elderly population who experience dif-

ficulties because of their status in society; for example, blacks, Mexican-Americans, native Americans, etc.

Natural group: A group organized by the members.

Needs: Basic requirements; in this context, specifically requirements for elderly people to secure and maintain maximum independence and dignity in a home or home-like environment.

Needs assessment: A means of systematically collecting   information about the problems and needs of older people and their service utilization pattern.

Objective: A statement of a precise, measurable outcome to be accomplished by a program within the program year and under the funds requested.

Old age: A phase of the life cycle, including the years 75 to death.

Older Americans Act: Basic federal law dealing with the older adult population.

Output objectives: The expected level of service or activities of a project.

Partialization: Breaking down a client's problem into manageable parts.

Physical aging: Physical changes associated with advancing years.

Planning: A process for fully determining a preferred course of future action.

Priority objective: An objective that has been evaluated against all other stated objectives and has been determined to be of greatest relative importance; it therefore will be ranked first in order of execution.

Protective services: Assistance provided by human services workers, usually under the jurisdiction or authority of a public social services agency, to assist persons who are being mistreated or exploited by others and are unable to help themselves. Adult protective services typically deal with older people as well as the mentally handicapped.

Reminiscence: Thinking and talking about occurrences of earlier years.

Role: A defined position within a group or in society that is associated with specific defined functions to be performed and expected behaviors as part of the position.

Self-determination: Permitting clients to decide and direct their own lives in a counseling situation.

Self-help group: A group through which older people become engaged in programs designed to help them deal with their problems, interests, or concerns themselves.

Social actions: Human behavior that is exhibited in groups or by classes of people without reference to specific individuals.

Social aging: The habits and roles of aging individuals as they relate to groups or society.

Social problem: A situation affecting a large number of people that they or others believe to be a source of difficulty or unhappiness.
Socialization: Learning of new behaviors and orientation as one moves into new positions in the social structure.
Status: Position in the social order.
Stereotype: Preconceived ideas about individuals or groups, generally not based on fact.
Strategy: The preferred course of action designed to best accomplish stated objectives.
Support services: Supplemental services provided by an agency to facilitate clients' ability to use the primary services of the agency.

Target population: A specific group or subgroup for which a program is intended or who is to benefit from a specific program.
Thanatology: The study of death and dying.

Unmet need: A need for which no service or resource exists, or for which the existing services are inadequate, inappropriate, or inaccessible.

Work plan: A detailed description, including tasks, of what is to be done, who is going to do it, and when it will be done.

For further definitions and explanations of concepts discussed in this book, the authors recommend the *The Social Work Dictionary*, (R.L. Barker. National Association of Social Workers, 1987.) and *The Seventeenth Edition of the Encyclopedia of Social Work*, (A. Minahan, et al. National Association of Social Workers, 1987)

bibliography

Aaron, Henry J., Barry P. Bosworth and Gary Burtless.
  1989   Can America Afford to Grow Old? Washington, D.C.: The Brookings Institution.

Ackerman, Nathan.
  1967   Expanding Theory and Practice in Family Therapy. New York: Family Service Association of America.

Ackerman, Nathan.
  1970   Family Therapy in Transition. Boston: Little, Brown.

Ackerman, Nathan.
  1982   The Strength of Family Therapy: Selected Papers of Nathan Ackerman. New York: Brunner/Mazel.

Alexander, Jo (ed.)
  1986   Women and Aging: An Anthology/by Women. Corvallis, Ore.: Calyx Books.

Atchley, Robert C.
  1977   The Social Forces in Later Life: An Introduction to Social Gerontology. 2nd ed. Belmont, Calif.: Wadsworth.

Atchley, Robert C. and Mildred M. Seltzer.
  1977   The Sociology of Aging: Selected Readings. Belmont, Calif.: Wadsworth.

Auerbach, Arnold.
  1976   "The elderly in rural areas: differences in urban areas and implica-
            tions for practice." In Leon Ginsberg (ed.), Social Work in Rural
            Communities. New York: Council on Social Work Education.

Baltes, P. and K. Warner Schaie.
  1974   "Aging and I.Q.: the myth of the twilight years." Psychology Today,
            March.

Bayles, Kathryn A.
  1987   Communication and Cognition in Normal Aging and Dementia. Bos-
            ton: Little Brown.

Bayles, F. H.
  1988   "You Must Remember This." in Health and You. West Columbia,
            S.C.: Lexington Medical Center.

Beauvoir, Simone de.
  1972   The Coming of Age. New York: Putnam.

Bengston, Vern L.
  1972   "A Conceptual framework for the analysis of the behavior of aging
            individuals in society." In Delivery and Administration of Services
            for the Elderly. Los Angeles: University of Southern California Press,
            1972.

Bengston, Vern L.
  1973   The Social Psychology of Aging. New York: Bobbs-Merrill.

Bennett, Louis L.
  1965   "Protective service for the aged." Social Science Review 39:283–51.

Berne, Eric.
  1969   Principles of Group Treatment. New York: Oxford University Press.

Binstock, Robert H. and Ethel Shanas (eds.)
  1985   Handbook of Aging and the Social Sciences. New York: Van Nos-
            trand Reinhold.

Bird, Caroline.
  1988   "The Jobs You Do." in Modern Maturity, Vol. 31, No. 6. December,
            1988-January, 1989. pp. 40–46.

Birren, James E. and K. Warner Schaie (eds.),
  1985   Handbook of the Psychology of Aging. New York: Van Nostrand
            Reinhold.

Birren, James E.
  1974   "Aging: psychological aspects." In Birren and Ruth Web (eds.), Cur-

riculum Development in Gerontology. Los Angeles: Ethel Percy Andrus Gerontology Center, University of Southern California.

Birren, James E. and Ruth Weg (eds.)
1974   Curriculum Development in Gerontology. Los Angeles: Ethel Percy Andrus Gerontology Center, University of Southern California.

Bittles, A. H. and K. J. Collins (eds.)
The Biology of Human Aging. Cambridge: Cambridge University.

Blanchard, Evelyn Lance.
1987   "American Indians and Alaska Natives," in Encyclopedia of Social Work, 18th edition. Silver Spring, Md.: National Association of Social Workers.

Boyd, Rosamond E. and Charles Oakes (eds.)
1969   Foundations of Practical Gerontology. Columbia, S.C.: University of South Carolina Press.

Brawley, Emilia E. Martinez.
1987   "Rural Social Work," in Encyclopedia of Social Work, 18th edition. Silver Spring Md.: National Association of Social Workers.

Brody, Elaine M.
1985   Mental and Physical Health Practices of Older People: A Guide for Health Professionals. New York: Spring Publishing Co.

Brody, Jacob A. and George L. Maddox (eds.)
1988   Epidemiology and Aging: An International Perspective. New York: Springer Publishing Co.

Brody, Stanley, Harvey Finkle, and Carl Hirsh.
1972   "Benefit alert: outreach program for the aged." Social Work 17:14–23.

Bross, Dorothy R.
1967   "Night college courses for older women." Adult Leadership 15:233–34.

Brown, David.
1987   Brown's Guide to Growing Grey. New York: Delacorte.

Browne, Colette and Roberta Onzuka-Anderson (eds.)
1985   Our Aging Parents: A Practical Guide to Eldercare. Honolulu: University of Hawaii Press.

Brubaker, Timothy H. (ed.)
1987   Aging, Health, and Family: Long Term Care. Newbury Park, Calif.: Sage Publications.

Burdman, Geri Marr.
1986   Healthful Aging. Englewood Cliffs, N.J.: Prentice Hall.

Burnside, Irene Mortenson.
1973   "Touching is talking." The American Journal of Nursing 73:2060–63.

Bush, Malcolm.
1988   Families in Distress. Berkeley: University of California Press.

Butler, Robert.
1975   Why Survive? Being Old in America. New York: Harper & Row.

Butler, Robert N. and Myrna Lewis.
1973   Aging and Mental Health. St. Louis: C. V. Mosby.

Caine, Lynn.
1988   Being a Widow. New York: William Morrow.

Caird, F. I.
1986   Drug-Induced Diseases in the Elderly: A Critical Survey of the Literature. New York: Elsevier.

Caso, Elizabeth and Harry T. Phillips.
1966   "Small-grant project in Massachusetts for the chronically ill and aged." Public Health Report 81:471–77.

Chen, Linda (ed.)
1986   Nutritional Aspects of Aging. Boca Raton, Fla.: CRC Press.

Chen, Yung-Ping.
1970   Income. Background Paper for the 1971 White House Conference on Aging. Washington, D.C.: U.S. Department of Health, Education, and Welfare, Administration on Aging.

Clark, Patch.
1985   Seniors on Stage: The Impact of Applied Theater Techniques on the Elderly. New York: Praeger.

Cohen, Carl I. and Jay Sokolovsky.
1989   Old Men of the Bowery. New York: The Gilford Press.

Consumers Union.
1983   The Medicine Show. Mount Vernon, N.Y.: Consumers Reports.

Cooper, Kenneth.
1985   Running Without Fear. New York: Bantam.

Cooper, Kenneth.
1978   The Aerobics Way. New York: Bantam.

Counts, Dorothy Ayers and David R. Counts (eds.)
  1985   Aging and Its Transformations: Moving Toward Death in Pacific Societies. Lanhan, Md.: University Press of America.

Cox, Harold.
  1984   Later Life. Englewood Cliffs, N.J.: Prentice-Hall.

Craik, F. I. M. and S. E. Trehub (eds.)
  1982   Aging and the Cognitive Processes. New York: Plenum.

Craven, Joan and Florence S. Wald.
  1975   "Hospice care for dying patients." American Journal of Nursing 75:1816–22.

Davis, Bernard and W. Gibson Wood (eds.)
  1985   Homeostatic Function and Aging. New York: Raven Press.

Davis, Patti and Maureen S. Foster.
  1987   Home Front. New York: Crown.

Davis, Richard H. (ed.)
  1974   Aging: Perspectives and Issues. Los Angeles: Ethel Percy Andrus Gerontology Center, University of Southern California.

Doress, Paul Brown and Diana Laskin Siegel.
  1987   Ourselves, Growing Older. New York: Simon and Schuster.

Dove, Mary.
  1986   The Perfect Age of Man's Life. New York: Cambridge University Press.

Eastman, Peggy.
  1989   "Child Care Field Seeks Older Hands." in AARP News Bulletin. Vol. 30, No. 1, January, 1989. p.1.

Ebersole, Priscilla.
  1985   Toward Healthy Aging: Human Needs and Nursing Response. St. Louis: Mosby.

"The Elderly: Prisoners of Fear."
  1976   Time Magazine, November 26, pp. 21–22.

Esposits, Joseph L.
  1987   The Obsolete Self: Philosophical Dimensions of Aging. Berkeley: University of California Press.

Estrada, Leobardo F.
  1987   "Hispanics," in Encyclopedia of Social Work, 18th edition. Silver Spring, Md.: National Association of Social Workers.

Finch, Caleb E. and Edward L. Schneider (eds.)
1985   Handbook of the Biology of Aging. New York: Van Nostrand Reinhold.

Foner, Anne.
1986   Aging and Old Age: New Perspectives. Englewood Cliffs, N.J.: Prentice Hall.

Forbes, Gilbert.
1987   Human Body Composition: Growth, Aging, Nutrition, and Activity. New York: Springer-Verlag.

Fulman, Terry T.
1987   Inadequate Care of the Elderly: A Health Care Perspective on Abuse and Neglect. New York: Springer Publishing Co.

Fyten, David.
1988   "High Tide at Street Level." in Tulanian, Winter 1988. pp. 13–19.

Gibbs, Nancy R.
1988   "Grays on the Go." in Time Magazine, February 22, 1988. pp. 66–75.

Ginsberg, Leon.
1988   "Shelter issues for the 1990's. The potential roles of adult foster care and community residential facilities." in Adult Foster Care Journal, Winter 1988.

Gioiella, Evelynn Clark.,
1986   Gerontology in the Professional Nursing Curriculum. New York: National League for Nursing.

Gioiella, Evelynn Clark.
1985   Nursing Care of the Aging Client: Promoting Healthy Adaptation. Norwalk, Conn.: Appleton-Century-Crafts.

Glefand, Donald E.
1982   Aging: The Ethnic Factor. Boston: Little, Brown.

Goffman, Erving.
1965   Stigma. Englewood Cliffs, N.J.: Prentice-Hall.

Greengard, Samuel.
1988   "Shop Till You Drop." in American Health, December 1988, p. 34.

Gutmann, David E.
1975   "Parenthood: A key to the comparative study of the life cycle." In Leon H. Ginsberg and Nancy Datan (eds.), Life-Span Development Psychology: Normative Life Crisis. New York: Academic Press.

Haley, Alex.
  1977   "Haley's Rx: talk, write, reunite." in Time magazine, February 14, p.
          72.

Harrington, Michael.
  1960   The Other America. Baltimore: Penguin.

Hayflick, Leonard.
  1977   "The biology of aging." Natural History 86:22–30.

Health of the Elderly.
  1977   Public Health Report 92:3–64.

Hendricks, Jon and C. Davis Hendricks.
  1981   Aging in Mass Society. Cambridge, Mass.: Winthrop.

Hendrickson, Michael C. (ed.)
  1986   The Role of the Church in Aging. New York: Haworth Press.

Hulsey, Steve.
  1975   "Working seniors prove their mettle." Manpower, June, pp. 23–25.

Hurley, Anne DesNoyers and Robert Sovner.
  1986   "Dementia, Mental Retardation, and Down's Syndrome." in Psychi-
          atric Aspects of Mental Retardation Reviews. Vol. 5, No. 8, August
          1986, pp. 39–44.

Jackson, Jacquelyne Johnson.
  1973   Proceedings of Black Aged in the Future. Durham, N.C.: Center for
          the Study of Aging and Human Development, Duke University.

Jacobs, Ruth Harriet
  1987   Older Women: Surviving and Thriving, A Manual for Group Leaders.
          Milwaukee: Family Service America.

Janicki, Matthew P. and Henryk M. Wisniewski (eds.)
  1985   Aging and Developmental Disabilities: Issues and Approaches. Balti-
          more: Brookes.

Johnson, Horton (ed.)
  1985   Relations Between Normal Aging and Disease. New York: Raven
          Press.

Kalish, Richard A.
  1975   Late Adulthood: Perspectives on Human Development. Monterey,
          Calif.: Brooks/Cole.

Kalish, Richard A.
  1977   (Ed.), The Later Years. Monterey, Calif.: Brooks/Cole.

Kaplan, Jerome, Caroline S. Ford, and Harry Wain, M.D.
  1967   "Assessing the impact of a gerontological counseling service on community health resources." Geriatrics 22:150–54.

Karlinsky, Harry.
  1986   "Alzheimer's Disease in Down's Syndrome: A Review." Journal of the American Geriatrics Society, 34:728–34.

Kass, Leon R.
  1975   "The pursuit of health." The Public Interest, No. 40, Summer.

Kastenbaum, Robert J. and R. Aisenburg.
  1972   The Psychology of Death. New York: Springer.

Kaufman, Sharon R.
  1986   The Ageless Self: Sources of Meaning in Late Life. Madison: University of Wisconsin Press.

Kessler, Julia Brown.
  1976   "Aging in different ways." Human Behavior 5:56–63.

Kingson, Eric R.
  1987   What You Must Know About Social Security and Medicare. New York: Pharos.

Kingson, Eric R., Barbara A. Hirshorn and John M. Cornman
  1986   Ties That Bind. Cabin John, Md.: Seven Locks Press.

Kitano, Harry H.
  1987   "Asian Americans," in Encyclopedia of Social Work, 18th edition. Silver Spring, Md.: National Association of Social Workers.

Kohut, Sylvester.
  1987   Reality Orientation for the Elderly. Oradell, N.J.: Medical Economics Books.

Kornblum, Seymour and Geraldine Lauter.
  1976   "The development tasks of middle age and aging and the implications for practice." Conference Papers, New York: Association of Jewish Center Workers.

Kosburg, Jordan.
  1975   "Methods of community surveillance on geriatric institutions." Public Health Report 9:144–48.

Kramer, Elaine and Joyce Unger.
  1967   "A survey of need in a public housing project for the aged." The Gerontologist, Part I 7:204–206.

Kubler-Ross, Elizabeth.
　　1970　　On Death and Dying. New York: Macmillan.

Lamden, Richard S. and Lawrence N. Greenstein.
　　1975　　"Partnership in out-patient day care." Hospital 49:87–89.

Lesnoff-Caravaglia, Gary (ed.)
　　1987　　Handbook of Applied Gerontology. New York: Human Sciences
　　　　　Press.

Lindsay, Inabel B.
　　1971　　The Multiple Hazards of Age and Race: The Situation of Aged Blacks
　　　　　in the United States. Senate Report 450, 92nd Congress, First ses-
　　　　　sion. Washington, D.C.: U.S. Government Printing Office.

Litwak, Eugene.
　　1985　　Helping the Elderly: The Complementary Roles of Informal Net-
　　　　　works and Formal Systems. New York: Guilford Press.

Locker, Rose.
　　1976　　"Elderly couples and the institution." Social Work 21:149–51.

Lowy, Louis.
　　1986　　Why Education in the Later Years? Lexington, Mass.: Lexington
　　　　　Books.

Lowy, Louis.
　　1962　　"The group in social work with the aged." Social Work 7:62.

McAdoo, Harriette Pipes.
　　1987　　"Blacks," in Encyclopedia of Social Work, 18th edition. Silver
　　　　　Spring, Md.: National Association of Social Workers.

McAuley, William.
　　1987　　Applied Research in Gerontology. New York: Van Nostrand Rein-
　　　　　hold.

McCarthy, Belinda and Robert Langworthy.
　　1988　　Older Offenders. New York: Praeger.

McGuire, Frances.
　　1986　　Computer Technology and the Aged: Implications and Applications
　　　　　for Activity Programs. New York: Haworth Press.

Maldonado, David Jr.
　　1975　　"The Chicano aged." Social Work 20:213–16.

Manney, James D., Jr.
　　1975　　Aging in American Society: An Examination of the Concepts and Is-

sues. Ann Arbor: The Institute of Gerontology, The University of Michigan–Wayne State University.

Markides, Kyriakios S.
1987   Aging and Ethnicity. Newbury Park, Calif.: Sage.

Mayadas, Nazneen, and Douglas Hink.
1975   "Group work with the aging." The Gerontologist 15:441–44.

Merlin, Debrah.
1975   "Home care project for indigent allows dignified care, cuts cost." Hospitals 49:77–78.

Meyer, Carol H. (ed.)
1986   Social Work with the Aging. Silver Spring, Md.: National Association of Social Workers.

Milloy, Margaret.
1964   "Casework with the older person and his family." Social Work 45:450–55.

Morris, Robert.
1970   Facilities, Programs and Services. Background paper for the 1971 White House Conference on Aging. Washington, D.C.: U.S. Department of Health, Education, and Welfare, Administration on Aging.

Morris, Robert and Robert H. Binstock.
1966   Feasible Planning for Social Change. New York: Columbia University Press.

Nader, Ralph.
1977   "The Older American." Morning Reporter, January 3, Morgantown, W. Va.

Nahemow, Lucille, Kathleen A. McCluskey-Fawcett and Paul E. McGee (eds.)
1986   Humor and Aging. Orlando, Fla.: Academic Press.

National Indian Council on Aging.
1981   Indian Elderly and Entitlement Programs: An Accessing Demonstration Project. Albuquerque, N.M.: National Indian Council on Aging.

Oakland California Health Services Administration.
        (Co-Sponsored by the Ethel Percy Andrus Gerontology Center, University of Southern California, and the Advisory Committee for Continuing Education: Services to the Black Elderly).
1974   The Black Elderly in Long Term Care Settings. Oakland, Calif.: Health Services Administration.

OECD.
1988   Aging Populations: The Social Policy Implications. Paris.

Palmore, Erdman (ed.)
1985   Normal Aging III: Report from the Duke Longitudinal Studies, 1975–1984. Durham, N.C.: Duke University Press.

Panitch, Arnold.
1974   "Advocacy in practice." Social Work 19:326.

Parke, James J.
1964   "Enlisting retired elderly persons for volunteer services." Hospital 38:66–68.

Peterson, David A., James E. Thornton and Donna E. Deutchaman (eds.)
1987   Education and Aging. Englewood Cliffs, N.J.: Prentice-Hall.

Peterson, David.
1987   Career Paths in the Field of Aging: Professional Gerontology. Lexington, Mass.: Lexington Books.

Peterson, Warren A. and Jill Quadagno (eds.)
1985   Social Bonds Later in Life: Aging and Interdependence. Beverly Hills, Calif.: Sage Publications.

Philibert, Michel.
1975   "Philosophies of Aging." In James Manney (ed.), Aging in American Society: An Examination of Concepts and Issues. Ann Arbor: The Institute of Gerontology, The University of Michigan–Wayne State University, pp. 9–10.

Phillips, Harry T. and Susan Gaylord (eds.)
1985   Aging and Public Health. New York: Springer Publishing Co.

Pifer, Alan and Lydia Bronte (eds.)
1986   Our Aging Society: Paradox and Promise. New York: Norton & Co.

Pillemer, Karl A. and Rosalie S. Wolf (eds.)
1986   Elder Abuse: Conflict in the Family. Dover, Mass.: Auburn House Publishing Co.

Pincus, Allen.
1970   "Reminiscence in aging and its implication for social work practice." Social Work 20:47–53.

Prado, C. G.
1986   Rethinking How We Age: A New View of the Aging Mind. Westport, Conn: Greenwood Press.

Pritikin, Nathan.
    1985   Diet for Runners. New York: Simon and Schuster.

Pritikin, Nathan.
    1980   The Pritikin Program for Diet and Exercise. New York: Bantam.

Rathbone-McCuan, Eloise and Betty Havens (eds.)
    1988   North American Elders: United States and Canadian Perspectives.
            Westport, Conn.: Greenwood Press.

Reagan, Michael (with Joe Hyams).
    1988   On the Outside Looking In. New York: Zebra.

Revis, Joseph S.
    1970   Transportation. Background paper for the 1971 White House Con-
            ference on Aging. Washington, D.C.: U.S. Department of Health, Ed-
            ucation, and Welfare, Administration on Aging.

Riley, Matilda W.
    1971   "Social gerontology and the age stratification of society." The Ger-
            ontologist 2:79–87.

Robbins, Ira S.
    1970   Housing the Elderly. Background paper for the 1971 White House
            Conference on Aging. Washington, D.C.: U.S. Department of Health,
            Education, and Welfare, Administration on Aging.

Rosen, Sumner, David Fanshel and Mary E. Lutz (eds.)
    1987   Face of the Nation 1987. Statistical Supplement to the 18th edition of
            the Encyclopedia of Social Work. Silver Spring, Md.: National Asso-
            ciation of Social Workers.

Rubin, Allen.
    1987   "Case Management," Encyclopedia of Social Work, 18th edition. Sil-
            ver Spring, Md.: National Association of Social Workers.

Salamon, Michael J.
    1986   A Basic Guide to Working with Elders. New York: Springer Publish-
            ing Co.

Satir, Virginia.
    1983   Satir Step by Step: A Guide to Creating Change in Families. Palo Alto,
            Calif.: Science and Behavior Books.

Schaie, Warner K. (ed.)
    1983   Longitudinal Studies of Adult Psychological Development. New
            York: Guilford Press.

Schnore, Morris M.
    1985   Retirement, Bane or Blessing? Waterloo, Ontario, Canada: Wilfrid Laurier University Press.

Schlesinger, Benjamin and Rachel Schlesinger (eds.)
    1988   Abuse of the Elderly: Issues and Annotated Bibliography. Toronto: University of Toronto Press.

Schmidt, Mary Gwynne.
    1975   "Interviewing the 'old, old.'" The Gerontologist 20:544–47.

Schultz, James.
    1970   Retirement. Background paper for the 1971 White House Conference on Aging. Washington, D.C.: U.S. Department of Health, Education, and Welfare, Administration on Aging.

Scott, Walter.
    1988   "Personality Parade." in Parade, September 4, 1988. p. 2.

Shanan, Joel.
    1985   Personality Types and Culture in Later Adulthood. London: Karger.

Shanas, Ethel.
    1971   "The sociology of aging and the aged." The Sociological Quarterly 12:159–76.

Shapiro, Harvey.
    1977   "Do not go gently . . . " The New York Times Magazine, February 6, pp. 36–41.

Shapiro, Isaac and Robert Greenstein.
    1988   "Holes in the Safety Nets." Washington, D.C.: Center on Budget and Policy Priorities.

Sharkey, Harold.
    1962   "Sustaining the aged in the community." Social Work 7:18–22.

Sherman, Susan R.
    1975   "Provision of on-site services in retirement housing." International Journal of Aging and Human Development 6:229–47.

Shover, Neal.
    1985   Aging Criminals. Beverly Hills, Calif.: Sage Publications.

Silverman, Phillip (ed.)
    1987   The Elderly as Modern Pioneers. Bloomington: Indiana University Press.

Simos, Bertha G.
  1973   "Adult children and their aging parents." Social Work 18:78–85.

Smithers, Janice A.
  1985   Determined Survivors: Community Life Among the Urban Elderly.
            New Brunswick, N.J.: Rutgers University Press.

Sobel, Irvin.
  1970   Employment. Background paper for the 1971 White House Confer-
            ence on Aging. Washington, D.C.: U.S. Department of Health, Educa-
            tion, and Welfare, Administration on Aging.

Sommers, Tish.
  1975   "Social security: a woman's viewpoint." Industrial Gerontologist,
            2:266–79.

Stanford, E. Percil (ed.)
  1974   Minority Aging. San Diego: San Diego State University Press.

Strauss, Anselm.
  1973   "Chronic Illness." Society 10:33.

Streib, Gordon F.
  1971   Retirement Roles and Activities. Background paper for the 1971
            White House Conference on Aging. Washington, D.C.: U.S. Depart-
            ment of Health, Education, and Welfare, Administration on Aging.

Sudnow, David.
  1967   Passing On: The Social Organization of Dying. Englewood Cliffs,
            N.J.: Prentice-Hall.

Tamarkin, Civia.
  1988   "A Home Not Her Own." in People, Vol. 30, No. 14, October 3, 1988.
            pp. 100–111.

Toufexis, Anastasia.
  1988   "Older—But Coming on Strong." in Time Magazine, February 22,
            1988. pp. 76–79.

Turner, Bryan S.
  1987   Medical Power and Social Knowledge. New York: Sage.

Ulatowska, Hanna K. (ed.)
  1985   The Aging Brain: Communication in the Elderly. San Diego: College-
            Hill Press.

Unger, S. (ed.)
  1977   The Destruction of American Indian Families. New York: Associa-
            tion on American Indian Affairs.

U.S. Bureau of the Census.
  1983   Statistical Abstract of the United States. Washington, D.C.: U.S. Government Printing Office.

U.S. Department of Health, Education, and Welfare.
  1980   Tuberculosis in the United States. Washington, D.C.: U.S. Government Printing Office.

U.S. Department of Health, Education, and Welfare.
  1971   Report of the National Protective Service Project for Older Adults. Washington, D.C.: U.S. Government Printing Office.

U.S. Department of Health, Education, and Welfare, Administration of Aging.
  1975   Facts About Older Americans. Washington, D.C.: U.S. Government Printing Office.

U.S. Senate Special Committee on Aging.
  1987   Developments in Aging. Vol. 1. Washington, D.C.: Government Printing Office.

Von Tassel, David and Peter N. Stearns (eds.)
  1986   Old Age in a Bureaucratic Society: The Elderly, the Experts, and the State in American History. Westport, Conn.: Greenwood Press.

War, Thomas T. H.
  1985   Well-Being for the Elderly: Primary Prevention Strategies. Lexington, Mass.: Lexington Books.

Warheite, George, Roger A. Bell, and John J. Schwab.
  1974   Planning for Change: Needs Assessment Approach. Washington, D.C.: The National Institute of Mental Health.

Watson, Ronald (ed.)
  1985   CRC Handbook of Nutrition in the Age. Boca Raton, Fla.: CRC Press.

Weg, Ruth B.
  1974   "The Changing Physiology of Aging." In James Birren and Ruth Weg (eds.), Curriculum Development in Gerontology. Los Angeles: Ethel Percy Andrus Gerontology Center, University of Southern California.

Whitbourne, Susan Krauss.
  1985   The Aging Body: Physiological Changes and Psychological Consequences. New York: Springer-Verlag.

Williamson, John B.
  1985   Aging and Public Policy: Social Control or Social Justice? Springfield, Ill.: C. C. Thomas.

Wilson, Gertrude and Gladys Ryland.
1949   Social Group Work Practice. New York: Houghton Mifflin.

Woodruff, Diana S. and James E. Birren.
1975   Aging, Scientific Perspectives and Social Issues. New York: Van Nostrand.

Woodward, Kathleen and Murry M. Schwartz (eds.)
1986   Memory and Desire: Aging—Literature—Psychoanalysis. Bloomington: Indiana University Press.

Worthington, Gladys.
1963   "Older persons as community volunteers." Social Work 8:71–75.

Wu, Frances Y. T.
1975   "Mandarin-speaking aged Chinese in the Los Angeles area." The Gerontologist 15:271–75.

index

Accidents, 150–151
Acquired Immune Deficiency Syndrome (AIDS), viii, 17
Administration on Aging, 181, 184, 187, 189
Adult foster care, adult residential care, 240–251 (reading), 257–258, 269-270
Advocacy, advocate, 152, 178–179, 215–224
African Americans, 54
Age-grading, 14
Age norms, 14–15
Aging, physical, 7–8
Aging, psychological, 9–10
Agriculture, U.S. Department of, 181, 186
Aid to Families with Dependent Children, 23, 234, 256
Alaska Natives, 55
Alcohol, alcoholics, alcoholism, 41, 111, 263–264
Alcoholics Anonymous, 302
Alzheimer's Disease, 150, 185, 252, 257–258
American Association of Retired Persons (AARP), 20–23, 186, 231, 238, 301
American Indians, 138, 187
Area agencies on aging, 179, 184
Arteriosclerosis, 252
Arthritis, 20, 252
Asia, viii
Asian Americans, 55–56, 138, 300

Biological perspectives, 1, 34–35
Blacks, 22, 37, 54, 56, 60–64 (reading), 138, 300
Block grants, vii
Blue Cross and Blue Shield, 253
B'nai B'rith, 299
Bush, George, vii, 21

Cancer, 153
Capitalist society, 35
Carter, Jimmy, vii
Case management, viii, 81, 102–103, 105
Census, U.S. Bureau of, 37, 150
Chicanos, 138
China, 33
Chinese, 34, 55
Civic groups, 299
Civil rights movement, 215
Commissioner on Aging, 177, 185
Commodities, 184
Communication process, 95

Community action programs, 85
Community mental health center, 104, 143, 261–262, 264
Confidentiality, 92
Congress (U.S.), 21, 184, 189
Congressional Budget Office, 181
Consumer Price Index, 184
Consumer protection, 231–232
Continuum of care, 264–265
Coronary disease, 153
Counseling, 81, 104, 141
Counselors, 154
Crime and criminals, 44–45, 59–60, 77–80 (reading), 210–214 (reading)
Cubans, 55–56
Cultural perspectives, 33

Death, 9, 15–16, 111, 147–174, 216, 224, 259
Demographics, 4
Developmental disabilities, 256–257
Diagnostic Related Groups, 256
Direct services, 81–174
Disability, 232–233
Discrimination, 38
Down's Syndrome, 257
Drug users, abusers, viii, 40, 263
Dukakis, Michael, 21

Eastern culture, 34
Economic Opportunity Act, 180, 186
Elderhostel, 303
Employment, employable, 6, 12, 38, 179, 185, 237
Escort service, 208
Ethnic groups, 22, 55–56, 138–139, 153, 291

Families, 5, 135–146
Family service agencies, associations, 143, 263–264
Family Service America, 263
Family Support Act, 234
Federal Council on Aging, 183
Filipinos, 55
Financial assistance, 145, 227–235
Food Stamps, vii, 235
Foster Grandparent Program, 25, 304
French Canadians, 56
Fuel assistance, 235
Functional approach, 104
Funerals, 155

Gay men, viii
Gerontologists, 109
Gestalt Therapy, 112
Gray Panthers, 222, 300–301
Great Society, (The), 21, 180
Green Thumb, 186
Group development, stages of, 114–120
Group dynamics, 120–124
Group services, 106–134
Group therapy, 112
Guamanians, 55
Guaranteed minimum income, 235

Halfway houses, 268
Harrington, Michael, 37
Health and Human Services, U.S.
  Department of, 183, 187
Health education, 260
Health insurance, 18, 20, 253–254
Hearing, 8, 19, 150, 252
Hip fracture, 259
Hispanics, 37, 55–56, 300
Homeless, Homelessness, viii, 40–41, 136,
  240–251 (reading)
Homes for the aging, 111, 263, 269
Hospice, 154
Hot lines, 264
Housing, 5, 37, 40–42, 136, 216, 240–251
  (reading)
Housing, public, 239
Hypertension, 252

Immigrants, 5, 57
Immigration, viii, 138
Incontinence, 258–259
Individual Retirement Accounts (IRAs),
  237
Industrialization, 5
Influenza, 150
Information and referral services, 203–205
Inner-city, 5
Institutionalization, Institutionalized
  elderly, 145, 216, 267–268
Intelligence, 12–13
Intergovernmental planning, viii
Interviewing, 91–102, 141

Jackson, Jesse, 21
Japanese, Japan, 55–56, 138
Jewish, 56, 138
Jewish Community Center, 297–298
Johnson, Lyndon B., 21, 180

Knights of Columbus, 299
Koreans, viii, 55, 138

Latin America, viii, 138, 148

Learning ability, 12
Legal services, 208
Leisure, leisure time, 19, 46–47, 140–141,
  156, 229–235, 269, 291–307
Life expectancy, 4
Life insurance, 228, 236
Life-span, 4, 148
Living will, 154–155
Lobby, Lobbyists, 24, 111, 218
Longevity, 4
Long term care, 188, 265–269, 273–285
  (reading)
Lost Chord group, 302

Masonic groups, 299
Mead, Margaret, 48–53 (reading)
Meals on Wheels, 44
Means test, 234
Medicaid, 254, 256, 265, 267
Medicare, vii, 18, 21, 24, 179, 230,
  254–256, 265
Mental capacity, 12–13
Mental health services, 156, 216, 261–264
Mental illness, mentally ill, 40, 258, 268
Mental institution, hospital, viii, 104,
  267–270
Mentally retarded, 257
Minority elderly, 54–56, 188

National Council on Aging, 301
National Institute on Aging, 36
Native Americans, 55–56
Natural disasters, 148
Needs assessment and identification,
  192–198
New Deal, vii
Nuclear family, 5
Nurses, 109, 150, 262, 269
Nursing homes, 45, 111, 258, 264–267,
  269, 273–285 (reading)
Nutrition, 183, 186

Occupational therapist, 109
Offenders, older, 59–60, 77–80 (reading)
Older Americans Act, 177–189
Old Gray Mare syndrome, 34
Ombudsman, 183, 188
Outreach services, 84, 86–89

Pacific Islanders, 55
Pan-Asian community, viii, 138
Partialization, 93
Peace Corps, 304
Pensions, 36–38, 238–239
Perception, 11
Personality, 13
Physical, physiological aging, 7–8

Physical therapist, 109
Physicians, 150, 253
Pneumonia, 150
Poverty, 17, 21, 36–37, 54
Preventive services, 259
Program planning, 175, 190–202
Protective services, 209, 215–224
Psychologists, 263
Psychomotor functions, skills, 11–12
Psychotherapy, 104
Public welfare, 144, 269

Reagan, Ronald, viii, 17, 21, 23, 40, 137, 181
Recreational activities, 216, 292–300
Recreation workers, leaders, therapists, 109, 263
Red Cross, 85
Referrals, 88–89, 101
Rehabilitation counselors, 263
Religion, religious, 33, 139, 299
Reminiscences, 107
Research and training (under Older Americans Act), 178, 185
Retired Senior Volunteer Program, 304
Retirement, 6, 15–16, 19, 34, 37–40, 46–48, 103, 140, 230–231, 237–239
Roles, 15–17
Roman Catholics, 138, 299
Rural areas, 5, 56
Rural elderly, 58–59

Salvation Army, 85
Samoans, 55
Savings, 236
Self-determination, 93
Self-help groups, 108, 302
Senility, 270–273 (reading)
Senior centers, 177–179, 183, 237, 297–298
Senses, Sensory, 8, 10–12, 83
Sex roles, 140–141
Sexuality and aging, 13, 15, 25–32 (reading), 142
Shelter, 41, 240–251 (reading)
Social action, 141
Social case work, 104
Social group work, 112
Socialization, 13–14, 16
Social perspectives, 1
Social Security, vii, 6, 20–24, 36, 46, 84, 229, 232, 237, 257, 300–301
Social services, 183, 216

Social workers, 21, 109, 150, 263
Socioemotional treatment, 107
Sociologists, 13
Special Committee on Aging, U.S. Senate, 179
Status, 16, 33
Stereotype, 15
Strokes, 150
Substance abuse, abusers, 40
Suicide, 16, 151–152, 264
Supplemental Security Income (SSI), vii, 40, 84, 232–234, 257
Support groups, 108
Support services, 44, 203–210

Target population, 84–85
Tax-sheltered annuities, 38, 236
Teachers, 109
Telephone reassurance, 205
Terminal illness, terminally ill, 147–174
Transportation, 42–43, 59, 88–89, 107, 136, 144, 178–179, 191, 205–207, 239–240
Treatment services, 103–105

Unemployment, 38, 228
United Way, United Fund, 196, 298
Urban elderly, 5, 85
Urbanization, 5
Urban League, 186

Veterans, 110, 300
Veterans Administration (U.S.), 109, 270
Veterans benefits, 40
Vietnamese, 55
Voluntary organizations, 175
Volunteer programs, 304–307
Volunteers, 206–207, 236
Volunteers in Service to America (VISTA), 304

Wage structure, 6
Waste product theory, 7
Wear and tear theory, 7
Weatherization, 236
Welfare system, viii
Western society, 34
White House Conferences on Aging, 187, 194
Women, older, 57–58, 64–77 (reading), 141

YMCA, YWCA, 298, 303